Resolving the European Debt Crisis

William R. Cline and Guntram B. Wolff, editors

PETERSON INSTITUTE FOR INTERNATIONAL ECONOMICS
BRUEGEL

Washington, DC
February 2012

William R. Cline has been a senior fellow at the Peterson Institute for International Economics since its inception in 1981. While on leave during 1996–2001, he was deputy managing director and chief economist of the Institute of International Finance. Since 2002 he has held a joint appointment with the Center for Global Development. He has been a senior fellow at the Brookings Institution (1973–81); deputy director for development and trade research, US Treasury Department (1971–73); Ford Foundation visiting professor in Brazil (1970–71); and lecturer and assistant professor of economics at Princeton University (1967–70). He graduated summa cum laude from Princeton University in 1963 and received his PhD in economics from Yale University in 1969. He is the author of 24 books, including *Financial Globalization, Economic Growth, and the Crisis of 2007–09* (2010), *Global Warming and Agriculture* (2007), and *The United States as a Debtor Nation* (2005).

Guntram B. Wolff is deputy director of Bruegel. He worked for the European Commission's Directorate General for Economic and Financial Affairs, where he researched on the macroeconomics of the euro area and the reform of euro area governance. Prior to joining the Commission, Wolff was an economist in the economics and research departments of the Deutsche Bundesbank, where he coordinated the research group on fiscal policy. He holds a PhD from the University of Bonn, where he was a research fellow at the Center for European Integration Studies (ZEI). He has taught economics at the University of Pittsburgh and is currently an adviser to the International Monetary Fund.

PETER G. PETERSON INSTITUTE FOR INTERNATIONAL ECONOMICS
1750 Massachusetts Avenue, NW
Washington, DC 20036-1903
(202) 328-9000   FAX: (202) 659-3225
www.piie.com

C. Fred Bergsten, *Director*
Edward A. Tureen, *Director of Publications, Marketing, and Web Development*

Typesetting by BMWW
Printing by Versa Press, Inc.

BRUEGEL
33 Rue de la Charité/Liefdadigheidsstraat 33
B-1210 Brussels, Belgium
Phone: +32 2 227 4210
Fax: +32 2 227 4219
www.bruegel.org

Jean Pisani-Ferry, *Director*

Printed in the United States of America
14 13 12   5 4 3 2 1

Library of Congress Cataloging-in-Publication Data
Resolving the European debt crisis / [edited by] William R. Cline and Guntram Wolff.
 p. cm.
 Papers presented at a conference held at a conference center near Paris, on Sept. 13–14, 2011.
 Includes index.
 ISBN 978-0-88132-642-0
 1. Debts, External—European Union countries—Congresses. 2. Financial crises—European Union countries—Congresses. 3. European Union countries—Economic policy—Congresses. 4. Euro area—Congresses. I. Cline, William R. II. Wolff, Guntram. HJ8615.R47 2012
 336.3'4094—dc23

 2012000905

Contents

Preface

More than three years after the most acute phase of the Great Recession and global financial crisis, the most severe stress on global financial and economic stability is centered in the sovereign debt crises and banking sector in the euro area. What began as a relatively localized Greek crisis in early 2010 soon escalated to envelop Ireland and Portugal, both of which lost capital market access and required emergency lending. By the second half of 2011, the contagion had spread to the far larger economies of Italy and Spain, which by late October had to pay sovereign risk premia on the order of 500 basis points and whose public finance sustainability was therefore at risk. Large maturities come due in the first few months of 2012 in both economies, and the first half of the year seems likely to witness either a new phase of more successful management of the debt crisis or a severe unraveling with major negative spillover effects on the world economy.

At each successive phase in this unfolding financial drama, European policymakers have taken incremental steps designed to reassure markets, only to find that the actions were widely regarded as too little too late. In 2010 precious time was lost discussing the pros and cons of financial support and International Monetary Fund (IMF) intervention and later the conditions for bailing in private creditors, but no concrete decision was taken on Greek debt restructuring. In 2011 the July decision to increase support to Greece and accept a modest "private sector involvement" in the reduction of the Greek debt was superseded by the late-October decision to require much deeper (50 percent) "haircuts" for private creditors, supplemented by an announced policy intended to build a firewall through major leveraging of the European Financial Stability Facility (EFSF). Then a landmark summit in early December committed EU members (except the dissenting United Kingdom) to a treaty-based tightening of the fiscal rules. The summit also announced a plan for

€200 billion in EU lending to the IMF, to be supplemented by corresponding lending by other economies (especially large emerging-market economies with ample reserves) for purposes of emergency support to euro area sovereigns.

In mid-2011, the Peterson Institute and Bruegel joined forces to plan a conference designed to contribute to the formulation of policies that could help resolve the euro area debt crisis. This volume presents the papers prepared for that conference, held in Chantilly, France, on September 13–14, 2011. Several of the papers have been updated to take account of developments through end-2011.

Sovereign debt crisis resolution turns crucially on political will, and the first set of papers accordingly examines the political context in each of five economies facing debt difficulties—Greece (Loukas Tsoukalis), Ireland (Alan Ahearne), Portugal (Pedro Lourtie), Spain (Guillermo de la Dehesa), and Italy (Riccardo Perissich)—as well as the two key stronger economies of Germany (Daniela Schwarzer) and France (Zaki Laïdi).

Two other papers review past experience with sovereign debt restructuring from the economic (Jeromin Zettelmeyer) and legal (Lee Buchheit) standpoints and consider implications for (and the special circumstances of) the euro area.

The two final papers, authored by the two editors of this volume, are parallel examinations of the set of policy options available. The salient issues in both include questions of debt sustainability, whether private sector involvement spurs contagion, the merits and drawbacks of alternative restructuring approaches, how to assemble a large emergency financing capacity in case it is needed for Spain and Italy, whether the European Central Bank (ECB) should perform the role of lender of last resort, whether joint-liability eurobonds would be feasible and desirable, and the implications of a possible breakup of the euro.

Following the views of George Soros, who presented the luncheon address, the final chapter (by Steven Weisman with Silvia Merler) describes a policy simulation game played on the second day of the conference by about fifteen market participants and experts representing the roles of governments, banks, and political sectors of the seven euro area nations as well as the ECB, IMF, G-7, and credit-rating community. Building on practice that is common in the financial community but very rarely applied to macroeconomic and macro-financial policy, this innovative approach was intended to shed light on the interdependence between policy decisions and market responses as well as on the interdependence and cooperation among policy players. Andrew Gracie of Crisis Management Analytics contributed to designing the simulation game, and then conducted it. Starting from the initial conditions of early autumn 2011, the game explored developments in the following quarters and the responses they triggered from the various players. The game engendered the deterioration of sovereign spreads in core euro area countries actually observed in the autumn and early winter. It also provided the possibility to test a particular proposal for leveraging the capacity of the EFSF through arrangements with the ECB. This proposal, arguably still relevant even though so far the ECB and euro area authorities have rejected it, resulted in a sudden and significant lowering of the sovereign spreads.

As of mid-January 2012, we are relatively sanguine about the prospects for managing the crisis without either breakup of the euro area or extensive defaults. One of us has argued that important new intervention power has been achieved through the swifter introduction of the European Stability Mechanism (ESM) and the new resources for the IMF, but has also cautioned that the heavy focus to date on fiscal rules has not yet come to grips with the inherent need to either authorize true lender of last resort action by the ECB, break the link between sovereign and bank risk through making bank regulation and resolution truly euro area wide, or embark on jointly liable eurobonds.[1] The other has emphasized that Europe is well on its way to completing the original concept of a comprehensive economic and monetary union; that, in the crunch, both Germany and the ECB will pay whatever is necessary to avert disaster; but that the process will be messy because it relies on financial market volatility to provide incentives that force solutions and that those markets will thus remain volatile.[2] We nevertheless share the assessment that, although decisions taken thus far are significant, the euro area has not yet escaped the danger zone and should recognize the need for more ambitious and comprehensive responses. This volume is a contribution to the debate about these responses.

The Peter G. Peterson Institute for International Economics is a private, nonprofit institution for the study and discussion of international economic policy. Its purpose is to analyze important issues in that area and to develop and communicate practical new approaches for dealing with them. The Institute is completely nonpartisan.

The Institute is funded by a highly diversified group of philanthropic foundations, private corporations, and interested individuals. About 35 percent of the Institute's resources in our latest fiscal year were provided by contributors outside the United States. We gratefully acknowledge funding from Tudor Investment Corporation and BlackRock Investment Management for the September conference and this volume. The views expressed in this publication are the sole responsibility of the authors and do not necessarily reflect the views of the funders, the Institute, Bruegel, or any of their respective officers.

The Institute's Board of Directors bears overall responsibilities for the Institute and gives general guidance and approval to its research program, including the identification of topics that are likely to become important over the medium run (one to three years) and that should be addressed by the Institute.

---

1. Jean Pisani-Ferry, *The eurozone and the streetlamp syndrome*, Bruegel, December 12, 2011; *The Euro Crisis and the New Impossible Trinity*, Bruegel Policy Contribution 2012/01, January 2012.

2. C. Fred Bergsten and Jacob Kirkegaard, *The Coming Resolution of the European Crisis*, Policy Briefs in International Economics 12-1, Peterson Institute for International Economics, January 2012.

The director, working closely with the staff and an outside advisory committee, is responsible for the development of particular projects and makes the final decision to publish an individual study.

Bruegel is an independent economic think tank. It contributes to European and global economic policymaking through open, fact-based, and policy-relevant research, analysis, and debate. Membership is composed of EU governments, leading international corporations, and institutions. The Bruegel Board consists of 11 members, all with distinguished backgrounds in government, business, civil society, academia, and media. The Board decides on strategy and adopts the research program and budget. The Board does not bear responsibility for research results—this remains with individual researchers, under the overall editorial oversight of the director.

The Institute and Bruegel hope that their studies and other activities will contribute to building a stronger foundation for international economic policy around the world. We invite readers of this publication to let us know how they think we can best accomplish this objective.

C. FRED BERGSTEN, Director
Peterson Institute for International
Economics

JEAN PISANI-FERRY, Director
Bruegel

January 2012

Overview

WILLIAM R. CLINE and GUNTRAM B. WOLFF

On September 13–14, 2011, the Brussels-based think tank Bruegel and the Peterson Institute for International Economics hosted a conference entitled "Resolving the European Debt Crisis." Held at a conference center near Paris, the event assembled about four dozen policy experts and practitioners, mainly from Europe and the United States. The conference was designed to articulate and clarify the implications of alternative approaches to resolving the crisis, in particular, the dynamics of interaction among various stakeholder groups as policy decisions evolve. It brought together leading former policymakers, academics, and market participants to discuss, interact, and learn from each other.

At the conference, Bruegel and the Peterson Institute explored an innovative technique for understanding complex policy issues: a dynamic policy simulation with a large number of players. Crisis simulation of this nature makes it possible to obtain a deeper understanding of the constraints and opportunities facing real policymakers, market players, and the public at large. Such a simulation permits grasping real-life decision making; it goes beyond the typical conference format in which participants present their views and ask and answer questions. A simulation game forces real interaction and real decision making on players in a short space of time, thereby revealing preferences for and constraints upon action.

This volume collects the papers that were presented at the conference and, in the final chapter, summarizes the central insights from the simula-

William R. Cline has been a senior fellow at the Peterson Institute for International Economics since its inception in 1981. While on leave during 1996–2001, he was deputy managing director and chief economist of the Institute of International Finance. Guntram B. Wolff is deputy director of Bruegel.

tion game. This opening chapter provides a short overview of the two-day conference.

Conference Structure

On the first day there were three panels aimed at providing a comprehensive understanding of the current and prospective situation surrounding the European debt crisis. The first of these assessed the current economic and political situation in the key euro area creditor and debtor nations and the associated constraints facing policymakers. The second focused on the lessons learned from past experiences of sovereign debt crises and their resolutions, including lessons having to do with legal and accounting issues, and their relevance for current European circumstances. The third analyzed the pros and cons, including the costs and benefits, of the different options available to policymakers for bringing the euro area debt crisis to a successful resolution.

On the second day, the simulation game took place among the conference participants in what amounted to a stress-test for European debt policy. Prepared with the assistance of experts from Bruegel and the Peterson Institute, the game was directed by Andrew Gracie of Crisis Management Analytics. No sitting officials participated, and the game was played under Chatham House rules. Participants played the roles of governments (of France, Germany, Greece, Ireland, Italy, Portugal, and Spain); of decision makers for the European Central Bank (ECB), International Monetary Fund (IMF), and United States; and of decision makers in commercial banks in the countries involved and nonbank financial market actors. In addition, in response to successive rounds of the game as it developed, other participants provided expertise in the areas of credit ratings, legal and accounting issues, and political repercussions.

Background and Policy Discussion

The papers on the political-economic environments in Greece, Ireland, and Portugal argued that there is a strong degree of domestic political support for fully honoring sovereign debt obligations and remaining in the euro. The papers and discussion on the recent market deterioration in the much larger economies of Italy and Spain underscored the need for euro area institutional reform providing for much greater fiscal integration. Such reform would make it possible to spread the umbrella of creditworthiness of the stronger countries by enforcing far more central control on fiscal policies. There was an accompanying sense that the time inconsistency between the immediate need to address the current emergency and the lengthy process of building new euro area institutions poses an unresolved problem.

The best vehicle for forceful action in the bridge period was generally seen to be the ECB. Several participants had misgivings about the ECB's involvement in sovereign debt purchases and the prospect that it might need to expand those purchases on a much larger scale, however; and others urged that the ECB send a strong signal that future support would be highly conditional on prompt fiscal adjustment. For France, the session revealed an intense commitment to sustaining the euro. For Germany, it revealed that any notion of exit from the euro remains very much a minority view.

Country Political-Economic Environments

Greece (Chapter 2)

Loukas Tsoukalis (University of Athens) observed that it remains to be seen whether Greece will prove to be the odd man out or the precursor of things to come elsewhere in Europe. Whereas early polls showed acceptance of the inevitability of austerity measures, Tsoukalis said, Greeks are growing increasingly angry and see no light at the end of the tunnel. He pointed to the need for a radical renewal of the political class, although at present the current government has the best chance of implementing the needed adjustment and reform.

The decisive battle in Greece today is about rationalizing a bloated and inefficient public sector. Tsoukalis called the July 2011 support package a great improvement but judged the private sector involvement (PSI) portion of it to be costly and cumbersome. In general discussion, it was argued that so far there had been too much austerity and too little reform (such as deregulation), and that cacophony in the euro area was making country adjustment efforts more difficult. It was agreed that, although there is little political consensus, there is widespread agreement within Greece that bankruptcy-type debt restructuring should be avoided and that Greece must remain in the euro area.

Ireland (Chapter 3)

Alan Ahearne (National University of Ireland, Galway) emphasized that Ireland has already carried out fiscal adjustment amounting to 13 percent of GDP and that the total adjustment will reach 20 percent. He stressed the degree of internal devaluation, citing a 15 percent cut in public sector wages over the past three years. He noted the strong consensus that the sovereign debt must be paid in full because Ireland, as a small economy dependent on international investment and trade, must honor contracts.

However, he also indicated the distinction in domestic political perceptions between sovereign debt resulting from budgetary deficits and exceptional debt attributable to emergency support of banks. At about 40 percent of GDP, the latter is larger than in almost any other international experience. Controversy about treatment of senior bondholders of bank debt had notably involved ECB opposition to any haircuts. However, except for a small portion of this debt, the government has put this issue in the past.

The current government has an unusually large majority in Parliament, and the next general election is in 2016. One point raised in the discussion was that the ECB had judged any savings through senior bank bondholder haircuts to be far too small to warrant the associated market disruption. More broadly, discussion during the course of the day tended to reiterate the view that Ireland has gone the farthest and fastest in its adjustment to the crisis.

Portugal (Chapter 4)

Pedro Lourtie (former Portuguese secretary of state for European affairs) emphasized that there is broad political support for the adjustment program and that the new government has a comfortable majority in Parliament. In assessing Portugal's performance before the global crisis, he argued that during its period of slow growth after 2001–02, the country entered a path of slow adjustment to the new euro monetary setting and of regaining lost competitiveness. He stressed that, with the sovereign debt crisis hitting the euro area, such a soft approach ceased to be an option. Furthermore, he underlined the risk of crisis contagion to the most vulnerable euro area economies during the current sovereign debt crisis and emphasized the importance of external events and euro area decisions in influencing market spreads for Portugal.

Lourtie emphasized that in 2011 Portugal entered a phase of hard adjustment, and he stressed that the country is following an ambitious road map of fiscal consolidation and structural reforms included in the adjustment program. Overall structural fiscal adjustment targeted over the 2011–13 period amounts to 9 percent of GDP, with half of that adjustment in 2011. He argued that Portugal has the political and economic conditions to come out stronger and more competitive from this adjustment, and emphasized that the continuation of strong export growth is a key element in a successful adjustment. He also underlined that the stabilization of the broader euro area is essential.

Italy (Chapter 5)

Riccardo Perissich (Council of the United States and Italy) began with the observation that although Italy's debt is large relative to GDP and in absolute size (where it is behind only the United States and Japan), Italy had maintained fiscal balance for a decade before the crisis and has large private savings. The economy has a strong manufacturing sector. Contagion from Greece in July 2011 forced a new fiscal package, which unraveled because of internal dissension in the majority party. In the face of heightened market pressure, by the end of August the government agreed to a new package cutting transfers to local authorities, raising the capital gains and value-added taxes, and renegotiating the social security system.

Spain (Chaper 6)

Guillermo de la Dehesa (Centre for Economic Policy Research) argued that euro area leaders made a serious mistake in seeing early IMF involvement in

Greece as a stigma, given that the United Kingdom, Italy, and Spain had IMF programs in the late 1970s. He stressed the strong growth record that Spain had achieved. Its fiscal position had been excellent in 2007 and its debt-to-GDP ratio was less than two-thirds the levels for France and Germany. Lower interest rates with adoption of the euro, along with massive labor immigration, had spurred Spain's growth. But large external imbalances resulted from fast growth (not an increase in relative wages), and the bursting of a property bubble in the financial crisis provoked a sharp recession.

The government responded with fiscal stimulus even as revenue was falling, leading to a budget deficit of 11 percent of GDP in 2009 (with about one-third attributable to unemployment benefits for 21 percent of the labor force). Adjustment is now under way, with the deficit to be cut to 6 percent of GDP in 2011 (although the actual outcome was 8 percent) and a target of 3 percent by 2013. A new constitutional rule limits growth of government spending to that of the economy. Labor reform will increase flexibility. The banking system is efficient and performed well in the recent stress test.

France (Chapter 7)

Zaki Laïdi (SciencesPo) focused on the tensions between the French anticapitalist tradition and the necessities of crisis management. Even the Socialist Party now agrees to the goal of a zero fiscal deficit. The president sheltered the French banks, and the public sees the banking system as a public service necessary to maintain. France sees an increasing role for Europe, and domestic support for the euro is increasing (polls show 61 percent favoring the euro, with those calling for a return to the franc falling to 29 percent from 38 percent in May 2010).

There is also support for financing Greece, and support for European fiscal federalism is increasing. Laïdi also stressed the unusually strong power of the president in the French system, an arrangement that facilitates decisions though not consensus building. The crisis has shown that the French model is vulnerable to market pressures, likely placing a premium on a technocratically sound candidate in the next election.

Germany (Chapter 8)

Daniela Schwarzer (Stiftung Wissenschaft und Politik [SWP]) began with the reminder that Germany accounts for 28 percent of euro area GDP. It has come out of the global crisis quickly, with 2.9 percent growth in 2011. Its fiscal deficit is down to 1.7 percent for 2011, and will be zero in 2014. In the present crisis, Chancellor Angela Merkel has committed to "do whatever it takes" to maintain the euro.

Although the government has a comfortable margin in Parliament, it is seen as weak. Its crisis management strategy has little public support and the coalition parties have lost regional elections. It was a great relief that the constitutional court approved the European Financial Stability Facility (EFSF), and the Bundestag is likely to ratify it despite two-thirds opposition to it in the polls. Much of the public feels it has lost the Economic and Monetary Union it once joined, and fears inflationary consequences of ECB intervention in the debt crisis. In the discussion, there was a sense that if fiscal federalism comes to the euro area, it will be on German terms. Some expressed concern that the consequence could be a contractionary bias.

Lessons from Past Restructuring Experience

With the partial exception of Greece, so far the peripheral euro area economies involved in the current debt crisis have not been forced to carry out formal debt restructurings. Nonetheless, past international experience in such restructurings can help shed light on the policy choices presently facing the euro area, especially if the official refinancing and other interventions to date prove to be insufficient.

Economic (Chapter 9)

Jeromin Zettelmeyer (European Bank for Reconstruction and Development) identified five lessons from restructuring experience in 1998–2008. First, collective action problems are overrated; excluding Argentina, creditor participation was high and average completion of restructuring took only 13 months. Second, purely voluntary exchanges rarely work. Restructuring in Uruguay in 2003 was soft but not voluntary. Third, market-perceived haircuts substantially exceed debt relief for the country because markets discount at a high "exit" risk premium, whereas the proper discount rate from the standpoint of the country is somewhere between the risk-free rate and the country's borrowing rate in normal times. Fourth, markets punish haircuts, especially if they derive from lack of willingness, rather than lack of ability, to pay. New research shows that a 20 point increase in the haircut boosts borrowing costs by 150 basis points in year 1 and 70 basis points by year 5. Also, a coercive approach to debt restructuring significantly reduces access of domestic firms to foreign credit. Fifth, preventing a banking crisis is the key to avoiding severe output loss from debt restructuring.

Legal (Chapter 10)

Lee Buchheit (Cleary Gottlieb) also emphasized avoiding a banking crisis as a consequence of restructuring, which is difficult to do where local banks are heavy holders of the government's debt. His list of lessons further included avoiding excessive delay before facing up to unsustainability of the debt; keeping accurate accounts of public debt, including off-balance-sheet provincial "quasi-sovereign" debt likely to be seen as public by foreign holders; asking for enough relief initially rather than needing three or four rounds of rescheduling, as in Latin America in the 1980s; calling on the IMF to help identify the right balance between financing needs and excessive relief; being efficient (and mark to market bondholders of the present have a greater incentive for speedy resolution than bank loan holders of the 1980s); and being evenhanded instead of discriminatory among creditor groups. He noted that peripheral Europe has a unique advantage in restructuring in that its debt is under national law rather than law of another jurisdiction. He emphasized that in a fair deal, national law could if necessary be amended to identify a high but manageable majority required for approval. He also noted that some calls for collateral against EU support could raise issues of negative pledge clauses in existing bonds and loan contracts. In discussion, Buchheit answered a query about contractual implications if the euro were to break up by indicating that, if the contract were under the law of a country that had exited, the country's obligation could be converted to the new local currency despite an original euro denomination.

Pros and Cons of Alternative Policy Options

Peterson Institute for International Economics (Chapter 11)

William Cline (Peterson Institute for International Economics) argued that the European debt crisis is primarily one of confidence. Examining the severity of the debt problem in each of the five countries, Cline first considered prospects for debt sustainability in Greece. He calculated that the July 2011 package provided the basis for reducing the gross debt-to-GDP ratio from 170 percent to 113 percent by 2020. He stressed that there is a misleading increase in gross debt from the collateral assets set aside for PSI exchanges and that Greek net debt shows considerably less burden, at 120 percent now, falling to 69 percent of GDP by 2020. Similarly, the interest burden falls from 7.2 percent of GDP to 5.2 percent by 2020 instead of rising to 9 percent without the interest relief in the EU package decided upon in July. The package involves an ambitious but feasible fiscal target (primary surplus of about 6 percent of GDP) as well as sizeable privatizations (€50 billion). The PSI package (€135 billion) and the lengthening of maturities for EU support remove the liquidity squeeze by covering amortization through 2020. Cline thus judged Greek debt to be sustainable given the new package.

Consideration of debt sustainability also finds Ireland and Portugal to be solvent. The sustainability test is that the primary fiscal surplus is large enough to equal or exceed the debt-to-GDP ratio multiplied by the difference between the interest rate and the nominal growth rate; both countries pass this test. Italy and Spain also meet this sustainability test. However, if they were to face a serious liquidity squeeze, the financing needs combined could be on the order of €1 trillion through 2015 for debt coming due.

Cline then examined a spectrum of restructuring and buyback policy options as well as three broader changes: expansion of the EFSF, issuance of eurobonds with joint guarantee by euro area members, and outright exit from the euro (either by weak countries or by strong countries establishing a new strong currency). Ireland and Portugal have the mildest options on the spectrum, official refinancing only; Greece, the next mildest, refinancing with voluntary PSI. More drastic options—restructuring with moderate debt reduction, like the Brady Plan's 35 percent haircuts, and restructuring with deep debt reduction, like Argentina's 70 percent haircut—Cline judged currently unnecessary even for Greece. At the moderate end of the spectrum, an important market-friendly option is repurchases of debt at a discount, by the country or by the ECB.

The need for the various approaches will depend on the future severity of the problems. Expansion of the EFSF threefold or fourfold could be necessary to deal with acute liquidity stress for Italy and Spain. For the eurobond alternative, Cline made a calculation relating risk spreads to country ratings and found that the weighted average spread for all euro area countries would be only 40 basis points above the German benchmark. The direct costs could be 0.3 percent of GDP annually in higher interest payments for Germany and France but with interest savings of 0.6 percent for Italy (in normal times), 1.3 percent for Ireland, 1.9 percent for Portugal, and 9.0 percent for Greece at its current low rating. After taking account of liquidity gains for the euro as an international currency, as well as gains in exports to partners in stronger economic health, net costs to France and Germany could be close to zero.

The paper closed with a matrix relating each policy approach to its impact on the five countries facing debt difficulties, on Germany and France, and on the rest of the G-7, showing an impressionistic index of the intensity and sign of the impact. The current policy programs, perhaps supplemented by market buybacks, show the most uniformly positive effects if they can succeed. The option of exit from the euro would be negative for the troubled debtors (ballooning domestic currency burden of euro debt), negative for France (for social-good reasons of high value attached to the single currency), and either negative or positive for Germany (depending on whether avoidance of lender-of-last-resort burdens were more or less valuable than the loss of competitiveness from appreciation of a new currency if Germany and France were to exit).

Bruegel (Chapter 12)

Guntram Wolff (Bruegel) took the opposite view on Greek solvency but argued that other euro area countries appear solvent. Citing other Bruegel work, he considered Greece to be insolvent and noted that many economists believe it requires a 50 percent haircut. More broadly, he saw the euro area challenged by both a debt overhang and a need for price adjustment.

In the case of Greece, he argued that debt haircuts need not be costly, especially if the primary deficit is zero and borrowing is no longer needed. Instead, Wolff saw the principal cost of sovereign debt haircuts as the impact on banking systems. By far the largest impact would be on the banking system of the country in question, according to the most recent stress tests conducted by the European Banking Authority (EBA). A 50 percent haircut for Greek debt would require only €25 billion in bank recapitalization funds, of which the financial assistance program for Greece already foresees €10 billion. Given the limited exposure of banks in other euro area countries, a haircut addressing Greek insolvency would cause relatively limited direct losses for Irish, Italian, Spanish, Portuguese, French, and German banks. Wolff argued that the ECB would need to change its collateral policy and accept debt of a government that had defaulted in order to provide the necessary liquidity to the banking system. Wolff then discussed further policy options, in particular with a view to avoiding self-fulfilling crises. The Blue Bond (euro area guaranteed)/Red Bond (not guaranteed) proposal includes joint and several liability (Delpla and von Weizsäcker 2010). Adopting this proposal would likely require a new EU treaty. He questioned the argument that this proposal would raise borrowing costs, and argued that greater liquidity could offset any higher interest costs. He further suggested that a "big bang" would be required to split each current bond into blue and red, because the alternative of gradual issuance of blue bonds would distort incentives and provoke legal challenges. Gradual introduction would also delay structural reforms.

Wolff argued that there is an internal contradiction involved in a major EFSF expansion: the large size that would be needed to address Italy (for example) would spur contagion to core countries, including France. He cited favorably a recent proposal of Daniel Gros to instead turn the EFSF into a bank with full access to ECB refinancing, placing debt management in the hands of finance ministers but ensuring a liquidity backstop.

Finally, Wolff considered euro breakup scenarios and argued that they would be prohibitively costly. A central concern of the current euro area, however, is the lack of competitiveness adjustments and the increasing deindustrialization of the euro area periphery. Practically, debt under home country law would convert to the new home currency. But under current EU law it would be illegal to leave the euro without also leaving the European Union. Describing the economic impact of the breakup of the euro, he stressed the likelihood of massive asset-liability mismatches and resulting chains of bankruptcies. Once one country left, markets would attack the next one most likely to leave. So overall a euro area exit even by one member would have severe economic repercussions for the union as a whole and would be a historic mistake economically and politically.

Discussion (Chapter 13)

Gertrude Tumpel-Gugerell (formerly a member of the ECB) and Rodrigo de Rato (chairman, Bankia, and former managing director, International Monetary Fund) served as the discussants of the two papers on policy alternatives in resolving the European debt crisis. Tumpel-Gugerell agreed with Cline's emphasis on diagnosing debt sustainability and restoring confidence to avoid self-fulfilling prophesies. She viewed expansion of the EFSF as the most realistic alternative for increasing financial backstopping. She disagreed with Wolff's view that restructuring Greek debt would not have direct adverse spillover effects on other euro area economies. De Rato argued that transition to a true economic and fiscal union would be necessary to ensure the survival of the euro area monetary union. His suggestions for action included strengthening the EFSF (including through leveraging with partial bond guarantees), implementing reforms to spur growth, imposing central coordination on fiscal policies, and possibly creating an IMF "debt facility" like the 1973 "oil facility."

The general discussion revealed sharp division on whether a default by Greece would spread severe contagion to other euro area economies. One participant observed that even the PSI in the July package had triggered rising spreads in Italy and Spain. Wolff replied that the Italian spreads had risen as markets focused on domestic disagreements on fiscal action. Discussion of concrete steps to be taken emphasized the tension between a horizon of perhaps five years for deep institutional change such as creation of a euro area treasury or development of eurobonds, and the need for action in the short term. The ECB was generally seen as the only entity capable of action in the near term. Some argued that the ECB was being overstretched, and that instead the EFSF could be used in more imaginative ways, such as insuring new bonds. It was also argued that the ECB does not have the comparative advantage in conducting fiscal monitoring, yet currently it is in effect conducting shadow adjustment programs. The contagion to Italy has intensified the short-term problem. One participant feared that in the absence of an EFSF guarantee for banks, European bank equities would be far more severely depressed by the first quarter of 2012. As discussed below, the evolution of the simulation game played on day 2 of the conference did indeed lead to imaginative uses of the EFSF and more forceful measures to guarantee the banks.

Luncheon Speech (Chapter 14)

In a luncheon speech, George Soros (Soros Fund Management) argued that the lack of a common treasury had been an inherent weakness in formation of the euro. An embryonic treasury, the EFSF is not properly capitalized and its functions are ill defined. Tailored for the three small crisis economies, it is inadequate to support Italy or Spain. The German Constitutional Court decision subjects approval of future support of other states to Bundestag approval. The absence of concessional rates for Italy or Spain, and of preparation for possible default and departure from the euro by Greece, casts doubt on government bonds of other deficit countries and euro area banks with large holdings of these bonds. The ECB purchase of Italian and Spanish bonds is not a viable solution; the same move for Greece did not have lasting success. If Italy had to pay 3 percent in risk premiums, its debt too would become unsustainable. An orderly Greek default and exit from the euro may be necessary; a disorderly default could precipitate a meltdown like that following the bankruptcy of Lehman Brothers, this time without a treasury to contain it. Even if catastrophe is avoided, pressure to reduce deficits will push the euro area into prolonged recession.

Four measures should be taken: bank deposits in Greece must be protected, or else a run on banks would spread to other deficit countries; some banks in defaulting countries have to be kept operating; the European banking system should be recapitalized and put under European instead of national supervision; and government bonds in other deficit countries have to be protected. These measures will require a new treaty turning the EFSF into a full-fledged treasury with the power to tax. Despite German public opposition to it, such a treaty must be approved; assets and liabilities are so intermingled that a breakdown of the euro would cause a meltdown the authorities could not contain. Default or defection of the three small economies would not mean their abandonment. The EFSF would protect bank deposits, and the IMF would help recapitalize banking systems. The ECB, indemnified from insolvency risks and with authorization from the European Council, could serve as the bridge during time-consuming institutional change. A solution in sight would help relieve markets. Because new arrangements would be on German terms, it would take a change in the German attitude toward anticyclical policies to allow resumption of growth.

Simulation Game (Chapter 15)

The strategic game undertaken on the second day of the conference was played in a large room at the conference center. About 50 people, stationed at tables labeled for each entity in the game, participated in or observed the simulation. The players included the ECB, the IMF, market participants, commercial banks, political analysts, and governments of Greece, Ireland, Italy, Portugal, Spain, France, and Germany. Also participating were players representing the rating agencies and the US authorities. The game unfolded over several hours as participants voted their preferences on policy and in the marketplace. These choices were informed by the periodic infusion of new data from market participants on interest rates, bond spreads, and other market developments.

The game drew on many of the insights reached in the earlier discussions and presentations, but with a different focus. Whereas day 1 concentrated on the broad political, economic, and legal challenges to the stability of the euro area, day 2 grappled with more immediate responses to the crisis. The goal was to address the deteriorating situation in the euro area caused by market pressure on several troubled economies. The participants ended up devising a collaborative mechanism to provide additional assistance to ailing countries in the euro area. The market reaction that unfolded in the game suggested that this approach could help quell the serious risk of contagion spreading from the periphery to the core of Europe.

The main feature of this innovative mechanism was a dramatic expansion in the lending capacity of the EFSF combined with collateralized financing from the ECB. The scheme would make available substantial additional resources through the new leveraged EFSF mechanism: depending on haircuts applied in repurchase agreements, the amount would be between €3 trillion and €5 trillion. The ECB played a pivotal role in the game in encouraging and helping the euro area leaders to set up this arrangement.

The primary initial beneficiary of the new EFSF lending mechanism was Greece, which was provided €100 billion in new loans. Athens could use these funds to buy back its existing debt at a premium over current market prices, still reducing its existing stock of debt by considerably more than €100 billion. This capacity was seen as easing Greece's solvency and budgetary concerns and encouraging the markets to offer it lower interest rates. In the game, the market reaction was to reduce these rates slightly. Diminishing risk for Greece was also seen as a significant contribution to overall stability in the euro area.

In a notable feature of the game, and in contrast to some of the discussions of the first day, no concerns surfaced among the players about a possible breakup of the euro area. Lingering wariness over the economic outlook in Europe was widespread, on the other hand.

The reaction of the market players indicated some confidence that the new facility could effectively address the liquidity crises of the ailing countries. For all these positive developments, many of the players expressed concerns that they fell short of solving the euro area's long-term growth and financial prospects. Many players warned that even as the short-term financing and budget problems of Greece were eased, all the debtor countries needed to continue on a path of fiscal consolidation and structural reform in the years ahead. The new mechanism would leave unresolved the issue of how structural reforms could be fostered and conditionality imposed. Ultimately, it would risk being tested by the market. There were also concerns expressed about a possible political backlash against such an extensive new lending program, particularly in Germany, where previous expansions of ECB and EFSF lending have also raised legal and constitutional concerns.

A striking feature of the game, many players agreed afterwards, was that the devised solutions were not effectively communicated, including to the markets. The workings of the proposed leveraged EFSF facility had to be explained repeatedly by those playing ECB and IMF officials. In side meetings, participants from the euro area countries, often convening separately to discuss their possible decisions, sometimes had difficulty in arriving at a consensus on how to proceed. The ECB and IMF came forward on several occasions with key suggestions to address the problems faced in Europe. The ECB also contributed a small cut in interest rates, as well as unlimited long-term liquidity, as the crisis deepened in the first phase of the game. These difficulties illustrated the well-known challenge of achieving effective decision making in the euro area and of communicating with the markets.

The large new lending facility was seen by some players as free money for errant countries without sufficient conditionality. But those devising and supporting the program argued that, on the contrary, it was mobilized to help countries that were on track in implementing their fiscal and structural reform commitments but needed assistance in order to cope with the adverse effects of a slowing world economy and other exogenous factors. A lesson from the game was that the euro area needs to better define the framework for precautionary EFSF operations in support of countries with credible policies.

A team from the United States participated in the game and made a series of announcements, including a maturity extension of the Federal Reserve's balance sheet, a third round of bond purchases (known as quantitative easing), and new dollar swaps with the ECB. These actions appeared to have little effect on the European situation. Players representing the United States pointed out that the new EFSF lending mechanism was somewhat similar to what the Fed and Treasury had established in the depths of the financial meltdown in 2008–09.

The simulation game thus turned out to be an innovative way to improve economic policy advice. It provided a dynamic and strategic setting in which players were faced with real and pressing choices. It revealed the difficulties that current policymakers face given the large number of actors. We hope that the insights derived from the simulation game will contribute to the ongoing development of policies to resolve the European debt crisis.

Postscript[1]

As this volume began production in early December 2011, major new developments had occurred in Greece, in Italy, and within euro area institutional arrangements. On October 27, EU leaders announced that representatives of private banks and insurers had voluntarily agreed to a 50 percent haircut in the face value of their claims on the Greek government. The EU leaders also agreed to recapitalize European banks, and to use leverage to increase the capacity of the EFSF. Two approaches were being considered to obtain EFSF leverage: use of EFSF funds to provide partial guarantees on sovereign bonds; and creation of coinvestment entities to mobilize international funding to purchase bonds of euro area governments. (The alternative emphasized in the Bruegel–Peterson Institute conference, EFSF leverage based on backing by the ECB, was specifically rejected by both the ECB and the euro area leaders, especially Germany.)

New uncertainty soon eroded the restoration of confidence from the EU summit results, however. In the face of domestic opposition to the Greek adjustment package, Prime Minister George Papandreou announced he would hold a referendum on it. The move, which raised the specter of the package's rejection, was condemned by euro area partners and a wide range of the do-

---

1. December 14, 2011.

mestic Greek political spectrum. After securing an implicit pledge to support the adjustment program from the main opposition party, the prime minister then withdrew the referendum proposal, committed to a unity government, and resigned to make way for a transitional coalition government that would be in place until new elections were held. Parallel political unraveling occurred in Italy. On November 8, after losing his coalition's majority support, Prime Minister Silvio Berlusconi announced that he would resign once Parliament passed austerity measures. By then interest rates on Italian 10-year government bonds had risen close to 7 percent, the level that had come to be associated with a spiral into debt crisis in the earlier cases of Greece, Ireland, and Portugal; and the following day they rose above this level.

A further development occurred at the December 9 Council of Europe meeting when the European Union heads of state reached agreement on a core set of actions affecting the debt crisis. The 17 euro area members agreed to a new legal framework on fiscal rules (although a veto by the United Kingdom, largely prompted by the special UK objectives regarding regulation and taxation of financial services, prevented formal revision of the EU treaty). Each government was to adopt a legal "golden rule" providing for a structural deficit no greater than 0.5 percent of GDP, subject to surveillance by the European Court of Justice and fines for countries with deficits exceeding 3 percent of GDP. The starting date for the €500 billion European Stability Mechanism (ESM, to replace the €440 billion EFSF) was moved forward to July 2012, and its clause requiring private sector involvement was removed—reflecting the growing perception that pressure for PSI in Greece had contributed to contagion to Italy and Spain.[2] The EU members planned to consider providing €200 billion in lending to the IMF, in principle to be supplemented by non-European governments, for the purpose of strengthening the financial "firewall" capacity aimed at curbing debt crisis contagion in the euro area. However, the agreement omitted any immediate movement on the issue of euro bonds, or on more robust assurances by the ECB that it stood ready to intervene forcefully in the sovereign bond market.

The papers in this volume on Greece and Italy provide a rich background for understanding the political crises that have unfolded in these two countries. The debate in the policy strategy analyses on the needed depth of Greek debt forgiveness and the associated risks of contagion similarly set the stage for the real-time developments under way as this volume went to press. The emphasis in the conference on the need to fortify the EFSF in order to deal with the much larger economies of Italy and Spain similarly resonates with the EU summit initiative in late October as well as the earlier date for the ESM and

---

2. European Council president Herman Van Rompuy stated that ". . . our first approach to PSI, which had a very negative effect on the debt markets, is now officially over." However, he also stated that "from now on we will strictly adhere to the IMF principles and practices" (European Council 2011). Considering that the IMF has at times been hawkish on PSI in country restructurings, the overall effect was ambiguous.

the special IMF-based initiative for crisis-related lending. Finally, the papers on lessons from past experience in sovereign debt restructurings will serve as a sobering reference if less-voluntary restructuring proves necessary in Greece and if restructurings spread to other euro area sovereigns.

References

Delpla, Jacques, and Jakob von Weizsäcker. 2010. *The Blue Bond Proposal*. Bruegel Policy Brief 2010/03. Brussels: Bruegel. Available at www.bruegel.org (accessed on November 15, 2011).

European Council. 2011. Remarks by Herman Van Rompuy, President of the European Council following the first session of the European Council. EUCO 155/11 (December 9). Brussels.

POLITICAL-ECONOMIC ENVIRONMENTS

I

2

Greece in the Euro Area: Odd Man Out, or Precursor of Things to Come?

LOUKAS TSOUKALIS

Greece has acted as a catalyst for the outbreak of the crisis of the euro area, following the bursting of the big bubble in the Western financial system. It remains today the most vulnerable link of the euro chain, even as the crisis has extended to other countries. Greece has also served as a test case for national and European policies in response to the crisis—more precisely, as a stress test for the domestic political system and the economy and society at large in the context of economic austerity, recession, and reform-induced change, as well as for the capacity of European institutions to devise new policies to deal with problems they had clearly not been prepared for.

Some believe that Greece is the odd man out among the beleaguered countries of the European periphery. If that is true, there is a wide variety of policy options that may follow, ranging all the way from special treatment and patience for a country expected to go through little less than a peaceful revolution amid punishing conditions, to orderly or less orderly default and/ or forced exit from the euro area. There are others who suspect or fear that Greece may be the precursor of things to come—as it has already been to some extent—or possibly the first in a series of domino effects that could eventually lead to the disintegration of the euro area. The stakes are high, indeed. Hence

Loukas Tsoukalis is professor of European integration at the University of Athens, president of the Hellenic Foundation for European and Foreign Policy (ELIAMEP), and visiting professor at the College of Europe in Bruges.

Figure 2.1 Holdings of Greek government debt, December 2007–March 2011

billions of euros

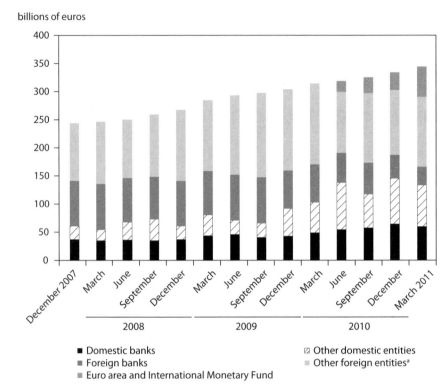

| | 2008 | 2009 | 2010 |

■ Domestic banks   ☒ Other domestic entities
■ Foreign banks   ▨ Other foreign entities[a]
▨ Euro area and International Monetary Fund

a. Including the European Central Bank.

Source: European Commission, *The Economic Adjustment Programme for Greece,* Fifth Review Draft, October 2011, p. 22, graph 21.

the disproportionate amount of international attention paid to Greece in comparison to its modest size, although admittedly the size of its public debt is less modest. As of June 2011, its public debt had risen to €354 billion, held in large part by foreigners, notably banks, other financial institutions, and increasingly European governments and the European Central Bank (ECB). The debt held by private institutions exceeded €200 billion (figure 2.1).

The Outbreak of the Crisis

It all began in October 2009, when the newly elected government of Greece, led by George Papandreou of the socialist party (PASOK), announced that the Greek budget deficit of 2009 was going to be much bigger than previously claimed by the outgoing center-right (New Democracy) government, well into double-digit figures. The announcement was not followed by serious

Figure 2.2   10-year interest rate spreads over German bunds, September 1992–June 2011

basis points

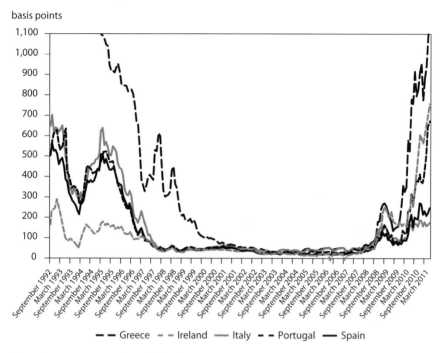

Greece   Ireland   Italy   Portugal   Spain

Source: Europe at a Crossroads, speech by Gikas Hardouvelis, Eurobank EFG, Belgrade, October 24, 2011, www.eurobankefg.rs.

measures to deal with the problem. Jittery markets, still under the spell of the Lehman effect, suddenly focussed on the prospect that the financial crisis could transform itself into a crisis of sovereign debt, as governments increased their borrowing to deal with the adverse effects on banks and the real economy. Spreads on Greek state borrowing rose fast as the Greek government and EU institutions dithered (figure 2.2).

Greece was the catalyst for the outbreak of the crisis of the euro area because it had the worst combination of three different deficits. First, it had a large budget deficit, which reached 15.4 percent of GDP in 2009 after a number of revisions (figure 2.3), on top of an already big public debt (at 127 percent of GDP in 2009, it was already the highest in the euro area). Second, it had an equally large, indeed unsustainable, deficit in its current account that was almost 15 percent of GDP in 2008 (figure 2.4)—a deficit of competitiveness, in other words. Finally, it had a serious credibility deficit, as people realized that Greek politicians had repeatedly been economical with the truth and creative with the use of statistics. Greece was surely not unique with respect to any of those three deficits among members of the euro area and the wider world. But

Figure 2.3 General government revenues and expenditures, 1988–2010

percent of GDP

Source: Europe at a Crossroads, speech by Gikas Hardouvelis, Eurobank EFG, Belgrade, October 24, 2011, www.eurobankefg.rs.

Figure 2.4 Current account balance, 1995–2010

percent of GDP

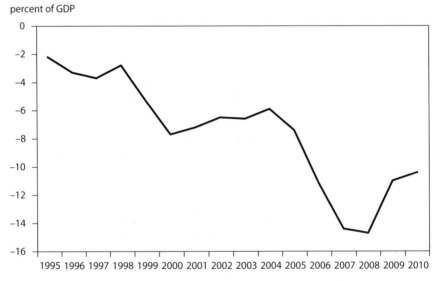

Source: Europe at a Crossroads, speech by Gikas Hardouvelis, Eurobank EFG, Belgrade, October 24, 2011, www.eurobankefg.rs.

Figure 2.5 Real GDP growth, 2003–12

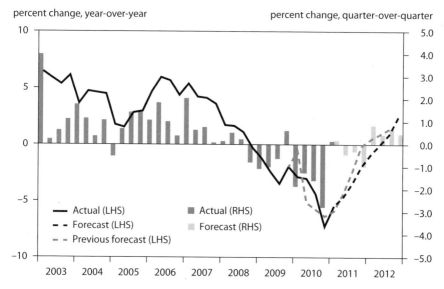

percent change, year-over-year   percent change, quarter-over-quarter

Legend:
— Actual (LHS)   ■ Actual (RHS)
- - Forecast (LHS)   ■ Forecast (RHS)
- - Previous forecast (LHS)

Sources: Hellenic Statistical Authority (EL.STAT.), www.statistics.gr; European Commission Services.

it had, undoubtedly, the worst combination of deficits when markets began to panic again, while governments, and notably Greece's own government, took their time in trying to get a grip on an admittedly very difficult situation.

The mess in which the country found itself stemmed from huge failures of government and political responsibility. Since Greece joined the euro in 2001, budget deficits have always exceeded the 3 percent Maastricht limit (figure 2.3), partly camouflaged through creative accounting but seen as manageable as long as nominal and real growth rates remained high (figure 2.5). They seemed manageable no longer when the international crisis hit. At the time, Greece had a weak government that, facing the prospect of early elections, allowed public finances to get completely out of control in 2008–09.

Greek politics is clientele politics par excellence: Political parties distribute money and favors to voters/clients. Greece is, of course, not unique in this respect. But the problem grew bigger with time: The quality of the Greek political class steadily deteriorated, the *"enrichissez-vous"* culture became dominant after many years of rapidly rising prosperity, and membership in the European Union, and the euro in particular, came to be perceived as an all-protective umbrella against adversity, as well as a provider of free or cheap money, rather than an agent for reform. The state became increasingly corrupt and dysfunctional, an instrument of parties in power and a victim of the clientele system which, if anything, grew stronger over the years. There was cheap money to spend. Organized interests and the forces of inertia in a basically conservative society that does not much like change combined to kill any attempt at structural reform. The result was a deadlocked country in many ways, although one still enjoying a steadily rising standard of living.

It had not always been like this. Greece is a country that underwent a remarkable transformation during the second half of the 20th century, from economic underdevelopment and deeply flawed democratic institutions, interrupted by a spell of dictatorial rule, to high standards of living (Greece was classified before the outbreak of the crisis among the top 25 countries of the world according to United Nations indicators) and a full-fledged democracy. It is the country that organized the highly successful, albeit extremely costly, Olympic Games of 2004, the only country of its size to do so for several decades, and the one that played an important stabilization role in the Balkan region after the collapse of communist regimes, with Greek banks and enterprises acquiring in the process an important foothold in the area. It could be argued that Greece has often tried to punch above its weight. This tendency has largely to do with history going back a long way.

But there is something else contributing to it: a Greek elite, consisting largely of expatriates, with a strong global presence in the arts and sciences, in finance, and in shipping, but not directly participating in the running of the country. From the peak of success and self-confidence only a few years back, Greece has suddenly come tumbling down. The fall has been big, sudden, and painful, and most Greeks now realize it is far from over yet: hence, a society in a state of deep shock.

Of course, if responsibility and blame are to be attributed for the derailment of Greek public finances and the steady loss of competitiveness during the period of euro membership, the buck cannot stop at the door of Greek politicians. No doubt the main responsibility lies with those who governed the country and indirectly with those who entrusted them with their votes: in other words, Greek society in general. But at least part of the responsibility also lies with EU institutions and Greece's European partners. Successive Greek governments pretended that public finances were in order and reforms were under way, and the other Europeans pretended for different reasons to believe them. Greece is not unique in this respect either. The surveillance mechanism for the euro set up at Maastricht clearly did not work: The Stability and Growth Pact was inadequate in its conception, and it was poorly implemented. And when the crisis came, we all discovered (or were just reminded) that the European Union had no mechanism to deal with it—some had apparently been afraid of moral hazard (Tsoukalis 2011a, 2011b).

There was also manifest market failure. Greek governments and others kept borrowing at very low interest rates—at times, at negative interest rates. Spreads over German bunds remained at very low levels for many years (figure 2.2), thus implying that Greek government bonds were perceived by markets as presenting almost the same risk as German ones. Markets did not bother to look at the figures, or ask awkward questions. To be fair, the possibility of sovereign default for a member of the euro area was not at all an issue until two or three years ago; it belonged to the category of unthinkables. Now markets know better, having often moved to the other extreme, and thus helping to make the nonsustainability of Greek public debt almost into a self-fulfilling prophecy.

The Weak Link of the Euro Chain

Much has happened since the late months of 2009, when the crisis hit. Rating agencies, markets, and analysts looked more closely at figures and institutional structures and began to doubt both the sustainability of Greek public finances and Europe's possession of either the instruments or the political will to deal with the more general problem that had arisen.

They placed their money accordingly. Those doubts were more pronounced in Wall Street and the City of London, where speculation about the viability of the euro, or even the European Union, has been particularly rife since the very beginning. There was surely an element of schadenfreude among people who had not welcomed the creation of the common currency in the first place, but a more complete explanation would require a much longer paper.

Many unthinkable things have happened since then—and in a big way. Crisis is, after all, the mother of change, helping to transform the unthinkable into reality. It has happened in Greece and in other vulnerable countries of the euro area. It has also happened in the countries of the European core, leading to the adoption of European measures that had been completely off the agenda only a short time ago. The trouble is that measures usually come late, they are often poorly implemented, and they invariably end up being judged by markets as insufficient. A growing number of critics now argue that the underlying strategy behind the adopted measures may also be flawed.

In Greece, PASOK was elected in October 2009 with a strong majority and a mandate to spend and to further strengthen the welfare state. Of course, PASOK should have known better. Lynched by reality (and the markets), it was forced to make a volte-face a few months later and ended up reducing the budget deficit by 5 percentage points of GDP in a year, something that had not happened in an Organization for Economic Cooperation and Development (OECD) country for decades. However, the deficit was still over 10 percent at the end of 2010 (European Commission 2011). The government raised taxes, cut public sector salaries and pensions, adopted fiscal and pension reform, changed the statistical service, and began to take measures to restore the international competitiveness of the economy. The latter included liberalization measures in the labor market and closed professions. Surely, these are not the kind of measures that most socialist parties identify with, especially not Greece's PASOK, with its strong populist tradition and with most of the party machine, or what is now left of it, safely and comfortably (or so its members thought until very recently) ensconced in the wider public sector. Internal resistance was, as expected, ferocious.

Macroeconomic adjustment, with the emphasis on fiscal consolidation, and structural reform were the Greek part of a deal reached at the level of

Figure 2.6   Greek banks' borrowing from the Eurosystem, 2004–11

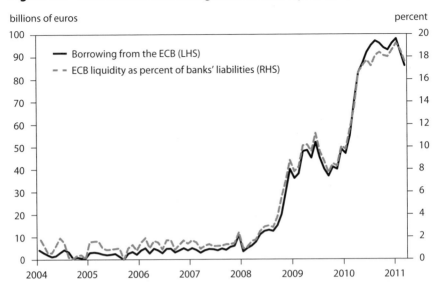

ECB = European Central Bank

Source: European Commission.

the euro area in May 2010. The deal was intended to provide Greece with the necessary finance (€110 billion) until 2013 in order to continue servicing and financing its public debt, while also helping it to restore sustainable public finances, encourage competitiveness, and establish the conditions for healthy long-term growth. Since then, Greece has been on European and International Monetary Fund (IMF) life support: Disbursements to the Greek government had reached €65 billion at the time of writing, with another €8 billion on its way.[1]

Support has also been extended to Greek banks through the ECB. The banks have been the victims of the Greek sovereign debt crisis, and not the other way round as happened in Ireland and several other countries. Greek banks are big holders of Greek state bonds. As a result of the crisis, they were cut off from interbank lending, while domestic deposits shrank by more than 20 percent and nonperforming loans increased substantially, thus leaving the ECB and the Greek central bank as a key source of liquidity. Total borrowing from these two sources is now between €90 billion and €100 billion, which represents about 20 percent of liabilities (figure 2.6).

After a lot of agonizing and difficult negotiations, a new financial support package was agreed to by euro area leaders on July 21, 2011, with more money

---

1. For the latest review of the economic adjustment program for Greece at the time of writing, see European Commission (2011).

Figure 2.7   10-year interest rate spreads over German bunds, January 2010–September 2011

percent

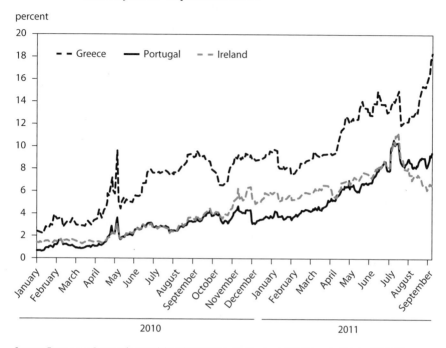

Sources: Europe at a Crossroads, speech by Gikas Hardouvelis, Eurobank EFG, Belgrade, October 24, 2011, www.eurobankefg.rs; Bank of Greece.

and new provisions for reduced interest burdens, extension of maturities, protection of Greek banks, measures to foster growth (including the frontloading of the use of EU structural funds in Greece), and some private sector involvement in the refinancing of Greek debt. It was another big package: a strong signal to Greece of European solidarity but also an attempt to correct some of the weaknesses and faults of the earlier package. A big taboo was also being broken with the provision for private sector involvement under strong German insistence. The intra-European debate on this highly controversial issue, pitting Germany against the ECB, had been highly destabilizing in terms of the effect it had on Greek spreads (and not only) before the July 21 decision. Figure 2.7 shows the evolution of those spreads, although they no longer mean very much since there is hardly a market for Greek sovereign bonds any more.

The decision of July 21, 2011, broke the taboo of sovereign debt default in the euro area, although it was only meant to reduce slightly Greece's debt burden. It proved difficult to implement, and it was soon superseded by another, much bolder decision, as the crisis took a turn for the worse in Greece and elsewhere in the euro area. In the early hours of October 27, 2011, the leaders of the euro area went much further, implicitly recognizing that the decision they had taken only three months earlier was no longer adequate. After a difficult negotiation with representatives of banks, an agreement was reached to proceed with a "voluntary" haircut of no less than 50 percent of the notional value of Greek sovereign debt held by private institutions. The objective was to bring Greek debt down to 120 percent of GDP by 2020, and thus make it more sustainable. They also agreed to a new multiannual assistance program for Greece that would add €100 billion to the amount already committed in May 2010, plus €30 billion as the official counterpart to the private sector involvement package: unprecedented amounts for an unprecedented crisis. Implementation of those decisions will not be an easy sail, judging from earlier experience.

The European system is slow and cumbersome, and implementation usually leaves much to be desired. Decisions reached at the European level are constantly prey to national politics, while there is less and less appetite for bailouts in the creditor countries or for any kind of "transfer union," a possibility that is haunting the minds of many German citizens and others. On the other hand, the task of convincing private creditors of Greece to accept a big haircut "voluntarily," thus averting a so-called credit event, will not be easy either. The crisis has already reached the bigger fish, most notably Italy.

There is also a question mark about Greece's capacity to deliver its part of the bargain. The Greek government has not proved to be strong on delivery on several fronts, even though much has already been achieved. The budget for 2011 has been off target, thus forcing the government under pressure from the "troika" (European Commission, ECB, and IMF) to pile on additional measures in order to fill the gap. More austerity, however, is increasingly difficult, if not impossible, as the recession is deepening (the decline in GDP is expected to be around 6 percent this year, substantially more than forecast), while unemployment is rapidly approaching 17 percent (figure 2.8). There is no end in sight as yet.

An austerity-recession downward spiral has been at work, reinforced by the shortage of liquidity provided by the banks. This situation is now recognized by the troika (European Commission 2011). On the other hand, it is true that the government was slow with structural reform intended to create an environment favorable to investment and growth, and that it was more willing to raise tax levels than cut expenditures. And these tendencies further penalized the private sector, at least those in it who pay taxes. The private sector has been shedding labor at a rapid pace as domestic demand shrinks fast. Experience suggests that structural reforms are particularly difficult in a rapidly worsening economic environment.

PASOK has been married to the state, and any ideas about even a velvet divorce are horrifying for many of its members. But the same is true of all political parties in Greece. The big and decisive battle today in Greece is about the restructuring and rationalization of a bloated, inefficient, and largely corrupt public sector. This will be the mother of all battles.

Figure 2.8   Employment and unemployment rate, 2007–January 2011

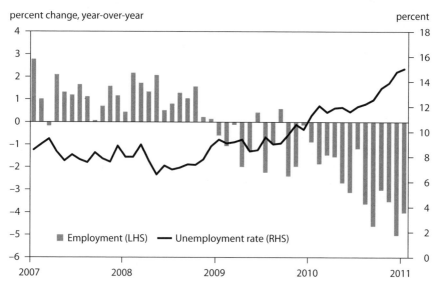

Sources: Hellenic Statistical Authority (EL.STAT.), Labor Force Survey, www.statistics.gr.

After long hesitation and much resistance, the PASOK government finally undertook to reduce substantially the numbers of those employed in public administration and the state-controlled enterprises, through shutdowns, restructuring, and extensive privatization. And the reaction from trade unions was fierce, as expected. The fight for a leaner state will be hard going, judging from earlier results and the strong opposition already encountered.

State assets are very large in Greece in comparison to many other European countries, for historical reasons among others. Hence the emphasis on the privatization program, which will bring money to the government coffers while also leading to a more efficient use of resources. The objective is to raise €50 billion by 2015, a highly ambitious target. A common objection to privatization is that carrying it out on a large scale will be selling Greece on the cheap—like holding a fire sale at a time when prices of stocks have hit rock bottom in the Athens exchange as a result of the crisis. This phenomenon has happened before in other countries in deep crisis, close to home in the Balkans after the fall of communism and the war in Yugoslavia, and also in the Far East following the financial crisis of the 1990s. There may be little choice in the matter, but it is still politically very difficult. It should be added, however, that most of the privatization will be in real estate and government concessions for mainly underutilized assets.

Tax evasion is a major problem. According to the OECD (2011), if Greece had the tax-collecting capacity of the average (not the best) member of the organization, its tax revenues would increase by almost 5 percent of GDP: not bad, since this would amount to more than half of the total fiscal adjustment still required. Tax evasion certainly stems from the poor state of tax collection in Greece, in turn the product of weak administrative capacity as well as corruption. But it also has to do with the structure of the Greek economy, which has the highest percentage of self-employed in the OECD, coupled with a predominance of small, family-run enterprises. Economic structures do not change from one day to the next. Tax collection may change more quickly, though, if the political will is there—and it should be.

Overall, there are indeed legitimate doubts about the will and capacity of Greece, notably its political system and society at large, to deliver what it has promised to its European partners and the IMF. There is, however, another side to the story. Greece's creditors have been arguably asking too much in a short space of time from a democratic government in a state of siege, while the frontloading of fiscal adjustment has been creating a deadly spiral for the economy, especially in the context of a deteriorating international economic environment. This situation may not change dramatically, whoever is in power in the country. The two sides of the story are not mutually exclusive. They are instead mutually reinforcing. Is there a way of getting out of the vicious circle?

Can Greece Do It?

The task facing Greece is simply enormous: fiscal adjustment of close to 13 percent of GDP in five years' time (2009–14), with about 7 percent still to go, depending on the final outcome of the haircut of its public debt. This is combined with the need for internal devaluation and structural reforms, including a major overhaul of the state machine and a wide range of liberalization measures. By the end of 2011, real GDP will have registered a cumulative decline of more than 10 percent since 2009. The decline is expected to continue in 2012, contrary to the forecasts made in the adjustment program. Admittedly, other countries have suffered a worse fate and survived.

The distribution of pain is crucial in political and social terms. The burden has so far fallen more than proportionately on the better off, although allowance has to be made for the still-large number of tax evaders. Dealing with tax evasion is a question of social justice as much as it is a question of macroeconomic balance. Unemployment is now hitting the middle classes, and the fat accumulated over the years of prosperity is being rapidly burnt.

We are dangerously close to the bone. Were it not for the Greek family, which remains by far the most efficient welfare provider in times of need, the social situation would be much worse. Young and less young Greeks are increasingly looking for job opportunities abroad, and there are also signs of a slow return from urban centers to the countryside, where there are better ways to survive a big economic crisis. A better utilization of the opportunities provided by Greece's comparative advantage in agricultural products would surely not be a bad thing. On the other hand, effective resistance to change does not come primarily from the weak. It is organized interests in the public sector and elsewhere (lawyers, pharmacists, owners of lorries and taxis, among others) that have been fighting hard to preserve privileges and rents acquired in the political domain. And they have people in parliament to defend their interests.

The decisions taken by the euro area leaders in July and October 2011 have broken the taboo about the sustainability of Greek public debt. International and EU organizations had until then produced different scenarios that tried to prove that under various assumptions Greece was illiquid but not necessarily insolvent. This was increasingly not the view adopted by markets and the majority of analysts.[2] The first, hesitant step toward accepting that Greek public debt was unsustainable was taken in July 2011 with a small "voluntary" haircut accompanied by expensive financial incentives offered to Greece's creditors. It was followed by a much more drastic step in October, with an agreement in principle for a 50 percent haircut of notional Greek public debt held by private institutions. If and when implemented, this step will cut more than €100 billion out of Greece's overall debt. Coupled with decisions taken in July concerning the reduction of the interest burden for the part of the debt owned by EU governments and institutions and the extension of maturities, this haircut will surely provide significant relief. But sustainability of the debt, of course, crucially depends on future growth, in turn a function of domestic reforms and the economic environment in Greece and outside. For a still relatively closed economy such as the Greek one, the export environment is not as important as it is for the Irish economy, for example. But it surely does matter. Greek exports have risen substantially since the outbreak of the crisis, thus partially closing a still unsustainable gap in the current account (figure 2.4). This is indeed one of the positive signs.

The Greek government generally adopted a low profile with respect to discussions about the restructuring of Greek public debt. The official line for some time was that Greece would meet all its obligations to debtors in accordance with the official statements made by its EU partners as well as by European and international institutions. The government seemed to mean it. In fact, this was one of the few issues on which the PASOK government and the main opposition party, New Democracy, were in agreement. The fact that the ECB was strongly opposed to any kind of debt restructuring surely played an important role in this stance, since the very survival of the Greek banking system remained entirely dependent on access to ECB liquidity. When, under pressure from Germany, the possibility of debt restructuring was opened, the Greek government continued to keep a low profile, which is more surprising. Allowing foreign governments and bankers to take the lead role in negotiating the restructuring of your debt is surely a big sign of weakness. The country had become marginalized.

At the time of writing, the crisis in Greece had reached a new climax. Following the European agreement of October 27, 2011, which was meant to offer Greece breathing space through a new multiannual rescue plan and a substan-

---

2. See also chapter 11 in this volume by William Cline.

tial haircut of its debt, Papandreou committed a fatal error of judgment. Having for two years led a government under siege, having introduced bold and painful measures—but having failed to develop and articulate a coherent and consistent strategy for economic reform and adjustment, and aware that his popularity and that of his party were sinking rapidly in the polls—he decided to call for a referendum on Greece's rescue package. This would inevitably turn into a referendum on Greece's continued participation in the euro. The negative reaction from inside and outside Greece was very strong, as markets saw Greece as the new Lehman Brothers. Papandreou was forced to take back the plan for a referendum and paid the price by leaving the office of prime minister.

These events were the catalyst for further political developments in Greece. Domestic politics has always been strongly partisan and confrontational. The credibility of the Greek political class has sunk very low, and it is increasingly being seen as part of the problem and not part of the solution. Papandreou's government has been replaced by a coalition government led by Lucas Papademos, former vice president of the ECB, which has the main task of putting Greece's side of the October 2011 agreement on track and preparing for early elections. Given the enormity of the task facing any Greek government for the next few years, the optimistic scenario is that this transitional government may lay the ground for broader consensus and coalition governments after the next elections.

The main opposition party is ahead in the polls, although far from certain of gaining an absolute majority. There is no doubt that the New Democracy party bears a huge responsibility for the mess that Greece finds itself in. After all, it was this party that governed the country between 2004 and 2009, while PASOK, in opposition then, competed in terms of populist rhetoric. Under a new leader, Antonis Samaras, New Democracy opposed the government of PASOK and the program agreed upon with the European partners and the IMF, arguing that the economic strategy was wrong because it produced a vicious circle of austerity and recession. It called for tax reductions as an incentive for investment and growth, but remained reluctant when it came to cuts in the public sector. Samaras basically argued that there is an alternative strategy, and implied that he could convince his European partners and creditors to go along with it when he comes to the negotiating table with a fresh popular mandate. He was forced to compromise earlier as a precondition for Greece receiving the next installment of financial aid from its European partners and the IMF, after the formation of the new government, led by Papademos, in November 2011, with support from three parties, including his own, and with people from New Democracy in the cabinet. The solidity of Samaras' conversion, forced or otherwise, remains to be tested.

Not surprisingly under the circumstances, populism has been on the rise in a country where many people feel increasingly desperate. The radical Left, including an old-style Communist party, with a strong anticapitalist platform and in favor of a debt moratorium, represents 20 to 25 percent of the electorate today. This group is in no mood to compromise with the government, the European Union, or anybody else. They largely represent the angry, the *indignados*, and the desperados, but they have no serious alternative to offer.

Although support for European integration has suffered as a consequence of the crisis, there is no big wave of anti-Europeanism in Greece. When it comes to the crunch, nearly all Greeks apparently still realize there is no future for Greece outside the European Union. There is also a clear majority in favor of keeping the euro (about two-thirds majority, according to the latest opinion polls), which is also reflected in the stance adopted on this strategically important issue by most political parties, including the two major ones: a kind of bottom-line consensus. Most Greek citizens realize that a return to the drachma would be tantamount to economic and political disaster for Greece, although most also realize that the possibility of this happening is coming closer by the day as long as Greece fails to deliver its side of the bargain. The minority arguing for the return to the drachma speaks more about the alleged benefits of regained sovereignty and less about the possible benefits of a devaluation of the new currency. This group includes those who are banging on the patriotic drum and others who expect to buy assets on the cheap after an economic collapse—an unholy alliance indeed.

Populist media have resorted to racist and xenophobic messages, often in direct response to their counterparts (of the *Bildt Zeitung* variety) in other countries and Germany in particular. The exchange of stereotypes and insults is depressing. But most Greeks still reluctantly accept that the crisis is basically of Greek making. Looking for scapegoats outside the borders remains therefore an exercise for those on the fringes of the political system, yet fringes that are increasingly occupying parts of the old core.

There is a culture of protest in Greece, coupled with a high degree of politicization of just about everything. Clientele politics is part and parcel of the political culture. Politics is high-adrenaline stuff—Greece is not Scandinavia. Street demonstrations and other forms of social protest have increased dramatically as a result of the crisis. Some have been unruly even by Greek standards. Anomie has become a real issue, and the rule of law is being stretched. The problem with the young generations is the most serious. With around 40 percent of young people in their early 20s out of a job, there is the grim prospect of a lost generation in Greece and in several other countries (IMF 2011). This situation is a time bomb waiting to explode.

The reluctant acceptance of the inevitability of austerity measures, which had been registered by opinion polls in the early stages of the crisis, has been progressively replaced by ever bigger majorities against. Greeks are angry and afraid; they see no light and no end of the tunnel. The political scene has become extremely fluid: Party allegiance has weakened remarkably, shifts within the political system are happening fast, while more than 30 percent of those polled consistently refuse to express a preference. There is a big political vacuum that waits to be filled. It has not happened for a long time or on such a scale. A large part of the Greek political class is likely to be swept away by the tsunami caused by the crisis. Most of them will not be missed.

Greece needs a radical renewal of its political class. Such a renewal is likely to happen within existing parties when the next election comes, a prospect that is not far away, and it may also happen with the creation of one or more new parties. An increasing number of opinion formers, intellectuals, and businesspeople in Greece are converging on the need for a reformist political movement, one cutting across traditional dividing lines between center-left and center-right, which would articulate and defend the vision of a reformed Greece. Whether the critical mass is already there and, perhaps more importantly, whether there will be somebody to lead it, remains to be seen. It could be a game changer.

Odd Man Out?

So, is Greece the odd man out in the euro area, a patient in the European intensive care unit with little chance of recovery? No doubt, the challenge of adjustment facing Greece is huge. I wrote above about the need for a peaceful revolution. Such a revolution would not just seek macroeconomic adjustment and regained competitiveness, as if those two tasks were not big enough. It would also offer a new model of economic development, a radical reform of the state, and the renewal of its political system. And it would finally promote a change of values.

Under normal conditions, the progress registered in the last two years or so—more than had been achieved for years—would have been truly impressive. But conditions are not normal. The country could end up with a disorderly default, while the possibility of an exit from the euro area is being openly discussed. If this exit were to happen, it would set Greece back many years and plunge it into uncharted territory.

Greece's political forces have had great difficulty in reaching any meaningful consensus, as the economy sinks and society is in a state of despair. In fact, Greece's political class, with some exceptions, is more part of the problem than of the solution. The country finds itself in that intermediate stage when the old is dying and the new has not yet been born. This stage could last for some time, but the trouble is that Greece may have little time left to avoid a major catastrophe.

The program imposed on Greece by its creditors is punishing, even though considerable improvements have been made in successive revisions of it. Arguably, it is still more than any government in a democratic country can deliver. And this is not meant as an excuse for the outgoing PASOK government, which wasted precious time, tried to protect the barons of the state sector at the expense of those working in the private one, sat on reform, and poorly implemented what it had itself legislated. At the time of writing, Greece had just entered the next phase, with a new government enjoying broader support in Parliament and with the task of setting the ground for the implementation of the European agreement reached on October 27, 2011. New elections are expected to be called a few months later. Now the ball is more in the court of the New Democracy party and its leader, Samaras. It remains to be seen how much the prospect of coming to power sooner rather than later will help to soften the rough edges of public stances taken while in opposition.

The European and international context does not always help—and this is a polite way of putting it. True, decisions adopted by the euro area leaders with respect to Greece would have been completely unthinkable only two years ago. They have paved the way for similar decisions for Ireland and Portugal. Yet the time and pain involved in reaching those decisions, the cacophony that often surrounds them, and the implementation gap that follows present real problems. Alas, such is the European decision-making system.

Euro leaders hoped in May 2010 that Greece would be a unique case requiring special treatment. They were proved wrong a few months later, when other countries followed Greece asking for European support. Again, in July 2011, euro leaders reiterated the same hope, while agreeing on a second and more generous rescue package for Greece. They took a big step further in October of the same year, by which time the crisis had reached Italy with no end in sight. While they have been trying to build a firewall around Greece, the fire has been spreading elsewhere.

Greece is, indeed, different and in several respects weaker than other countries of the euro area. But if Greece does not make it in the end, other countries could follow. The fear of the domino effect is in everybody's mind. Many of the problems Greece is facing are far from unique. The euro area will need to move further along the road of fiscal union as the necessary counterpart to the single currency. This being a long and painfully slow process, the role of the ECB (and the European Financial Stability Facility) will be crucial in the meantime. If the euro area crisis continues to get worse, nothing short of the ECB intervening on a large scale as a lender of last resort will be strong enough to restore calm in the financial markets. In a double-dip recession, existing European mechanisms will come under heavy pressure, while resistance to austerity will grow in many places. And Greece could then once more be the precursor of things to come. This is indeed a scary scenario.

References

European Commission. 2011. *The Economic Adjustment Programme for Greece.* Fifth Review—October 2011 (Draft). Brussels.

IMF (International Monetary Fund). 2011. *Greece: Fourth Review Under the Stand-By Arrangement and Request for Modification and Waiver of Application of Performance Criteria.* IMF Country Report No. 11/175. Washington.

OECD (Organization for Economic Cooperation and Development). 2011. *Economic Survey of Greece.* Available at www.oecd.org/eco/surveys/greece (accessed on December 5, 2011).

Tsoukalis, L. 2011a. The Delphic Oracle on Europe. In *The Delphic Oracle on Europe: Is There a Future for the European Union?* ed. L. Tsoukalis and J. A. Emmanouilidis. Oxford: Oxford University Press.

Tsoukalis, L. 2011b. The Shattering of Illusions—And What Next? *Journal of Common Market Studies* 49 (issue supplement S1): 19–44.

3

Political-Economic Context in Ireland

ALAN AHEARNE

The economic crisis that has affected the Irish economy over the past three years owes its severity to the interaction of domestic and international factors.[1] Economic activity has slumped and unemployment surged since 2008, as the housing bubble deflated and the badly overheated construction sector shrank. The housing bubble and related credit boom over the previous decade resulted in an overindebted household sector, and ongoing efforts to repair household balance sheets have put a drag on consumer spending. The global recession added to the downturn, as exports declined in 2009, although exports have since recovered to hit new record highs in recent quarters.

The drop in domestic demand was exacerbated by necessary fiscal adjustment. At the peak of the boom, nearly one-third of government revenues were directly related to the property market. This overreliance on asset-related revenues was accompanied by rapid increases in government spending during the boom. The bursting of the housing bubble exposed a large structural budget deficit of more than 11 percent of (potential) GDP.[2] Reducing this deficit to sustainable levels has necessitated a multiyear program of substantial spending cuts and revenue-raising measures.

Alan Ahearne lectures in economics at the National University of Ireland in Galway. He is also a nonresident research fellow at Bruegel and a member of the Board of the Central Bank of Ireland.

1. See Regling and Watson (2010) for an excellent discussion of how different factors interacted to cause the crisis.

2. The IMF estimate is for 2008 (IMF 2011, 26).

The combination of the housing bust and the global financial crisis also exposed deep problems in Ireland's banking sector. Lending by Irish banks surged 21 percent annually on average between 2002 and 2007, with most of the growth concentrated in speculative property lending (Nyberg 2011). The downturn revealed huge losses on these loans. Moreover, this rapid expansion in bank lending was funded largely by borrowing from international wholesale money markets (Honohan 2010). Concerns about banks' prospective loan losses and the tightening in international credit markets following the collapse of Lehman Brothers in September 2008 and the Greek crisis in May 2010 resulted in the eventual withdrawal of most of this foreign funding. This funding has been replaced by borrowing from the European Central Bank (ECB) and the Central Bank of Ireland.

Ireland entered the crisis with very low levels of government debt. Gross government debt was 25 percent of GDP in 2007, while net government debt was only 12 percent of GDP.[3] Large fiscal deficits and the substantial cost of rescuing the banking system resulted in a rapid increase in gross government debt to an estimated 110 percent of GDP in 2011. After spiking at 6 percent in March 2009, the cost of long-term Irish government borrowing gradually eased back to 4.5 percent by April 2010. However, European sovereign debt markets were unsettled by the Greek crisis in May 2010 and the Deauville Agreement in October 2010, leading to a sharp rise in risk premia on the debt of peripheral economies. Amid investor concerns about the rising cost of the banking rescue and the slowdown in global economic growth in the second half of 2010, yields on Irish government debt rose to unsustainable levels. Under pressure from the ECB, Ireland requested financial assistance through an EU-International Monetary Fund (IMF) program on November 21, 2010.[4]

Summary Description of the National Political Situation and Near-Term Outlook

Parliamentary elections held on February 25, 2011, returned a new coalition government of Fine Gael and the Labor Party. The new coalition government holds more than two-thirds of the seats in Parliament, the largest majority in Ireland's history (see table 3.1).

The next general election is due in 2016 at the latest.

Current Governing Coalition

During the election campaign, both Fine Gael and Labor promised a significant renegotiation of the terms of the EU-IMF program, which had been

---

3. The difference between gross and net government debt reflected financial assets held by the state, including €21 billion in the National Pension Reserve Fund and nearly €5 billion in cash balances (FitzGerald and Kearney 2011).

4. The program was subsequently approved by the Council of the European Union on December 7, 2010, and by the IMF board on December 16, 2010.

**Table 3.1   General election results,
February 25, 2011**

Party	Seats
Fine Gael	76
Labor	37
Fianna Fáil	20
Independents and small parties	19
Sinn Féin	14
Total	166
Fine Gael–Labor coalition	113

Source: Election 2011 Results: National Summary, RTÉ News,
www.rte.ie/news/election2011/results/index.html.

agreed upon with the previous Fianna Fáil–led government. Both parties' campaigns included promises to impose losses on senior bondholders in Irish banks. Since the election, some changes to the EU-IMF program have been agreed to with the troika (European Commission, ECB, and IMF) and the new government has shown a strong willingness to meet the program's targets. In the last quarterly review of the program, in October, the troika concluded that "programme implementation continues to be strong."

Minister for Finance Michael Noonan said recently that Ireland had shown that it "can and will meet demanding fiscal targets." He added that the EU-IMF program provided a "clear path of sustainability," and that "at a political level, the willingness to meet the targets is underpinned by the new government which has such a large parliamentary majority."

There have been some public differences recently between Fine Gael, a center-right party, and Labor, a center-left party, over relatively minor aspects of the EU-IMF program. Some political analysts worry that more serious tensions between the coalition parties may emerge as the government faces up to a range of unpalatable decisions in coming budgets. For example, another round of public sector pay cuts would undermine support for Labor among its political base. Labor will come under particular pressure from smaller left-wing parties who oppose the EU-IMF program.

There is also some concern that the size of the government's majority may lead to indiscipline and that some backbench members of Parliament might not support difficult measures that affect their own areas, thereby weakening the resolve of the government.

Opposition

The main opposition party, Fianna Fáil, lost three-quarters of its seats (dropping from 78 to 20 seats) in the February election. Fianna Fáil was in government from 1997 to 2011, and voters blamed the party for the economic boom and bust. Fianna Fáil supports the implementation of the EU-IMF program, which it negotiated with the troika in November 2010 when in government.

Sinn Féin, a left-wing republican party, strongly opposes the implementation of the EU-IMF program, as do most independents. In particular, they oppose most spending cuts that affect low- and middle-income citizens. They also believe that the fiscal cost of recapitalizing the banks has pushed the public debt to unsustainable levels, and they have called for burden sharing with senior bank bondholders to reduce the debt.[5]

How Is the Debt Crisis Debate Framed in the National Public Arena?

The main feature of the economic backdrop to the debate over the debt crisis is the significant ongoing reductions in disposable income resulting from the deep recession and budgetary adjustments.

■ Real GDP has dropped 15 percent from its peak in 2007; nominal GDP is down 20 percent.[6]

■ Real personal consumption is down 12 percent from the peak in the fourth quarter of 2007.[7]

■ The unemployment rate has jumped to 14.5 percent, up from 4.5 percent in 2007.[8]

■ Budgetary adjustment measures of €21 billion (13 percent of GDP) have been implemented since summer 2008.[9] An additional €10 billion (6 percent of GDP) of adjustments are planned over the next three years to reduce the deficit to 3 percent of GDP by 2015.[10]

■ A primary budget deficit of 6.6 percent of GDP is expected for 2011 (IMF 2011, 25).

■ Nominal wages per employee in both the public and private sectors have fallen. Average public sector wages have been cut by 14 percent over the past three years (Department of Finance 2010, 66).

---

5. Sinn Féin's finance spokesperson, Pearse Doherty, said recently that "the economics of austerity and socialising the losses of private banks is not working."

6. Central Statistics Office, www.cso.ie/en/index.html.

7. Ibid.

8. Ibid.

9. Data are from the Department of Finance (2010). These adjustment measures have been partly offset by large increases in spending on social protection as a result of rising unemployment as well as higher interest costs on the national debt.

10. FitzGerald and Kearney (2011) argue that Ireland is likely to outperform this target, in part because of the reduced debt burden resulting from the decision at the EU summit on July 21, 2011, to lower the interest rate on borrowings from EU funds from 5.8 to 3.5 percent.

Table 3.2   Public resources used to recapitalize Irish banks

Public capital injections into banks	Billions of euros
Total	62
Of which:	
Going-concern banks	27
Nonviable banks in run-down	35
Total as a share of 2010 GDP	40 percent

Source: Central Bank of Ireland.

Ireland's ratio of gross public debt to GDP is expected to peak at around 115 percent in 2012–13.[11] There are mixed views among Irish economists and commentators in the media as to whether this projected level of debt is sustainable.[12]

A key feature of the popular discourse on public debt is the distinction that many commentators make between increased indebtedness that has been incurred because of fiscal deficits (excluding banking outlays) and that which has resulted from the bank bailout. Table 3.2 shows that public funds amounting to around €62 billion (40 percent of GDP) have been used to recapitalize Ireland's banks. More than half of this amount has been injected into Anglo Irish Bank and Irish Nationwide Building Society (INBS) (largely in the form of promissory notes counted as part of Ireland's gross government debt), which are nonviable institutions that have been merged and are being run down.[13]

As a result of the capital injections, the Irish state owns 15 percent of the country's largest bank, Bank of Ireland, and essentially 100 percent of Ireland's other large bank, Allied Irish Bank (AIB). Bank of Ireland's market capitalization peaked in 2007 at around €18 billion, while AIB's market capitalization reached more than €20 billion. Of course these values in part reflected expectations of continued elevated profits associated with the property bubble. It is very hard to say what value the state may eventually realize from the sale of these stakes, but it is clear that the future value of the banks will depend on the strength of the economic recovery. It is expected that €3 billion of "excess" capital that the state injected into the banks this July will be repaid to the state in 2014.

---

11. The Irish authorities hold significant liquid financial assets composed of cash deposits and liquid investments at the National Pension Reserve Fund. Taking these assets into account, the ratio of net public debt to GDP is expected to peak at around 105 percent.

12. See FitzGerald and Kearney (2011) for an examination of Ireland's debt dynamics.

13. The management of Anglo Irish Bank has said recently that the final cost of bailing out the bank could be up to €4 billion lower than previously expected.

Bailing Out the Banks

There is a strong political consensus—which seems to be shared by the general public—that the country's "sovereign" debt (that is, government debt resulting from fiscal deficits, excluding banking outlays) must be honored in full. It is well understood that Ireland is a small open economy that relies heavily on international trade and foreign direct investment. The county's reputation for honoring contracts is viewed as important for future economic growth.[14]

However, there is significant public dissatisfaction with the bailouts of the banks. The public attitude is shaped by several factors:

- For starters, the cost to Irish taxpayers of rescuing the banks is very large. As shown in table 3.3, the scale of public resources used in Ireland to recapitalize the banks is unprecedented. An important question for Ireland's debt sustainability relates to how much of these up-front costs the state will eventually recover. It is interesting to note that Chile in the 1980s recorded gross recapitalization costs of about 34 percent of GDP, but recovered most of these outlays within five years. In contrast, Indonesia in the 1990s had gross recapitalization costs of 37 percent of GDP and zero recoveries, so the net cost was 37 percent of GDP. Maximizing the recovery value of the state's stakes in the banks should be a priority for the Irish government.

- It is perceived that the sustainability of the sovereign debt may have been put in question by the scale of the bank bailout.

- In popular discourse, the focus is mainly on the banks' creditors, who have benefitted from the bailout at the expense of taxpayers. The view that tends to dominate in the public debate is that the bailing out of (mainly foreign) bank bondholders has been unfair, and that financial institutions that invested in the bonds of reckless Irish banks during the boom should be required to bear some of the banks' losses. There does not appear to be a public appetite for burden sharing to extend to ordinary depositors.

- In the public mind, Irish bank bonds are largely owned by German and French banks. This gives rise to a perception that Irish taxpayers are being asked to bear a huge burden to rescue the European banking system.[15] This distribution of the costs is perceived in Ireland as unfair. In addition, it was

---

14. Ireland's prime minister, Enda Kenny, recently wrote in the *Irish Times,* November 2, 2011: "Default would mark us out as a country that 'won't' rather than 'can't' pay our debts, killing off foreign direct investment and resulting in even higher borrowing costs for the State and Irish businesses that would strangle recovery and lower living standards for a generation."

15. The rescue of Anglo Irish Bank, a monoline property lender, has been particularly expensive for Irish taxpayers, with state injections of capital approaching €30 billion (19 percent of GDP). In an interview in March 2011, when asked what would have happened had the Irish government allowed Anglo to collapse, Central Bank of Ireland Governor Patrick Honohan replied: "There would have been a lot of problems. This would have been problematic for Europe as well, it would have been a European Lehmans."

Table 3.3   Bank recapitalization costs

Country	Start date of crisis	Gross recapitalization cost (percent of GDP)	Net recapitalization cost (percent of GDP)
Ireland	2008	40.0	n.a.
Indonesia	1997	37.3	37.3
Chile	1981	34.3	6.5
Turkey	2000	24.5	24.5
Korea	1997	19.3	15.8
Thailand	1997	18.8	18.8
Advanced economies			
Finland	1991	8.6	6.9
Japan	1997	6.6	6.5
Norway	1991	2.6	0.6
Sweden	1991	1.8	1.5

n.a. = not available

Note: Net costs refer to gross costs minus five-year recoveries.

Sources: Author's estimates for Ireland; Laeven and Valencia (2008) for all others.

widely reported in the Irish media in October 2010 that Russian billionaire Roman Abramovich owned bonds issued by INBS. The term "bondholder" is therefore often associated with large foreign banks, hedge funds, and megarich individuals.

■ The Irish public is aware that financial regulation in Ireland utterly failed during the boom years. But they do not believe it necessarily follows that the Irish taxpayer should bear the full burden of bailing out banks' creditors. In the public mind, authorities in countries whose banks invested in Irish banks' bonds also failed to regulate properly.[16]

■ There is an (incorrect) view among sections of the public that fiscal austerity is being implemented in large part to generate funds to put into the banks. "You are taking money from me to put into the banks" was a common charge put to government politicians during the February 2011 election campaign. In fact, the budget deficit of about 10 percent of GDP

---

16. The public mood is well reflected in a letter from former Irish prime minister John Bruton to European Commission President José Manuel Barroso in January 2011: "I agree the main responsibility does rest with Irish institutions, the Irish Government, the Irish Central Bank, the Irish banks, and the Irish individuals who borrowed irresponsibly. But you should know that this is not the whole story. British, German, Belgian, American, French banks, and banks of other EU countries, lent irresponsibly to the Irish banks in the hope that they too could profit from the Irish construction bubble. These banks, who lent to the Irish banks, were supervised by their home Central banks, who seemingly raised no objection to this lending, which was so ill advised. So these non-Irish Central Banks must take some share of responsibility for the mistakes that were made. Yet the non-Irish banks, who so foolishly lent to the Irish banks, are now being spared any share in the losses, because the Irish taxpayer is bailing them out."

in 2011 largely reflects the gap between government spending (excluding banking-related costs) and revenues.

- Several official investigations into possible criminal wrongdoing in the banking sector during the boom are ongoing, but progress has been slow. There is frustration among the public that no bankers have been called to account for their actions. More generally, there is a perceived lack of accountability over the banking collapse that has not been appeased by several inquiries into the causes of the crisis. There seems to be a public demand for vengeance.

Sharing the Burden of Bank Losses

Large losses have been imposed on both bank shareholders and holders of subordinated bonds.

- Shareholder equity in the Irish banks peaked at €25 billion in 2007, all of which has been wiped out (Nyberg 2011, 42). The banks have been recapitalized largely by the state and in the case of Bank of Ireland by injections of private capital.

- Subordinated loan capital peaked at just over €20 billion in 2007. Subordinated debt has been bought back by the banks for discounts generally ranging between 70 and 90 cents on the euro. Holders of these bonds have absorbed about €16 billion in losses.

To date, no losses have been imposed on holders of senior bank bonds.

- Senior bank bonds were included in the two-year blanket state guarantee of banks' liabilities introduced on September 28, 2008. Senior bank bonds that matured after the introduction of the guarantee and before September 28, 2010, were covered by the guarantee and repaid in full.

- Since September 2010, senior bank bonds that had been issued before September 2008 have no longer enjoyed a state guarantee. Nonetheless, those (unguaranteed) bonds that have matured since September 2010 have also been repaid in full. It has been widely reported in Ireland that the ECB is firmly against default on senior bank bonds. Therefore any burden sharing with senior bondholders would have to be executed against the wishes of the ECB. Given the significant support that the ECB is giving to the Irish banking system, both the previous government and the new government have said that they will not act unilaterally on the issue of senior bank bonds.[17]

---

17. Total Eurosystem lending (that is, ECB lending and Emergency Liquidity Assistance [ELA] lending from the Central Bank of Ireland) to resident Irish banks has been running around €130 billion over the second and third quarters of 2011.

Table 3.4   Irish Bank senior bonds, February 2011 (billions of euros)

Institution	Senior bonds guaranteed	Senior bonds unguaranteed, secured	Senior bonds unguaranteed, unsecured
Allied Irish Bank	6.1	2.8	5.9
Bank of Ireland	6.2	12.3	5.2
EBS	1.0	1.0	0.5
ILP	4.7	3.0	1.2
Anglo Irish Bank	3.0	0	3.1
Irish Nationwide Building Society	0	0	0.6
Total	21.0	19.1	16.5

Source: Central Bank of Ireland.

■ Senior bank bonds issued after December 2009 continue to be covered by a state guarantee.

Table 3.4 shows the amounts of outstanding senior bank bonds. A state guarantee covers €21 billion of bonds. There are €35.6 billion of unguaranteed senior bonds, of which €19.1 billion are secured on banks' assets and €16.5 billion are unsecured.

The new government has said it will not impose losses on the senior bondholders of the so-called pillar banks, that is, the merged AIB/EBS bank and Bank of Ireland. Finance Minister Michael Noonan has said the "last red cent" of debt owed by the government and the two pillar banks will be repaid.

That leaves the question of whether losses will be imposed on the unguaranteed, unsecured senior bonds of the two nonviable banks that are being run down, Anglo Irish Bank and INBS.[18] As shown in table 3.4, there were €3.7 billion of such bonds outstanding in February 2011. Roughly €720 million of these bonds were repaid in full on November 2, 2011. A further €1.25 billion are scheduled to be repaid in January 2012. The government said that it had wanted senior bank bondholders to share in the losses of these two institutions, but was not prepared to go against the wishes of the ECB on this matter.[19] Instead, it seems that the government is hoping to reduce the cost of the banking rescue by securing low-cost, long-term financing of the banking-related debt.

---

18. Anglo Irish Bank and INBS were merged in July 2011.

19. Finance Minister Michael Noonan in June 2011 said: "We don't think the Irish taxpayer should redeem what has become speculative investment—we don't believe it should be redeemed at par." The government argued that most of these bonds have probably been sold on secondary markets to hedge funds at significant discounts over the past couple of years. On the other hand, according to the *Irish Independent* (July 14, 2011), "officials from the ECB have warned the Government that any efforts to force losses on senior bondholders at Anglo Irish Bank and Irish Nationwide could lead to the withdrawal of €50bn of central bank liquidity for the two institutions."

The Public Attitude to Euro Area–Wide Solidarity

A poll conducted in December 2010, shortly after Ireland's entry into the EU/IMF program, showed that 51 percent of people welcomed the bailout deal, while 37 percent did not (figure 3.1). The public recognized that Ireland could not borrow from capital markets and that the budget deficit would have to have been eliminated immediately without bailout funds.

There was general consensus among economic commentators that the interest rate of 5.8 percent charged on the EU/IMF loans was excessive. Complaints about the interest cost of the loans have abated since July 21, when EU leaders agreed to cut the interest rate on EU loans from 5.8 to 3.5 percent and to lengthen maturity terms.

There does appear to be public recognition that the country is receiving relatively low-cost funding from Europe in the form of funds from the EU/IMF program as well as large amounts of liquidity support (around €130 billion) from the Eurosystem to Irish banks at 1.5 percent.

The December 2010 poll also revealed that 56 percent of people believed that sovereignty had been surrendered, against 33 percent who said it had not. The new coalition government has regularly over the past six months justified the introduction of unpopular measures by saying that the government has no choice since the measures are contained in the EU/IMF program.

It is difficult to gauge how the public attitude to Europe has changed over the past year. On the one hand, the public recognizes that without help from Europe, the government would have run out of money to keep the country running. The public may also be encouraged by recent reports in the international media praising Ireland's efforts in adhering to the program and by signs that the Irish economy is stabilizing.

On the other hand, there are several areas in which dissatisfaction with Europe is evident:

- It is widely perceived that Ireland's membership in the single currency contributed to the country's property bubble. Interest rates in the euro area were too low for the strongly growing Irish economy during the boom. In addition, entry into the EMU gave Ireland's banks increased access to funding from international capital markets, which facilitated their catastrophic ramping up of lending to the property sector. That said, the view that the euro is partly to blame for the unsustainable boom does not seem to translate into a desire to leave the euro area.[20]

- Many commentators put the lion's share of the blame for the high cost to taxpayers of rescuing the banks on the introduction of the state guarantee

---

20. In an informal poll in May 2011 for a Sunday newspaper, 80 percent of people said that Ireland should stay in the euro area.

Figure 3.1 Irish attitude toward bailout

a. Do you welcome the European Union/International Monetary Fund deal?

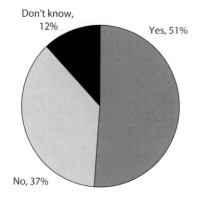

Don't know, 12%

Yes, 51%

No, 37%

b. Has sovereignty been surrendered?

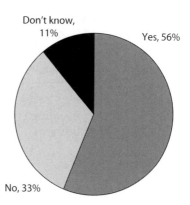

Don't know, 11%

Yes, 56%

No, 33%

Source: Stephen Collins, "Majority Back Bailout but Say Sovereignty Lost," *Irish Times*, December 18, 2010, www.irishtimes.com.

of banks' liabilities in September 2008.[21] However, the public debate on burden sharing since the blanket guarantee scheme expired last September has focused on the unguaranteed bank bonds, especially those issued by Anglo Irish Bank and INBS. Media reports have regularly pointed to the government's efforts to force losses onto these bonds being blocked by the ECB.[22]

- Pressure on the Irish government earlier this year from French president Nicolas Sarkozy to change Ireland's corporate tax rate was widely criticized in the media in Ireland.[23] Prior to the July 21, 2011, EU summit agree-

---

21. The state guarantee covered some subordinated debt, senior bank bonds, and depositors. Large haircuts of 80 to 90 percent were eventually applied to subordinated debt when the guarantee expired in September 2010. It is not clear that haircuts could have been applied to senior bank bonds had they been excluded from the guarantee, given the objections of the ECB.

22. For example, on February 8, 2011, Bloomberg reported the following comments by then finance minister Brian Lenihan: "No unguaranteed senior debt has been dishonored in the euro area to date. That has been the practice and that has been the consistent message we have received from the European Central Bank. I couldn't see the European Central Bank contemplating discounts on senior debt at present. But again in the context of the winding up of an institution or the gradual winding down of an institution these options can be put on the table. I pressed for it in the context of a multilateral discussion with Europe. It is an issue and we have an ongoing dialogue with the bank and with the European authorities." Available at www.bloomberg.com.

23. The *Irish Times* on January 14, 2011 reported President Sarkozy as saying: "I deeply respect our Irish friends' independence and we have done everything to help them. But they cannot continue to say 'come and help us' while keeping a tax on company profits that is half [that of other countries]." Available at www.irishtimes.com.

ment, the interest rates attached to Ireland's borrowings from EU rescue funds were higher than those charged to Portugal and Greece. There was much criticism of President Sarkozy's insistence that a lower interest rate be contingent on Ireland raising its corporate tax rate. There were several dimensions to this criticism: First, Ireland's corporate tax rate is seen as a crucial policy tool in attracting inward foreign direct investment and very important for economic recovery. Second, it was widely believed that President Sarkozy was taking this approach solely for domestic political purposes.[24] Third, media reports pointed to the fact that France's effective rate of corporate tax was actually lower than Ireland's rate.[25] Fourth, it was perceived that, having "taken one for the team" in bailing out the euro area banking system (including French banks), Ireland was now in a vulnerable position and was being victimized.

Conclusion

It is worth repeating several key features of the domestic political situation that are relevant to how developments in the European debt crisis might be received in Ireland. First, the current government has a huge parliamentary majority, and the next general election is not due until 2016. This should give the government the political space to continue to implement the country's demanding adjustment program. Regaining Ireland's access to international sovereign debt markets would be a huge political win for the government. Second, public anger over the crisis is largely directed at the previous government, with polls showing that voters are still taking a benign view of the new coalition. Finally, disquiet over the cost of the banking rescue remains an important part of the public debate.

References

Department of Finance. 2010. The National Recovery Plan 2011–2014 (November).

FitzGerald, John, and Ide Kearney. 2011. *Irish Government Debt and Implied Debt Dynamics: 2011–2015*. Research article. Dublin: Economic and Social Research Institute.

Honohan, Patrick. 2010. *The Irish Banking Crisis—Regulatory and Financial Stability Policy 2003–2008*. Available at www.bankinginquiry.gov.ie.

---

24. The *Irish Times* on March 21, 2011 reported former minister for finance Brian Lenihan as saying that internal politics was the reason why France was being so insistent. "As in many European matters, this comes back to local politics and the position of different politicians in their own state. I believe President Sarkozy is pushing this situation solely for domestic purposes." The paper reported that Lenihan urged his successor, Michael Noonan, and Taoiseach Enda Kenny to stand firm against any attempts by France or Germany to use Ireland's corporate tax rate as a quid pro quo for a reduction in the interest rate on the EU-IMF loan. Available at www.irishtimes.com.

25. The *Irish Times* on March 21, 2011 reported that the French Agency for International Investment cites an effective tax rate of 8.2 percent in advertising literature aimed at attracting foreign business to France, compared with an effective tax rate of more than 11 percent in Ireland. Available at www.irishtimes.com.

IMF (International Monetary Fund). 2011. *Ireland: Third Review Under the Extended Arrangement.* Country Report no. 11/276 (September). Washington.

Laeven, Luc, and Fabian Valencia. 2008. *Systemic Banking Crises: A New Database.* IMF Working Paper 08/224. Washington: International Monetary Fund.

Nyberg, Peter. 2011 *Misjudging Risk: Causes of the Systemic Banking Crisis in Ireland.* Report of the Commission of Investigation into the Banking Sector in Ireland. Dublin.

Regling, Klaus, and Max Watson. 2010. *A Preliminary Report on the Sources of Ireland's Banking Crisis.* Available at www.bankinginquiry.gov.ie.

4

Understanding Portugal in the Context of the Euro Crisis

PEDRO LOURTIE

On April 7, 2011, Portugal became the third euro area member state to request international financial assistance from the European Union and the International Monetary Fund (IMF). Roughly one year after the European Union had approved the first financial aid package to Greece, and five months after Ireland had requested international financial assistance under the temporary crisis mechanisms that had in the meantime been set up by the European Union (the European Financial Stabilization Mechanism, or EFSM) and by the euro area (the European Financial Stability Facility, or EFSF), Portugal could no longer resist the pressure from the financial markets on the financing conditions of its economy.

The past year had been one of resisting that outcome as a sovereign debt crisis unfolded in the euro area and market pressure increased on the area's most vulnerable economies. This paper gives an account of the context for, and the events that shaped the period leading up to, Portugal's request for international financial assistance, and it attempts to draw conclusions from that experience. It is an account based on public information and reports, but experienced from up close. The first section briefly looks at factors that have shaped divergent perceptions of the crisis, which have had a considerable influence on the political management of the sovereign debt crisis in the European Union. The second section considers the economic situation in Portugal,

Pedro Lourtie is the former secretary of state for European affairs of Portugal (2009–11). Prior to this position, he was chief of staff to the Portuguese prime minister from 2006 to 2009 and diplomatic adviser in the prime minister's office from 2005 to 2006.

in particular developments during the 2002–08 period, before the global crisis. The third section gives an account of the crisis as it unfolded, seen from a Portuguese perspective and looking at the evolution of European decisions and market sentiment. The last section tries to draw lessons from the Portuguese experience and looks at the economic and political conditions for implementing the current economic and financial adjustment program in Portugal.

Euro Area Crisis versus National Crises

Divergent perceptions of the sovereign debt crisis have influenced its political management within the European Union and the euro area. That this is a euro area crisis was not a view accepted by many political leaders, especially in central and northern European countries. It was often (and still is) depicted as a crisis of the fiscally profligate states. This is certainly partially the case. Those countries with higher public deficits and debts were and are the most vulnerable to this crisis. But this view misses an important point: that this crisis is structural and political, as well as economic, and that it is closely linked to how the euro was built.

Early on in the crisis, specific circumstances were influential in shaping divergent political perspectives of the crisis and in singling out individual situations and solutions at the expense of a more global and determined euro area approach.

A Greek Crisis

The first reason for the country-specific view can be traced to the origins of the sovereign debt crisis. The European Union had tackled in a coordinated manner and with single purpose the global financial crisis in 2008 and the global economic recession in 2009. The general view was that those crises had originated in the United States and had spilled over to Europe. Not the 2010 sovereign debt crisis. This was triggered in the European Union and, in particular, in Greece. It was, of course, bad enough economically that the newly elected Greek government found out in November 2009 that the country's public deficit that year would exceed 12 percent of GDP, doubling the level announced by the previous administration. Here was a country with a precrisis public debt level of 105.4 percent of GDP in 2007, the highest in the European Union, in serious fiscal crisis.

True, euro area budget deficits and public debts had dramatically increased. The same had happened in the United States (where the public debt level rose from 62 percent of GDP in 2007 to 93.6 percent in 2010) and in Japan (where the rise was from 167 percent of GDP in 2007 to 199.7 percent in 2010). Moreover, increased public spending had been the EU policy for avoiding an economic depression in 2009, as is clear from the European Council conclusions at the time (see box 4.1). Economic recession, automatic

Box 4.1   One year of European Council conclusions
(December 2008–December 2009)

December 11–12, 2008

§8. The financial crisis is now impacting on the economy. The euro area, and indeed the Union as a whole, are threatened with recession. . . . It will mobilize all the instruments available to it. . . . In that context, Member States' policies on social protection and inclusion also have a vital part to play.

§9. The European Council agrees on a European Economic Recovery Plan. . . . It is based on an effort equivalent in total to around 1.5 percent of European Union GDP.

June 18–19, 2009

§11. It is imperative for the EU to continue to develop and implement the measures required to respond to the crisis. This should be done by building on the important achievements of the past months in line with the European Economic Recovery Plan agreed last December, which will amount to an overall budgetary support of around 5 percent of GDP in 2009/2010.

October 29–30, 2009

§26. The incipient recovery needs close monitoring and the supporting policies should not be withdrawn until the recovery is fully secured.

December 10–11, 2009

§6. The economic and financial crisis . . . resulted in the most difficult economic downturn since the 1930s. . . . The support measures have been crucial in restoring confidence in financial markets and ensuring their proper functioning as well as dampening the impact of the crisis on growth and employment.

§8. Fiscal consolidation should start in 2011 at the latest, earlier in some Member States where economic circumstances make this appropriate, provided that the Commission forecasts continue to indicate that the recovery is strengthening and becoming self-sustaining.

Source: European Council, "Conclusions," www.european-council.europa.eu (accessed on October 23, 2011).

stabilizers, stimulus packages, and bailouts of some insolvent banks added up to considerably higher public deficits and debts. Even the most fiscally conservative countries in Europe saw their debt-to-GDP ratio jump by more than 10 percentage points between 2007 and 2010 (see table 4.1). As a matter of fact, by 2010 every single euro area country had been put under an excessive

Table 4.1   General government gross debt, 2007–10 (percent of GDP)

Country/group	2007	2008	2009	2010	Percent change
Euro area	66.2	69.9	79.3	85.1	18.9
European Union	59.0	62.3	74.4	80.0	21.0
Belgium	84.2	89.6	96.2	96.8	12.0
Germany	64.9	66.3	73.5	83.2	18.3
Ireland	25.0	44.4	65.6	96.2	71.2
Greece	105.4	110.7	127.1	142.8	37.4
Spain	36.1	39.8	53.3	60.1	24.0
France	63.9	67.7	78.3	81.7	17.8
Italy	103.6	106.3	116.1	119.0	15.4
Netherlands	45.3	58.2	60.8	62.7	17.4
Portugal	**68.3**	**71.6**	**83.0**	**93.0**	**24.7**
Finland	35.2	34.1	43.8	48.4	13.2
United Kingdom	44.5	54.4	69.6	80.0	35.5
Japan	167.0	174.1	194.1	199.7	32.7
United States	62.0	71.0	84.3	93.6	31.6

Sources: Eurostat database, http://epp.eurostat.ec.europa.eu; Organization for Economic Cooperation and Development.

deficit procedure, with the exception of Luxembourg.[1] But Greece's budgetary problems were of another order of magnitude altogether.

Additionally, the Greek government's admission that national statistics had for years been unreliable had a devastating political effect. This admission brought to mind the 2004 episode when, after close EU scrutiny, the Greek government conceded that the country's budget deficits had not been below the Maastricht criteria of 3 percent since 1999, not even as Greece adopted the euro in 2001, and it compounded suspicions not only from the international financial markets but also from the European partners that Greek statistics were not to be trusted. This fact poisoned the debate within the European Union and had an out-of-proportion effect on the way the sovereign debt crisis was dealt with politically.

Divergent Economic Performances in Europe

But that was not the only reason why for so long many insisted that the troubles (and the solutions) were restricted to the euro area peripheral countries.[2] The second reason had to do with diverging postrecession economic performance. In 2010, many euro area countries were coming out of the recession. The central and northern euro area countries all posted annualized growth

---

1. Estonia entered the euro area on January 1, 2011.

2. I use the expression "peripheral countries" throughout this paper to describe Greece, Ireland, Portugal, and Spain. Not only does it match those countries' geographical positions in Europe, it also seems a more elegant alternative to expressions (or acronyms) used elsewhere.

figures above 2 percent in the second quarter of 2010 (Finland, 5 percent; Slovakia, 4.7 percent; Germany, 4.4 percent; Belgium, 2.8 percent; Austria, 2.4 percent; and the Netherlands, 2.1 percent).[3] In the periphery the picture was quite different, with Greece (–4 percent) and Ireland (–0.7 percent) deep in recession and Spain (0.2 percent) barely growing. Only Portugal showed healthier indications (1.6 percent).

The situation fed into the narrative of the "after-party bust" that became popular and seemed to fit well with the economies of Greece, Ireland, and Spain, which had seen strong growth in the past decade even as they saw their international competitiveness and current account balances deteriorate. Portugal had a slightly different story. Indeed, external balances had continued to be highly negative since 1996, but strong growth had not been registered since 2001.

Ring-Fencing Strategy

The third reason that the crisis was not seen as affecting the entire euro area was that the EU leaders decided to treat each country individually. Naturally, this approach was not to the liking of the country negatively singled out at a specific moment. Greece, Ireland, and Portugal consecutively all had their situations described as substantially different from those countries considered to be next in line. This treatment was an attempt to ring-fence the countries in bigger trouble from those that could themselves soon be in big trouble, as the speed of the crisis and the danger of contagion became clear and difficult to control. And, as a matter of fact, the situation and the gravity of the financing difficulties were (and are) considerably different from country to country. However, it was clear that contagion was not going to be stopped by this ring-fencing strategy alone. The situation was all too reminiscent of the 1992 Exchange Rate Mechanism (ERM) crisis, in which a problem that had at first seemed limited to the British pound exchange rate ended up reaching the French franc and becoming a full-blown ERM crisis.

The Central Role of Sovereign Moral Hazard

As the crisis unfolded, the environment in the European Union was tense. Arguably with a lot of help from the tabloid press and populist politicians, mistrust increased, national prejudices were reinforced, and intra-European solidarity weakened. In the fear of creating moral hazard by benefiting irresponsible fiscal behavior, the debate was often entangled in moral duality. This was the case when officials initially priced the financial assistance packages at considerably higher levels than, for example, interest rates in the European balance of payments facility used to assist non-euro EU members.

---

3. Figures are for real GDP growth rate, percent change over fourth quarter of the previous year (Eurostat database, http://epp.eurostat.ec.europa.eu).

2002–08: The Portuguese Economy

Out of Sync with the Periphery

Unlike Greece, Ireland, or Spain, where economic growth had been sustainably high before the crisis, Portugal had experienced low growth since 2001. In 2003, Portugal went into recession (–0.9 percent), the only euro area country beside Germany (–0.2 percent) to register negative growth that year. That same year, Greece's economy expanded by 5.9 percent, Ireland's by 4.4 percent, and Spain's by 3.1 percent.[4] The difficult Portuguese case, described in Blanchard (2006), was one where productivity growth was anemic, economic growth very low, the budget deficit large, and the current account deficit very large.

The prospect of euro accession in the second half of the 1990s had led to a sharp drop in interest rates, with real interest rates approaching zero at the end of the decade. This triggered an unprecedented and substantial wealth effect strongly felt by all domestic agents, leading to rapid internal demand growth and a decrease of private saving. Nontradable uncompetitive rent-seeking sectors surged, diverting investment from tradable sectors and thus contributing to low productivity growth. With domestic demand sustaining the economic boom, unemployment shrank to less than 5 percent, and this decrease exerted a considerable upward pressure on wages. The economy became overvalued, and current account deficits grew increasingly larger.

In addition to the macroeconomic consequences of a difficult adjustment to the new monetary setting, two important asymmetric shocks hit the Portuguese economy in the late 1990s, adding considerably to Portugal's external competitiveness deficit.

It had been anticipated that enlargement of the European Union to the central and eastern European countries would have adverse economic effects on Portugal. In fact, repercussions were already being felt in the second half of the 1990s, as the European Union entered into Association Agreements with central and eastern European countries before their actual accession in 2004. The agreements tended to divert foreign direct investment (FDI) and trade that had come Portugal's way since its own accession in 1986. Much higher skill and educational levels of the workforce, lower labor costs, and a central geographical position relative to Europe's main markets meant that those countries, once within the EU framework, had considerable advantages in attracting FDI and being more trade competitive.

Additionally, with the new century, China, India, and other emerging low-cost economies entered the world market and competed in labor-intensive areas that the Portuguese economy had historically specialized in. The end of the Multi-Fiber Arrangement following the World Trade Organization

---

4. Figures reflect the real GDP growth rate and give the percentage change from the previous year (Eurostat database, http://epp.eurostat.ec.europa.eu).

Figure 4.1   Investment in construction, 1996–2010

percent yearly change

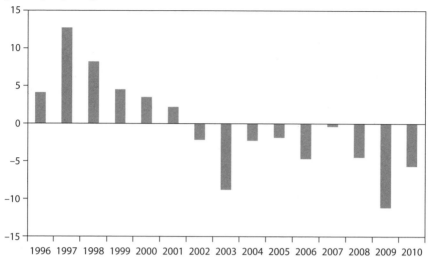

Source: National Statistics Institute.

Uruguay Round negotiations had an enormous impact on Portugal's textile industry, its main export sector. The textile sector represented 33 percent of total Portuguese exports in 1990. It accounted for only 13 percent in 2006.[5]

Developments in the macroeconomic context and in international trade meant that Portugal was not in a good position to profit from rapid European and world expansion in the 1990s and 2000s. When private domestic demand dropped sharply in 2001–02, the engine of recent economic growth also stalled. The country's landscape had changed immensely, with public investment notably devoted to roads and other public infrastructures spanning north to south. Consumption patterns had also changed dramatically in the past 10 years, and property ownership had increased substantially. As household indebtedness weighed on families that had been used to traditionally high rates of private saving, and a new (2002) political cycle underscored the country's need to curtail past excessive consumption and spending, households' expectations adjusted suddenly. An example of the drop in domestic spending is clearly seen in the evolution of investment in construction (figure 4.1). Portugal is the only European country to register a decline in investment in construction in every year from 2002 until today.

5. Data are from a presentation by Paulo Vaz, director-general of ATP (Textile and Clothing Association of Portugal), May 2007, www.citeve.pt.

Slowly Getting Back on Its Feet?

By 2002 Portugal had been through the full cycle of boom, overvaluation, and slump—well before the other peripheral economies in the euro area, which completed that journey when their rapid expansion came to a sudden halt during the 2008–09 global recession.

To get back to growth, with domestic demand stalling, Portugal needed to regain competitiveness. To a large degree this had been done through currency devaluation in the 1970s and 1980s, but that solution was no longer available. The solutions available this time were salary disinflation and stronger productivity growth. Both actually occurred to an extent.

Lowering Wage Costs

Beginning in 2002, the growth of wage costs slowed down considerably. The accumulated real effective exchange rate in relative unit labor costs grew by 3.6 percent in Portugal from 2003 to 2008. This compares with 11 percent in the euro area, 11.4 percent in Greece, 12 percent in Spain, and 26.8 percent in Ireland.[6] The increase in Portugal was still far from Germany's real competitive disinflation of –4 percent for the same period, but below the euro area average.

The measurement of nominal unit labor costs for the total economy confirms a very different profile from 2003 onward. While before labor costs had grown at a considerably faster rate than in the euro area and in the European Union as a whole on average, starting in 2003 the trend clearly reversed (figure 4.2).

Increasing Productivity Growth

As regards productivity growth, the picture also started to change. Labor productivity in the second half of the last decade was catching up to EU levels, which it was not for at least a decade. The indicator for labor productivity per person employed in purchasing power standards in relation to the EU-27 average at 100 registered an increase from 72.6 in 2005 to 77.2 in 2010, while it had stalled, and even slightly declined, in the previous decade, dropping from 71.1 in 1995 to 69.6 in 2004.[7] The same trend for labor productivity is also seen in the hours worked indicator (once again with the EU-27 average at an index of 100), which rose from 62.7 in 2005 to 65.2 in 2010 (62.3 in 1995 and 60.2 in 2004). Real labor productivity per person employed, a more reliable indicator for international productivity comparisons,[8] confirms this trend (figure 4.3). In the second half of the 2000s, for the first time in more than a decade, productivity in Portugal was again growing above the EU average.

---

6. Annual Report, 2010, Bank of Portugal, www.bportugal.pt.

7. A break in the Eurostat series makes 2004–05 comparisons difficult.

8. There are limitations to international comparisons of productivity indicators based on purchasing power standards.

Figure 4.2 Nominal unit labor costs, total economy, 1997–2010

index, 2000 = 100

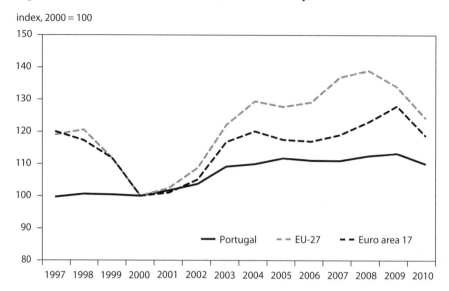

Note: The figure shows performance relative to the rest of 35 industrial countries. Calculations use double export weights.

Source: European Commission, Directorate General for Economic and Financial Affairs.

Figure 4.3 Real labor productivity per person employed, 2000–10

index, 2005 = 100

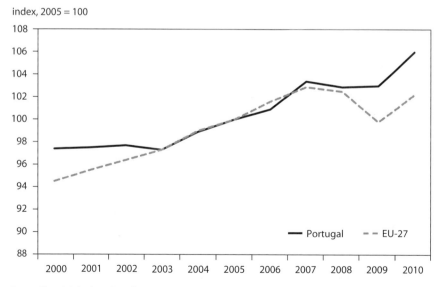

Source: Eurostat database, http://epp.eurostat.ec.europa.eu.

Structural Reforms

In terms of policy, the rate and span of badly needed structural reforms also increased during the period of low economic growth in Portugal. The country was not only in a macroeconomic quagmire but also had, and still has, substantial structural deficiencies that need to be tackled if it is to successfully change the profile of its economy and the instruments of its competitiveness. The results recently achieved in some areas are worth noting.

Education. Education and skills have been Portugal's biggest, and arguably costliest, deficit. In economic terms, this was the heaviest burden left from a 48-year dictatorship that democracy has been addressing, albeit not at the desired pace. In this context, recent reforms in education have achieved visible and important results. The percentage of early leavers from education and training has been on a sustained and accelerated path of reduction toward the EU average since 2002. That year, a staggering 45 percent of the population aged 18–24 with at most a lower secondary education had left education or training, while the corresponding EU average was 17 percent. In 2010, the figures were 28.7 percent and 14.1 percent, for Portugal and the EU average, respectively (figure 4.4). Portugal was also the Organization for Economic Cooperation and Development (OECD) country that most progressed in the three areas (reading, mathematics, and science performance) of the 2009 PISA (Program for International Student Assessment) tests, with Portuguese students ranked for the first time among the OECD average countries (the United Kingdom, Denmark, Sweden, Germany, France, Ireland, and Hungary).[9] Moreover, tertiary educational attainment has more than doubled, from 11.3 percent in 2000 to 23.5 percent in 2010.[10]

Research and Development. Investment in research and development (R&D), another deficient area, has sharply increased, from 0.53 percent of GDP in 1995 to 1.66 percent in 2009. The rate at which Portugal has approached the EU-27 average (which moved from 1.8 percent of GDP in 1995 to 2.01 percent of GDP in 2009) has recently accelerated substantially (figure 4.5). These figures put Portugal, in terms of R&D, ahead of Spain (1.38 percent), Italy (1.27 percent), Greece (0.58 percent[11]), and all the more recent EU member states except Slovenia (1.86 percent), and almost on par with Ireland (1.77 percent). It is relevant that the weight of private sector expenditures in Portugal represented more than 50 percent of total R&D expenditures in 2007, up from little more

---

9. See OECD, *PISA 2009 Results: What Students Know and Can Do: Student Performance in Reading, Mathematics and Science,* volume 1, 2010, www.oecd.org (accessed on October 23, 2011).

10. Eurostat database, http://epp.eurostat.ec.europa.eu.

11. The figure for Greece is from 2007, the latest year for which data are available.

Figure 4.4   Early leavers from education and training, 2000–10

percent

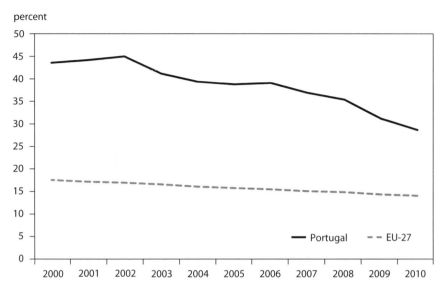

Note: Figure shows percent of the population aged 18–24 with at most lower secondary education and no further education or training.

Source: Eurostat database, http://epp.eurostat.ec.europa.eu.

Figure 4.5   Gross domestic expenditure on R&D, 1995–2009

percent of GDP

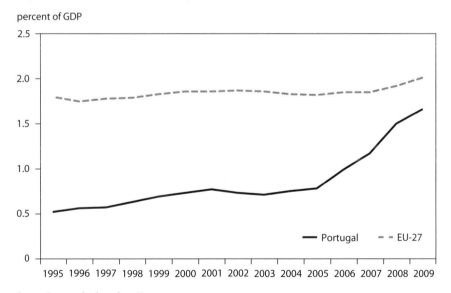

Source: Eurostat database, http://epp.eurostat.ec.europa.eu.

Figure 4.6 Electricity from domestic renewable sources, 2003–July 2011

percent of total electricity production plus net imports

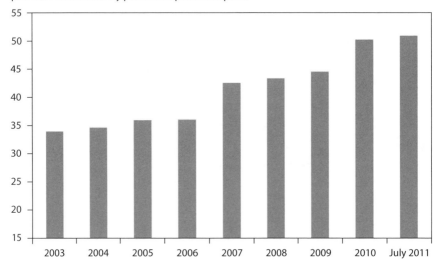

Source: Portuguese Ministry of Economy, Directorate General for Energy and Geology.

than 20 percent in 1997.[12] This trend has had a positive impact on the export profile (leading toward more incorporation of knowledge and value added) and has also led to a technology balance improvement.

Energy Dependency. Reducing energy dependency is also an area critical to Portugal. Energy imports account currently for almost half of the trade deficit. The recent rapid promotion of renewable energies is thus a significant contribution to the correction of the economy's external imbalances. Electricity generated from renewable sources accounted for 50.2 percent of total electricity production plus net imports in 2010, up from 33.9 percent in 2003 (figure 4.6).

Public Administration and Business. The modernization and reform of public administration—including cutting red tape, improving e-governance and the business environment, and reducing bureaucracy—is a fourth area where significant improvements have occurred. Portugal rose from the 48th to the 7th position in the ranking of availability of services online (West 2007) and, according to the European Commission, became in 2009 the leading EU country in terms of availability and sophistication of online public services,[13]

---

12. Statistical Summaries—IPCTN.08, Survey on National Scientific and Technological Potential (2011), Office for Planning, Strategy, and International Relations, Portuguese Ministry of Science, Technology, and Higher Education, www.gpeari.mctes.pt.

13. See European Commission, Directorate General for Information Society and Media (2009).

Figure 4.7   Changes in employment protection in OECD countries, 2003–08

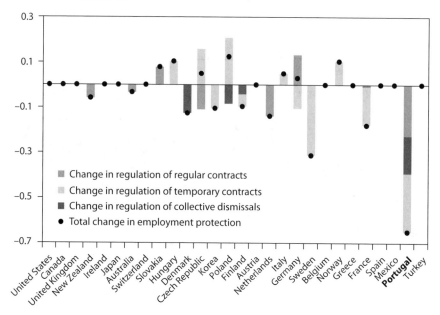

Note: Data for Portugal and France are for 2003–09. See figure 4.8 for scale.

Source: Venn (2009).

up from number 16 in 2004. Portugal also moved to the top of the scale for ease of starting business, with more than 60 percent of companies now being created in less than an hour.[14]

Labor Market. Finally, it is worth noting that Portugal has changed labor market legislation to increase flexibility, reversing the tendency of the previous 30 years. Labor legislation was changed in 2003 and, more substantially, in 2009; the result is that labor market flexibility increased more in Portugal than in any other OECD country, according to the organization's indicators (figure 4.7).[15] The latter changes came into law on February 17, 2009, and included

14. The "company in the hour" measure earned Portugal the stamp of "Top Reformer" in the World Bank's *Doing Business 2007* report; see www.doingbusiness.org.

15. The OECD overall employment protection indicator is a qualitative index ranging from 0 to 6. It is compiled from 21 items quantifying the costs and procedures involved in dismissing individuals or groups of workers or hiring workers on fixed-term or temporary work agency contracts. The overall summary indicator is made up of three subindicators quantifying different aspects of employment protection: (1) individual dismissal of workers with regular contracts; (2) additional costs for collective dismissals; and (3) regulation of temporary contracts. See Venn (2009).

Figure 4.8 Strictness of employment protection, 2008

scale from 0 (least restrictions) to 6 (most restrictions)

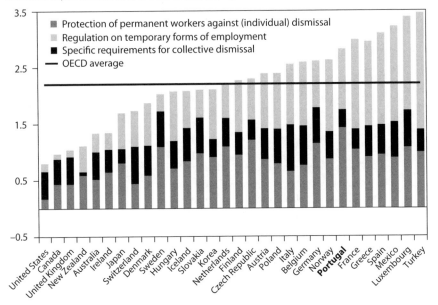

Note: For France and Portugal, data refer to 2009. This indicator refers to version 3 as defined in the methodology.

Source: Venn (2009); OECD Indicators on Employment Protection; see methodology at www.oecd.org/employment/protection.

(1) reducing the delay before the notice period starts by simplifying administrative procedures for individual and collective dismissal; (2) reducing notice periods for workers with short tenure (e.g., from 60 to 15 days for workers with tenure of nine months) and increasing them for workers with long tenure (e.g., from 60 to 75 days for workers with tenure of 20 years); (3) reducing compensation paid to workers and the right to reinstatement where the dismissal was found to be irregular only because administrative procedures were not properly followed, and introducing government funding for the cost of back pay exceeding one year in unfair dismissal cases if the court takes longer than one year to rule on a case; and (4) reducing the maximum time allowed for employees to make a complaint of unfair dismissal from one year to 60 days. These reforms meant that the OECD indicator of employment protection for Portugal fell from 3.4 to 2.7 (within a range of 0 to 6), but still remained above the OECD average, mainly due to the rigidity of individual dismissal regulations (figure 4.8). In 2011, a new proposal for further reform of labor market legislation was presented to Parliament and is currently under discussion.

Vulnerability of Budgetary Consolidations

Portugal was part of the group of countries that created the European single currency in 1999. At first budget deficits met accession targets (though by a slim margin: 2.7 percent in 1999) and public debt was reduced from 59.1 percent of GDP in 1995 to 48.5 percent in 2000 (in comparison, Spanish public debt was reduced from 63.3 to 59.3 percent during the same period). But these budgetary figures were mainly sustained by rapid economic growth at the time.

As growth stalled from 2001 onward, Portugal was confronted with the difficulties of having to adjust late in budgetary terms to the new monetary regime. In fact, between 2002 and 2008, while Portugal was trying to consolidate budgets in a context of low economic growth, next door Spain was managing very low public deficits (under 1 percent) or surpluses under strong economic growth conditions.[16]

During this period, Portugal underwent two phases of budget moderation/consolidation, both in contexts of low economic growth: 2002–04 and 2006–08. These coincided with the two times before 2009 when the country was subject to the corrective arm of the excessive deficit procedure under the Stability and Growth Pact of the euro. In the 1996–2001 period, public consumption contributed annually on average 4.0 percentage points to GDP growth, while this was lowered to 1.5 percentage points in the 2002–04 period and 0.1 percentage points in 2006–08.[17] It was during the 2006–08 period that total government expenditure actually decreased, from 45.8 percent of GDP in 2005 to 43.6 percent of GDP in 2008.[18] Structural reforms in the area of public spending with longer-term impact were also implemented during this time. Two reforms, in particular, are worth noting.

Social Security Reform

The first is social security reform. This reform had three main pillars: (1) it harmonized retirement age at 65 (previously 60 for public servants) and eliminated special schemes; (2) it introduced a sustainability factor that took into consideration the evolution of life expectancy when determining pension value, effectively resulting in an automatic annual increase in retirement age for workers wanting to access their full pension; and (3) it introduced a new

---

16. The exception was in 2008, when the Spanish deficit took off to –4.2 percent, coinciding with the burst of the real estate bubble.

17. Statistics Portugal, www.ine.pt.

18. According to the IMF, figures for public debt were as follows: 45.8 percent (2005); 44.5 percent (2006); 43.7 percent (2007); 43.6 percent (2008). See *World Economic Outlook: Slowing Growth, Rising Risks* (April), www.imf.org. Eurostat figures (after the March 2011 guidelines revision) differ slightly: 45.8 percent (2005); 44.5 percent (2006); 44.4 percent (2007); 44.7 percent (2008). See Eurostat database, http://epp.eurostat.ec.europa.eu. Here I use the former figures for easier comparison with previous years, since the Eurostat revision focused on 2007 onward.

Table 4.2   The prospective long-term increase in age-related expenditure, 2007–60 (percent of GDP)

Country/group	Pension spending	Total
Greece	12.5	16.0
Spain	6.2	8.3
Ireland	5.9	8.7
Belgium	4.5	6.6
Netherlands	4.0	9.4
Slovakia	3.6	5.5
Euro area average	2.7	5.1
Finland	2.6	5.9
United Kingdom	2.5	4.8
Germany	2.5	5.1
EU-27 average	2.3	4.6
Portugal	**1.5**	**2.9**
Austria	1.0	3.3
France	0.6	2.2
Italy	–0.4	1.6

Source: European Commission (2009).

pension update rule indexing pensions to inflation (only for lower pensions) and the real GDP growth rate.

In 2009, the European Commission considered Portugal to be one of the EU countries to have implemented substantial pension reforms, with important effects on the country's long-term fiscal sustainability (European Commission 2009). Increased age-related expenditures (table 4.2) and improved public finance sustainability (figure 4.9), as calculated by the European Commission in 2009, placed Portugal above the EU average position.

Public Administration Reform

One other major area of reform was public administration. Public sector employment in Portugal had steadily increased since the 1970s and became overblown relative to output and to average European levels. Mainly through tougher restraints on admission into public sector employment, the period after 2005 witnessed the reversal of this upward trend. By 2010, the number of public servants was back to the levels of the late 1990s, with total numbers coming down approximately 10 percent, from almost 750,000 in 2005 to below 670,000 in 2010 (figure 4.10). Furthermore, the introduction of quota assessment systems and the end of automatic progressions also helped to reduce spending on compensation for public employees, from 13.9 percent of GDP in 2005 to 12 percent in 2008. Although an increase to 12.6 percent occurred in 2009, the downward trend resumed in 2010 (12.2 percent).[19]

---

19. Statistics Portugal, www.ine.pt.

Figure 4.9 Sustainability gap S2 calculated by the European Commission, 2009 (baseline scenario)

percent of GDP

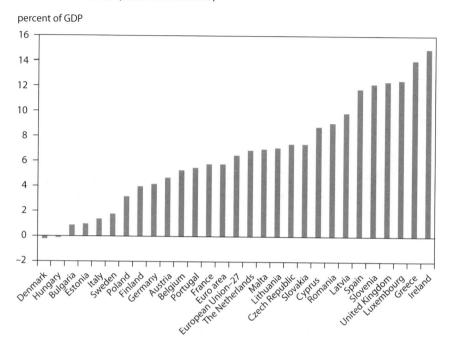

Note: The European Commission sustainability gap S2 indicator shows the adjustment to the structural primary balance required to fulfill the infinite horizon intertemporal budget constraint, including paying for any additional expenditure arising from an aging population. It thus quantifies the gap that must be closed to ensure the sustainability of public finances. The larger the value of the gap indicator, the greater the necessary adjustment to the structural primary balance to ensure sustainability.

Source: European Commission (2009).

2009: Budget Deficit Swells

In 2009, public deficit consolidation efforts came to a halt. The deficit in 2009 increased to 9.3 percent of GDP, up from 2.7 percent in 2008.[20] The evolution of the 2009 budget projections shows that initial figures for revenue were

---

20. For better comparison, these are prerevision figures. Following a Eurostat guidance note on financial defeasance structures (March 16, 2011, http://epp.eurostat.ec.europa.eu) and guidelines on the administrative public sector budgetary perimeter, the National Statistics Institute revised, in March and April 2011, the recent years' figures for Portugal's budget deficits. Final numbers from September 2011, reflecting Eurostat guidelines, are 3.5 percent for 2008 and 10.1 percent for 2009. The new figures were the result of including within the state's accounts budgetary perimeter financial assistance to banks (Banco Português de Negócios and Banco Privado Português), three public transportation companies (REFER, Metropolitano de Lisboa, and Metro do Porto), and three public-private partnerships for toll-free motorways which, following the introduction of tolls, had to be considered public assets and be registered as investment expenditure (Eurostat database, http://epp.eurostat.ec.europa.eu).

Figure 4.10   Number of public sector employees, 1996–2010

number of employees

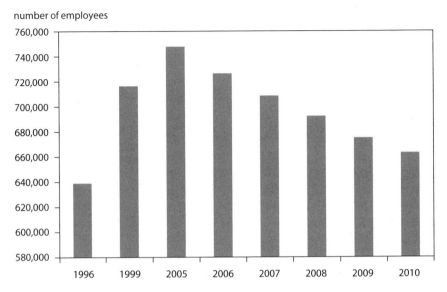

Source: Portuguese Ministry of Finance, 2011 State Budget Report.

clearly too optimistic, notably in an already declining economy. This miscalculation, combined with an expansionary expenditure projection—to which the European Union's Investment and Employment Initiative added further expenditures—led to a drastic increase in the deficit in 2009 (table 4.3).

Soft Approach to Correcting Imbalances

When economic growth stalled in 2001, Portugal had no option but to confront the economy's large structural deficiencies and declining external competitiveness, as well as adjustments to fiscal policy required by the new monetary regime within the euro area. In previous years, the country had been growing on the back of rapidly increasing domestic demand, and before that it had sustained external competitiveness mainly through currency devaluations. However, domestic demand was exhausted and currency devaluations were no longer feasible.

The year 2002 marked the beginning of a period of slow adjustment to this new reality. As was seen above, labor costs progressed at slower rates, and were below the EU average, between 2002 and 2008. Starting in 2005, the productivity growth trend rose above the EU average. Public expenditure was substantially less expansionary than in the past (the exception during this period was 2005; public expenditure was contractionary only in 2006, with a –0.6 percentage point contribution to GDP growth). Structural reforms were also

Table 4.3 Evolution of 2009 budget projections

Component		Budget, 2008	Budget, 2009			
		January 2010	October 2008	(+IEI) January 2009	May 2009	January 2010
Deficit	Millions of euros	−4,456.1	−3,850.5	−6,652.4	−9,659.0	−15,366.2
	Percent of GDP	2.7	2.2	3.9	5.9	9.3
Revenue	Millions of euros	71,978.3	75,997.7	74,562.5	71,112.0	65,507.6
	Percent of GDP	43.2	43..8	44.1	43.6	39.7
Expenditure	Millions of euros	76,434.5	79,848.2	81,214.9	80,771.0	80,873.9
	Percent of GDP	45.9	46.0	48.0	49.5	49.1
GDP	Millions of euros	166,436.9	173,683.8	169,092.5	163,073.0	164,879.6

IEI = The Investment and Employment Initiative, a stimulus package that the Portuguese government approved in January 2009, in the context of the European Economic Recovery Plan agreed at the European Council level. The initiative's impact on the national budget was initially foreseen at 0.8 percentage points of GDP (0.5 percentage points in increased expenditure and 0.3 percentage points in reduced revenue). More information on the IEI is available at www.min-financas.pt.

Source: Portuguese Ministry of Finance.

implemented with a view to increasing the sustainability of public finances and the economy's potential and productivity.

Export Growth

Export figures in the second half of the last decade indicate that the economy had indeed entered a period of recovering competitiveness. In the 2006–10 period, for the first time in a decade, exports grew on average above the EU-15 average, regaining a trend that had been lost since the second half of the 1990s (figure 4.11). The export-to-GDP ratio steadily increased, from 27.8 percent in 2005 to 32.4 percent in 2008, its highest proportion ever in the Portuguese economy. After a steep decline in 2009 (28 percent), consistent with the fall in world trade, this ratio recovered its upward trend in 2010 (31 percent) and projections, as well as evidence in 2011, indicate that exports should continue to rapidly increase as a share of the Portuguese economy, an essential de facto precondition to redressing external deficits. Furthermore, and contributing

Figure 4.11   Export growth differential, Portugal versus EU-15

change in percentage points

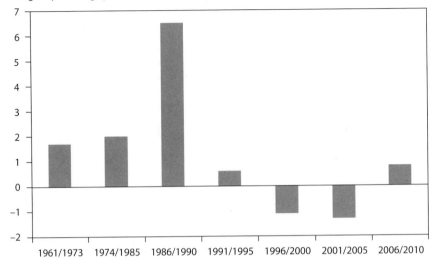

Source: European Commission, *Statistical Annex of European Economy,* spring 2011.

to more rapid export growth, Portugal diversified export markets toward the fastest-growing emerging economies. The European Union's share in total exports was reduced from a peak of 84.6 percent in 1999 to 74.4 percent in 2008 (figure 4.12).

The growth of exports in the second half of the 2000s is consistent with gains registered in productivity and with lower growth in unit labor costs. But there is also longer-term structural change in Portugal's economy that is worth noting. In the past 20 years, medium- and high-technology exports as a percentage of total exports have increased, from around 37 percent in 1990 to almost 65 percent in 2010.[21] This change is also a reflection of a rapidly changing workforce. While in the beginning of 1998 only 19.6 percent of the total workforce had completed secondary education, figures for the first quarter of 2010 put this number at 33.9 percent.[22]

High Current Account Deficits

Nevertheless, the economy's external deficits remained very high even after 2002. Current account deficits surged after 1995 (figure 4.13), an increase that at first look seemed to be the result of higher private productive investment looking for higher returns in a faster-growing economy in the context of the

---

21. Statistics Portugal, www.ine.pt.

22. Ibid.

Figure 4.12   Exports to the EU-27, 1993–2009

percent of total exports

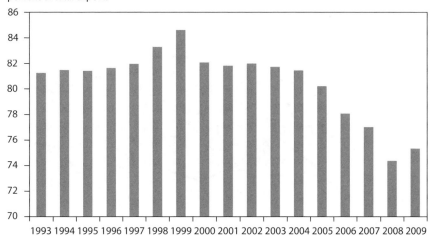

Source: National Statistics Institute.

Figure 4.13   Current account deficit, 1995–2010

percent of GDP

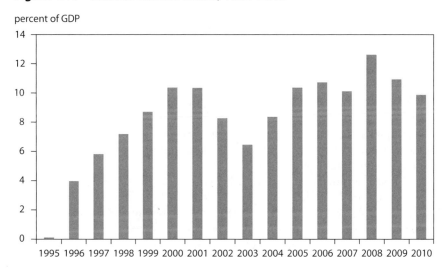

Source: IMF, *World Economic Outlook* database, April 2011.

euro area. However, in hindsight, it was clear that the increase was largely the result of the economy's overvaluation effects on higher private consumption and higher nonproductive investment.

The economy showed signs of correcting the competitiveness deficits, with stronger productivity growth, lower unit labor costs growth, and conse-

Figure 4.14   Trade and income accounts, 2000–10

percent of GDP

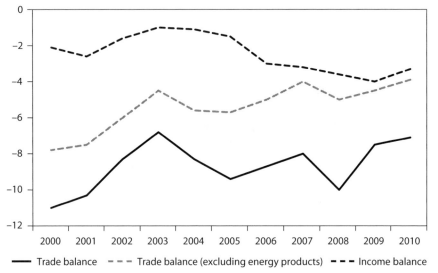

Sources: National Statistics Institute; Portuguese Ministry of Economy, Directorate General for Energy and Geology.

quently more dynamism in exports, notably in the second half of the 2000s. Goods and services trade deficits, excluding energy products, were halved during the decade between 2000 and 2010, corresponding to an improvement of approximately 4 percentage points of GDP. Still, current account deficits remained extremely high, as gains in export growth were offset by higher energy prices, in particular for oil (the share of energy products imports in total imports grew from 9.6 percent in 2002 to 16.8 percent in 2008), and the income account deteriorated due to the accumulation of external debt and higher interest rates (figure 4.14).

The correction of the external deficits could have been accelerated by stronger internal devaluation. This could have been accomplished, as was recently suggested by the IMF (2011) in the context of the current financial assistance program in Portugal, by substantially lowering the existing single social tax on workers' wages paid by employers and compensating the loss in revenue with higher value-added taxes (VATs). However, a change in the single social tax rate that was large enough to have a significant short-term impact on competitiveness and exports would have been difficult to compensate on the fiscal side—problematic at a time when Portugal was subject to an excessive deficit procedure and was trying to reduce its budget deficits.

The challenge of fighting twin deficits (external and fiscal) within the euro area meant that a faster correction of current account deficits would have needed a stronger downward adjustment of Portuguese domestic de-

Figure 4.15 International investment position, 1996–2010

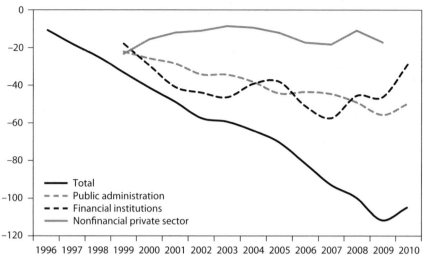

percent of GDP

Note: The figure does not separately calculate monetary authorities' (gold reserves) positive and rather stable international investment position; but these data are reflected in the total. The point is to show that the overall investment position is mostly dependent on the public administration and financial institution sectors.

Source: Bank of Portugal.

mand through a more contractionary fiscal policy (since a tighter monetary policy would have been difficult, as the single monetary policy is adjusted to the conditions of the wider euro area and, in particular, its larger economies). A look at the recent development of Portugal's international investment position shows that after 2002, public sector and financial institutions tended to offset each other's contraction in international financing needs (figure 4.15). Consequently, the international investment position of the economy continued to deteriorate throughout the period. In 2004–05, after the 2003 Portuguese economic recession, financial institutions deleveraged, but the state did not. In turn, in 2006–07, it was the public sector that deleveraged, but the international investment position of the financial institutions deteriorated considerably as borrowing from abroad rose in response to stronger economic sentiment and higher consumer confidence. The trend reversed itself again afterward, with the exception of 2010, when the whole economy deleveraged, a trend that is expected to continue in future years. The only year in the 2002–08 period when both state and financial institutions curbed their international financing needs was 2003, and at that time the country went into a countercyclical recession.

During this period, a faster correction of the Portuguese current account deficits could have been achieved only by means of a much more contractionary fiscal policy. This, in turn, would have probably led to relatively prolonged recession. With exports only around 30 percent of GDP in Portugal, an abrupt decline in internal demand would not likely be compensated, in the short term, by even a significant growth in exports. At a time when Europe and especially comparable economies were growing at very solid rates, such policies would have been politically very challenging to sustain. The option of a strong internal devaluation of the economy through lower wage taxes would have made fiscal targets more difficult to achieve in the short term. Still, it is an option that could have been gradually pursued, along with productivity- and growth-enhancing reforms, in order to accelerate the economy's adjustment.[23] The need for correcting Portugal's budget deficits limited the options available to tackle the external deficits.

In sum, to preserve the fiscal consolidation targets and at the same time tackle the current account deficit would in the short run have entailed a strongly contractionary fiscal policy, which would probably have led to an economic recession. Portugal took the soft approach to correcting its imbalances, when a soft approach was still an option. It was, however, too late and too slow to be sufficient once the global crisis hit.

Facing the Sovereign Debt Crisis

End-2009: Portuguese Bonds in Calm Waters

The 2010 Portuguese budget was presented to Parliament in January, approved in March, and entered into force only in May, having been delayed by elections. Unlike the old government, the new government (also of the Socialist Party, or PS) did not have parliamentary majority support, but the two main center-right opposition parties (PSD and CDS-PP) abstained so as to allow the budget's approval.[24]

The initial budget included a small reduction of the deficit by 1 percentage point, to 8.3 percent of GDP. Consolidation would start, but slowly, since it was still substantially an expansionary budget given that the economy had come out of recession in the second quarter of 2009. The consolidation was, however, one that was consistent with European guidelines as approved by the European Council in December 2009. The council had agreed that "fiscal consolidation should start in 2011 at the latest, earlier in some Member States where economic circumstances make this appropriate, provided that the Commission forecasts continue to indicate that the recovery is strengthening and becoming self-sustaining."[25] (See box 4.1.)

---

23. In particular, a gradual move in that direction could have been made instead of the 1 percentage point reduction in the main VAT rate that occurred in mid-2008.

24. The PS, or Socialist Party, is center-left; the PSD, or Social Democratic Party, is center-right; and the CDS-PP, or Democratic and Social Centre–People's Party, is center-right.

25. European Council, "Conclusions," December 10–11, 2009, www.european-council.europa.eu (accessed on October 23, 2011).

In the sovereign debt market, 10-year Portuguese government bond yields actually decreased in the second half of 2009,[26] in a pattern similar to that of Spanish and Italian bonds; the difference from German bonds was back at less than 100 basis points during that period. Portuguese bonds had not accompanied the wider divergence of Greek and Irish bonds from German bonds that had started at the end of 2008.

Early 2010: Greece Is Bailed Out; Portugal Enters the Spotlight

The situation changed early in 2010 when the magnitude of Greece's difficulties became obvious. At the beginning of February, Greek 10-year bond rates spiked to more than 7 percent, and Portuguese rates reached 4.725 percent on February 4. Contagion from the Greek problems affected Portuguese bonds more than bonds in the other peripheral countries, mainly because Portuguese figures for 2009 made public at the time indicated a much higher than foreseen deficit of 9.3 percent of GDP, resulting, in particular, from an abrupt fall in revenues in the fourth quarter of 2009 (total state budget revenues in 2009 fell below 2006 revenues in nominal terms). In some respects, this was a turning point for Portugal, which up to then had been at par with Spain and Italy and had not suffered as much pressure from international markets on its debt as Greece and Ireland.

The informal meeting of heads of state and government that took place in the Solvay Library on February 11, the first chaired by Herman Van Rompuy, was dominated by the financial pressure on Greece. The message was that euro area member states would take determined and coordinated action, if needed, to safeguard financial stability in the euro area as a whole. The emphasis was on Greece, whose government denied having requested any financial support.[27] This was as much a message to the financial markets as it was to the electorates of Germany and other central and northern European countries that opposed any bailout of Greece.

Pressure on Portuguese bonds eased in February and March, while for Greece it mounted again at the end of February in anticipation of the Hellenic government's austerity package. On March 25, at the meeting of the European Council, the heads of state and government of the euro area confirmed the strategy of strong national austerity in Greece to reduce the deficit and fight off market pressure, recognizing the ambitious consolidation measures taken by Greece and effectively hoping that these would be enough to regain market confidence.

But by the March 25 European Council it was obvious that Greece would need international financial assistance. Despite some European partners' resistance to any form of bailout, euro area member states announced their

---

26. Data for 10-year government bond yields are from Bloomberg.

27. See European Council, "Statement by the Heads of State or Government of the European Union," February 11, 2010, www.european-council.europa.eu (accessed on October 23, 2011).

readiness to contribute to coordinated bilateral loans as part of a package involving substantial International Monetary Fund financing.

The conditions, however, reflected the skepticism that such a mechanism raised in some capitals. The mechanism would be used only as an *ultima ratio* and in case market financing proved insufficient. Disbursement on the bilateral loans would be decided by unanimity subject to strong conditionality. And it was made clear that financing would not be provided at average euro area interest rates, but rather under the assumption that incentives were needed to induce a return to market financing as soon as possible through risk-adequate pricing.[28] The fear of moral hazard was behind the debate on pricing, with skeptical countries afraid they would be rewarding profligate budgetary behavior if they set much-lower-than-market interest rates.[29]

Euro area negotiations followed, and finance ministers reached an agreement on a €45 billion package, one-third of which was coming from the International Monetary Fund, the rest being bilateral loans from euro area member states. This figure would rise to €110 billion on May 2, after Greece demanded that the euro area/IMF loans be activated.[30] Because the package agreement depended on national parliamentary confirmation by most participating member states, many of which were overtly skeptical about a bailout of Greece (the Slovak government decided not to participate at all), and because public anger was mounting in Greece at the scale of cutbacks, market pressure on Greece continued to increase, with 10-year bond interest rates spiking above 12 percent on May 7. The contagion affected all of the most vulnerable euro area economies, Portugal, Ireland, and Spain in particular, and interest rates on Portuguese bonds reached 6.285 percent at market close on May 7.

That day, the EU heads of state and government came together at an emergency meeting in Brussels and agreed on the European Financial Stability Mechanism and the European Financial Stability Facility, totaling €500 billion (€60 billion and €440 billion, respectively), due to expire after three years. Interventions by the EFSM and the EFSF would be coupled with another €250 billion in IMF funds for a final total of €750 billion. Ecofin (Economic and Financial Affairs Council) ministers were left on Sunday, May 9, to hammer out the details, which they did after a long and tense meeting that ended just before the opening of the Asian markets on Monday. The immediate effect was positive, with interest rates lowering considerably for all the peripheral economies in the euro area and falling to 4.5 percent for 10-year Portuguese bonds.

---

28. See European Council, "Statement by the Heads of State or Government of the Euro Area," March 25, 2010, www.european-council.europa.eu (accessed on October 23, 2011).

29. The March 25, 2010, European Council also launched the debate on the new governance of the euro area, which would lead to an important agreement at the October 28–29, 2010, European Council on mechanisms to reinforce budgetary discipline, introduce effective macroeconomic supervision, and strengthen economic coordination in the context of the "European semester."

30. See "Statement by the Eurogroup," May 2, 2010, www.consilium.europa.eu.

At the margins of the May 7 meeting, Portugal, as well as Spain, responded to market pressure by signaling austerity at home. At the final press conference, new targets of 7.3 percent and 4.6 percent for the 2010 and 2011 deficits, respectively, were announced by the Portuguese prime minister, lowering the previous targets by 1.0 and 1.5 percentage points. Domestically, new measures were taken to adjust to the new target in 2010, notably through tightening government expenditure and personnel costs, as well as frontloading revenue side measures.

What followed was a period of apparent relative calm. Interest rates for Greece, which had been put under the umbrella of international financial assistance, quickly started to rise again, actually reaching the May 7 level early in September. Rates decreased in July for both Portugal and Ireland.

Irish Troubles, European Hesitations, Portugal under Pressure

But by August, concerns with the Irish banking sector turned the pressure on again. The decision by the Irish government, at the end of September, to bail out the Anglo Irish Bank gave rise to a new spike in interest rates in Ireland and, by contagion, in Portugal, with 10-year government bond yields closing a little short of 6.5 percent on September 29. Pressure eased on Portugal only with the government's presentation of the 2011 austerity budget to Parliament on October 15.

A few days later, in the run-up to the October European Council, Angela Merkel and Nicolas Sarkozy met in Deauville. On that occasion, they issued a declaration stating that the establishment of a permanent crisis management mechanism, to take over the temporary EFSF and EFSM in 2013, was conditioned on amending the EU treaties to provide for adequate participation of private creditors.[31] The same line would be taken days later in the October 28–29 European Council, where it was decided that the future mechanism should have a role for the private sector.[32]

Private sector participation made perfect sense from the theoretical point of view. After all, taxpayers had been bailing out banks and private investors in virtually every European country since the beginning of the financial crisis. Arguably, private sector moral hazard—in particular the financial sector's irresponsible risk-taking behavior and unique "talent for privatizing gains and socializing losses"[33]—had led to the 2007–08 financial crisis. However, to introduce that idea in the midst of an extremely volatile market and without detailing how it would work was like adding fuel to the flames.

Indeed, borrowing costs soared both for Ireland and Portugal after the Deauville meeting and continued to rise after the October 28–29 European

---

31. See "Franco-German Declaration," October, 18, 2010, www.elysee.fr.

32. See European Council, "Conclusions," October 28–29, 2010, www.european-council.europa. eu (accessed on October 23, 2011).

33. Martin Wolf, "Regulators Should Intervene in Bankers' Pay," *Financial Times,* January 15, 2008.

Council. Even the agreement reached late in the evening of Friday, October 29, between the Portuguese government and the main opposition party (PSD) on the strong austerity 2011 budget, after very difficult and tense negotiations, had no positive effect on bond prices. It was clear by then that good news at the national level could always be trumped by bad news at the European level, which made the fate of the more-vulnerable countries dependent not only on their own deeds but on those of their European partners as well.

With continued pressure from markets, and as the Irish public debt incurred by taking over enormous liabilities from bad banks swelled, on November 22 Ireland requested access to the EFSF for support to its financial system. An €85 billion package was agreed upon by the Eurogroup and Ecofin ministers on November 28, with emphasis on an immediate strengthening and a comprehensive overhaul of the Irish banking system.[34]

At the margins of that meeting, the Eurogroup issued a statement—meant to allay market fears on the issue of private sector participation in the future European Stability Mechanism (ESM)—announcing its agreement on the main guidelines for that mechanism. It was decided that the ESM would provide for case-by-case participation of private sector creditors, consistent with IMF policies. In this context, ministers made a clear distinction between solvent countries, for which private sector creditors would be encouraged to maintain their exposure according to international rules and fully in line with the IMF practices, and insolvent countries, which were required to negotiate a comprehensive restructuring plan with their private sector creditors in order to restore debt sustainability. It was decided that standardized and identical collective action clauses (CACs) would be included in all new euro area government bonds. Furthermore, it was made clear that any private sector involvement, including the use of CACs, would not become effective before mid-2013.[35]

Portugal: Next in Line

In less than 10 months, by the end of 2010, the European Union had agreed on fundamental changes to its economic governance and had achieved what one year before would have been considered little short of a revolution in terms of crisis management mechanisms. Political agreement had been obtained on the new elements of economic governance, including new and stricter sanctions linked to budget discipline and macroeconomic supervision. A new framework for economic coordination in the context of the European semester was about to take off in the beginning of 2011. Perhaps more surprisingly, financial assistance facilities had been agreed upon and set up, and were now being used

---

34. See "Statement by the Eurogroup and Ecofin Ministers," November 28, 2010, www.consilium.europa.eu.

35. See "Statement by the Eurogroup," November 28, 2010, http://consilium.europa.eu (accessed on October 23, 2011).

to help euro members in difficulty. Moreover, agreement had been reached that these temporary facilities would be replaced by a permanent mechanism in 2013. These were, without any doubt, important structural decisions.

Nevertheless, the feeling in December was that the European Union had been running behind events and sometimes even provoking them, as had been the case with the dispute over private sector involvement. In reality, political agreement had been, and continued to be, extremely difficult to achieve. Perceptions about the crisis, as well as economic situations, diverged considerably between the countries in the periphery and the central and northern European countries. In addition, interests were also different. Some euro members were not only posting healthy economic growth figures but were also far from suffering negative effects on their financing from the sovereign debt crisis. On the contrary, Germany and some central and northern European countries actually saw lower interest rates on their debts, considered safe havens by investors fleeing riskier bonds.

Furthermore, a significant part of the electorates in those countries saw the crisis almost entirely as the result of fiscal mismanagement, an idea fueled by much of the press and some political parties trying to profit from populist nationalistic sentiments. This perspective obviously made European solidarity harder to achieve and increased tension in the European political debate.

For Portugal, the Irish bailout and the November 28 statement by the Eurogroup on private sector involvement meant some interest rate relief, however short, from just above 7 percent to just below 6 percent. It was not a comfortable feeling, however. With Greece and Ireland under financial assistance programs, all eyes were now on Portugal as next in line. Portugal was certainly the most vulnerable euro area member still financing itself in the markets.

In November 2010, the Portuguese Parliament approved the toughest austerity budget in almost 30 years, targeting a 4.6 percent deficit by the end of 2011, the equivalent to a reduction of 5 percentage points of the structural deficit. On expenditure, public sector salaries suffered an overall reduction of 5 percent, admissions into public administration were essentially blocked, and promotions or any salary progressions were forbidden. Social benefits and allowances were reduced, and pensions were frozen. The National Health Service and public investment programs were particularly targeted for cuts. On the revenue side, measures included a 2 percentage point increase in the standard VAT rate and a 1 percentage point increase of employees' contribution to the civil servants social security scheme.

Early in 2011, indicators revealed that the 2010 deficit would be close to 6.8 percent,[36] thus lower than the 7.3 percent target set in May, and that the Portuguese economy had grown at the reasonable rate of 1.3 percent in 2010,

---

36. Including a one-off measure: For the transfer to the state social security of the pension fund of Portugal Telecom's workers the state received in 2010 approximately €2.8 billion (roughly equivalent to 1.6 percent of GDP), in exchange for assuming responsibility for future pension payments for those workers.

although the pace had been slowing down throughout the year, with the last quarter of 2010 registering negative quarterly growth.

Nevertheless, market sentiment clearly held that Portugal would soon have to request international financial assistance. In the beginning of 2011, a series of news reports, most based on anonymous senior euro area sources, reinforced that sentiment by repeatedly reporting either that core member states were pressuring for financial assistance and that Portugal would not hold out for long, or that a plan was somewhere being prepared for the imminent request for financial assistance. A good example is the January 8 report in *Der Spiegel* that Germany and France were trying to persuade Portugal not to postpone an inevitable bailout. This report was denied by the three governments mentioned, but four days later, when Portugal had its first government bond auction of the year, the international press waited in Lisbon for the inevitable, which did not occur. The three-year bonds were placed at the relatively high price of 5.396 percent, but below secondary market prices and with a bid-to-cover ratio of 2.6.

It was evident that fending off market pressure would be extremely hard. The prevailing line within the European Union was that any assistance would be of last resort, and several governments rejected outright other solutions seen to pull together the weight of the whole of the euro area, and especially of its strongest members, in order to calm market fears. As a result, Portugal would be facing market sentiment essentially on its own and would have to rely on itself to turn it around. In December 2010, Jean-Claude Juncker's and Giulio Tremonti's defense of eurobonds as a systemic response by the euro area to the crisis[37] was met with extreme skepticism even within some strongly pro-European circles.

The vulnerabilities of the Portuguese economy, and its recent history of low growth and very high external deficits, reinforced negative market sentiment. That Ireland, not Portugal, had asked for financial assistance while Portugal's structural problems were far greater (in spite of the Irish banking problem), seemed to puzzle many in the global English-language media.

The fact that Portugal was a small economy in the European context did not make things easier either. After Ireland had gone under the international assistance umbrella, and although Portugal was considered next in line, the main concerns did not seem to concentrate on Portugal but rather on Spain. It was the possibility of having to bail out Spain that really scared European leaders.

Portugal Resisting: National Austerity and EFSF Flexibility

The sentiment in financial centers, communicated by market analysts and journalists on a daily basis, was that Portugal could not resist. Unlike Greece

---

37. See Jean-Claude Juncker and Giulio Tremonti, "E-bonds Would End the Crisis," *Financial Times*, December 5, 2010.

or Ireland, Portugal experienced no single decisive event to undermine market sentiment. Contagion and Portuguese economic vulnerabilities had added up to form negative market perceptions.

However, Portugal had reasons to resist pressure from markets. Most importantly, the government deemed that Portugal did not require international financial assistance. Fiscal consolidation advanced in 2010 and the 2011 budget implied aggressive cuts, which would inevitably be reflected in budgetary results. Indeed, budget implementation showed a substantially reduced deficit by the beginning of the year, with both a decrease in expenditure and an increase in revenues.

Moreover, asking for a bailout would not be financially profitable for Portugal under existing conditions at the time. International financial assistance interest rates were high (around 5.2 percent for Greece and 5.8 percent for Ireland) and not much better than market conditions at the time for Portugal. Also, Portugal's implicit sovereign debt interest rate stood at 3.5 percent, lower than that of Belgium (3.6 percent) or of Italy (3.8 percent), for instance, which meant that there was margin to handle higher interest rates for some time. Simulations under the scenario that the entire 2011 bond issuance would be made at 7 percent showed that by the end of the year, the implicit funding cost would still be below 5 percent.[38] Ten-year government bonds were issued in January at 6.716 percent interest, and because emerging economies had revealed an interest in Portuguese debt, some diversification was possible.

Additionally, although European leaders were certainly more concerned at the prospect of an eventual Spanish bailout, it was by then obvious that the ring-fencing strategy was not working. Putting Greece under international financial assistance had not stopped contagion, nor had the Irish bailout calmed markets down. On the contrary, not only did secondary market yields continue to increase substantially for Greek and Irish bonds, but market fears seemed to turn their attention to the next country in line. With contagion so obviously occurring, it was unlikely that financial assistance to Portugal would ring-fence it from Spain. It could, on the contrary, concentrate pressure on Spain and possibly on other economies like Italy and Belgium.

Domestically, resisting the bailout was supported by a majority of the population, marked by the memories of the two previous IMF interventions in Portugal (in 1978 and 1983) following balance of payment crises. It was generally understood that such an outcome would hurt Portugal's European and international credibility for a long time to come and would, in the short run, dampen the minority Portuguese government's already very slim policymaking margin of maneuver.

These reasons meant that it made economic and political sense for Portugal to continue access to international markets, while expecting that good

---

38. See Portuguese Treasury and Government Debt Agency, "Republic of Portugal: Economic Outlook and Debt Management Strategy," January 2011, page 14, www.igcp.pt.

results, continued reforms at home, and good decisions at the European level would start turning market sentiment around.

Indeed, although it was difficult to shake off a feeling of frustration at the lack of more-decisive European decisions, member states' positions had evolved throughout 2010 as events unfolded and the crisis deepened. The fact that ambitious proposals like the emission of Eurobonds were being put forward and supported by high-level European politicians in office (albeit rejected by several others) signaled that Europe was still trying to find the right balance to respond to the sovereign debt crisis. At the margins of the December 16–17 European Council, euro area heads of state and government declared that elements of the euro area strategy, including ensuring the availability of adequate financial support through the EFSF pending the entry into force of the permanent mechanism, would be further developed in the coming months as a comprehensive response to any challenges and as part of the new economic governance.[39] What this statement meant, even in the somewhat watered-down final version insisted on by hardliners during the summit, was that the door was not closed to the possibility of increased flexibility in EFSF support, notably through direct interventions in the debt markets.

The European Council met again on February 4, 2011, in a summit intended to focus on energy and innovation. Instead, the center of attention was a new Franco-German idea to create what at the time was called a "competitiveness pact." Although details of the pact were left for later negotiations between "sherpas," euro area leaders endorsed the idea of increasing economic policy coordination in the euro area to improve competitiveness, leading to a higher degree of convergence. The pact was targeted at euro members, although nonmembers were invited to participate.[40] The idea of a pact, presented to journalists by Angela Merkel and Nicolas Sarkozy in Brussels on the day of European Council, was aimed at stronger policy coordination but also at creating a blueprint for countries to converge toward the German competitiveness model, targeting four main areas: unit labor costs (by abolishing wage indexation schemes); pension systems (by raising retirement ages); tax harmonization (by creating a common base for corporate taxes); and fiscal discipline (by making it a constitutional violation to exceed limits on national debt).

Implicit in the European Council discussions, but explicit in the negotiations that followed on the competitiveness pact (or the Euro-Plus Pact, as its final version would be called), was that the pact would be part of a larger package that would include bolstering the capacity and flexibility of the EFSF—the so-called grand bargain to be agreed upon at the European Council at the end

---

39. See "Statement by the Heads of State or Government of the Euro Area and the EU Institutions," annex 3 of European Council, "Conclusions," December 16–17, 2010, www.europeancouncil.europa.eu (accessed on October 23, 2011).

40. See "Statement by the Heads of State or Government of the Euro Area and the EU Institutions," annex 1 of European Council, "Conclusions," February 4, 2011, www.european-council.europa.eu (accessed on October 23, 2011).

of March. This was seen as especially important by many favoring a systemic euro area response. Interventions in Greece and Ireland had failed to calm down markets, and it was generally accepted that the EFSF did not have the capacity to handle a possible bailout of Spain in case it requested financial assistance.

Strengthening the EFSF intervention capacity by raising its capital to match its initially announced capacity of €440 billion had been in the cards since December. EFSF's triple-A grade meant that the initial capital of €440 billion (agreed on in May 2010) was equivalent to a borrowing capacity of only around €255 billion, since only 6 were triple-A countries among the 17 euro area members.

More importantly, increasing the flexibility of the intervention modalities of the EFSF—notably by allowing it, under conditionality, to directly access primary and secondary bond markets, and in doing so relieving the European Central Bank (ECB) from its "nonstandard" and contentious bond-buying program—was seen by many, including Portugal, as essential to stabilizing the euro area sovereign bond markets. It was to this, not to the Euro-Plus Pact, whose effects would be long term only, that markets' attention had turned after the European Council meeting.

For Portugal, something else was also at stake during the February 4 summit. Portugal had managed successful emissions of bonds and treasury bills in January with decreasing, albeit high, rates. One-year Treasury bills had been subscribed at 4.029 percent on January 19 and at 3.71 percent on February 2. But market pressure and volatility were very high, and rates on 10-year bonds in the secondary market remained just below 7 percent throughout the month. The ECB had assisted in reducing volatility by continuing its bond-buying program early in January, as news reports of Portugal's imminent bailout disrupted markets, although it went on to temporarily suspend bond buying in mid-January.[41]

Bond buying by the ECB was not popular among hardliners, but the ECB's actions were effectively the best euro area tool against market volatility. Portugal's austerity 2011 budget, negotiated between the two largest Portuguese parties in Parliament, gave the ECB assurances that Portugal was firmly on the track of fiscal consolidation. The macroeconomic scenario within the budget proposal presented to Parliament in mid-October 2010 included a 0.2 percent GDP growth projection for the country, which was considered too optimistic, but a more cautious assumption of –0.7 percent growth had been taken as the underlying scenario for fiscal revenues.

However, international institutions' forecasts coming later in 2010 and in the beginning of 2011 were more pessimistic than the –0.7 percent underlying assumption. In its autumn economic forecast, released on November 29, 2010, the European Commission predicted a –1.0 percent GDP economic recession for Portugal. The Bank of Portugal's winter economic bulletin, made public

---

41. See "ECB Forced to Buy Portugal Bonds," *Financial Times,* February 10, 2011.

on January 11, 2011, forecasted a 1.3 percent fall in GDP. Weak fourth-quarter growth indications and the austerity measures included in the 2011 budget were being factored in by the institutions and were reflected in more negative scenarios for 2011. Different forecasts meant that there was a gap between the Portuguese government's and the EU institutions' fiscal projections for 2011 that would meet the 4.6 percent deficit target.

Concerns with this gap were behind one of the paragraphs in the euro area statement of February 4. A part of the "grand bargain" global package to be finalized in March was the assessment by the European Commission, in conjunction with the ECB, of progress made by euro area member states in the implementation of measures taken to strengthen fiscal positions and growth prospects.[42] It was a message for Portugal to speedily put forward contingent measures that took into account the lower growth projections.

After the February 4 summit, market pressure increased with news of German resistance to strengthening and extending the flexibility of the EFSF; and the ECB started buying Portuguese debt again in an attempt to contain yields that went above 7 percent for 10-year bonds.[43] Simultaneously, Portuguese government officials sat down in Lisbon with European Commission and ECB officials to discuss the 2011 fiscal gap as well as the magnitude of the measures needed to meet the 2012 and 2013 deficit targets of 3 percent and 2 percent of GDP, respectively.

January 2011 had been the longest month so far in the crisis for Portugal, and very few had thought the country could have resisted up to this point. Positive preliminary indications for the 2011 budget implementation and the show of national political resolve to fend off market pressure were signs to EU institutions and important European partners that Portugal's bailout could perhaps be avoided. This slight change of mood was not, however, accompanied by a change in market sentiment.

If signs of a slight mood change were going to be translated into stronger and more vocal support from European partners and, possibly, a reversal of the trend in market volatility, the Portuguese government needed to definitively address the concerns of the EU institutions. Preliminary information relating to the implementation of the budget in the first two months was consistent with the defined targets. Year-on-year tax receipts had increased by around 10.5 percent, and total state expenditure had decreased by 3.6 percent, with expenditure in wages decreasing by 5.2 percent.[44] But it was imperative

42. See "Statement by the Heads of State or Government of the Euro Area and the EU Institutions," annex 1 of European Council, "Conclusions," February 4, 2011, www.european-council. europa.eu (accessed on October 23, 2011).

43. On Germany and the EFSF, see "Berlin Resists Call for Extended EFSF Role," *Financial Times,* January 28, 2011; on the ECB's actions, see "ECB Forced to Buy Portugal Bonds," *Financial Times,* February 10, 2011.

44. Directorate-General for Budget, Portuguese Ministry of Finance, Budget Implementation Synthesis Report, March 2011, www.dgo.pt.

that Portugal take a precautionary view on increased economic risks stem-ming from austerity and market volatility, which the international institu-tions had underlined in their forecasts.

Closing the Gap

In this context, the Portuguese government agreed on expenditure-side mea-sures that corresponded to a further cut of 0.8 percent of GDP to be taken immediately in 2011 as a precaution. Moreover, measures to meet the 2012 and 2013 targets needed to be detailed ahead of the March 11 euro area sum-mit, where the global package was going to be discussed, advancing the regular April timetable for stability programs' presentation. Concrete assurances by the Portuguese government on meeting fiscal targets and a positive assess-ment by the EU institutions on the credibility of the measures taken in 2011 and planned for 2012 and 2013 were part of the global package.

On March 11, hours before the summit in Brussels, the Portuguese gov-ernment announced the guidelines for meeting the 2011, 2012, and 2013 fiscal consolidation targets.[45] For 2012 and 2013, the government anticipated an expenditure reduction of 2.4 percent of GDP (1.6 percent in 2012 and 0.8 percent in 2013) and an increase in revenue of 1.3 percent of GDP (0.9 percent in 2012 and 0.4 percent in 2013). On the expenditure side, it included freezing salaries and most pensions as well as reducing higher pensions in proportion to the 2011 salary cuts, plus savings in health, education, social benefits, pub-lic sector enterprises, and local authorities. On the revenue side, there would be a reduction in fiscal benefits, review of lower VAT rates, increase in excise taxes, and total convergence of pension and salary taxes.

The government also committed to further structural reforms in the ju-diciary, competition rules, and housing. On labor market reform it proposed changes—agreed upon with social partners before the March 24–25 European Council—to allow decentralizing certain collective bargaining aspects to com-pany level, to lower worker compensation in future contracts in case of dis-missal, and to increase flexibility in the use of temporary layoff instruments.

On the day of the March 11 summit, the presidents of the European Commission and of the ECB issued a press statement supporting the policy package,[46] and euro area leaders did the same in the summit conclusions. A positive mood in relation to Portugal had been achieved around the European Council table.

---

45. See "Note on Policy Guidelines and Measures that the Portuguese Government Will Adopt to Address Main Economic Challenges," March 10, 2011, www.portugal.gov.pt.

46. See "Joint Press Statement by the European Commission and the European Central Bank on the Measures Announced by the Portuguese Government," March 11, 2011, http://europa.eu (accessed on October 23, 2011).

Limited EFSF Flexibility

The summit agreed on a Pact for the Euro. The Pact for the Euro, joined by Poland, Bulgaria, Denmark, Romania, Lithuania, and Latvia two weeks later at the March 24–25 European Council to become the Euro-Plus Pact, laid out guidelines for convergence between its members in competitiveness, employment, public finances, and financial stability, areas that would be monitored in the context of the reinforced economic governance through specific agreed-upon indicators.

There was also an agreement on reinforcing the crisis mechanisms. The effective financing capacity would be increased in the case of both the ESM (to €500 billion) and the EFSF (to €440 billion). A first step was taken toward lowering the price on ESM and EFSF loans, with Greece being given lower interest rates (100 basis points less) and longer maturities (7.5 years). But the increased flexibility of these instruments did not meet the expectations of those betting on a systemic game changer for the euro area. There was a reference to the possibility of ESM and EFSF interventions in the debt primary market, but only exceptionally and in the context of a full assistance program with strict conditionality. No reference was made to secondary market intervention. The decision on flexibility fell short of what was needed to give the euro area an instrument to fight market disruptions. It remained in the hands of the ECB alone to try to do that job.

Request for Financial Assistance

As part of the European semester, the Portuguese government adopted on March 19 the Stability and Growth Program for 2012–14 (known as PEC IV[47]), prepared on the basis of the austerity guidelines announced days earlier. On March 23, the Portuguese Parliament rejected PEC IV. The political outcome was inevitable: The country headed to early elections.

Although the PS, PSD, and CDS-PP, the only parties to plausibly be part of a future government, clearly declared full allegiance to fiscal consolidation and structural reforms, markets nonetheless reacted badly to political instability, and interest rates for Portuguese bonds soared. In little more than a week, between March 24 and April 4, rating agencies lowered Portugal's rating. Fitch took it from A+ to BBB–, and Standard and Poor's from A– to BBB–. Besides the agencies' interpretation of the March 24–25 European Council conclusions that "sovereign debt restructuring is a potential pre-condition to borrowing from the ESM,"[48] they pointed to political instability and possible difficulties for Portugal in acceding to timely European support. Elections still

---

47. The program's Portuguese initials are PEC and this is the fourth version of the program.

48. Standard & Poor's Research Update, "Republic of Portugal Ratings Lowered to BBB–/A-3 on ESM Lending Conditions," March 29, 2011, www.standardandpoors.com (accessed on October 23, 2011).

being two months away, a possible financial assistance agreement would have to be negotiated by the caretaker government. Furthermore, bailouts had become an issue in the Finnish elections, with the nationalistic True Finns party apparently benefiting in the polls from its radically negative stance. Yields on 10-year government bonds moved from 7.367 percent on March 23 to 8.767 percent on April 5.

Adding to the gloomy picture, on March 31 and again on April 24, following a Eurostat guidance note on financial defeasance structures and guidelines on the public sector budgetary perimeter, the National Statistics Institute revised upward the recent years' figures for Portugal's budget deficits and public debts. Although several other European countries were also affected, for Portugal these corrections implied 2009 and 2010 public deficit figures of 10.1 and 9.1 percent of GDP, respectively, instead of 9.3 and 6.8 percent of GDP. Numbers for public debt were also raised to 83.0 and 93.0 percent for 2009 and 2010, respectively.

The new figures were the result of including within the state's accounts budgetary perimeter financial assistance to banks (Banco Português de Negócios and Banco Privado Português), three public transportation companies (REFER, Metropolitano de Lisboa, and Metro do Porto), and three public-private partnerships for toll-free motorways which, following the introduction of tolls, had to be considered public assets and registered as investment expenditure.

With the financing conditions collapsing for both Portugal and its banks and companies, on April 7 the Portuguese government took the inevitable step of asking for international financial assistance from the European Union and the IMF.

Financial assistance negotiations took place during the preelection period between the caretaker government and a technical team composed of the European Commission, the ECB, and the IMF (the troika), with step-by-step consultations with the main opposition parties. The end result is a vast economic and financial adjustment program[49] that the three main political parties agreed to and that includes strong budget consolidation, ambitious structural reforms, and reinforcement of the financial sector. It came with a financing package of €78 billion, of which €12 billion is for possible recapitalization of banks.

Conclusions and Looking Ahead

By 2002, with domestic demand stalling, Portugal had entered a phase of low economic growth. It was the third stage of a cycle of boom, overvaluation, and slump that had started in the mid-1990s with the prospect of euro accession, and that was brought about by insufficient fiscal policy adjustment to the new

---

49. See "Portugal: Memorandum of Understanding on Specific Economic Policy Conditionality," May 17, 2011, www.min-financas.pt (accessed on October 23, 2011).

monetary setting, compounded by the diverting impact of EU enlargement on FDI and trade and by the competitiveness effects on the most important Portuguese exporting sectors of large emerging economies' entry into the world market.

It was argued above that with growth stalled, and the country economically out of sync with comparable European economies, Portugal took a soft approach to correcting imbalances and regaining economic growth conditions. The country entered a phase of budget moderation/consolidation and structural reforms. Labor costs were contained, productivity grew above EU average, and the economy slowly recovered competitiveness.

Export growth was above EU average in the 2006–10 period, a level not achieved for a decade. Still, that period is evidence of the difficulties of correcting current account imbalances, and especially twin deficits, within a single monetary union. Despite stronger export growth (which was largely offset by higher energy prices and higher interest rates), the international investment position of the economy continued to deteriorate. Evidence shows that when the private sector deleveraged, the public sector overcompensated with larger budgetary deficits, and that when the public sector consolidated, private sector borrowing boomed. A stronger internal devaluation of the economy, notably via lower wage taxes paid by employers, would have contributed to a faster adjustment of the economy. However, it would have made fiscal targets more difficult to achieve, a problem for a country in excessive deficit procedure. This option could have been followed gradually, and indeed it would reinforced the country's progress toward regaining competitiveness; but its impact on the external deficit would have been slower. The conclusion is clear: Portugal would have needed a relatively prolonged recession brought about by a considerably more contractionary fiscal policy if it were to rapidly redress its current account imbalances without jeopardizing its fiscal targets.[50]

---

50. It is interesting to recall, for context, a passage from the founding document of the Economic and Monetary Union in Europe. In 1970, the Werner Report indicated that "For such a Union only the global balance of payments of the Community vis-à-vis the outside world is of any importance. Equilibrium within the Community would be realized at this stage in the same way as within a nation's frontiers, thanks to the mobility of the factors of production and financial transfers by the public and private sectors . . . . For influencing the general development of the economy, budget policy assumes great importance. The Community budget will undoubtedly be more important at the beginning of the final stage than it is today, but its economic significance will still be weak compared with that of the national budgets, the harmonized management of which will be an essential feature of cohesion in the union. The margins within which the main budget aggregates must be held both for the annual budget and the multi-year projections will be decided at the Community level, taking account of the economic situation and the particular structural features of each country. A fundamental element will be the determination of variations in the volume of budgets, the size of the balance and the methods of financing deficits or utilizing any surpluses. In order to be able to influence the short term economic trend rapidly and effectively it will be useful to have at the national level budgetary and fiscal instruments that can be handled in accordance with Community directives" (Werner 1970).

Portugal followed a soft approach to correcting its imbalances when politically it still had that alternative. When the sovereign debt crisis hit the euro area, that ceased to be an option. The result of the adjustment program agreed upon with the international institutions is a hard approach to redressing Portuguese economic imbalances (already implied in the 2011 budget) within the euro single currency area context.

The precrisis evolution showed an economy changing its profile and slowly regaining competitiveness. These trends need now to be dramatically reinforced. Positive signs are being registered. The positive trend in exports, which indicates growth at a sustainably strong rate since the beginning of 2010,[51] is an essential element in the necessary rebalancing of the Portuguese economy. The inevitable retrenchment of domestic demand, visible since the beginning of 2011[52] and expected to accelerate further at least during the first part of the program's implementation, needs to be compensated to an extent by strong net export growth in order for the program to succeed.[53]

The economic and financial adjustment program negotiated between Portugal and the troika is an ambitious roadmap for fiscal consolidation and structural reforms. The program targets a 5.9 percent budget deficit in 2011, 4.5 percent in 2012, and 3 percent in 2013, corresponding to an overall structural adjustment of over 9 percentage points (4.5 percentage points in 2011; 4.6 percentage points in 2012–13). Moreover, the Portuguese government has recently indicated deficit targets of 1.8 and 0.5 percent for 2014 and 2015, respectively (implying a further 1.1 percentage point reduction in the structural deficit).[54] The programs' macroeconomic scenario forecasts an economic contraction of 2.2 percent in 2011 and 1.8 percent in 2012, with annual growth returning in 2013. Inevitably, implementation of the program will be very challenging.

The new government that resulted from the June 5, 2011, elections is supported by a large majority in Parliament—132 members out of 230 (PSD has 108; CDS-PP has 24)—and is committed to the full implementation of the program. The PS, which supported the previous minority government and is now the main opposition party, elected 78 members to Parliament and has also declared its engagement with the adjustment program and its targets. Politically, it is relevant that parties representing 206 out of the 230 members

---

51. Export growth in 2010 was as follows: first quarter 9.2 percent; second quarter 9.6 percent; third quarter 8.5 percent; fourth quarter 7.8 percent. For 2011, the figures are first quarter 8.4 percent; second quarter 8.4 percent (Statistics Portugal, www.ine.pt).

52. Internal demand growth in 2010 was as follows: first quarter 1.3 percent; second quarter 2.0 percent; third quarter –0.8 percent; fourth quarter 0.2 percent. For 2011, the figures are first quarter –3.1 percent; second quarter –5.2 percent (Statistics Portugal, www.ine.pt).

53. Import growth in 2010 was as follows: first quarter 6.2 percent; second quarter 9.6 percent; third quarter 1.2 percent; fourth quarter 3.7 percent. For 2011, the figures are first quarter –0.9 percent; second quarter –5.4 percent (Statistics Portugal, www.ine.pt).

54. Ministry of Finance, "Budgetary Strategy Document 2011–2015," August 31, 2011, www.min-financas.pt (accessed on October 23, 2011).

of Parliament are committed to the implementation and success of the adjustment program, despite their political differences.

Portugal has the domestic political conditions to achieve timely implementation of the program and the economic conditions to succeed and come out stronger and more competitive economically. With parliamentary elections planned only for 2015, a stable majority government in place, and the largest opposition party firmly engaged, the political conditions are in place for a successful implementation of the economic and financial adjustment program. Implementation is imperative, as Portugal will be facing years of economic and social hardship and of hard economic adjustment. Unemployment will continue to rise, and wages in the whole economy will inevitably continue to suffer downward pressure. Exports will need to be the essential element of economic growth and will see their share in GDP increase considerably as external demand takes the place of internal demand. However, the balance between export growth and internal retrenchment is more difficult to achieve in Portugal than, for instance, in Ireland (or in the Baltic countries). A relatively low share of exports to GDP (little above 30 percent in 2010) means that even strong export growth will not be enough, in the first two years, to compensate for the foreseen decrease in internal demand. Furthermore, Portugal is a small open economy in the euro area and the European Union. For this hard adjustment to occur in a relatively balanced way, it is essential that the European Union avoid a double-dip recession in 2012–13.

One of the lessons from the current sovereign debt crisis is that Portugal's fate is not dependent on its decisions alone. For Portugal, success will also depend on the financial stabilization of the euro area, which, in turn, will depend on how the European Union continues to address the current crisis. This chapter began by suggesting that the European Union first approached this crisis on the basis of divergent and partially misguided perceptions. However psychologically and politically understandable, the emphasis on sovereign moral hazard was clearly overrated. Events in Portugal and Ireland, where governments resigned and were defeated in national elections provoked directly by the management of austerity or bailout scenarios, are witnesses to that fact.

Moral duality has affected the management of this crisis. Indeed, the economic, political, and institutional roots of this crisis can be found not only within the most affected countries but also in the construct and in the political management of the euro area as a whole. The narrative according to which some euro area countries are being punished for their sins is certainly not helpful in encouraging a balanced approach. Nor does it correspond to reality. In fact, the problem was as much one of insufficient rules and mechanisms as it was one of disregard for existing rules (by many within the euro area).

It is clear from the unfolding of the crisis and the timeline of events (table 4.4) that, once the crisis began, EU and euro area decisions influenced its course. From examining the Portuguese experience, in particular, it is reasonable to ask whether Portugal would have needed to resort to a bailout if the

Table 4.4   Timeline of crisis: Causes and effects

Date	Main cause	Other causes	Effects on Portuguese debt market
October 2008	*United States* • Global financial crisis. • Lehmann Brothers bankruptcy.		Portuguese vs. German bond spread widens, but is less than Greek, Italian, and Irish bond spreads.
Throughout 2009			Portuguese debt market calm. Portuguese vs. German 10-year (10Y) bond spread lowers back to less than 100 basis points in second half of the year.
January 2010	*Greece* • Greek deficit swells. • Uncertainty as to Greek figures.	*Portugal* • Portuguese budget deficit is bigger than expected	Portuguese 10Y bond yields above 4 percent.
February 4, 2010	*European Union* • EU heads of state or government (HSG) meeting proclaims coordinated action to safeguard financial stability in euro area.		Portuguese 10Y bond yields peak at 4.725 percent. Pressure lowers in February and March.
April 2010	*European Union* • European skepticisms about bailout mechanism. • Need for unanimous agreement, including national parliaments. *Greece* • More austerity in Greece, which demands financial help.		Pressure strongly increases on Portuguese debt.
May 7, 2010	*European Union* • EU HSG meeting agrees on EFSF/EFSM.	*Portugal* • Portugal signals austerity at home.	Rates drop immediately after Portuguese 10Y bond yields peak at 6.285 percent. A calmer but still volatile period follows. Trend is upward in May and June, but downward in July.

(table continues next page)

Table 4.4   Timeline of crisis: Causes and effects *(continued)*

Date	Main cause	Other causes	Effects on Portuguese debt market
September 2010	*Ireland* • Concerns with Irish banking sector. • Ireland bails out Anglo-Irish Bank.		Portuguese 10Y bond yields rise, though less than Irish ones.
October 2010	*European Union* • Franco-German (October 18) + European Council (October 29) decision to include private sector in future crisis mechanism. *Ireland* • Magnitude of Irish debt swells.	*Portugal* • Portuguese government presents tough austerity budget (October 15). Government and main opposition party agree to approve it in Parliament (October 29).	European news on private sector involvement trumps austerity agreement in Portugal. Pressure continues and Portuguese 10Y bond yields are at 7 percent or close.
November 28, 2010	*European Union* • Eurogroup clarifies private sector involvement. Separation between solvent and insolvent countries.		Pressure immediately decreases with Portuguese 10Y bond yields momentarily falling below 7 percent.
December 2010, January–February 2011		*European Union* • Ambiguity at EU level, with possibility of EFSF strengthening and increased flexibility receiving contradictory reactions. • Start of Euro-Plus Pact negotiations. *Portugal* • Portuguese government determined to resist a bailout. • Positive public deficit indications for 2010. • Negative economic growth forecast. *Markets* • Market sentiment and news reports negative on Portugal's prospects of avoiding a bailout.	Volatility remains and rates resume upward trend in December, January, and February.

(table continues next page)

Table 4.4   Timeline of crisis: Causes and effects *(continued)*

Date	Main cause	Other causes	Effects on Portuguese debt market
March 11, 2011	*Portugal* • Portuguese government announces further cuts for 2011, and austerity plans for 2012, 2013. • Doubts as to whether package will be approved in Portugal. *Europe* • Eurogroup HSG welcome Portugal's commitment. • Euro-Plus Pact is agreed upon.		Markets await developments in Portugal.
March 23–April 7, 2011	*Portugal* • Portuguese Parliament rejects package proposed by government.	*Markets* • Agencies plunge Portugal's ratings. *Portugal* • Revision upwards of Portuguese deficit and debt figures for 2009 and 2010, following Eurostat guidelines.	Yields on Portuguese debt spiral. Portugal requests international financial assistance.

European Union had managed to anticipate the far-reaching decisions taken in the July 21, 2011, meeting of the heads of state and government of the euro area and implement them on time. For Portugal, especially, the growing financial market pressures of 2010 and 2011 were to a great extent due to causes outside Portugal's domestic economic situation. Certainly, the country has substantial structural problems and imbalances that have put it under the spotlight and that need to be addressed. But contagion effects are obvious from the crisis timeline. Stopping contagion and preserving the stability of the whole area is the European Union's most pressing objective, and has now finally begun to be recognized as such.

Moreover, structural change in the euro area needs to be oriented not only at making similar crises much more unlikely—and the groundbreaking new economic governance rules do that—but also at ensuring that the euro area pulls its weight in solving any future crises. Europe has reasonably managed the former but not yet the latter, and it is the latter that is most urgent now if the euro area is to find its way back to stability. In this sense, the agreed-upon decisions of the July 21 meeting, which indeed amount to an important leap forward, need to be rapidly implemented. To build a system to avoid crises is smart and necessary. To believe that any system can make the occurrence of crises impossible is naive. This understanding, as well as the clear perception of the advantages of the euro for the whole of Europe, needs to supersede the moral duality in which the debate has often been entangled.

References

Blanchard, Olivier. 2006. *Adjustment within the Euro: The Difficult Case of Portugal* (November 11). Available at http://econ-www.mit.edu/files/740.

European Commission. 2009. *Sustainability Report 2009*. Luxembourg. Available at http://ec.europa.eu.

European Commission, Directorate General for Information Society and Media. 2009. *Smarter, Faster, Better e-Government*. Available at http://ec.europa.eu.

IMF (International Monetary Fund). 2011. *Portugal: First Review Under the Extended Arrangement.* Country Report No. 11/279 (September). Washington.

Ministry of Finance. 2010. *2011 State Budget Report*. Lisbon. Available at www.dgo.pt.

Venn, Danielle. 2009. *Legislation, Collective Bargaining and Enforcement: Updating the OECD Employment Protection Indicators*. OECD Social, Employment and Migration Working Paper 89. Paris: OECD. Available at www.oecd.org/els/workingpapers.

Werner, Pierre. 1970. *Report to the Council and the Commission on the Realisation by Stages of Economic and Monetary Union in the Community.* Bulletin of the European Communities, Supplement 11/1970.

West, Darrel M. 2007. *Global E-Government, 2007.* Center for Public Policy, Brown University (August). Available at www.insidepolitics.org.

5

Italy and the Euro Crisis

RICCARDO PERISSICH

The acronym PIGS—for Portugal, Ireland, Greece, and Spain—was created at the start of the euro crisis to indicate those countries that were, or were likely to be, in trouble: the weak links of the euro chain. The Italians were quick to point out that the "I" stood for Ireland and not for Italy. Not everybody was convinced, and some suggested that a second "I" should be added. However, the majority—in Brussels, Frankfurt, and the EU capitals—thought that there was little to gain in pointing to the problems of Europe's fourth-largest economy. Granted, Italy's stock of public debt, at 120 percent of the country's GDP, was the largest in Europe after that of Greece and one of the largest in the world in absolute terms. More worrying was the fact that after having declined somewhat following the launch of the euro, it had started to grow again and had now reached pre-euro levels.

The primary surplus, more than 5 percent of GDP when the country joined the euro, now is at or below zero. On the other hand, Italy's public finances have been kept reasonably under control throughout the period: At 4 percent of GDP the deficit is not high by current euro standards, and it is lower than France's. Given the still high (but declining) level of private savings, the net external debt is one of the lowest in Europe. Unlike Spain, let alone Greece or Portugal, Italy has a strong "real economy"; it has the second-largest manufacturing sector in Europe and has not suffered from a housing bubble. Its banks, partly because they had been slow to internationalize, were not seriously affected by the financial crisis of 2008. Notwithstanding all this, the official display of confidence has not been as solid as it pretended to be. Even

Riccardo Perissich is executive vice president of the Council for the United States and Italy at the Italian branch.

Giulio Tremonti, the all-powerful finance minister, was heard saying while defending the first Greek bailout in Parliament, that Italy had to save Greece because if it fell, Italy could be next in line.

The Euro Crisis Reaches Italy

The first two years of the euro crisis were relatively calm for Italy. Although its financial sector was less affected than that of other countries, Italy suffered from the same economic slowdown as most of its European partners. The spread between Italian bonds and German bunds, although increasing, remained manageable at little more than 200 basis points. Italian debt was "in negative outlook" for the rating agencies, but it had been that way for quite some time. Commentators who wrote about "contagion" mentioned Spain (the S in PIGS) more often than Italy. In order to preempt possible turbulence, Tremonti announced that a supplementary budget, requested by "Europe," would be put to Parliament in September. Then, at the end of June 2011, there was a sudden change. First came an attack on Italian banks, whose shares were losing much more than their European counterparts. The only plausible reason—a deeply worrying one—was that they owned a lot of Italian public debt. After a few days the spread between Italian bonds and German bunds jumped to more than 300 points; to the dismay of most Italians, it quickly became larger than that between Italian and Spanish bonds. The contagion, like the rats spreading the Black Death, had reached the Italian shores from the east. In the 14th century, a succession of poor harvests made the population susceptible; this time, it was a sluggish economy and weak leadership.

Under pressure from Brussels and from Giorgio Napolitano, Italy's president, the government decided to move up the parliamentary debate to mid-July. A new budget was voted on in just two days. The center-left opposition voted against it but in a show of national solidarity helped to accelerate the debate. On the face of it, the budget was an impressive move: the most ambitious since the extraordinary measures that had been taken in 1992 by the Amato government to confront the crisis of the lira. Public finances were to be improved by a total of €48 billion over three years, with the objective of reaching a balanced budget by 2014. Admittedly, most of the improvement would come from more revenues. Some of the cuts to expenditures were particularly controversial insofar as they disproportionately affected regional and local authorities, a move that seemed to fly in the face of the proclaimed objective of transforming the country into a federal state. More importantly, most of the improvement would take place in 2013 and 2014, i.e., after the next general election, scheduled for 2013. Nevertheless it was hoped that the new budget, promptly welcomed by Brussels, could calm the markets. But the truce lasted for only a few days; the spreads quickly jumped to close to 400 points and remained consistently larger than Spain's. PIGS had by now clearly inherited a new "I." The rising spreads supported the growing view that Italy would be the field on which "the final battle [for the euro] will be fought."[1]

On August 5, in an unprecedented move, Jean-Claude Trichet, president of the European Central Bank (ECB), and Mario Draghi, governor of the Bank of Italy and Trichet's designated successor, wrote a letter to Prime Minister Silvio Berlusconi. Unlike previous messages from "Europe," it had not been discussed in advance with Tremonti, and many suspected that it had not been written in Frankfurt but in Rome. The text was kept secret, but its general content became known. It asked Italy to do several things: adopt additional fiscal measures to achieve a balanced budget in 2013; take a number of pro-growth measures, including a bold new drive to liberalize and privatize professional and public services at the national and local levels, improvement of flexibility of the labor markets, pension reform; and introduce a balanced-budget clause in the constitution. Berlusconi, once again pushed by Napolitano, announced that Parliament would be reconvened and that new measures would be decided in a matter of days. Although this was not explicitly included in the Trichet/Draghi letter, he also said that such measures were needed so that the ECB could start buying Italian bonds.

A new decree was adopted on August 13. This time the total effort amounted to €60 billion. In order to reach the balanced budget in 2013, the primary surplus was projected to be 5.9 percent in 2013 and 6.3 in 2014. This time Brussels's routine endorsement was less warm than usual, and it politely pointed out what most commentators were already writing in Italy. The balance between increased revenues and cuts in expenditures had further deteriorated: Now more than two-thirds would come from additional revenues, probably three-quarters if local authorities decided to compensate the lost transfers with new taxes. The projected fiscal pressure now stood at an unprecedented 50 percent of GDP. Gains predicted from an effort to fight tax evasion were deemed at best theoretical. A full €20 billion was supposed to come from a yet-undefined, radical reform of the fiscal and social security system; otherwise this amount would be replaced by linear cuts in all existing fiscal incentives, a measure that would primarily affect social incentives. The most important criticism, however, was that while the decree coped, albeit imperfectly, with the "fiscal" part of Trichet's letter, nothing had been decided on the "growth" part. Furthermore, the budget's estimates were based on the government assumption of an average 1.5 percent growth of GDP, which was deemed totally unrealistic.

The ECB started to buy Italian (and Spanish) bonds and, again for a few days, the markets became less aggressive. Many Italians thought that the worst was over, only to be confronted with the most absurd political psychodrama in the history of the republic. Under the constitution, the decree-law adopted on

---

1. Edward Altman and Maurizio Esentato, "Italy will fight last stand in debt crisis war," *Financial Times*, June 20, 2011.

August 13 was effective immediately, but would lose force unless confirmed by Parliament within 60 days. Immediately after that mid-August weekend, the consensus within the majority started to unravel. The main battlefield was a 3 percent surcharge on high incomes designed to raise some €4 billion. Given the high level of tax evasion, it was immediately labeled "the honest people's tax," a particularly apt name given that it would concern less than 1 percent of all taxpayers. Many, including the main employers' federation, advocated a wealth tax, which was deemed to be less discriminatory and easier to collect. Berlusconi was known to favor an increase in the value-added tax (VAT) rate, which was fiercely opposed by Tremonti on inflationary grounds. A second battlefield concerned pensions. Many wanted to complete reforms already enacted, by raising the legal retirement age and eliminating the existing possibilities for early retirement. This path was strongly opposed by the Northern League, the junior partner in the coalition.

When Parliament finally approved a modified version of the decree on September 6, Berlusconi had obtained the VAT increase, the surcharge on high incomes survived in a much softer form, and a modest step was taken to align women's legal retirement age with that of men. At the same time, the lobbies had been at work to eliminate or emasculate some measures aimed at liberalizing the professional services, a constituency that represents a significant part of the center-right majority. Public opinion was particularly incensed by the disappearance of any measure to reduce the costs of the political system—something that is of relatively little economic importance, but that carries enormous symbolic value with a public generally disaffected with the political class (the *casta*, as it is commonly called). Finally, still absent were measures aimed at improving Italy's growth and competitiveness. The opposition had a field day in describing the government as antisocial, divided, and inefficient. The ECB continued to buy Italian bonds, but the spreads remained in the 350–400 point range. Finally, the government pledged to enshrine in the constitution the principle of a balanced budget, something many people say has always been there and never complied with.

Understanding the Crisis in Italy

Such are the events that occurred in July and August. The question is, why did they unfold as they did and, more importantly, why then? Nobody, even among the most critical market analysts, ever suggested that Italy was facing insolvency in the foreseeable future; contagion was necessarily of a different nature from the disease affecting Greece, Ireland, Portugal, and even Spain. The reason for the emergence of the new "I" had to be different. The answer was this: lack of growth. As the respected analyst Carlo Bastasin[2] has noted, Italy is less a "fat p[i]ig" than a "lazy cat." Italy's economic performance had

---

2. Carlo Bastasin, *Italy: Fat PIIG or Lazy Cat?* RealTime Economic Issues Watch, Peterson Institute for International Economics, April 15, 2010, www.piie.com.

been lagging behind that of most other euro area countries not for 1 or 2 years, but for more than 10. Unlike in Germany and France, in Italy the growth of productivity had stopped. Some industrial sectors could still produce a good export performance, but overall the economy had been stagnant for a long time. Despite the relative success in keeping the deficit under control, the markets were saying that in the absence of stronger growth, the huge stock of public debt would never be reduced; rising interest rates could then make it, albeit in the long run, unsustainable.

But why did the crisis occur then and not before? Many Italians were slow to understand two factors that are critical in the political context of the euro crisis. First, if the country did not address its debt problem, it could become the vehicle of contagion to French banks that had large amounts of Italian debt on their balance sheets; the same was of course true for Greek debt, but on a different scale. Second, Germany's domestic political debate had made it very difficult for the government to agree to (limited) measures of solidarity for Greece, Ireland, and Portugal. If Italy, a member of the G-7 and the third-largest euro area economy, was perceived to be on the way to joining the group of potentially insolvent countries, Merkel's task would become impossible; hence the Trichet/Draghi letter. The ECB could provide temporary liquidity, but the structural problems affecting the country's competitiveness needed to be addressed by Italy and Italy alone.

These structural problems have been known for a long time, and many were explicitly mentioned in the Trichet/Draghi letter. The labor market had historically been affected by strong rigidities and by frequent conflicts with militant unions. In the early 1990s, as part of the drive to join the euro, the Amato and Ciampi governments succeeded in negotiating with the unions and the employers' federation a pact that included the end of indexation, a more flexible method of adjustment, and wage moderation. In exchange, the unions obtained the promise that nationwide contracts would remain the main pillar of the system of industrial relations. This pact served the country well, and it was a nonsecondary element that allowed Italy to fulfill its ambitious bid to join the euro from the start.

In the following years, pressure mounted to introduce more flexibility, particularly more freedom to hire and fire. Successive governments, as well as many employers, feared that this could compromise wage moderation. Instead, reforms were enacted that increased the scope for temporary and part-time contracts. Italy now has a dual labor market, with overprotected but declining permanent jobs and an expanding "precarious" job market that concerns primarily the young and women. An instrument designed to facilitate entry into the labor market has become for many people a permanent way of life, one offering little stability and limited hope for an adequate pension. As a result, many have dropped out of the official market to enter the unofficial or black market. More recently, some large companies have started to campaign for more decentralization in industrial relations, at both the company and geographical levels, a request that is seen by some (but not all) unions as an attempt to demolish the "national" contract. Given the present state of industrial relations, progress is not impossible, but it would require the presence of a determined and credible government, as was the case for the pact of 1993. The problem is also closely related to another critical issue, that of social security and pension reform.

Italian social expenditure, at 22 percent of GDP, is not particularly high by European standards, but it is unbalanced. Two-thirds of it goes to pensions, and not enough is left to finance unemployment benefits and the modern active labor market policy that would be necessary to increase employment. This is one of the reasons why the labor market remains rigid. The problem has distant roots. Italian pensions are not high, but they have been too generously awarded to people who are too young. Early retirement, particularly from public service, has been used as an electorally popular form of patronage. Many early retirees have found their way into the black economy. Measures to restrict the practice have been taken in the last decade, but there is still a long way to go. More than €17 billion is still spent every year to pay pensions for people between the ages of 40 and 59. What should be required now is a gradual increase of the age for legal retirement, in line with changes in life expectancy. What was decided in the last decree was only the acceleration, requested by European law, of the alignment of the legal age for women (60) and men (65). This change in turn would also require an improvement in services to assist working mothers, services that are particularly deficient in Italy and that help to explain the low rate of female participation in the labor market. Health care is another component of social expenditure that has been out of control for many years. Responsibility has been transferred to the regions, and some of them have accumulated enormous debts. Reforms have been announced, most recently with the August decree, but they will take time to produce effects and will probably have to be strengthened further.

Until the early 1990s, state control was stronger and more pervasive in Italy than in any other European country. Nearly all the banks and a significant part of big industry were in public hands. All sectors enjoyed a high level of protection. As European integration progressed, the situation became untenable. In the following years and under pressure from Brussels, mainly center-left governments implemented a massive program of privatization and liberalization. The results have been mixed. Part of the system has adapted well and has shown remarkable dynamism. In other cases, an entrepreneurial class characterized by a culture of (protected) small and medium-size business, combined with a still-archaic financial sector, prevented Italian industry from achieving the scale and technological innovation required by European and later global competition. There still is considerable scope for further privatization and liberalization at both the national and local levels: This is one of the main points mentioned in the Trichet/Draghi letter. The service sector, particularly the professional and retail services, is dominated by powerful corporate interests; this is another area that calls for further liberalization.

Finally, the fiscal system is deeply flawed. Nearly everybody agrees that it is biased against labor and production. As a result, while Italian take-home wages are relatively low, unit labor costs are high. Still more important is the exceptionally high level of tax evasion: According to some estimates, it could concern up to 30 percent of GDP. Although still in vague terms, both problems are addressed in the August decree.

If visible, determined, and sustained progress could be achieved on all these fronts, the impact on competitiveness would be considerable. The Italian economy has already shown itself in the past to be resilient and capable of exploiting what is probably the country's main richness: a vast pool of entrepreneurial spirit. However, for a revitalization of competitiveness along these lines to occur, other problems would have to be addressed, problems that go beyond the scope of economic policy, such as the impact of organized crime in large parts of the country, the inefficiency of the public administration and of the judiciary, and a dysfunctional institutional system for both, with too many layers of responsibility, each capable of blocking a decision. In recent years, much needed public and private investment in infrastructure, from transport, to energy, to waste disposal, has been delayed by budgetary problems, but also by legal, bureaucratic, and institutional obstacles.

Response to the Crisis

Most of the reforms described above need time to produce their effects and require a strong government capable of commanding broad political support over a long period of time. In the case of Italy, they should probably be the task of more than one parliament. However, immediate and determined action on any one of them would probably help to improve business confidence and break the vicious circle in which the country is trapped. The lack of such action is the main reason why market confidence in Italy has suddenly started to crumble. Disappointment in the performance of the present government and particularly the prime minister is not a new thing. Berlusconi has been elected three times with the promise of a "liberal revolution" that would unleash the animal spirits that are present in Italian society, and he has governed for most of the last decade. To epitomize his objective of preparing the country for the 21st century, he labeled his program the "three Is": "Impresa, Internet, and Inglese" (Enterprise, Internet, and English). The sad reality is that productivity has declined, Italy is among the lowest in broadband penetration in Europe, and some government ministers can barely speak Italian, let alone English.

As far as structural reforms are concerned, the results have been modest to say the least. The decline in competitiveness has not been reversed. Berlusconi's main promise was to lower the tax burden; an ill-advised step in that direction at the beginning of the decade had the effect of wiping out the primary surplus that he had inherited from the previous center-left coalition. Fighting tax evasion remained a declared objective of the government, but the prime minister's public statement that he "understood" tax dodgers undermined the government's credibility. Finance Minister Tremonti was allowed to pursue a policy of budgetary austerity, but otherwise the government looked rudderless. As Berlusconi gave the impression of being principally absorbed by his numerous legal problems, his image deteriorated in Italy and abroad. Nevertheless, his political support remained strong, if only because the opposition did not seem to be able to provide a viable alternative.

The situation began to change at the end of 2010, when Berlusconi's party started to experience open internal conflict, including defections of some of its leaders. The majority was becoming increasingly restless. The turning point came in the spring when the center-right lost important local elections, including in some of its traditional strongholds in the north, the most advanced and productive part of the country. Many of Berlusconi's allies drew the conclusion that the master campaigner had lost his magic. Electoral defeat in the north also had the effect of destabilizing the Northern League, the junior member of the coalition whose support is vital for the survival of the government. This party, a mainly populist movement that supports independence for the north and strong anti-immigration policies, had adopted the very skillful strategy of supporting the government while distancing itself from Berlusconi's personal behavior and focusing mainly on the objective of obtaining more political and fiscal power for the regions of the north. The party thought it had found a win-win strategy where success would benefit the entire coalition, while failures would affect only Berlusconi's party. However, in the spring elections both parties lost votes. At the same time, the budgetary austerity enacted by Tremonti was cutting into resources available to local authorities and risked transforming the goal of a federal Italy into an empty promise. The Northern League started to worry.

Berlusconi's business empire was built on commercial television and implicitly on advertising and the prospect of ever-expanding private consumption. Optimism and consumer confidence are not only the basis for his business, they are the foundation of his political message and one of the main reasons for his popularity. Such a person is ill equipped to cope with a crisis. At the beginning he denied that there was a crisis, then he pretended that it would not affect Italy, and finally he blamed all the problems on the international situation. The message that emerged from the elections was clear: Empty promises and increasing economic and social pain compounded by a policy of budgetary austerity left little room for optimism. The tide also started to turn against Tremonti, until then the strongest member of the government. Many in the government, tired of the cuts that were imposed with little or no discussion and of his sometimes arrogant style, started to revolt. He has been openly accused of being the cause of the defeat. In the eyes of the markets, Italy, with a declining prime minister, a fractious and paralyzed coalition, the prospect of new elections not too far away, and no clear alternative in sight, was losing its main asset: perceived political stability.

The agonizing debate that accompanied the July and August decrees had not been provoked by the opposition, or by mass protests as in the case of

Greece, but had been entirely internal to the majority coalition. The message was clear: The government had no leadership. The Northern League was adamant in opposing reform of the pension system, which would primarily affect its popular electorate in the north. Taxes on the rich, in any form, even a new determined effort to fight tax evasion, was seen by Berlusconi as undermining the electoral message that had put him in power. Liberalization of the professional services and retail trade touched on important electoral interests of his party. Judicial reform was compromised by his perceived attempt to use it as a pretext to solve his own judicial problems. Difficulties like these should not be insurmountable; they are the staple of any government—but not when the coalition is divided and the leadership declining. Worse, even the policy of budgetary rigor, so important for the country's credibility in Europe, had been put into question. Tremonti had managed to preserve it, but his image was tarnished.

The markets have continued to impose on Italy larger spreads than in the case of Spain. Their opinion seems to be that, with structural reforms blocked, the austerity policy will be self-defeating: It will only lead to even slower growth, the need for yet more austerity, and more discontent. In this view, Italy is not quite like Greece, but is on the same trajectory. This analysis may be simplistic, but it is not easy to contradict. Many observers think that Berlusconi should follow the example of José Luis Rodríguez Zapatero and seek the support of the opposition for a credible reform package, announce early elections, and declare that he will not stand again. He has adamantly refused to do that. Instead, the government has announced that structural reforms will be proposed very soon and that Parliament will see his natural end, scheduled for 2013. So far, the parliamentary majority, although shrinking, is holding together. The question is, for how long?

One notable feature of this situation is that, unlike other European countries, Italy doesn't seem to have experienced a significant rise of euro skepticism. Opinion polls do signal a decline in support for the European Union and the euro, but much smaller than in other countries. If one looks closely at the figures, Italians are disappointed by "too little Europe" rather than, as in other places, by "too much of it." Criticism has focused mainly on the perceived weakness of the European Commission, on Germany's "egoism" and reluctance to act, and on the "arrogance" of the Franco-German "axis." The idea of eurobonds (whatever that means) is very popular. The euro has sometimes been blamed for the increase in prices after its introduction, and some people in industry regret having lost the capacity to devalue. However, the predominant view is that without the euro, Italy would face a Latin American rather than a European future.

Open euro skepticism is indeed concentrated mainly on the fringes of the radical left and the extreme right. The center-left parties are traditionally strongly pro-Europe. The picture for the center-right is a bit different. The Northern League, true to its populist roots, has often played with euro skepticism, as has Berlusconi himself. Newspapers close to him have occasionally endorsed the representation of the European Union as "a socialist plot." However, as the crisis unfolded, all this has declined rather than increased. Tremonti has played an important role. Known for having made euro-skeptical remarks in the past, in recent years he has decided to position himself as the indispensable link between Brussels and Rome and consequently as the guardian of European orthodoxy. He claims copyright on the idea of euro-bonds. Paradoxically, sympathy for Germany's economic model has increased, at least among the informed public, since the markets started to focus on Italy. Newspapers occasionally publish articles by leading critics like Paul Krugman, Merkel continues to be criticized for her "lack of courage," but the predominant view is that the message from Berlin is basically sound. Led by influential people like Giorgio Napolitano, Mario Draghi, and Mario Monti, most commentators support the view that there should be "more Europe" and that European instruments (the ECB in particular) can help Italy in this direction, but that the effort should be primarily an Italian one; in addition, they believe that Italy must act not only in its own interest, but also to fulfill its responsibility to the euro area as a whole.

Of course, this mainstream current of opinion does not automatically lead to political action, but it is nonetheless significant. Italians, deeply disappointed by their political class, in fact do not resent being driven by Europe. As Guido Carli, a long-time governor of the Bank of Italy, wrote in his memoirs, "Almost all the reforms that have been successfully accomplished were implemented under pressure from Europe."[3]

Postscript[4]

As with the decree adopted in July, the decisions taken on September 6 did not elicit enthusiasm in the markets. The spread with German bunds has remained in the range of 350 to 400 points and well above Spain's (figure 5.1). Worse, the decree did not prevent the long-anticipated downgrading by the rating agencies.

Downgrading of Italian banks followed. The government reacted with dismay but confirmed that a "bill for growth" would be put to Parliament shortly. In a display of open hostility to Tremonti, Berlusconi entrusted the task of drafting it to the minister for economic development, a lackluster personality from his business empire. Two animated discussions have once again shaken the majority. The first concerns Tremonti's adamant insistence that the bill should not include additional costs. He seems likely to prevail, though the debate is still ongoing. The second concerns possible additional sources of revenue; some in the majority, including the unions and Confin-

---

3. Guido Carli, *Cinquant'anni di vita italiana* (Rome: Laterza, 1993).

4. October 31, 2011.

Figure 5.1   Italy and Spain: Interest rate spreads above German bunds

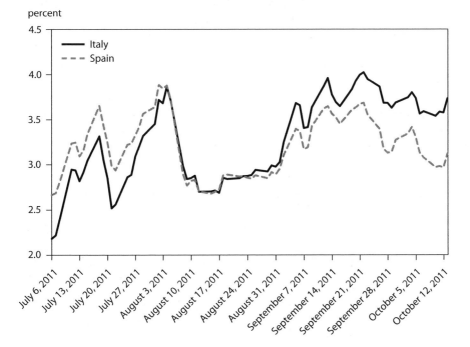

percent

Sources: Lavoce.info and Datastream.

dustria, the main employers' federation, support a wealth tax; Berlusconi continues to reject it. As an alternative, members of the majority propose a "fiscal amnesty." This is a traditional Italian way to raise money; it has been criticized as an open encouragement to moral hazard that would lead to more tax evasion in the future. Tremonti, who in the past was guilty of implementing similar measures, this time appears to be firmly against the approach. The proposal has been met with rage by the opposition and by most commentators and would probably be rejected by Brussels. Berlusconi has said in public that he does not support it, but he allows people close to him to state that he could go along with it. Even long-overdue decisions, like the appointment of the successor of Draghi (who will leave for Frankfurt on November 1), have been dealt with as part of a depressing political bargain. Tremonti has also scored another victory by securing government approval for the allocation among the various departments of the cuts that had been included in the August decree.

Between October 23 and 26, there were two crucial EU and euro area meetings. On the 23rd, Berlusconi went to Brussels empty-handed; Merkel, Sarkozy, Herman Van Rompuy, and even the usually mild José Manuel Barroso gave him a rough time. Clearly, as the crisis goes on European leaders are learning to be less complaisant with each other. He came back having promised to detail his commitment to reform within the next two days. To add insult to injury, Merkel and Sarkozy looked openly skeptical about Italy's commitment at their joint press conference; those images made the tour of the world and were received in Italy as a severe humiliation. The next two days were spent drafting a long letter detailing the Italian government's plans. Allegedly, several drafts were delivered to Brussels and sent back with requests for more details. When Berlusconi finally left for Brussels on October 26, he brought with him a letter that had been agreed to as the minimum that "Europe" could accept. It contains a long list of all the reforms that were already in Trichet's letter and that most observers had been suggesting; many of them have been part of the government program for a long time.

Tremonti appears not to have been involved in the draft and his signature does not appear on the letter. He has not commented on it, but some observers think that this is because he believes that the commitments are unlikely to be fulfilled. Two points were immediately noted. On pensions, the letter confirms the intention to gradually increase the legal retirement age to 67 by 2026, but nothing is said about closing the remaining windows for early retirement, something that is still deemed unacceptable by the Northern League. The paragraph on the reform of the labor market was drafted in a way to appear deliberately provocative to the unions and part of the opposition. The center-left has shown deep divisions, and a large part of it promptly fell into the trap of appearing to oppose the measures even before they were detailed. Furthermore, the letter is drafted in a way to constitute a government program for the best part of 2012. All in all, from a domestic point of view it was a subtle political move, allowing the government to appear determined to work for the good of the country and the opposition to seem unprepared to back up its vocal support for Europe with concrete facts.

The question is this: Is the government capable of delivering? The markets seem to think that it is not, and the spread has continued to widen. Many people think that Berlusconi should follow Zapatero's example: Seek the support of at least part of the opposition in exchange for the commitment to leave the government. Tremonti, in an off-the-cuff remark, seemed to agree when he said that Zapatero's pledge to exit was the reason Spanish bonds were performing better than those of Italy. Berlusconi firmly rejects this option. He seems convinced that he can deliver the reforms that he has promised in Brussels and then carry on until the natural end of the Parliament in 2013. Although it is always dangerous to underestimate Berlusconi's resources, few believe that that such a course is possible. The government has narrowly passed a new vote of confidence, but strains within the majority are increasing. Nobody can predict what will trigger the crisis, but most think that it will happen sooner rather than later, probably early next year. Many support the idea of a transitional government, possibly under a respected technocrat like Mario Monti, which would be entrusted with the task of adopting the necessary economic measures and of reforming the electoral law, universally considered inadequate.[5]

Acute and increasing polarization of the political discourse nevertheless makes this option difficult. Early elections held under the present law may well result in a victory for the center-left opposition, which is still divided and doesn't have a clearly agreed-upon leader. It is impossible to judge the opposition's policy for the simple reason that its program doesn't yet exist. Such a government would probably confirm its European credentials, but might find it very hard to agree on a common line on matters like pension and labor market reforms. Elections could also result in a hung Parliament that would lead to a government of national unity, of course without Berlusconi. Ideally, this may well be the best option, but it would have to solve the hurdle of leadership and, more importantly, of economic policy.

In the meantime, social discontent and disaffection with the entire political system are mounting. In recent years Italy has acquired the dubious distinction of topping the European league in inequality of wealth and income distribution. Most Italians never heard of John Rawls's *Theory of Justice*, but they instinctively know that the situation is not politically sustainable. Contempt for the perceived privileges of the political class, for widespread corruption, and for the high level of tax evasion is universal. Grassroots protest movements have now emerged, following the example of Spain and the United States. Notably, the slogans of Italy's *indignados* are directed not only against the government and the banks, but also against the ECB. It is too soon to say if this is an important development that could affect bipartisan support for fiscal austerity.

On the other hand, the most popular political figure in the country is Giorgio Napolitano, the president of the republic, with approval ratings close to 80 percent; his constitutional powers are limited, but so far he has played his cards with great skill, and his role will be enhanced if and when there is a government crisis. He is also increasingly active at the international level, both in Washington and in Europe. An elderly gentleman well into his 80s, he is perceived in Italy and abroad as the acceptable and modern face of the country. In a highly unusual move, Angela Merkel apparently had a long telephone conversation with him before she met Berlusconi in Brussels on October 26. This is hopefully an indication that what Italians are really looking for is leadership capable of giving them a sense of direction or, as they say in the United States, a convincing "narrative" that could replace the failed one offered by Berlusconi.

---

5. *Editors' note*: In the first week of November 2011, spreads above German bunds for 10-year government bonds reached over 500 basis points. After losing the majority on a key vote in Parliament, Prime Minister Berlusconi announced that he would resign once Parliament passed the economic reforms promised to EU partners. On November 12, the reform measures passed and Berlusconi resigned. President Napolitano invited Mario Monti to serve as prime minister in an interim government, with elections to be held no later than early 2013.

6

Spain and the Euro Area Sovereign Debt Crisis

GUILLERMO DE LA DEHESA

Historical experience and empirical evidence show that deep financial crises tend to produce sovereign debt crises, given that bank bailouts, automatic stabilizers, and extrafiscal impulses increase budget deficits and debt of the general government.

At the end of 2007, when the financial crisis started, the fiscal position of Spain was apparently excellent. According to Eurostat, it was better than that of the other three largest euro area member states. It had a consolidated total government budget surplus of 1.9 percent of GDP, the third-highest after Finland (5.2 percent) and Luxembourg (3.7 percent). Three other euro area member states were also in surplus, Germany (0.3 percent), the Netherlands (0.2 percent), and Ireland (0.1 percent).[1]

The rest were in deficit: Slovenia, which had joined the euro area that year (–0.1 percent), Belgium (–0.3 percent), Austria (–0.9 percent), Italy (–1.5 percent), France (–2.7 percent), Portugal (–3.1 percent), and Greece (–6.4 percent). Cyprus, which would join in 2008, also had a surplus (3.4 percent), as did Estonia, which would join in 2011 (2.5 percent). But Slovakia, which would join in 2009, and Malta, which would join in 2008, were in deficit (–1.8 and –2.4 percent, respectively). The average euro area deficit that year was 0.7 percent.[2]

Guillermo de la Dehesa is chairman of the Centre for Economic Policy Research (CEPR), a member of the Group of Thirty, and chairman of the IE Business School.

1. Eurostat, Government Finance Statistics, 2011, http://epp.eurostat.ec.europa.eu.

2. Ibid.

The total government debt-to-GDP position of Spain was also quite good and also much better than that of the other three largest member states of the euro area. Spain had a debt-to-GDP ratio of 36.1 percent, compared with France with 63.9 percent, Germany with 64.9 percent, and Italy with 103 percent; all three were above the 60 percent Stability and Growth Pact ceiling. The best positions were those of Ireland (24.9 percent), Luxembourg (6.7 percent), Slovenia (23.1 percent), Finland (35.1 percent), and the Netherlands (45.3 percent). By contrast, Austria (60.7 percent), Portugal (68.3 percent), and Belgium (84.2 percent) were above the 60 percent ceiling. The member states that joined later were all below the ceiling (except Malta, which had 62 percent): Estonia (3.7 percent), Slovakia (29.6 percent), and Cyprus (58.3 percent). The average debt-to-GDP ratio of the euro area that year was 59 percent.[3]

A Long Period of High Growth

Spain had reached an excellent fiscal position after growing at an average of 3.7 percent per year, for a period of 14 years (since 1994), while the euro area as a whole had grown at an average of 2.3 percent.[4] This boom was mainly due to two factors. The first was the Spanish entry into the Economic and Monetary Union (EMU), which produced a dramatic fall in Spanish interest rates once investors discounted the end of the exchange rate risk of the peseta (which Spain had devalued several times before joining the EMU). Average short- and long-term rates fell, respectively, from 13.3 and 11.7 percent in 1992 to 3.0 and 2.2 percent in 1999 and to 2.2 and 3.4 percent in 2005.[5] That decline produced a large expansion of credit, investment, and growth. At that time, investors did not apply sovereign risk spreads, because the probability of default in Europe was extremely low, given that, since the 1930s, no EMU member had defaulted.

The second factor arrived when, between 2000 and 2007, 3.6 million immigrants, most of them of working age, entered Spain, and the immigrant population grew from 923,000 in 2000 to 4.5 million in 2007. Immigration continued after 2007 and reached its peak in 2010 with 5.7 million, 12.2 percent of the total population and 15 percent of the total labor force; these new workers generated large contributions to social security.[6] This huge inflow supported the boom by contributing to 80 percent of the population growth and giving a large push to the working-age population; it also contributed, on average, to GDP growth of 36 percent during that period. Immigrants were

---

3. Ibid.

4. European Commission, Directorate General for Economic and Financial Affairs, *Statistical Annex of European Economy,* spring 2011, http://ec.europa.eu (accessed on October 25, 2011).

5. Banco de España, *Boletín Estadístico,* 1993–1996, Madrid.

6. Instituto Nacional de Estadística, *Anual Populación Censas,* 2011, www.ine.es.

attracted by the housing and construction boom as well as by an expanding tourist sector.[7]

Nevertheless it should be recalled that Spain had been growing at a high rate, and catching up fast to rich partner economies, for much longer. In the last 50 years, since its first deep structural reform in 1959 (the Stabilization Plan), Spain, after Ireland, has been the member state of the euro area with the second-fastest average growth; during this period it has also been the sixth-fastest growing country in the world, after Korea, Japan, Singapore, Hong Kong, and Ireland.[8]

Between 1961 and 2010, the fastest-growing euro area member state was Ireland, with an average growth rate of 4.46 percent, followed by Spain (3.80 percent), Greece (3.70 percent), Portugal (3.56 percent), France (3.00 percent), the Netherlands (2.98 percent), Austria (2.90 percent), the average for the 12 original euro area members (2.86 percent), Belgium (2.76 percent), Italy (2.74 percent), and Germany (2.46 percent). The EU-15 including noneuro members grew at 3.12 percent. Outside the euro area, Korea has been growing the fastest, with an average rate of growth of 4.5 percent, followed by Japan (4.18 percent), the United States (3.16 percent), and the United Kingdom (2.30 percent).[9]

Internal and External Imbalances

Spain's high average growth rate of 3.7 percent between 1994 and 2007 has turned out to be 0.7 percentage points above its average potential growth rate, which was, over that period, around 3 percent, according to several estimates. As a result, Spain's first imbalance was that its average annual rate of inflation during this period was 2.7 percent, compared with an average of 1.8 percent in the euro area—that is, 0.9 points higher every year.[10] This differential rate of inflation has been even higher since the introduction of the euro, 2.9 percent versus 1.8 percent, that is, 1.1 percentage points higher.[11] This differential has produced a loss of competitiveness versus the euro area average.

It is also important to remember that the European Central Bank (ECB) inflation target is based on the harmonized index of consumer inflation (HICP), weighted by the relative GDP of each member state in the euro area. In the first years of the euro (2000–2005), the three largest economies constitut-

7. Oficina del Presidente, *Inmigración y Economía Española, 1996–2006,* Presidencia del Gobierno, Madrid.

8. European Commission, *Statistical Annex of European Economy,* spring 2011, http://ec.europa.eu (accessed on October 25, 2011); International Monetary Fund, *World Economic Outlook,* various years, www.imf.org.

9. Ibid.

10. European Commission, *Statistical Annex of European Economy,* spring 2011, http://ec.europa.eu (accessed on October 25, 2011).

11. Ibid.

ing two-thirds of total euro area GDP were growing at dismal rates (Germany at 0.6 percent and Italy at 0.5 percent) or modestly (France at 1.6 percent). Consequently, the ECB kept policy rates low.

These policy rates were not low enough for Italy and Germany, with their low growth and inflation rates, and at the same time not high enough for the faster-growing member states, such as Spain (3.3 percent), Ireland (5.4 percent), and Greece (4.0 percent), which had higher inflation rates than the central member states. As a result, real interest rates for Spain were close to zero, a situation that generated several excessive booms.[12]

First, given that Spanish household wages were growing with the inflation rate while real interest rates were close to zero or even negative, households understandably thought that it was the right time to take a mortgage and buy a home. Banks also thought that it was the perfect time to push the sale of mortgages. The housing boom was also fueled by the inflow of almost 4 million immigrants. As a result, while nominal GDP was growing at 6.5 percent per year, mortgages were growing at 32 percent, almost five times the nominal GDP, when historical experience shows that credit should not grow more than the double of nominal GDP.

Second, the construction sector was booming, reaching 16 percent of GDP and generating close to 20 percent of the total employment in the economy. Between 1998 and 2007, construction contributed to 20 percent of GDP, 23 percent of employment, and 53 percent of investment.[13] Moreover, in both 2006 and 2007, 700,000 new homes were started, an even larger number than in the United States, which was experiencing another housing boom, but with 7.5 times the population of Spain.

Third, total growth was achieved mainly through the accumulation of labor and, to a lesser extent, of capital, due to the rapid expansion of the construction sector, which has a lower output per worker than manufacturing and tradable services. As a result, labor productivity growth was very low, and total factor productivity growth was close to zero or even negative, depending on the year. For instance, the Spanish level of labor productivity per person employed, measured in purchasing power parity, fell from 110.6 in 1995 to 103.7 in 2007 (with the European Union equal to 100 in both years) while averages of the euro area fell from 116.0 to 109.3. Spanish labor productivity levels per hour worked, again with the EU equal to 100, came down from 110.7 in 1995 to 105.8 in 2007, a fall similar to that for the euro area from 120.1 to 114.4 (mainly due to Germany's enlargement and growth in immigration), but starting from a lower level.[14]

Fourth, starting in 2007, structural and cohesion funds from the EU budget were starting to diminish at a quick rate, having been, since 1987, almost

---

12. Ibid.

13. BBVA, *Situación Espuma,* 2009.

14. Eurostat, Government Finance Statistics, 2011, http://epp.eurostat.ec.europa.eu.

1 percent of total GDP per year. Finally, internal demand grew at an average of 4.7 percent during that period. Consumption grew at 4.2 percent per year, investment in equipment goods at 5.5 percent per year, and investment in construction at 6.7 percent per year. Internal supply also grew during the same period but at a lower rate, 3.8 percent, based on employment creation through immigration and also a much higher participation rate by women in the labor market.

The end result was a very large external imbalance. Spain's current account deficit reached 10 percent of GDP in 2007, one of the world's largest in percentage of GDP and the second largest in total dollar volume, after that of the United States. It must be said that the US current account deficit was produced by a large fall in the savings rate and a relatively constant investment rate, while in Spain the savings rate was almost constant, at around 20 percent of GDP during that period and the investment rate went up to 30 percent of GDP—almost as if it had been an Asian emerging country. Moreover, in Spain, most if not all of the current account deficit was invested, either by households buying homes or by firms buying equipment goods, buying other companies, and establishing themselves abroad. In other countries, like the United States from 2000 onward, a larger part was consumed.

The main long-run problems for Spain were that most of its current account deficit was financed with foreign savings, mostly in euros and from other euro area member states (notably Germany and France), and that these foreign savings were mostly invested in "bricks and mortar" businesses instead of tradable goods and services, which could later have generated foreign revenue to pay for servicing the extra foreign debt accumulated.

The Financial Crisis and Spanish Vulnerability

The financial crisis caught Spain in a highly vulnerable position: First, it had a lot of private external debt owed by both firms and households, which had not been fully compensated by higher savings by the government sector, so that this debt had to be mostly financed with external savings. Second, its real estate and construction sectors were absorbing a large part of total investment and of total households' and firms' wealth.

Spain was also vulnerable because of a large and sustained increase in internal demand, due, in part, to price pressure, after the economy grew much faster than in the rest of the euro area, which appreciated the Spanish real exchange rate versus that of the euro area. The euro area was absorbing 57 percent of Spanish exports of goods and services.

Finally, Spain was vulnerable because it had experienced a large increase in employment and disposable income, which generated a credit boom (for both houses and consumer durables), given the low risk premium and the low level of nominal and, above all, real interest rates. According to the Bank of Spain, this private debt accumulation could be justified only if households' and firms' income were to increase at above 2 percent per year over 10 years—double their growth at that moment, and even much higher than the present rate.[15]

Thus in 1996, the Spanish economy did not need any foreign financing, given that it had a surplus of 0.8 percent of GDP in its net foreign balance with the rest of the world; but by 2007, its net foreign balance had accumulated a deficit of 9.7 percent of GDP. This balance consisted of a deficit of 11.1 percent of GDP for nonfinancial firms, a deficit of 2.7 percent of GDP for households, and a surplus of 2.2 percent of GDP for the public sector.

Real estate and construction were the two main drivers of debt accumulation, as households bought houses and firms built houses and other buildings. The number of real estate transactions increased to almost 1 million in 2006 and 2007, and the total number of houses increased at a rate of 2.7 percent per year, increasing the total housing stock from 18.3 million to 25.1 million between 1996 and 2007. Another million houses were added in 2008–09.[16]

There were also large speculative investment flows in houses as investors were attracted by their expected upside value, while financial income out of financial products was very low because of very low interest rates. These speculators were buying a house before it was built, making a down payment of 10 percent of the total price, and selling it when it was finished; they generally earned a huge return of several hundred percent.

Residential investment grew from 5 percent per year in the period 1990–98 to 6.8 percent per year in the period 1999–2007, a higher rate of growth than in the United States, which grew at 5.0 percent, and much higher than in the euro area, which grew only 0.1 percent per year. House prices increased at an average of 11 percent per year between 1997 and 2007.[17] Real house prices increased 118 percent over the same period. Household real estate wealth increased by 18 percent in real terms between 2003 and 2006, and its share in total wealth reached 80 percent, while in Italy this share was 75 percent and in the United States it was 44 percent of GDP.

When the financial crisis started in 2007, the gross nonconsolidated stock of private debt, both internal and external, was 405 percent of GDP. Households' accumulated debt was 88 percent of GDP, nonfinancial firms' 190 percent of GDP, and financial institutions' 127 percent of GDP; but net consolidated private foreign debt was only 84 percent of GDP. Credit achieved 170 percent of GDP, versus 120 percent for the euro area average. By contrast, total consolidated government debt was only 36 percent of GDP, one of the lowest percentages in the euro area. One of the reasons for this low level of debt was that the real estate bubble had provided large tax revenues, mainly to the Spanish regional governments but also to the central government.[18]

---

15. Banco de España, *Informe Anual*, 2010, www.bde.es.

16. Ibid.

17. "Checking the Engine: Is the Worst Over for America's Economy? *Economist,* June 7, 2007.

18. Eurostat, Government Finance Statistics, 2011, http://epp.eurostat.ec.europa.eu.

Unfortunately, the central government did not do anything to prevent the housing bubble, such as increasing regulation on land use and urbanization. On the contrary, it maintained the very favorable interest deduction on personal income tax for household mortgages on the first home. The Bank of Spain, by contrast, invented "dynamic provisioning," now very popular among regulators, by which banks provision every loan or credit when it originates and not when it becomes nonperforming. Banks were very upset by this requirement, but they were forced to build so-called "generic provisions" of more than €40 billion, which were an important cushion when the financial crisis hit and nonperforming loans started to increase.

Moreover, Spanish banks had financed most of the debt of the private sector, both household mortgages and company loans. At the end of the bubble, both types of loans had extremely favorable terms for households and firms. Banks then refinanced them in euros in foreign euro financial markets by issuing covered bonds for the mortgages as well as other securitizations for firms and placing senior debt. Unfortunately, when the crisis started, many investors stopped buying any financial product related to mortgages because of the "subprime" meltdown, even though covered bonds were rated triple A and not securitized but maintained in the banks' balance sheets.

The euro-covered bond market was then renationalized, so that German investors were buying only *Pfandbriefe* and French investors only *obligations foncières*, and neither were buying Spanish *cédulas hipotecarias*. Later, after Lehman's default, the interbank market came to a standstill, making it more difficult to tap foreign savings. Spanish banks engaged in a rush to buy deposits to finance their loans, paying very high rates as well as appealing to the ECB for liquidity through repurchase agreements for government debt. In the end, these developments generated a credit crunch that is still alive and well today.

The Buildup of the Sovereign Debt Crisis

Today, it is clear that the euro area sovereign debt crisis is mainly due to two things: On the one hand, financial markets have finally realized the design failures of the euro area as a true monetary union, and on the other hand, governments were first in denial and then reacted too late with too little to support Greece—and this foot-dragging has led to massive contagion within the euro area.

At the time of writing this chapter, the sovereign debt crisis has worsened, and the chances of a European monetary union failure continue to increase, as euro governments continue moving slowly and reacting too little and too late. This is most probably the worst performance by governments in crisis management since the Great Depression, and I have no doubt that, whatever the final outcome of the crisis, it will be a teaching subject for a long time in most schools of government, political science, and economics.

It is very clear that bad management by the euro leaders has played a major role in the crisis, but it is also clear that some member states undertook larger spending booms than others. Spain became so used to many years of economic, financial, and fiscal revenue booms that most people in government, but also in the society at large, wrongly thought that this trend could last forever. The Spanish reaction to the recession that followed the financial crisis was a fiscal stimulus, mainly through investments in small infrastructure, conducted at the same time as fiscal revenue was falling.

Spain went, in a very short period of time, from a general government budget surplus of 1.9 percent of GDP in 2007, to a budget deficit of 11.2 percent of GDP in 2009, a change of 13.1 percentage points of GDP in only two years.[19] Part of this swing was due to a large fiscal stimulus and part to a large fall in fiscal revenue following the recession and the puncture of the housing bubble; but most of the deterioration of government finances was due to the working of the built-in automatic stabilizers.

On the expenditure side, automatic stabilizers represented 66 percent and fiscal stimuli 33 percent of the total fiscal swing from surplus to deficit.[20] Therefore, Spain was not a "profligate member state," or at least it did not waste public fiscal resources, as a few other member states now think.

The financial crisis shows the great mistake of not having introduced true labor market reform for many years, a failure that produced a rate of unemployment of 21 percent, more than double the euro area average. The yearly cost of such a high rate of unemployment was close to 4 percent of GDP in the first two years, and it is now 3 percent of GDP, mainly in unemployment subsidies both contributive and noncontributive.

The fall in government fiscal revenue has been very great, mainly due to the recession but also due to the burst of the real estate and construction bubble, which had been generating large fiscal receipts for many years, mostly for the regional governments but also for the central government. In sum, there was on the one side inefficient investment by the private sector in construction, and on the other side inefficient stimuli by the government. In principle, this situation should have been manageable because Spanish finances did not offer much to worry about; Spain's debt-to-GDP ratio was still below 60 percent of GDP and today is around 66 percent of GDP.

Nevertheless, the shocking mismanagement of the Greek crisis produced a huge contagion effect. Greece's fiscal problems—the country had a 12.5 percent of GDP budget deficit in October 2009—could have been managed from the start by the International Monetary Fund (IMF) alone, since Greece was one of its 187 members. Moreover, by now, the IMF would have managed to restructure its debt without any large market reaction or contagion effect. Unfortunately, without any reason, the euro area leaders thought that IMF involvement in the affairs of a euro area member state was a "stigma" for the euro area and did not let the IMF do its job.

---

19. Banco de España, *Informe Anual*, 2010, www.bde.es (accessed on December 29, 2011).
20. Ibid.

The euro area leaders did not know or did not remember that the IMF intervened in the United Kingdom in 1976, in Italy in 1978, and in Spain in 1979 without any interference from European partners. Moreover, they took such a decision without having any knowledge of how to manage debt crises, and what is even worse without any funds to inject into Greece in exchange for imposing a conditionality program. Since then, every decision taken by the European Council not only has failed to create confidence in the markets but has produced more uncertainty, less confidence, and a greater contagion effect, so that the crisis is finally reaching some of the core member states of the euro area.

Now it appears that, having realized the increasing risk of contagion to large member states like Spain and Italy, euro area decision makers are more focused on the real issues and are not exploiting nationalism to win votes by telling voters about bad, profligate, and lazy member states versus good, saving, and hard-working member states.

This kind of moral argument is totally wrong, given that most so-called profligate member states had a budget surplus at the time the financial crisis hit. It has mainly been the recession, provoked by the financial crisis and the activation of the automatic stabilizers, that has created a large budget imbalance.

Spain's Serious Steps to Avoid Contagion

Spain has undertaken a number of fiscal adjustment measures and structural reforms to strengthen growth and debt sustainability in the face of contagion. These include pension reform, constitutional fiscal rules, labor market reform, regulatory reform, privatizations, and savings bank restructurings.

Strong Fiscal Contraction in the Short and Medium Term

Between 2009 and 2011, the general government budget deficit was reduced from 11.1 percent of GDP to about 6.0 percent of GDP—that is, 5.1 percentage points of GDP in two years.[21] Spain is strongly committed to reducing it another 3 percentage points of GDP in the next two years. Today, 60 percent of the fiscal contraction needed to cut the budget deficit to 3 percent of GDP in 2013 has already been achieved, and most of the contraction is affecting expenditure.

In 2009, the general government budget balance was −11.1 percent of GDP, of which the central government represented −9.3 percent of GDP, the autonomous regional governments −2 percent of GDP, and the local governments −0.6 percent of GDP. Social security was in a surplus of 0.8 percent.[22]

---

21. Ibid.

22. European Commission, *Stability Program, Spain, 2011–14,* table 4.1, http://ec.europa.eu (accessed on December 29, 2011).

In 2010, the general government deficit was reduced to 9.2 percent of GDP. The central government deficit was reduced to 5.0 percent of GDP, the deficit for the autonomous regional governments was increased to 2.8 percent, the local governments remained at 0.6 percent, and social security went into a deficit of 0.2 percent of GDP.[23]

By the end of 2011, the general government budget deficit will be reduced to 6.0 percent of GDP, with the central government deficit accounting for 2.3 percent of GDP, that of the autonomous regional governments 3.3 percent, and that of the local governments 0.5 percent, with social security again in a surplus of 0.4 percent of GDP.[24]

The main concern today has to do with the budget deficits of the regional governments. These governments are committed to a maximum budget deficit of 1.3 percent of GDP for 2011 as a whole. In the first quarter they had reached 1.2 percent on average—only 0.1 percent below the full-year target. Unfortunately, most of the regional governments held elections and spent much more in the second quarter, so at the end of June, 7 of the 17 regional governments had already exceeded the target for the year of 1.3 percent, another 5 had reached the half-year target deficit of 0.75 percent (compatible with the 1.3 percent at the end of the year), another 4 were below 0.75 percent, and 1 was in surplus.

The central government has warned those regions that they still need to reach their target at the end of the year, and it has introduced three different stages of authorization controls over new debt issuance. Today, regional governments require authorization for debt issuance depending on their compliance with their budget rebalancing plan of the previous year. Every region needs to present a rebalancing plan if its budget deficit is above 0.75 percent of its regional GDP. Regions without a rebalancing plan will have to achieve a balanced budget by 2014. Finally, the central government has already introduced its maximum expenditure ceiling for 2012, which is a drop of 3.8 percent from the 2011 budget.

Better Fiscal Sustainability in the Long Term

The first step in ensuring long-term fiscal sustainability was the approval of pension reform in July 2011. The reform calls for a gradual increase in the statutory retirement age from 65 to 67 years and limits retirement at 65 to employees with a long history of pension contributions. It also calls for a tightening of the conditions for early retirement and for making partial retirement more expensive.

In addition, it reinforces the relationship between contributions and benefits. On the one hand, the pension is now computed as a function of the last 25 years of career, representing an increase of 15 years over the previous

---

23. Ibid.
24. Ibid, table 5.1.

system. On the other hand, the number of working years needed to achieve full pension entitlement is increased to 37 years.

Finally, to increase its long-term sustainability, the parameters of the new system will be automatically adjusted to the changes in life expectancy every five years from 2027 onward. The expected yearly reduction in social security system costs after 2030 will be 1.4 percent of GDP.[25]

The second step was the approval of a constitutional fiscal rule of budget stability, which limits the structural deficit and debt; the rule was approved in September 2011 by both houses of Parliament by more than a two-thirds majority. It limits the maximum growth of general government expenditure to the reference growth of the Spanish economy, using the simple average of annual growth rates of real GDP over the past five years and projected growth rates over the next four years, plus an unchanged rate of inflation at 1.75 percent. Eligible expenditure does not include interest payments and nondiscretionary unemployment benefits.

The exact limits are left to an organic law, to be approved before June 2012, which also needs two-thirds of the total votes; this arrangement is intended to keep the constitutional article from being overly detailed. In principle, the proposed limit to the structural deficit (over the cycle) will be 0.40 percent of GDP (0.26 percent for the central government, 0.14 percent for the regional governments, and 0.0 percent for the municipal governments). The rule will be fully enforceable in 2020, but deficit limits will be established in the period 2015–18. The maximum debt limit will be set at 60 percent as determined in the EU treaty.

The path for the Spanish debt-to-GDP ratio is as follows: In 2010 debt reached 60.1 percent of GDP; at the end of 2011 it will reach 67.3 percent of GDP, in 2012 68.5 percent of GDP, and in 2013 69.3 percent. In 2014 it will go down to 68.9 percent of GDP, fairly close to the 60 percent limit of the EU treaty.[26]

Faster Adjustment in the Housing Sector

Residential investment, which in 1995 accounted for 4.4 percent of GDP, increased to 9.3 percent of GDP in 2006. At the end of the second quarter of 2011, it was already below the percentage of GDP for 1995. Its year-on-year growth has been –16.8 percent in 2010 and –5.0 percent in 2011, which reduced GDP growth by 1.0 and 0.2 percentage points, respectively.[27]

The average real price housing adjustment up to the first quarter of 2011 was a decline from peak levels by 27.6 percent, its dispersion being from 20 percent to 35 percent in different regions, and the stock of unoccupied hous-

---

25. Ibid, p. 36.

26. Ibid, table 5.3.

27. National Statistics Institute (INE), 2011, National Accounts Database, www.ine.es/en (accessed on December 29, 2011).

ing was on average 2.7 percent, ranging between less than 1.0 percent and 5.0 percent in different regions.[28] The average yearly demand for housing is around 350,000 units, but the stock of finished and unsold houses is twice the yearly demand at around 700,000. The fall in real estate prices is reducing household leverage, given that the homeownership rate in Spain is 84 percent of total households, one of the highest in the world. The same reduction is occurring for real estate firms, which were also highly leveraged.

Important Structural Reforms[29]

The labor reform, approved in September 2010, tries to achieve the following targets: First, it seeks to foster hiring by offering a new definition of the causes of fair dismissal and by lowering severance costs for employers. Second, to avoid labor dismissals or suspensions, it offers incentives to reduce daily working hours, through a similar system to the German reduced work schedule. Third, to avoid the firing of workers by small and medium-size companies under stress, it enhances internal flexibility and facilitates opting out of the application of higher-level collective agreements. Fourth, it offers incentives for hiring young workers through the introduction of a training contract and also by forbidding, for the next two years, any limits on rolling over temporary contracts.

The collective bargaining reform, approved in August 2011, encourages firm-level collective bargaining (versus bargaining at the provincial, regional, and national levels) by allowing firms under certain circumstances to opt out of their collective agreements and by giving incentives to negotiate new collective agreements before the previous ones expire.

These measures try to reduce the traditional excessively high responsiveness of employment to negative activity shocks. The measures are already facilitating adjustment in the labor market by means different from firing, such as short-term working contracts and wage flexibility within firms.

Active labor market policies were deployed in February 2011. The unemployment rate is still excessively high (21.2 percent)[30] mainly due to the difficulty of reallocating the 4 percent of the total labor force that lost construction sector jobs after the housing boom went bust and is unqualified for other jobs. These policies include incentives for hiring young people on a part-time basis by reducing social security contributions paid by the hiring

---

28. Ministry of Finance, www.fomento.gob.es (accessed on December 29, 2011).

29. Unless noted otherwise, data in this section are from Spanish Public Treasury (Tesoro Público), Update on policy measures towards a sustained and balanced growth path, December 7, 2011, www.thespanisheconomy.com (accessed on December 29, 2011).

30. National Statistics Institute (INE), 2011, *Economically Active Population Survey,* www.ine.es (accessed on December 29, 2011).

firms; personalized career advice to the young unemployed, older, long-term unemployed, and unemployed construction industry workers; establishment of an unemployment assistance grant, conditional upon completing training courses, once the unemployment benefit has expired; and allowing private employment agencies to compete with government ones.

Product market reforms, approved in December 2010 and July 2011, help small and medium enterprises (SMEs) by lowering their tax rate to between 20 percent and 30 percent; reducing the maximum time needed for them to incorporate to five days; accelerating payments in arrears by municipalities; exempting capital gains tax for entrepreneurial projects by business angels; improving the viability of companies undergoing difficulties through agreements with creditors; and introducing a free amortization scheme for new investments.

Privatization of airports took place in February 2011. The reform approved the separation of airport operation and traffic control, and determined that Madrid and Barcelona airports would be given on concession to private operators. Due to the worsening economic situation, privatization has been rescheduled. In the first quarter of 2012, 49 percent of the National Airport System will be privatized, with expected revenue between €3 billion and €4 billion.

Privatization of the national lottery took place in May 2011. A new gambling law was approved, separating regulation and operation and regulating online gambling. In November 2011, 30 percent of the national lottery will be privatized, with expected revenue of between €7 billion and €9 billion. Unfortunately, the present large fall in equity markets prices has led to a postponement of the initial public offering (IPO) until the first quarter of 2012.

Telecommunication reforms in July 2011 approved the introduction of technological neutrality in the usage of the telecommunication spectrum, the reallocation of the terrestrial digital television extra-spectrum to telephone services, and a spectrum auction, with expected revenues between €1.8 billion and €2.0 billion.

Savings bank system restructuring has been a multistep process and is described here in detail. Savings banks, which have been around for over 200 years, suffered very few casualties until recently by sticking to their territory—they knew every one of their clients well, so their nonperforming loan ratio was very low. At the same time, as they were not quoted and did not have shareholders, they were making a payout of only around 25 percent of their profits in the form of a "social dividend" that was invested in the region and was much appreciated by citizens, while quoted banks' dividend payout was 50 percent on average.

As they were so well liked by their customers, they were able to pay less for deposits and to charge more for loans than other banks. Thus they had good profits and low payout, so that they never had a shortage of capital. Their main problem was that of governance, since their boards were mainly formed by local and regional politicians, who in some cases redirected loans to projects that ended up unpaid.

This nice picture changed when, during the 14-year boom period, many savings banks decided to increase lending outside their own region, with higher economic and political risk, and to cover other regions across Spain with branches or even establish a foreign presence, notably in Latin America. This fast increase in their activity made them into a slightly larger group than the rest of Spanish banks, both in deposits and loans, but also increased their risk, mainly in the real estate and housing sectors, more than they had expected.

Unfortunately, in the middle of this expansion they were caught by the financial crisis and the burst of the housing bubble. Something similar happened to small and medium-size banks, which had decided to grow faster during the housing and growth boom.

The first step to reform savings banks taken by the central government and the Bank of Spain was to create the Fondo de Reestructuración Ordenada Bancaria (FROB), a government fund with €36 billion (that could be increased to €99 billion) in order to liquidate nonviable entities and to support the restructuring of the viable ones. The support was conditional on cutting 25 percent of branches and 18 percent of employment.

Of the existing 47 savings banks, only 4, of significant size, were insolvent and taken over by the FROB; another 4 have been temporarily nationalized because they were not able to find private capital to meet the 10 percent capital requirement imposed by the Bank of Spain. Of the first four, two have been restructured and sold in an auction to other savings banks, and a third one is in the process of being auctioned.

The second step was to reform the regulation of the savings banks. All were required to consolidate as much as possible and to become quoted banks within a year by means of an IPO, with at least 40 percent coming from institutional investors and a maximum of 60 percent from retail investors.

Of the 47 original savings banks, only 15 remain, and the number may continue to fall. In 4 of the 15 final groups after consolidation, the FROB did not need to give financial support; in another group the quantity was minimal. In total, the FROB's financial support so far has been around €10 billion, which is a very low figure compared to the amounts paid by most other euro area member states. Overall there are around 7,000 banking institutions in the European Union; Germany has the largest number, with around 2,400, of which around 1,400 are owned by the state governments or the public sector. Spain is going to end 2012 with a total of around 60 banks, including cooperatives and rural savings banks.

The third step has been to increase the minimum capital requirements of all the converted savings banks, as well as the rest of banks, to as much as 8 percent of total weighted assets, or to as much as 10 percent for banks that depend more than 20 percent on wholesale funding or that have more than 20 percent participation of third parties in their total equity. Capital requirements to reach these thresholds in 13 large banks reached €17 billion. The FROB may intervene as a backstop, providing capital in the form of preferred shares convertible into common equity before December 2014.

The fourth step has been to carry out the Spanish banking stress test. This was conducted in 2011 under the supervision of the new European Banking Authority and was one of the most comprehensive of similar tests conducted in Europe, including as it did 25 Spanish banks, representing 28 percent of the total sample of European banks subjected to the test and 93 percent of all Spanish financial sector assets. When considering key mitigating instruments, generic provisions, and convertible debt, and under very harsh assumptions (such as a fall in GDP of 2.1 percent in 2011 and 2012, a fall in house prices of 21.9 percent, and a fall in commercial real estate of 46.7 percent in the two-year period), the 25 Spanish banks passed the test.

Finally, in October 2011, the FROB and the Bank of Spain completed the recapitalization of the Spanish banking system by temporarily nationalizing three savings banks that were solvent but lacked access to private capital to meet the new high solvency requirements of 8 percent and 10 percent core capital ratios. This brings to an end the restructuring of the Spanish banking system. The recapitalization of nine savings banks and four medium and small banks cost a total of €13.4 billion, with €5.8 billion coming from private investors and €7.6 billion from the FROB in preferred shares. In addition, one savings bank (CAM) is no longer nationalized after it having invested and lost the FROB's €2.8 billion in preferred stock; this bank needs to be auctioned as soon as possible, and some serious screening of its management practices should also be undertaken.

The total exposure of Spanish banks to the government debt of Greece is €448 million, to that of Ireland is €79 million, Portugal is €5,492 million, and Italy is €7,408 million, for a total €13,427 million. These amounts are small in comparison to total bank assets of €3.8 trillion (end-2010).[31]

Reasonable Level of Competitiveness

One of the most important issues raised by the European Union's new Euro-Plus Pact for competitiveness reforms concerns labor productivity, with the pact's competitiveness evaluation based on unit labor costs (ULCs). But in this pact, as in everything else, the benchmark is Germany, as if there were

31. Banco de España, *Financial Stability Report, May 2011*, www.bde.es (accessed on December 29, 2011).

a high correlation between competitiveness and bond spreads. Of course, if the benchmark is Germany, then every member state is apparently not competitive, because Germany is the only member state that entered the euro area voluntarily with a high exchange rate and later needed to do a real devaluation by reducing wages; with internal demand flat or negative during many years, Germany needed exports to grow at a faster rate.

Nevertheless, real data show that there is very little relation between ULCs on the one hand and exports and export market shares on the other. Spain is one of the member states that lost more competitiveness in the euro area according to different measures of relative prices; but counterintuitively, its export performance within the euro area and worldwide has been quite good.

The World Trade Organization provides the following data on the Spanish market share of total world merchandise exports: Between 2000 and 2010, Spain lost 0.4 percentage points of market share, from its peak in 2004. That is, it went from 2 percent of the total in 2004 to 1.6 percent of the total in 2010. In terms of its ranking among top world exporters of merchandise, Spain has lost three positions, going from 15th to 18th.[32]

But other euro area members have also lost market share, mainly because of the eruption of China and other emerging exporters. Germany has lost market share from its peak of 9.9 percent of the world total in 2004 to 8.3 percent of the world total in 2010, that is, 1.6 percentage points; and in terms of ranking it has lost two positions, from first in 2004 to third in 2010, after China and the United States.

France has lost 1.6 percentage points of market share, from its peak of 5.0 percent of the total in 2004 to 3.4 percent of the total in 2010. In terms of ranking, it has lost two positions, from fifth to seventh. Italy has lost 1.1 percentage points of market share from its peak of 4.0 percent of the total to 2.9 percent in 2010, but it has maintained the eighth position.

In world total exports of commercial services, Spain has lost 0.6 percentage points of world market share from its peak in 2004—that is, it has gone from 3.9 percent in 2004 to 3.3 percent in 2010, but it has kept its world ranking position at number seven. Germany has lost only 0.2 percentage points of world market share since its peak in 2004, going from 6.5 percent of the total to 6.3 percent in 2010; and it has gained one position, moving to number two. France has lost 1.9 percentage points from its peak in 2000, going from 5.7 percent of the world total to 3.8; and it has lost two positions, moving from third to fifth. Italy has lost 1.4 percentage points, going from 4.0 to 2.6 percent, and it has lost 6 positions, moving from number 6 to number 12.

Within the euro area, overall data are available only up to 2009. From 2000 to 2009, the Spanish market share of total merchandise exports in the euro area was maintained at 3.5 percent. In the same period, Germany increased its market share 0.2 percentage points, from 13 percent to 13.2 per-

---

32. World Trade Organization, "World Trade in 2010," chapter 1 of *World Trade Report 2011,* www.wto.org.

cent. France lost 1.3 percentage points, from 8 percent to 6.7 percent of the total; and Italy lost 0.6 percentage points, from 5.5 percent to 4.9 percent of the total. According to the balance of payments calculations by the Bank of Spain, in 2010 the Spanish goods export share in the euro area increased to 3.9 percent, an increase of 0.4 percentage points in one year.[33]

In the period 2000 2010, the real effective exchange rate for Spain appreciated compared to the euro area average by 9.7 percent measured by the relative consumer price index, by 4.6 percent measured by relative export prices, and by 12.6 percent measured by the relative unit labor costs in manufacturing. How is it then possible that, with such a loss of real competitiveness, Spain maintained its market export share in the euro area and even improved it in 2010 by 0.4 percentage points? (The euro area is Spain's most important market for goods and manufactures, absorbing 57.3 percent of its total exports.)

Several explanations are possible:

The first is that competitiveness within the euro area seems to be more correlated with internal demand than with productivity and ULCs. The argument is that if labor productivity growth is considered permanent, it produces a permanent increase in workers' income, so there will be an increase in internal demand both in consumption and investment. As a result, labor may become scarce and wages go up, reducing competitiveness.[34]

Yet internal demand has been growing much faster in Spain during these 10 years than in any of the other three largest member states of the euro area. Therefore, this explanation does not work for Spain because Spain has maintained its export market share in the euro area.

Conversely, external demand within the euro area grew faster for Germany and Italy than for France and for Spain. Against a base of 100 in 2000, by 2009 the external demand index was 115 for Italy, 113 for Germany, 110 for Spain, and 109 for France.

The second explanation is that Spanish goods may have been improving in terms of quality and therefore in terms of value enough to compensate for the loss in price and cost competitiveness. Determining whether this is the case depends on computing hedonic prices within the euro area, which cannot be done at this time.

The third relates to the relative composition of exports. Some recent and very interesting research done by Goldman Sachs on the euro area relative export performance constructs a "revealed price elasticity index" of each exported product by member state and finds that members with price-sensitive exports, such as Greece and Portugal, suffer substantially more than member countries with price-insensitive exports, such as Spain. If, on average, countries run a quantity trade surplus in a low-unit-value good, then the market

33. Banco de España, The Spanish Balance of Payments and International Investment Position 2010, www.bde.es (accessed on December 29, 2011).

34. Daniel Gros, *Europe's Competitiveness Obsession*, CEPS Commentary, 2010, Brussels, Center for European Policy Studies.

for that good is price dominated. If, on the other hand, countries run a surplus in a high-unit-value good, the implication is a quality-dominated product through vertical differentiation.[35]

The most quality-dominated products are chemical products, rubber, plastics, motor vehicles, and pharmaceuticals. Germany is the most relatively skewed toward capital goods but also toward chemicals and motor vehicles; Spain scores well in all these kinds of goods. Moreover, Spain is the member country with the highest price insensitivity index, followed by Germany, Belgium, and Sweden. With 100 the most inelastic, Spain scores 59.9, followed by Germany (58.0), Belgium (57.5), Sweden (57.0), Austria (56.0), Ireland (55.0), France (54.5), and Italy (52.2). Greece and Portugal are below 50.

The Balassa indicators used by the Organization for Economic Cooperation and Development, which are based on the sectoral technological intensity of exports, tend to confirm these results. Spain specializes in medium- to high-technology intermediate products for which there is less competition or which are produced offshore, so that the subsidiary manufactures products for the parent company without competition. Spain also specializes in other products of medium to low technology, such as agricultural products (fruit and vegetables), fish products, wine and tobacco, textiles, leather, and shoes, but with a known trademark.

Moreover, Spain has very important multinational companies that are established in Europe and in the United States as well as in emerging countries, notably in Latin America. Its main sectors are banking and insurance, telecommunications, travel and tourism, construction and infrastructure management, technology, and energy production and distribution. Foreign direct investment by Spanish companies reached 44.2 percent of Spanish GDP in 2009.

More broadly, the Spanish current account deficit has been reduced from 10.0 percent of GDP in 2007 to 3.8 percent of GDP in 2011, and is expected to be reduced to 2.2 percent of GDP in 2016, according to the IMF. Thus the overvaluation of the Spanish real exchange rate seems much less of a problem now than before.[36]

Serious Issues Still Pending

Serious issues remain, however. First, growth is positive but very low, with internal demand still negative due to the process of general government fiscal contraction and private sector deleveraging. Growth in 2011 is probably going to be less than the expected 0.7 percent, according to the latest forecasts, and it is going to be exclusively based on external demand through exports. The same situation is expected in 2012, when growth will be around 1 percent,

---

35. Goldman Sachs, "Eurozone Competitiveness: Beyond Costs," *European Weekly Analyst* 11/02, January 13, 2011.

36. International Monetary Fund, *World Economic Outlook*, September 2011, www.imf.org.

not high enough to produce net employment; growth may start to reduce the unemployment rate only in the second half of the decade.

Second, the present unemployment rate is at 21 percent of the labor force, more than double that of the euro area average. Unfortunately, it has also been double the euro area average in every previous recession: 1974, 1981, and 1993–94. Spain has carried out several labor reforms during the last 33 years of democracy, but these have always been insufficient or wrong. Now is the time to solve this structural problem, which has very little to do with the rate of growth and a lot to do with inefficient structures for the labor market and collective bargaining.

The two largest political parties are aware of this problem, and they should jointly reform inefficient labor market structures in-depth as soon as there is a new government (after the November 20, 2011 elections). The duality of the labor market, dominated by insiders versus outsiders and indefinite versus short-term labor contracts, needs to end as soon as possible. A single new indefinite contract should be imposed for all new labor contracts, either full-time or part-time, with firing costs increasing with years of service until reaching the euro area average.

The same structural reform needs to be implemented in the present system of collective bargaining, where SMEs are forced to close down and fire employees because they must comply with collective agreements in which they have not participated and in which they have had no say. There should be a new law allowing any firm that has met with trade union advisors and that has the support of the majority of its employees to deviate from the collective agreement so it can avoid firing employees or closing down.

The cost of unemployment subsidies for the 21 percent unemployed has been around 4 percent of GDP per year throughout the recession. It is now coming down to 3 percent of GDP because some of the subsidies for workers have expired, but they are being either extended to avoid social unrest or replaced with a much lower noncontributive subsidy. If Spain had been able to achieve a lower rate of unemployment after putting these reforms in place, no fiscal contraction would have been necessary, and employment would be growing now at a reasonable rate.

Another structural reform that is absolutely necessary involves the different layers of the Spanish government and the system of financing. Today there are still four layers: central government, autonomous regional governments, provincial governments, and municipal governments. The large majority of the Spanish population lives in cities (under municipal governments), but the political and budgetary power is in the other upper layers. Autonomous regions mostly receive transfers from the central government that they spend without having the responsibility of levying or collecting taxes on their own citizens; they thus break the essential rule of "no taxation without representation."

These autonomous regions do not have the right alignment of incentives and therefore tend to spend more than they should. The regions have even abolished certain taxes, such as taxes on wealth and inheritance, that used to be collected by the central government but were turned over to the regions in a move toward decentralization. They have also neglected to use some tax tranches or brackets that were transferred to them by the central government. Moreover, there is no clear division of responsibilities among the different governments, so that much spending is duplicated by the different layers, resulting in extremely inefficient public expenditures. Finally, provincial governments need to disappear for good.

So long as the autonomous regions do not have the responsibility of collecting taxes from their citizens, and citizens do not exert control over the way regions spend this tax revenue by means of regional parliaments and elections every four years, the incentives will not be the right ones at the time the tax money is spent.

While the economy's external competitiveness is holding on rather well, internal competitiveness is still low, so that there are still barriers to exit and to entry, notably in services and in professional sectors and organizations. These barriers need to be tackled as soon as possible to accelerate the entry of new entrepreneurs into the market and to create jobs.

Conclusion

During its membership in the monetary union and in the euro area, Spain has generated large fiscal, credit, and current account imbalances. These are partly the result of the one-size-fits-all single monetary policy of the euro area, which has tended to produce bubbles and fiscal and competitiveness imbalances in the faster-growing member states and notably in Spain, but they are also the result of positive external shocks, notably immigration in the case of Spain, that need to be corrected as soon as possible.

Even if Spain is making increasing progress in reducing most of these imbalances, four main problems remain that need to be addressed: low growth, extremely high unemployment, inefficient distribution of tax collection and revenue expenditure across different layers of government, and a low level of internal competition.

From the growth performance point of view, Spain has been the second-fastest growing member state of the euro area (after Ireland) during the last 50 years, and it should regain a normal rate of growth in the next five to six years. It is also a member state with a relatively low debt-to-GDP ratio, but its general government deficit needs to be brought to 3 percent of GDP by the end of 2013. It is also one of the few member states with a higher effective age of retirement and one of the very few with a balanced budget rule and a top-level-of-debt clause in its constitution.

From the competitiveness point of view, Spain has one of the most consolidated, efficient, and recapitalized banking systems in the euro area, and stock prices of Spanish banks have fallen much less than those of other euro area banks. Its external competitiveness is quite high, according to its market shares of exports both within the euro area and worldwide. By contrast, it still lacks necessary freedom of entry and exit in its internal nontradable services market and needs more reforms to enhance it.

Finally, Spain is one of the member states that is trying to implement more structural reforms (not all of them successful) to improve its growth potential and recover growth. In spite of all these efforts and reforms, Spain is also one of the member states paying higher spreads when placing its debt in the financial markets, because contagion continues to be rampant. So long as euro area political leaders do not seriously tackle the roots of the sovereign debt crisis and introduce a credible firewall between insolvent Greece and the remaining (solvent) member states, the latter will have to pay extremely high spreads, until eventually they, too, become insolvent. If that occurs, then the cost for the euro, the euro area, the European Union, and the rest of the world will be huge.

In contrast, because the contagion felt by Spain has been more severe than warranted by fundamentals, if a firewall is put in place, sooner or later markets will recognize this fact and Spanish debt should recover.

Postscript[37]

On December 30, 2011, the newly elected government took extraordinary economic measures to reduce the general government deficit, which came in higher than the target set for end-2011: 8 percent of GDP instead of the official 6 percent target. This came as a shock to the markets because the central as well as the regional and municipal governments had been on target at the end of the third quarter, with only social security being 0.6 percent of GDP below target. The maximum excess of the deficit above the target for the whole year 2011 was expected to be 0.6 or 0.7 percent of GDP, a reasonable overshooting by about one-tenth.

It is important to remember that when these targets were set in 2010, in agreement with the European Commission and the European Council, Spanish GDP growth in 2011 was expected to be 1.3 percent; instead it will be only 0.6 or 0.7 percent. The situation will be no different in 2012; in fact it could be worse. The agreed target deficit of 4.4 percent of GDP for 2012 was based on expected GDP growth of 2.3 percent this year, but according to latest forecasts, growth could be minus 0.7 percent.

It will thus be impossible for Spain to meet the original deficit targets in 2012 and 2013, unless the country is forced to meet them at any cost, at the risk of producing a very deep and protracted recession. Most of the other euro area member states are in the same situation. The only way to avoid another euro area recession is to measure these deficit targets in structural terms or for euro area members to delay meeting these targets for a couple of years.

When definitive data are published at the end of January or early February 2012, they are likely to show that most of the huge deviation from the 2011

---

37. January 8, 2012.

deficit target (by 2 percent of GDP) was attributable to very large deviations in the regional governments' deficits from their targets. Most of Spain's regional governments have highly rigid costs because they are responsible for almost all the social expenditures: on education, health, and noncontributive transfers to the poor and to the long-term unemployed who have lost their contributive unemployment subsidies. In addition, regional governments have created a very large number of public companies and part of the unanticipated deficits could have arisen in them.

The new central government has decided to force regional governments to cap their deficits and debts and report their yearly total budget estimates to see if they exceed the cap, in which case they will be rejected.

7

France, the State, and Globalization

ZAKI LAÏDI

Everyone recalls the famous Stalinist expression "socialism in one country." In a very different context I will argue that the French strongly support globalization provided that it does not modify their way of life or alter their social model. Their preference is for globalization in one country. But there is a strong paradox: They are the westerners most reluctant to embrace the market economy and globalization, which is regarded as a source of social disorder; but at the same time they have expressed a real capacity to cope with its constraints. Why is this so? What implications does this reality have for the European crisis and for French conduct? These are the main questions I will explore.

The Specificities of the French Political System

At the institutional level, it should be noted that France has a unique political system compared to the rest of Europe. This system is commonly described as "presidential" or "presidentialist." However, these terms are misleading because the French presidency substantially differs from the American presidency; counterweights to executive power are much weaker in France than they are in the United States. Unlike all the other European systems, the French one is characterized by a very marked subordination of the legislative to the executive. This feature is all the more remarkable as it stems not from

Zaki Laïdi is professor at Sciences Po Paris and founder of the French think tank Telos.

constitutional texts, but rather from political practices that have been established now for nearly 60 years.

Indeed, a comparison between France and Germany shows that the French parliament formally has no less power than the Bundestag to control government action. Why does the French parliament not play its full part? Why does it fail to use its constitutional powers to its advantage? There are two explanations. The first and most important one by far derives from the practice, in place since 1962, of electing the president of the republic by direct universal suffrage. Everything proceeds from the president, including the Parliament's legitimacy.[1] The trend towards a stronger presidency has increased in recent years. President Sarkozy has been described as a hyperpresident because he has sought to maximize his power while reducing the powers still held by the prime minister.

The second source of voluntary subordination of the Parliament to the executive can be found in another French particularity: the accumulation of mandates, whereby a politician may simultaneously hold national and local office. This unique feature, which dates back to the 1970s, means that a deputy is never fully dedicated to parliamentary work. The deputy's added political value is accordingly diminished. If the deputy is part of the presidential majority, he or she is basically expected to rubber-stamp the government's decisions. The parliamentary majority thus has little power of initiative; by definition, the opposition has even less, despite a constitutional reform designed to increase its power. For example, it is of great significance that two of the main presidential candidates from the opposition Socialist Party (Martine Aubry and Ségolène Royal) are not members of Parliament. The former was defeated during the 2002 legislative elections, but this did not prevent her from becoming the first secretary of the Socialist Party. The latter chose to hold local rather than national office. The fact that nobody has challenged this state of affairs confirms the power of the presidency over the French political system, and even over the opposition that claims to combat the imbalance.

How does this very distinctive configuration affect political decision making during periods of crisis such as the one we are currently experiencing?

First and foremost, it grants the executive considerable room to maneuver compared with the legislature. It is unimaginable, for instance, that a French debate on eurobonds would take place in the Parliament, let alone that Parliament's opinion would be heard. Parliamentary subordination was further seen in August 2011 in the middle of recess, when the government proposed a series of new austerity measures, which called into question a good number of economic and fiscal policies enacted by the Parliament since 2007. Nobody in France thought to ask how these policies could be overturned without

---

1. The exception is when the parliamentary majority is different from the presidential one. This situation has occurred only three times in 30 years. Its chances of occurring are now very low because the presidential elections take place before the legislative elections; moreover, the terms of the National Assembly and of the president of the republic are now the same length.

consulting the Parliament. In the subsequent formal vote, amendments to the government package were very limited.

The centrality of the executive has a second consequence. It grants the executive discretionary power, not only regarding national representation, but also with regard to the French administration. There has been a lot of talk about the length of Christine Lagarde's tenure as finance minister, since in the 10 years before Nicolas Sarkozy was elected in 2007, the average tenure of a minister at the Ministry of Finance was not more than one year.

However, one should not be under any illusions about this longevity. It is primarily due to the minister's extreme submission to the Elysée's authority. In no way does this detract from her skills and qualities. The fact nonetheless remains that because Lagarde did not have any national political mandate, she was automatically dependent on the authority of the head of state. The presidency's power over economic decision making has continued to grow as the state has seen its power in economic matters diminish. The residual power naturally went to the Elysée. This development is striking at the economic level, and it partially explains why widening public deficits have not been addressed within the system. It is very tempting to make discretionary use of the sovereign privilege of public expenditure, especially when it is not financed. Unrestrained use over the past 30 years eloquently testifies to this.

Decision Making versus Consensus Building

It is important to emphasize this institutional and political reality as it allows the head of state to very easily commit France to initiatives with its partners. Nicolas Sarkozy has often been annoyed or irritated by Angela Merkel's legendary caution towards his proposals. Their different approaches have been attributed to undeniable differences of temperament, but these do not explain everything. In Germany, the chancellor must constantly compromise with her coalition members, with the parliamentary majority, and with all the *Länder*. The French president of the republic does not have to consult with anyone other than his advisors, who owe him their positions. In times of crisis the French political system may seem to be operationally efficient because it reacts more quickly than other countries, as is made clear by the extreme speed with which France implemented an anticrisis plan in the aftermath of the 2008 crisis. Could one therefore deduce that this centralized system is just as efficient when more painful tradeoffs are involved, such as the reduction of public deficits?

This question requires a nuanced response. While the French political system's centralization is conducive to rapid decision making, the flipside is a difficulty in producing consensus. The French system knows how to make a decision, but not how to build consensus. It is much easier to decide by oneself to spend (French debt has quadrupled in the past 40 years, and public expenditure accounts for 56.2 percent of GDP) than to reach a consensus to reduce public spending. This is where another significant difficulty in the system comes into play: the preference for a plebiscite over a consensus. Any time a president is in difficulty, he can always appeal to the people to settle the issue.

The state's inability to pursue a sound policy of public deficit reduction can also be explained by the extremely strong ideological direction of most of the debates in France. This ideological strand is the historical product of the interplay between the state and its creation of political identity. In France, the state's retreat is more or less associated with national decline. In the best case this retreat may be considered a necessity but rarely a salutary choice, even according to the French Right. The valorization of the state stems from French political culture since the French Revolution, and it at least partially transcends the Left-Right divide. Indeed, the French Right remains incomparably more statist than the other European right-wing parties, albeit slightly less statist than the French Left. Moreover, the differences between the Right and Left are in degree and not in kind. All this can only be understood by reference to a political culture that is historically rooted and built around a basic hostility to liberalism.

French Defiance of the Market

Upon taking office, Nicolas Sarkozy claimed that he would change this reality. The break did not take place, however. Sarkozy himself has never purported to be a liberal. He has repeatedly extolled state proactivity and expressed condescension towards those seeking to reduce it.[2] The Left's reflex is identical. A politician of the Left calling for a reduction in public expenditures would be marginalized and suspected of right-wing drift. One can moreover be both right-wing and antiliberal in France. There is a deep divide between what could be called cultural liberalism, which is overwhelmingly accepted and promoted by both the Left and Right, and economic liberalism, which is verbally attacked by the Left and half-heartedly defended by the Right.

The renowned GlobeScan poll about attitudes towards free enterprise and the market economy revealed a French particularity.[3] Over a set of 20 countries, 61 percent of respondents considered the free market system to be the best possible system, while the average dropped to 36 percent in France, compared to 65 percent in Germany and 74 percent in China. Among the 20 selected countries, France ranked last in terms of support for the market economy. Since the 2008–09 crisis this aversion has grown. A comparative study conducted in December 2010 highlighted that only 15 percent of the French believe that the market economy and capitalist economy work well and

---

2. Seventy-eight percent of the French believe that politicians have the power to change society. CSA, "La politique peut-elle encore changer la vie? [Can politics still be life-changing?]," May 2011, www.csa.eu (accessed on November 15, 2011).

3. GlobeScan, "20-Nation Poll Finds Strong Global Consensus: Support for Free Market System But Also More Regulation of Large Companies," January 2006, www.globescan.com (accessed on November 15, 2011).

Table 7.1   Opinions concerning capitalist/free market system, by political orientation (percent of respondents)

Country	Supporters of the Left			Supporters of the Right		
	A system that functions well on the whole and should be conserved	A system that functions poorly on the whole but should be conserved because there is no alternative	A system that functions poorly and should be abandoned	A system that functions well on the whole and should be conserved	A system that functions poorly on the whole but should be conserved because there is no alternative	A system that functions poorly and should be abandoned
United States	55	32	13	63	28	9
Germany	48	46	6	66	30	4
Great Britain	40	44	16	57	41	2
Italy	15	70	15	45	44	11
France	4	44	52	32	62	6

Source: IFOP, *Regards croisés sur la mondialisation dans dix pays,* 2011, www.ifop.fr.

should be conserved. Even Italy had a higher percentage (26 percent), as did Germany (46 percent), the United States, and China.[4] The issue is understood differently across the political spectrum in each country but it is in France that commitment to capitalism is socially weakest (table 7.1).

This cultural reluctance to accept the market economy was further confirmed in a comparative study on the relationship between consumers and their bankers. The comparison between the United States and France is especially telling. When the French were asked what they expect of their banker, 66 percent responded that a banker should serve his client's best interests.[5] The figure for the United States is only 49 percent. This difference reveals quite a bit about attitudes towards the market. Most Americans do not expect their banker to serve their best interests because they fundamentally know that the latter is primarily driven by self-interest. Above all, Americans expect that the rules of the game be transparent and the banker accountable. The French see this as a relatively secondary concern. French political culture reflects the idea that all agents, be they political or economic, first and foremost need to be vested with a mission of general interest. The French first turn to the state to assume this mission. However, when the state is not able to do so, it is not easy for the French to resign themselves to the idea that market actors might

---

4. IFOP, "Regard sur la mondialisation dans 10 pays" ["Outlook on globalization in 10 countries"], January 2011, www.ifop.com (accessed on November 15, 2011). The text figures are aggregates; table 7.1 provides a breakdown by political orientation.

5. All the data for this study are extracted from the IFOP opinion poll.

not be able to manage it, either. Banks are regarded by a majority of French citizens as a public utility (*service public*). All these ideas are not necessarily clarified or formalized in the minds of citizens, but they do mold their vision of the world. The French people's tepid support for the market nevertheless has an important political counterweight that is important in the current European context. A majority of the French remains strongly supportive of redistribution mechanisms, which the French deem to be indispensable market correction mechanisms.

It therefore comes as no surprise that they are among the greatest proponents of aid to Greece, for example. In June 2011, 59 percent of the French supported an aid package for Greece, compared with 58 percent of Spaniards and 73 percent of Italians.[6] Of course, this generosity can be explained by France's relative vulnerability. In Germany, for example, support for Greece does not exceed 41 percent. It is generally the countries in most danger that are calling for redistribution at the European level. While there is some truth to this explanation, it does not completely explain why most of the French support a policy of aid to Greece and to other counties in the euro area facing serious threats. The French are very comfortable with the idea of redistribution, regardless of their political affiliation.[7] As a result, French commitment to Europe has remained strong and has not crumbled. On the contrary, 61 percent of the French remain attached to it despite the hard times; only 29 percent call for a return to the franc, compared to 38 percent in May 2010.

The Gap Between Overall Perception and Individual Assessment

Aggregate data do not by themselves convey the complexity of the French case. French public opinion on all these subjects consistently shows a significant gap between the general perception of a problem and the way in which the French individually grasp the gravity of the problem. That is, French public opinion is systematically very worried, very pessimistic, and very negative when it comes to assessing the market economy, capitalism, and globalization, whereas the results are more nuanced when the French are asked to assess the consequences of this reality in their lives. According to one poll, 68 percent of French employees believe that globalization is a bad thing for them as workers.[8] However, when employees were asked to assess the impact of globalization on the company in which they work, the figures became less stark:

---

6. IFOP, "Europeans and the Euro Crisis," June 29, 2011, www.ifop.com (accessed on November 15, 2011).

7. This preference is confirmed by the BVA poll on aid to Ireland, which received greater support than aid to Greece, even though aid to Ireland followed aid to Greece. See BVA, "Les Français et l'aide de l'UE à l'Irland," November 2010, www.bva.fr (accessed on November 15, 2011).

8. All the figures on workers' attitudes towards globalization are extracted from TNS-Sofres, "Mondialisation et emploi," June 21, 2011, www.tns-sofres.com (accessed on November 15, 2011).

45 percent believe that globalization offers them some positive prospects, versus only 30 percent holding the opposite view. The "citizen employee" is hostile to globalization but the "individual employee" is much less so.

Another illustration of this discrepancy between overall perception and personal perception can be found in French views on the economic future of France. Here again, the figures are enlightening. The French are not only hostile to the market economy but foresee an extremely gloomy future. A comparative study in 2010 underlined that 3 percent see greater prosperity in the future, while the global average is 38 percent.[9] On the flipside, 36 percent see the future in negative terms, and 61 percent anticipate no change in either direction. When these same questions were not asked generally but rather were applied to the individual situation of each respondent, the results improved: 15 percent of respondents believe their situation in the future will be better (versus 3 percent at the general level) and 48 percent estimate it will remain unchanged. A recent study on social perceptions of the crisis underscores this same disconnect between a negative global perception and a more nuanced individual perception. Some 61 percent of the French fear contagion by the Greek crisis, while the share is only 56 percent in Italy, which is more directly concerned, and 34 percent in Germany. However, when the French were asked about the effects of contagion on their individual situations, the outlook was less dour: Only 59 percent believe that the crisis will personally affect them. This may be a high figure, but it is lower than the European average (71 percent). As seen above, the Italians are collectively less pessimistic than the French, but the reverse is true at the individual level.

Major problems like unemployment bring out this same discrepancy. According to the BVA poll just cited, 67 percent of the French believe that the employment situation will further deteriorate. However, only 40 percent think that this deterioration is likely to personally affect them.

This gap is significant because it serves as a mechanism that enables French society to adapt to the globalization process. In other words, the social and political behaviors and attitudes of the French do not necessarily reflect their spontaneous preferences. Rather, they reflect the French people's capacity to adapt to a reality from which they cannot escape but in which they cannot recognize themselves. Nothing is more alien to French political culture than the idea of an imposed reality that cannot be overcome. Cultural resistance, however, does not preclude the ability to adapt to market constraints. This discrepancy explains how the French can be very protectionist even while France remains a country that is hardly protectionist.

---

9. All the data on visions of the future cited in this paragraph and the next are extracted from BVA's Voice of the People opinion poll: "International Survey Conducted in 53 Countries: 2011 Economic Outlook," January 3, 2011, www.bva.fr (accessed on November 15, 2011).

The Political Implications of French Particularity

What are the political consequences of the French particularity only briefly summarized here?

The first and most important one is that political actors have to make sure that any government effort to confront the constraints and rigors of the market is not considered or perceived as mere political capitulation to the market. State heroism in dealing with the market is a hallmark of French political culture even if it affects the left-wing electorate more than the right-wing electorate. Accordingly, combating public deficits must be sold to the public using political rhetoric when neither budgetary rigor nor the reduction of state expenditures receives strong approval from a majority of the French. The preferred route to overcoming constraint is the redistribution of earnings and wealth. This is striking in the discourse of the Left, which exclusively attributes deficits to the Sarkozy government's alleged systematic favoritism of certain groups to the detriment of the middle class. The Left therefore advocates correcting social disequilibria by increasing the tax burden on the wealthiest. Even in 2011, the idea that France might have a bloated civil service is simply rejected by the Left, especially in an electoral period.[10] It must be said that the civil service has considerable leverage over left-wing parties.

The Left has officially promised to revisit the decision taken by Sarkozy's government to not renew half the posts of retiring civil service employees. It has also continued to promote the creation of government jobs as a means of boosting economic growth; increasing the tax burden of the wealthiest is a means of financing these jobs. Therefore, the crisis cannot be said to have truly changed the Left's attitude towards public action and the market. If the Left manages to win the 2012 elections—and this is far from a foregone conclusion, despite Sarkozy's disastrous poll numbers—it will reproduce the gap between what is said and what is done. When Lionel Jospin was in power, for example, he became the prime minister who was most intent on privatizing public companies. As a leftist, though, he could not clearly assume responsibility for this aim and has always refused to emphasize this part of his legacy. This is why one should be cautious when speaking of "archaic socialists," as this assessment takes into account only positions of principle. The political agenda of the Left is admittedly not very bold, but it would be a mistake to believe that discourse is the only window into left-wing leaders' views on economic issues. In a country where, as was mentioned above, all submission to market rules is seen as capitulation or even utter catastrophe, left-wing leaders continue to pretend to believe in state proactivity, which is the Left's major point of differentiation from the Right. This does not mean that, once in power, the Left

---

10. Reducing the number of civil servants is not very popular in France, even among the right-wing electorate, most of which does not want to go beyond the nonrenewal of half the positions of retiring civil servants. See IFOP, "The French Face the Debt," June 29, 2011, www.ifop.com (accessed on November 15, 2011).

would not deal with the huge constraints that currently hamper the French economy.

The gap between words and action is not only a prerogative of the Left, which has not exercised national power for over 10 years now. The Right has constant recourse to it, but to different ends. At the beginning of the 2008 crisis, President Sarkozy took positions that were extraordinarily hostile to the capitalist system and financial capitalism. He did not hold back on using political terminology close to that traditionally used by the Left and even the Far Left. His denunciation of financial capitalism did not prevent him, however, from adopting a very conservative attitude towards protecting the French banking system: Financial capitalism was denounced, but the French banking sector was shielded.

The gap was also manifest in the management of the Greek crisis, when the French government very clearly sought to protect French banks that were heavily exposed in Greece. Indeed, all governments legitimately seek to protect their national interests, including the ones that coincide with those of the private sector. From this perspective, Nicolas Sarkozy did not behave very differently from Angela Merkel, except that Merkel never used the words and terms that Sarkozy used to denounce the capitalist system.

What should be recalled here is that at the beginning of the crisis in 2008, many of the French, and especially their leaders, tried to convince themselves that the crisis revealed the strength of the French model, based on the central role of the state. France was resisting in a world that was damaging itself for lack of market distrust. This is the narrative par excellence that the French would have liked to see spread throughout the world. It is true that at first the effects of the crisis were relatively well contained in France, notably through the implementation of a recovery plan.

Has this perception changed since the Greek crisis? This question calls for a nuanced answer. Without a doubt, the deepening crisis no longer allows the French and their government to believe that the French model is immune to market pressures. France is experiencing weak growth, high unemployment, and explosive debt. The French are not witnessing the collapse of capitalism as they might have thought in 2008, but rather its supremacy over states.[11] In fact, the antimarket rhetoric has toned down, even within the Left. While the Left continues to fiercely fight against the famous golden rule on balancing public finances, it now does so with political arguments and not economic ones. That is, the Left rejects the principle of the golden rule to avoid being politically trapped by President Sarkozy, whom it accuses of being primarily responsible for worsening deficits. However, it no longer substantively challenges the principle of this rule and is careful not to attack the rating agencies at a time when they are threatening to downgrade French debt. Here again, French society is ambivalent in its relations to the crisis and market. It

---

11. On public attitudes towards the worsening debt crisis, see IFOP, "Europeans and the Euro Crisis," June 29, 2011, www.ifop.com (accessed on November 15, 2011).

maintains its firm and resolved opposition to the prevailing economic system. Many of the French (59 percent) even believe that they have consented to enough sacrifices over the past 10 years to not have to consent to any more.[12] At the same time, all the opinion polls show that voters systematically favor candidates who avail themselves of classical economic expertise. This is very striking on the Left, where the electorate's voting intentions have clearly swung from Dominique Strauss-Kahn towards François Hollande, to the detriment of Martine Aubry. The swing occurred because Hollande, like Strauss-Kahn before him, is (rightly or wrongly) seen as incarnating the responsibility and competence required to confront the crisis. This does not prevent France from being the only country in Western Europe where a crazy debate on deglobalization has emerged.

Nevertheless, the fact that this debate remains marginal within the electorate, including the Left, testifies to both the gravity of the situation and the left-leaning electorate's tendency to be extremely prudent and to reject radicalism, be it only verbal. As a case in point, all the parties to the left of the Socialist Party are currently weak even though the worsening crisis should have automatically burnished their credentials.

In the coming months, three political events of great significance will unfold.

The first is the selection of the Left's presidential candidate after a completely unprecedented primary in France. The conditions and results of this selection, which will occur in October, are not negligible, since presidential election polls currently show that the Left has a lead over the incumbent president. If the Socialist primaries are successfully carried out (without any contestation and with participation exceeding 1 million voters) they will automatically enhance the prospects of the Left's candidate. If this candidate happens to be Hollande, his political prospects will be enhanced by his ability to draw on Left and centrist electorates that already view him favorably.[13] This is only an indication, though; traditionally, winners of polls taken one year before presidential elections are systematically beaten. This has nothing to do with the quality of the polls, but rather the vicissitudes of public opinion, which very often solidifies only in the last months of the campaign.

The second event, which may occur in October 2011, is the vote on the "golden rule" designed to constitutionalize balanced budgets, albeit in a relatively loose manner. It is far from certain that Sarkozy will submit this proposal to Congress because of the uncertainty of the outcome.[14] The head of

---

12. Ibid.

13. *Editors' note:* On October 16, 2011, François Hollande won the Socialist Party nomination.

14. In France, the Congress refers to the joint session of the National Assembly and the Senate. The two bodies must together vote with a three-fifths majority to pass an amendment to the constitution. *Editors' note:* Following the September 25, 2011, elections for half of the seats in the Senate, which gave the Senate majority to the left-wing opposition parties, the vote on the golden rule was postponed *sine die.*

state will need explicit or implicit (abstention) support from the Socialists to constitutionalize this rule. As mentioned above, the latter have decided to vote against the measure for essentially political reasons. This situation is a golden opportunity for the incumbent president, at least in theory. If the golden rule passes he will be able to build on a very strong political consensus to intensify deficit reduction measures and enter the next presidential elections in a position of strength, despite the sacrifices imposed on voters. French public opinion wholeheartedly supports the golden rule, which is another interesting paradox in a country where opposition to market dictatorship is so strong. The rule would also allow him to strike a number of decisions he has made since 2007 that have undeniably increased deficits. In the opposite scenario, wherein the Socialists refuse to vote for the proposal, or even to abstain, the head of state could appeal to public opinion by emphasizing that Socialist stonewalling could harm France's established credibility. But a boomerang effect against the president cannot be excluded.

If the markets detect an American scenario—where the political class is deemed to have a very weak capacity to reach consensus on managing debt—they will not hesitate to downgrade France's rating. The question is how public opinion would respond to such a development. The incumbent president could attribute responsibility to the Left, while the Left could denounce the president for deliberately using market pressure to get reelected. The risk would then be of falling into a vicious circle that could be catastrophic for the country if it spiraled out of political control. Political actors are currently playing a very delicate game of brinkmanship. What seems certain is that if the Left hardens its opposition to the golden rule, it will need to prepare a compelling response in the event of a downgrade. Hollande has said that if elected he will propose to the new Parliament a vote on the golden rule. Even if no downgrade occurs, the debate over the political credibility of public finance restructuring will remain crucial and will most likely dominate the presidential campaign.

The presidential elections are the third and last great event that will take place in France in the next few months. They will proceed under unprecedented circumstances, given the French economy's extreme vulnerability. However, the result will not be automatically determined by economic constraints. At the moment two equal forces are animating the French social body. The first is the desire to harshly punish the incumbent president of the republic despite the Left's weak economic credibility. The second is the realism that is conducive to continuity and thus benefits the power of the incumbent. The novelty is that this tension exists not only between the two camps that traditionally dominate French political life, but also most likely within every French citizen, whose points of reference have been blurred by the crisis.

8

The Political Economy of Germany in the Sovereign Debt Crisis

DANIELA SCHWARZER

After the downturn in 2008–09, there was a strong economic recovery in Germany in 2010 and the first half of 2011. But in the context of an economic deceleration expected for the Organization for Economic Cooperation and Development countries, the German economy will probably slow down considerably in the second half of 2011 and in 2012. Export growth is likely to weaken as key export markets cool down, partly due to fiscal tightening in Germany's main trading partners. Domestic demand is also expected to decline as consumers and businesses become more cautious. Private consumption growth is forecast to accelerate to 1.6 percent in 2011 from 0.4 percent in 2010, but will then stay at around 1.4 percent on average in 2012–15.[1]

Germany's current account surplus is expected to fall moderately, from 5.7 percent of GDP in 2010 to 4.1 percent in 2011, and could stabilize at around 3 percent of GDP from 2013 to 2015. Germany's large export sector makes it vulnerable to a possible slowdown in major trading partners, both in the euro area and in the Asian and US markets. The reduction of Germany's surplus may reduce political tensions in a period in which the new

Daniela Schwarzer is head of the research division of European integration at the German Institute for International and Security Affairs, Stiftung Wissenschaft und Politik (SWP), in Berlin.

1. Economist Intelligence Unit, *Country Report: Germany,* September 2011, www.marketresearch. com.

Box 8.1   Germany's debt brake

The debt brake limits the possibility of running cyclically adjusted deficits (structural deficits) at the federal as well as the state level. Changes to the constitution were necessary for the debt brake to come into force. Thus the Bundestag as well as the Bundesrat had to pass the legislation. The debt brake provides guidelines for the reduction of budget deficits beginning in 2011. Its focus is on the cyclically adjusted budget to allow for automatic stabilizers to work. The limit for the annual federal cyclically adjusted budget, set at 0.35 percent of GDP, will become binding in 2016, and the states won't be allowed to run any deficits from 2020 onwards. Catastrophes such as natural disasters and deep recessions are exceptions to this rule.

mechanisms for economic policy coordination within the euro area (part of the recently adopted legislative "Six-Pack"[2]) will run their first test in 2012.

Employment is expected to expand, which will support domestic demand, but real wages are expected to grow only slowly. Government consumption is likely to grow only moderately, given self-imposed austerity and the recently enacted debt brake (see box 8.1). But around the time of the general elections (presumably in September 2013), public spending may temporarily be increased.

Forecasts see growth slowing to 1.4 percent in 2012, and to an average of 2 percent between 2013 and 2015.[3] But these assumptions do not take into account the impact of the euro area debt crisis, the evolution of a banking crisis, or a breakup of the currency. Hence, there are considerable downside risks for the German economy.

Forecasts see relatively strong inflation in 2012–13. Inflation in Germany was low in 2010, averaging 1.1 percent, but it may reach 2.3 percent as capacity constraints increase and wage growth accelerates moderately in a tightening labor market. Inflation is expected to average about 1.8 percent in the period from 2012 to 2015.

The euro is likely to display considerable volatility. Interest rate differentials are continuing to support the euro. But investors will remain concerned about the ongoing debt, banking, and governance crises and about the developments in the region's periphery, so downward pressure could occur. This would fuel German exports. Sharp movement in the other direction, mean-

---

2. The six legislative texts were voted on by the European Parliament on September 28, 2011, and officially agreed upon by the Economic and Financial Affairs Council on October 4, 2011. See European Commission, Economic and Financial Affairs, "EU Economic Governance," http://ec.europa.eu (accessed on November 14, 2011).

3. Economist Intelligence Unit, *Country Report: Germany,* September 2011, www.marketresearch.com.

while, would probably be supported more easily by Germany than by many other euro area member states, including France, given Germany's high degree of competitiveness.

Budgetary and Economic Policy Priorities

One important priority of the current government is to come close to eliminating the fiscal deficit over the next four years. The government's focus is on consolidating public finances, with the aim of moving to a balanced budget in the medium term. After a deficit of 3.3 percent of GDP in 2010, the general government deficit may narrow to 1.7 percent of GDP in 2011 and be almost in balance by 2015. The government's 2012 budget and 2013–15 financial plans foresee gradual declines in the federal budget deficit, due mainly to slow expenditure growth and strong revenue expansion from the economic upswing. Public and political support for good public services, with priority given to education and research, will remain high.

Under pressure from the liberal coalition partner Free Democratic Party (FDP), the government in November 2011 agreed to implement a tax cut of €6 billion in the election year 2013 and in 2014, but the Finance Ministry, led by the Christian Democratic Union (CDU), seems determined not to allow this to worsen public finances materially. In August 2009, Germany introduced a debt brake that—if respected—will impose tight constraints at the federal and state levels. Within the euro area, the German government seems to be determined to make others follow its own example (see the discussion on governance reform below), not only by pushing governments toward austerity, but also by driving the debate on domestic fiscal rules and national debt brakes in the euro area.

A second major concern of Germany's government is to stabilize the financial sector after the 2008 crisis and at a time when it may face further losses. The weakness of some German banks will remain a major issue, particularly given their exposure to the euro area sovereign debt crisis. Renewed restructuring could well make additional state support necessary, especially given the need for higher capital ratios under the Basel III agreements at the same time.

Reform of financial sector regulation is under way: A key element is a law of November 2010 intended to provide a method for tackling the possible insolvency of systemically important banks. A bank levy to finance a €70 billion fund to support the German financial sector in future crises has also been introduced.

The Political Situation in Germany

Since autumn 2009, Germany has been governed by a coalition of three parties: the center-right CDU; its Bavarian sister party, the Christian Social Union (CSU); and the FDP. Together, the coalition partners hold a rather comfort-

Table 8.1   2009 election results and voters' current intentions

Party	Seats in Parliament	Electoral results[a] (percent)	Voters' choice if general elections were held now[b] (percent)
CDU/CSU	237	33.8	35
SPD	146	23.0	28
FDP	93	14.6	4
Die Linke	76	11.9	7
Die Grüne	68	10.7	20

CDU = Christian Democratic Union; CSU = Christian Social Union; FDP = Free Democratic Party; Die Linke = the Left; Die Grüne = the Greens; SPD = Social Democrats

a. All other parties together reach 6 percent.
b. "Now" refers to September 2011.

Source: Infratest Dimap, "ARD-Deutschland-Trend," September 2011, www.infratest-dimap.de.

able majority of 330 seats (237 CDU/CSU and 93 FDP) out of the 620 seats in the Bundestag, Germany's lower house (see table 8.1).

Since the first decisions were made about the rescue packages in spring 2010, there have been severe tensions within the coalition over the way to cope with the sovereign debt crisis. Regional elections, in particular the elections in the largest regional state, North Rhine–Westphalia, were one of the determinants of the government's reluctance to act more swiftly in the sovereign debt crisis in spring 2010.[4] But interestingly, the parties' positions on euro area crisis management seemed to have little impact on the electoral turnout and—according to polls—would have little impact on voters if general elections were held now (see table 8.1). Actually, the two parties that have criticized the acting government for its insufficiently pro-European stance and that have sought more German engagement in the sovereign debt crisis, the Greens and the Social Democrats (SPD), have been able to increase their support and could record good election results in upcoming regional elections. The FDP, meanwhile, lost elections and support in opinion polls—even though it ran a campaign against eurobonds. For more details on the respective positions of the major parties on the proper response to the euro area debt crisis, see box 8.2. There is today widespread distrust in the present German government: 66 percent believe that the German federal government is on the wrong track with regard to the crisis. A similar percentage of people (65 percent) thinks that the federal government did not take the correct decisions in the euro and debt crisis.[5]

Despite the tensions and the decline of support for the coalition, the next general elections are not likely to be moved forward, in particular because

---

4. One more regional election is coming up before the general elections, in Schleswig-Holstein on May 6, 2012.

5. Infratest Dimap, "ARD-DeutschlandTREND," September 2011, www.infratest-dimap.de (accessed on November 14, 2011).

Box 8.2 Key positions of political parties in the Bundestag

The conservative *Christian Democratic Union* (CDU) is pro-European but divided about how to best tackle the debt crisis. The latest dispute has been about the future role of national parliaments in the governance structure of the EFSF and later ESM. Parliamentary members have harshly criticized Chancellor Merkel and Minister of Finance Schäuble for apparently trying to keep the national parliament out of future decisions about financial assistance to be granted (a criticism all parties share). An influential member of Parliament, Wolfgang Bosbach, openly stated his intention to vote against the EFSF in late September. Whether Merkel will be able to get a majority of her own coalition is not certain. Another contentious issue is the introduction of eurobonds. While Merkel and Schäuble have stated that eurobonds need to go hand in hand with a deeper integration of fiscal policy across the euro area, many members of the CDU want a general rejection of the very idea of eurobonds.

The smaller but still influential sister of the CDU, the more conservative *Christian Social Union* (CSU) (present only in Bavaria) has a harder stance toward eurobonds. It rejects them altogether, arguing that interest rate differentials are the only way to discipline national budgets. Nonetheless it supports Merkel in her attempts to stabilize the euro area. It also supports the introduction of debt brakes in all euro area member states, a financial transaction fee (announced together with French president Nicolas Sarkozy), and improved fiscal policy coordination.

The *Free Democratic Party* (FDP) consists of free-market liberals who reject any instrument that promotes debt reduction or debt collateralization, even though they eventually gave in to the mounting pressure of installing the EFSF. Like members of the CDU/CSU, they demand ongoing involvement by the Parliament in the EFSF and in future ESM decisions. FDP's Frank Schäffler has been the first (and remains one of the few) to openly demand a split from the euro area. The FDP criticizes the European Central Bank (ECB) for buying government bonds on the secondary market, which is a form of collateralizing the debt as well as turning the ECB into a bad bank. Very recently, party chairman Philipp Rösler refused to rule out Greece's bankruptcy and exit from the euro area as a policy option.

The *Social Democrats* (SPD) point out that the debt crisis arose out of a financial crisis via the bailout of banks. SPD members therefore make a strong case for financial regulation. They blame Chancellor Merkel for the spread of the crisis, saying she postponed crucial decisions due to state elections. In their view the austerity program for Greece is counterproductive because it kills off economic growth and thus makes an end to the crisis in Greece unlikely. Current account imbalances are seen as one of the core flaws of the monetary union and are attributed to excessively low real wage settlements (a view that all opposition parties share).

(box continues next page)

the junior coalition partner FDP would risk not making it over the 5 percent threshold (see the last column of table 8.1).

The weak performance of the governing CDU/CSU-FDP coalition in regional elections in the years 2010 and 2011 has had three major implications. First, the coalition is in the minority in the upper house, the Bundesrat, which comprises representatives of regional governments. The coalition must therefore compromise with the opposition on laws that require ratification by the Bundesrat. Second, the CDU party leader, Angela Merkel, is seen as weakened, although she does not face a serious challenger at present. The FDP leadership has changed from Guido Westerwelle (Germany's foreign minister) to Philipp Rösler (now minister of the economy). The party has become increasingly critical of the rescue measures agreed upon during the debt crisis. It is also likely to hold a member referendum on Germany's participation in the debt crisis resolution mechanisms. Such a move could cause a breakup of the coalition if the FDP leadership withdraws support for Merkel's crisis management strategy. But the bad results the FDP scored in the Berlin elections (it received 1.9 percent of the votes, which means it is no longer present in the regional parliament) have not made this scenario very probable.

In the Bundestag's vote on the European Financial Stability Facility (EFSF) on September 29, 2011, the governing coalition agreed to the law with 315 votes, which means that the chancellor had her own majority. Further tests will be the Bundestag vote on the second rescue package for Greece, scheduled for the end of 2011, and the vote on the future European Stability Mechanism (ESM), presumably coming up in early 2012. Despite the rising criticism of how the euro area crisis has been managed, there is so far no profoundly anti-European party for those voicing the criticism to turn to. Interestingly, and quite in contrast to the development of public opinion, the Social Democrat and Green opposition supports rescue mechanisms as much as or more than the German government.

German policymakers regularly refer to the state of public opinion in order to explain the core positions the government insists upon both in debt crisis management and in euro area governance reform. In fact, 1.5 years into the sovereign debt crisis, public opinion is critical but not anti-European. But given German sensitivities surrounding the abandonment of the Deutsche mark, this crisis is particularly delicate to handle.

Before the outbreak of the sovereign debt crisis, political leaders did not seem to miss Germany's postwar currency, but on the contrary outlined the euro's benefits, in particular at the celebrations of the single currency's 10th anniversary in 2009. But even then, the broad public evaluated the euro more critically. Since the outbreak of the sovereign debt crisis, this tendency has intensified.

The percentage of citizens that sees disadvantages in the euro climbed from 45 percent of those polled in 2001 to 63 percent in April 2010. Roughly a third of German citizens think that the euro has more advantages than disadvantages; only 6 percent think advantages and disadvantages are equal.[6]

Yet 63 percent of Germans are in favor of "a European economic and monetary union with one single currency, the euro,"[7] and 88 percent think that it is a matter of the German national interest to keep the euro stable.[8]

Among the German public, distrust of the European Union generally outweighs trust (55 percent compared to 35 percent).[9] As stated above, distrust of the German government is likewise significant.

Overall, there is criticism of the role of the euro during the crisis: 40 percent of Germans agree that "the euro has cushioned the effects of the economic crisis" (7 percent totally agree, 31 percent tend to agree), whereas 50 percent disagree (19 percent totally disagree, 33 percent tend to disagree).[10]

6. Infratest Dimap, "ARD-DeutschlandTREND," April 2010, www.infratest-dimap.de (accessed on November 14, 2011).

7. European Commission, Standard Eurobarometer 75, "Public Opinion in the European Union. Annex," August 2011, p. 63, http://ec.europa.eu (accessed on November 14, 2011).

8. Infratest Dimap, "ARD-DeutschlandTREND," December 2010, www.infratest-dimap.de (accessed on November 14, 2011).

9. European Commission, Standard Eurobarometer 75, "Public Opinion in the European Union," August 2011, p. 44, http://ec.europa.eu (accessed on November 14, 2011).

10. European Commission, Standard Eurobarometer 75, "Public Opinion in the European Union. Annex," August 2011, p. 133, http://ec.europa.eu (accessed on November 14, 2011).

As to countries that do not have their public finances under control, Germans prefer strict rules: 56 percent are of the opinion that these countries should be excluded from the euro area, whereas 40 percent do not think so.[11] Forty-seven percent of Germans think that the state of EU members' finances is one of the (two) most important issues that the European Union faces today (compared with the EU-27 average, which is only 22 percent).[12]

But Germans are in favor of a stronger Europe: 64 percent wish that European countries would develop more common policies and act together more effectively,[13] and 93 percent agree with the statement that "EU Member States should work together more in tackling the financial and economic crisis" (59 percent totally agree, 34 percent tend to agree).[14] Large majorities among the Germans polled for the Eurobarometer actually support more integration, including the following:

- "a stronger coordination of economic policy among all the EU Member States" (82 percent judge this an effective approach to tackling the crisis),
- "a closer supervision by the EU when public money is used to rescue banks and financial institutions" (85 percent in favor),
- "a stronger coordination of economic and financial policies among the countries of the euro area" (83 percent in favor),
- "a closer supervision by the EU of the activities of large financial groups/most important international financial groups" (85 percent in favor), and
- "a more important role for the euro in regulating financial services" (75 percent in favor).[15]

But concerning the enlargement of the euro rescue fund (EFSF), German public opinion is rather skeptical: 66 percent think that Germany's federal parliament should vote against the proposal (30 percent think that it should vote in favor of it). And when it comes to the highly politicized issue of eurobonds, a majority of 55 percent opposes German participation (compared to 35 percent in favor).[16] The proposal of Ursula von der Leyen (CDU labor min-

---

11. Infratest Dimap, "ARD-DeutschlandTREND," December 2010, www.infratest-dimap.de (accessed on November 14, 2011).

12. European Commission, Standard Eurobarometer 75, "Public Opinion in the European Union," August 2011, p. 25, http://ec.europa.eu (accessed on November 14, 2011).

13. Infratest Dimap, "ARD-DeutschlandTREND," September 2011, www.infratest-dimap.de (accessed on November 14, 2011).

14. European Commission, Standard Eurobarometer 75, "Public Opinion in the European Union. Annex," August 2011, p. 139, http://ec.europa.eu (accessed on November 14, 2011).

15. European Commission, Standard Eurobarometer 75, "Europeans, the European Union and the Crisis," August 2011, p. 20, http://ec.europa.eu (accessed on November 14, 2011).

16. Infratest Dimap, "ARD-DeutschlandTREND," September 2011, www.infratest-dimap.de (accessed on November 14, 2011).

Figure 8.1   Annual average inflation rate, euro area and Germany, 1997–2010

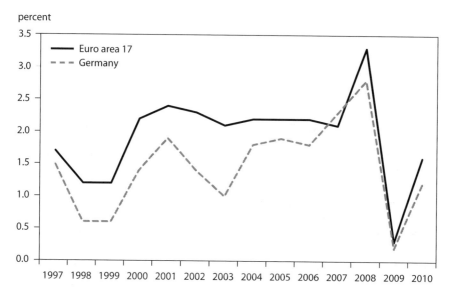

percent

Source: Eurostat database, http://epp.eurostat.ec.europa.eu.

ister) for a "United States of Europe" is welcomed by 42 percent (compared to 53 percent against).

Overall, Germans have a rather pessimistic outlook on the near future: Despite the measures already taken, a large majority of Germans (80 percent) thinks that the worst part of the crisis is still to come; 76 percent worry about a negative effect on wealth caused by the crisis.[17]

Inflation is a constant concern to the Germans. In February 2011, 61 percent of the German people believed that prices were rising more rapidly than in the years before (28 percent thought that the pace was not different from before).[18] Fears of inflation were actually the major concern in the first decade in which the Economic and Monetary Union (EMU) existed. Tabloids often nickname the euro the "teuro" (a pun on *teuer*, German for "expensive"), reflecting the sentiment that prices have risen strongly since its arrival. Inflation data for Germany contradict this perception: from 1999 to 2010, German inflation has on average been 1.5 percent.[19] Euro area inflation has been in line with the European Central Bank's (ECB's) inflation target of 2 percent on average from 1999 to 2010. As figure 8.1 shows, German inflation ranged below

17. Ibid.

18. Infratest Dimap, "ARD-DeutschlandTREND," February 2011, www.infratest-dimap.de (accessed on November 14, 2011).

19. Author's calculation based on Eurostat data.

the ECB's target of 2 percent in all years since the start of the EMU except for 2008 (2.8 percent) and was lower than the euro area average in all years but 2007 (Germany 2.3 percent, euro area 2.1 percent).

While price stability has been a major issue for the public and is likely to continue to be one in the medium-term future, public opinion traditionally pays little attention to growth performance, for instance to the fact that the German economy for several years was among the weak performers in the euro area, with only Italy doing worse.

Germany's Management of the Sovereign Debt Crisis

The German chancellor has made a commitment to do "whatever it takes" to support the euro. Thus the government has to maintain public support for the euro project and overcome deep domestic resistance, in particular in the Parliament, to Germany's assuming responsibility for other countries' debt. So far, German policymaking during the debt crisis has prioritized political considerations over a fundamental solution to the underlying problem.

Domestic and foreign observers have paid a lot of attention to the fact that the German government was not proactive with regard to Greece in spring 2010; they argue that it did not show a convincing commitment to the decision of the informal European Council of February 11, 2010, which promised to help member governments in need to refinance their debt. In the view of many observers, this attitude increased nervousness in the financial markets and led to a worsening of the crisis, for which the parliamentary opposition has severely criticized the German chancellor.

A lack of political leadership has also invited irresponsible polarization in the German tabloid press. With an unparalleled degree of hostility, the tabloids have depicted Greek citizens as lazy, corrupt, irresponsible, and the like. While there have been efforts by other media to draw a more realistic picture of the situation in Greece, at least for a few weeks the situation in the German media remained unbalanced.

There are probably four reasons why decision makers in Berlin did not give earlier rescue promises to Athens. One was to exert as much public pressure on the Greek government as possible in order to push and support Prime Minister George Papandreou's reform agenda. The assumption among policymakers that rescue packages create a moral hazard problem is very much part of the German debate, which is one of the reasons why the government requested high interest rates for credit given to the highly indebted countries. Second, there is a strong principled belief that the euro area should function according to the rules Germany had sought to implement with the Maastricht Treaty: as a monetary union founded on monetary stability, sound public finances, and a no-bailout clause (see box 8.3). Breaking these rules and hence letting the euro area slip away from these principles is seen as a major mistake by many Germans, even in times of crisis. The third concern was hostile public opinion, and in particular no willingness on the part of the government to

Box 8.3   Looking back 15 years: Germany adopts the euro

Many of the arguments (and emotions) that have arisen in the course of managing the sovereign debt crisis parallel those surrounding the introduction of the euro in 1999. At that time, Germany experienced an emotional debate on whether and under which conditions it should give up the Deutsche mark. Those arguments provide an important background to understanding the debate over Germany's involvement in the current management of the debt crisis and governance reform.

The Deutsche mark had become the symbol for the postwar Wirtschaftswunder and helped the country reemerge as a European and global player. The economic success, the stable currency, and the related international recognition were among the few things Germans dared to show pride in after World War II.

In the 1990s, the debate over giving up the Deutsche mark grew particularly intense when it became clear that the currency union would probably start with a rather large group of countries, including Italy, Spain, and Portugal, the so-called Club Med.[1] Concerns about the future stability of the euro revealed deeply rooted fears of a society that had lived through hyperinflation in the early 20th century, the effects of which were a root cause for the emergence of the racist and belligerent Nazi regime.

The critics of the incipient Economic and Monetary Union (EMU) were divided into two groups. While some opponents did not want the EMU to happen at all, other critics, including then-president of the Bundesbank Hans Tietmeyer argued for a political union to ensure in particular that national budgetary policies would not undermine monetary stability. In order to reassure an increasingly nervous public, the acting government underlined the strong degree of independence of the European Central Bank, whose statutes could be changed only by a unanimous decision of the member states, hence not against the will of the German government. By pushing through the Stability and Growth Pact in 1997, the German government succeeded in hardening fiscal rules and the Pact made it possible to sanction member states in order to complement the Maastricht Treaty. Furthermore, it explained that the no-bailout clause ensured that no government would be liable for public debt accumulated by other member states in the EMU. These provisions were not only relevant for the public debate, but also the basis upon which the German Constitutional Court ruled that the Maastricht Treaty was compatible with German Basic Law.

---

1. In 1997, in Baden-Württemberg, Social Democrat Dietmar Spöri ran an unsuccessful campaign for regional prime minister on an anti-euro platform.

attempt to convince the public of Germany's self-interest in granting support to Greece before North Rhine–Westphalia, Germany's largest state, went to the polls on May 9, 2010. The fourth and strongest concern was probably that German participation in a rescue package, which could not be justified with the argument that the stability of the euro was at stake, could be challenged before the German Constitutional Court. Policymakers were deeply concerned by the scenario that a European rescue package could be ruled unconstitutional in Germany, and that this would cause substantial instability in the financial markets.

With market tensions spreading to Italy and Spain, the ECB was forced to take further unconventional measures in early August 2011. It first injected liquidity into money markets.[20] The ECB then resumed its Securities Markets Program on August 8, 2011, making significant purchases of Italian and Spanish bonds for the first time in a bid to lower yields.

Such measures are particularly controversial in Germany and with the Germans in the ECB's governing council. A major concern is the potential difficulties of "sterilizing" large bond purchases, as well as the impact on the ECB's balance sheet of any future sovereign debt restructuring. Officially, the ECB is expecting that the EFSF will assume responsibility for purchasing bonds of struggling euro area countries beginning in October 2011, but expanding the EFSF's volume to a sufficient scale will be politically and technically difficult. Hence a continued role for the ECB is likely.

The German debate on the role of the ECB in crisis management, specifically its independence and potential inflationary pressure in the euro area as a consequence of its intervention, surged in August and September 2011. While Chancellor Merkel silently backs the European Central Bank's secondary market purchases, Jens Weidmann, her former advisor and now Bundesbank president, has openly criticized the program—just like his predecessor Axel Weber, who resigned from the Bundesbank in protest against the ECB's role in managing the sovereign debt crisis and thus gave up the possibility of becoming the next president of the ECB after Jean-Claude Trichet's term ended in November 2011.

The departure of Jürgen Stark on September 9, 2011, from his position as ECB chief economist and one of six ECB board members—also in protest over the bond purchases—not only came at a critical point in time with regard to the evolution of the sovereign debt crisis but also marked an important point in the German debate. There is now a widespread perception that the original conception of the euro area—built around Germany's preference for stability and in the style of the old Bundesbank currency union—seems to be coming to an end. Stark himself embodied the Bundesbank's stability orientation and represented important political and administrative continuity as former

---

20. The bank reopened an unlimited six-month credit facility, and said it would continue to offer a "full allotment" of liquidity at shorter durations throughout 2011, with support likely to be extended in 2012 and beyond.

> **Box 8.4   Implications of the Constitutional Court ruling of September 7, 2011**
>
> A crucial milestone for the reform and implementation of the European Financial Stability Facility (EFSF) and the European Stability Mechanism (ESM) was the German Constitutional Court ruling of September 7, 2011, on the legality of the first Greek rescue package and the EFSF. The court found that the parliamentary decisions on the recue measures are compatible with German Basic Law, but that every rescue measure with a large impact on the budget has to be approved by the Parliament. It is not possible for Germany to participate in an automatic and unmanageable guarantee mechanism that might include eurobonds.

deputy president of the Bundesbank. It is probable that Stark, who has been rather outspoken even as an ECB board member, will continue to play an important role in the public debate. The opposition in Germany against the current approach to the management of the sovereign debt crisis is likely to gain momentum. The current government's euro defense policy is coming under increasing pressure, and Stark's departure may turn out to be another element weakening the German chancellor and her finance minister. They will thus be under fire from two sides, the "pro-European Left" and the increasingly outspoken EMU skeptics.

At the same time it handles public opinion and constitutional constraints, the government has to convince financial market participants that the stronger euro area members (mainly northern stability-oriented countries led by Germany) are prepared to give full backing to the single currency. A crucial moment was the parliamentary vote on the EFSF and in particular the Constitutional Court's decision calling for Parliament's future involvement when the EFSF takes major actions (see box 8.4). The next crucial vote is on the second Greek rescue package and the new ESM. Meanwhile, the overarching debate, on whether the rescue mechanisms are at all sufficient, continues. Even if the extended EFSF is insufficient to handle a deteriorating crisis, securing the ratification of its amendments and of the ESM treaty was an important first step. If there are ratification difficulties in major countries, these are likely to lead to a worsening of the crisis.

Germany and Economic Governance Reforms

The sovereign debt crisis shattered German mantras like an earthquake. The European Central Bank is buying sovereign debt on a large scale, which has made German commentators tag it as Europe's largest bad bank that has lost its independence. The Stability and Growth Pact has continued to lose credibility, in particular since Greece and some other EMU member states have become candidates for a possible sovereign default. The no-bailout clause has de facto been given up. The perception is widespread that the ordoliberal framework of the Maastricht Treaty has been undermined, and that a transfer union has de facto been installed, in which those member states that have sound budgetary policies end up paying for those that cheat and behave irresponsibly.

In parallel to the negotiation of rescue packages for euro area members in spring 2010, a profound debate on the reform of the budgetary and economic governance mechanisms has developed. Germany pursued its traditional policy on euro area governance questions, namely a rules-based approach involving nominal targets and sanctioning mechanisms, a low degree of risk sharing, and very little room for political discretion—a policy that is not shared by all of Germany's EMU partners.

Ever since the Maastricht negotiations, Germany sought an integration of monetary policy that, in the absence of a political union (which the French government at the time objected to), would be backed by budgetary policy coordination. The aim was to prevent unsound fiscal policies from undermining monetary stability. This resulted in the inclusion of the so-called excessive deficit procedure in the Maastricht Treaty to insure budgetary policy surveillance and coordination. In 1996, the German government put forward an additional proposal, called the Stability Pact, to enhance budgetary policy coordination, which was deemed insufficient after two years of applying it and even before the euro was launched. Similar concerns are reflected in the position presented by the government to the Van Rompuy task force, which was set up to sketch out a reform of the euro area. One example is the German proposal to withdraw voting rights from member states that break the rules of the Stability and Growth Pact. Another example is German political leaders' opposition to the creation of a regular euro area summit, as had been repeatedly suggested by the French government; the fear was that such an institution and closer coordination among the euro area governments could lead to more-discretionary policies, which could contradict Germany's stability concerns and the ECB's independence. Despite the pressing problems that are unique to the euro area, the German government's position was initially that fiscal and economic governance should be improved in the EU-27.

This changed only under the severe pressure of the sovereign debt crisis, which made Germany accept the idea of a euro area summit, whose policy agenda it swiftly tried to fill with a detailed proposal for a "Pact for Competitiveness," later the Euro-Plus Pact. The new understanding in Berlin is now that top-level involvement in the coordination of budgetary and economic policy is necessary in order to strengthen the rules-based approach.

Furthermore, it has become a widely shared assumption in the German debate on euro area governance reform that private sector involvement in the case of highly indebted member states should be institutionalized under the ESM and should occur at an early stage of crisis management. But the worsening of the sovereign debt crisis, which has been attributed in part to the

Box 8.5   Consequences of likely reforms for euro area and EU economic governance

It becomes more and more manifest that the euro area will be equipped with "its own" governance mechanisms, strengthening the institutional base of policy coordination among the 17 members of the Economic and Monetary Union (EMU-17). This is a chance to increase the ability of the EMU-17 to effectively cope with the crisis and to improve policy coordination, and it should be seized. Some of the policy coordination proposals consist of potentially strong interference with domestic policymaking. Constraints imposed on member states are growing.

It will be difficult to gain support among all 17 EMU countries. And it may be impossible to gain support from all EU-27 members. So the most likely way toward economic and budgetary policy coordination will be a "euro area only" approach for which Germany now seems to be prepared. This trend will consist in a further shift of policy debates from EU-27 fora to EMU-17 fora, similar to the shift from the Economic and Financial Affairs Council (Ecofin) to the Eurogroup ever since the introduction of the latter. Hence, EU-27 formats dealing with issues that are subject to EMU-17 coordination in the Eurogroup or during EMU summits should include a short debriefing on EMU debates. This arrangement concerns the Ecofin (where this is already implemented), the European Council (dealing with crisis management), and in particular the spring Council devoted to competitiveness/growth strategy, the Competitiveness Council.

German debate on private sector involvement, has also made decision makers more prudent on this issue. In particular, the ECB has been fairly present in the German debate in order to raise the awareness of de facto and potential contagion effects. On this crucial matter, there is a deep-running difference between German and French positions: While German economists tend to see private sector involvement as key to preventing moral hazard, French observers tend to point out the risks of contagion involved in such a step.

Since spring 2010, a broad reform of the economic governance mechanisms in the euro area has been under way, in parallel to ongoing crisis management (box 8.5). The current situation is as follows:

- The six legislative acts of the Rehn package were agreed to in September 2011.[21] The legislative acts change the Stability and Growth Pact, improve economic governance coordination, and set a common framework for the member states' fiscal constitutions. Some elements will have to be defined upon implementation, for instance elements of the economic scoreboard.

---

21. In September 2010 the European Commission had presented six legislative proposals on economic governance, the so-called Six-Pack. Ollie Rehn is the EU Commissioner for Economic and Monetary Affairs.

- The European semester was implemented for the first time in 2011.[22] The next round will be launched in the first half of 2012.
- The Euro-Plus Pact was agreed to on March 11, 2011. Twenty-four member states have signed the pact.[23]
- The special euro area summit on July 21, 2011, put forward further ideas for reforms, notably to improve working methods and crisis management in the euro area (until October 2011) and to reduce the role of credit rating agencies in the EU regulatory framework and found a European agency.
- The euro summit of October 26, 2011, reached major decisions on the governance structure of the euro area: There will be a semiannual meeting of euro area heads of state and government after the European Council. More frequent meetings can be convened if necessary. The euro summit will also have a permanent president. The administrative backup of the Eurogroup and the euro summit will be decisively improved.
- The European Commission has been asked to present proposals for further governance reform, including a treaty change, in December 2011.

Another sensitive topic in the debate on the euro area's reform is how to address growing economic imbalances as a result of diverging degrees of competitiveness. These imbalances have been identified as one of the root causes of the current euro area crisis. There is a broad European consensus that countries with large external deficits need to implement far-reaching structural reforms in order to improve their competitiveness.

However, on March 15, 2010, the Eurogroup acknowledged for the first time that surpluses also need to be critically reviewed.[24] This is a very sensitive point for Germany, which has repeatedly been criticized for relying too much on exports and too little on domestic demand as engines of growth.[25]

Some critics argue that Germany has pursued competitive real devaluation as unit labor costs have stagnated and reductions of the financial burden on the corporate sector have improved its competitiveness. Meanwhile, the increase of the value-added tax to 19 percent weighs on domestic consumption. German reactions to such criticism are strong, because many Germans

---

22. The European semester is a cycle of economic policy coordination during a six-month period beginning in March of each year when the European Council identifies the main economic challenges facing the European Union. In April, member states present medium-term budgetary and structural reform strategies. Then in July the European Council and the Economic and Financial Affairs Council (Ecofin) provide policy advice prior to finalization of member state budgets for the coming year.

23. The countries that are not yet signatories are the United Kingdom, Denmark, the Czech Republic, and Hungary.

24. "Eurogroup Meeting of March 15, 2010," http://consilium.europa.eu (accessed on November 21, 2011).

25. See, for instance, the interview with Christine Lagarde, *Financial Times*, March 15, 2010, www. ft.com (accessed on November 15, 2011).

interpret the criticism as a request by Germany's partners that the country "do worse." Comparisons with the German football team, which could not possibly be asked to score less for the sake of its neighbors, have been drawn,[26] and economic performance in the euro area has been depicted as a competitive race. In general, the debate on German export competitiveness often is much more focused on global markets than on the euro area or the EU-27, which may explain why economic policymakers in Germany tend not to understand their European partners' concerns over Germany's real devaluations.

Nevertheless, the question of whether Germany needs to do more for domestic demand is regularly raised in political debates in Berlin, and will be raised even more often if export-driven growth decelerates in the years to come. There is a rising concern (for instance among some Social Democrat and Green politicians in the German Parliament, as a number of public hearings in parliamentary committees show) that Germany will have to do more for domestic demand in its own interest.[27] There are two major arguments why. First, Germany has a clear self-interest in seeing the euro area return to robust growth and sustainable public finances, for which a strongly growing German economy is a prerequisite. Second, if the euro area partners substantively increase their competitiveness, Germany as a consequence may lose market share in certain segments and therefore have to rely more on domestic demand.

Germany in the European Union under the Lisbon Treaty

The simultaneous implementation of the Lisbon Treaty, the management of the crisis, and the implementation of economic governance reforms have considerably changed the political functioning of the European Union. Power relationships have shifted toward the European Council (heads of state) and, in particular, to the larger member states. At the core of the system is Germany: the main guarantor of the EFSF and the future ESM, with a share of 28 percent in guarantee commitments; the strongest-performing economy of the euro area in the last two years; and a country whose chancellor probably has the most direct and influential access to council president Herman Van Rompuy.

The most relevant change for the question of leadership and power relationships was the installment of the permanent president of the European Council. The European Council has become particularly active in defining the reactions to the sovereign debt crisis. On the ministerial level, the most relevant forum is the Eurogroup. The European Commission has had to struggle for its standing. The seizure of longer-term policy orientations and strategic

---

26. See, for instance, Herman-Otto Solms's statement at the Economic Committee hearing of June 16, 2010, www.bundestag.de.

27. See, for instance, Heiner Flassbeck, Gustav Horn, and Sebastian Dullien, "Europa hat noch eine Chance," *Financial Times Deutschland,* May 5, 2010, 24.

reflection by the European Council have challenged the Commission's role both in crisis management and in the process of economic governance reform. This trend may continue.

The European Parliament, in contrast, is one of the institutions that benefits most from the Lisbon Treaty. With the new treaty, the codecision procedure has now become the ordinary legislative procedure, a change that puts the Parliament on an equal footing in all related legislative procedures. Throughout the first year of treaty, the Parliament strove for an equal footing with the council in the European Union's institutional triangle. In September 2009, in an unprecedented move, it committed Manuel Barroso, who was candidate for a second term as president of the European Commission, to detail his key political projects for his second term as commission president before the European Parliament. This gave the Parliament's power to approve all 27 members of the European Commission, including its president, a new quality and can be seen as an attempt to have a say in the setting of long-term policy priorities—which it formally does not have, despite its strengthened role under the Lisbon Treaty.[28]

But despite the upgrade of the European Parliament and despite the strengthening of leadership at the European level, many observers conclude that the European Union has recently become more intergovernmental; some have even observed a move toward renationalization.[29] This impression is mostly a result of the strengthening of the European Council in the management of the crisis and the governance reform process, for instance by the Van Rompuy task force. In particular, small and medium-sized member states are skeptical and criticize the dominant role of the large member states more and more openly. In 2010, the Franco-German Deauville compromise on the reform of the euro area provoked criticism in other European capitals, and in particular those that held or were going to hold the rotating presidency. Neither France nor Germany consulted its partners before presenting the proposal at the subsequent European summit.

Rather involuntarily, Germany has slipped into a new leadership role in the EMU: It has strongly shaped the euro area reform debate, and it sets the pace for other member states through its ambitious consolidation agenda.

---

28. This practice and other elements that strengthen the European Parliament as an actor in the institutional triangle of the European Union are laid down in the revised "Framework Agreement on Relations between the European Parliament and the Commission" of October 2010. This agreement of course does not alter the European Parliament's role as enshrined in primary law, but it is widely seen as being an important tool for the Parliament to further extend its influence over the running legislature.

29. However, even if the European Union has become relatively more intergovernmental, there are to date—apart from the opt-out cases of the Schengen Agreement—no cases in which an actual renationalization has taken place and in which the community method has actually been pushed back. At least in 2010, intergovernmental approaches were chosen in those fields where the community method does not apply, and hence can be read as a way for the European Union to expand its scope of action.

Germany's partners, including France, seem to feel considerable pressure to follow Berlin's policy choices as markets sanction domestic developments much more sensitively since the sovereign debt crisis. The intensified debate over whether EU countries should introduce domestic fiscal rules somewhat similar to Germany's debt brake is no coincidence.

There are striking parallels to the pre-EMU situation, when Germany's partners shadowed the Bundesbank's monetary policy in order to maintain exchange rate stability to the Deutsche mark: Currently, Germany's budgetary and economic policy decisions raise the stakes for other governments that may diverge in their assessments of suitable policies, as financial markets measure all other governments against the German one (a practice made clear by interest spreads between German government bonds and those of Germany's European partners). If this trend persists, the question is how politically sustainable the situation will be in the long run.

In the near future, Germany may increasingly be confronted with a new debate on its responsibility for the economic development of the euro area. This will not be an easy discussion, in particular because Germany's successful growth model is the result of an adaptation process whose components—tough structural reforms, wage restraint, and fiscal austerity—were justified (and broadly accepted) as a necessary consequence of reunification and Germany's entry into the EMU at an overvalued exchange rate.

The fact that the euro area's internal divergences may not be solved solely "if the others do their homework, too" will require sensitive and far-sighted debates between Germany and its EMU partners.[30] A particularly strong role is again to be taken by Germany—and by France, given that the two together account for almost 48 percent of euro area GDP.

References

Artus, Patrick. 2009. *La politique économique de l'Allemagne est-elle un problème pour les autres pays européens?* Natixis Flash 538. Paris: Natixis.

Lallement, Rémi. 2010. *Le régime allemand de croissance tirée par l'exportation: Entre succès et remise en cause.* Working paper. Paris: Centre d'Analyse Stratégique. Available at http://gesd.free.fr/lalmen10.pdf (accessed on December 21, 2011).

---

30. In Germany, comparatively little attention is paid to the intense debate on the German growth model that has developed in France both in the media and in the academic sphere. See, for instance, Lallement (2010) and Artus (2009).

II

LESSONS FROM PAST DEBT CRISES

9

How to Do a Sovereign Debt Restructuring in the Euro Area: Lessons from Emerging-Market Debt Crises

JEROMIN ZETTELMEYER

It is often argued that the obstacles standing in the way of a comprehensive solution to Europe's debt crisis are primarily political, not substantive or technical. This may be true, but political and policy preferences themselves are influenced by assumptions about what works and what does not. These assumptions, in turn, are often based on historical experiences.

In the area of sovereign debt restructuring, there is a lack of recent experience in Europe. Although historically Europe has led the world in sovereign defaults (Reinhart and Rogoff 2009), there has been no major restructuring of privately held sovereign debt in advanced European countries in the postwar period. Perhaps for this reason, the initial reaction of most European governments and the European Central Bank (ECB) in the Greek crisis was to reject any form of debt restructuring as un-European, and the idea that debt restructurings can be conducted in an orderly way as "Panglossian" (Bini-Smaghi

Jeromin Zettelmeyer is director for policy studies at the European Bank for Reconstruction and Development. He thanks, without implication, Mario Blejer, Bill Cline, Mitu Gulati, Christian Kopf, Christoph Trebesch, Shahin Vallée, Winfried Zettelmeyer, and participants at the September 13–14, 2011 Bruegel–Peterson Institute conference on resolving the European debt crisis, for comments and suggestions. The views expressed in this chapter are strictly the author's and should not be attributed to the European Bank for Reconstruction and Development.

2011). While the latter contains an element of truth—debt restructurings in distressed situations are rarely if ever cost free—the resulting unwillingness to consider debt restructuring as one among several possible options to resolve Europe's debt crisis has not been helpful, and has indeed by now been overtaken by events.

The objective of this chapter is to distill some lessons from recent historical experience in emerging-market debt crises for Europe. The selection is both subjective and incomplete.[1] Furthermore, it is clear that these lessons cannot be transposed one-for-one: There are essential differences between the situation of debt-ridden European countries today and typical emerging-market debt crises in the last 15 years. However, this does not mean that past lessons are not useful for Europe—only that specific European circumstances need to be taken into account when applying these lessons. Doing so leads to surprisingly clear-cut conclusions, which are presented in the final section of this chapter.

Five Lessons from Past Experience

1. Collective Action Problems Are Overrated

The fear of a debt restructuring in Europe today seems to be driven by two main concerns. The first is the fear of contagion across sovereigns and from sovereigns to the financial sector. The second is the notion that in the absence of a legal framework to restructure sovereign debt—either of a statutory nature, or in the form of modification clauses in debt contracts, which do not currently exist in the bonds of many euro area countries (see below)—any restructuring would be a legal and practical nightmare and take a long time. The first concern is well founded, but the second one is not.

The fear that "collective action problems" would stand in the way of an orderly resolution of debt crises has a long tradition in modern economic and legal thought, going back to the first signs of sovereign debt troubles in the early 1980s, and gaining prominence after the shift from bank to bond finance in the early 1990s (Rogoff and Zettelmeyer 2002). In light of the difficulties of coordinating even a small number of creditor banks during debt restructuring negotiations in the 1980s, coordinating thousands of bondholders was viewed as a virtual impossibility. Furthermore, the trading of debt in the secondary market made it much easier for distressed debt funds (sometimes known as "vulture funds") to acquire defaulted debt expressly for the purpose of litigation or extraction of a settlement under the threat of litigation. Indeed, the Brady deals of the early 1990s did give rise to a number of lawsuits by "holdout" creditors, some of which were successful.

---

1. For more comprehensive accounts, see Sturzenegger and Zettelmeyer (2007a); and Panizza, Sturzenegger, and Zettelmeyer (2009). The debt crisis of the 1980s is covered by Cline (1995).

The result was a number of policy proposals, by the mid-1990s, to create new institutions or legal frameworks that would facilitate the collective representation of bondholders, in the form of a bankruptcy law for sovereigns, or changes in bond contracts; calls to change European law or the terms of European bonds today are very much in the same vein.[2] However, none of these proposals was realized in time for the next generation of debt crises. As several large emerging-market issuers began to experience debt servicing problems in the late 1990s (Russia, Ukraine, Pakistan, Ecuador, and eventually, in 2001, Argentina), debt market participants faced a series of potentially daunting restructuring challenges without the benefit of virtually any of the institutional improvements that the literature and the official policy community had been urging.

It thus came as a surprise that, with one significant exception (Argentina's external debt restructuring, completed in 2005), all major bond restructurings in the last decade achieved very high levels of creditor participation (over 90 percent) and did not lead to significant litigation. In addition, bond restructurings were completed relatively quickly, with an average delay of only 13 months, compared to 31 months during the era of bank debt restructurings (Trebesch 2010). They were also no more "coercive than those of the earlier bank restructurings," either in terms of the debtor country's approach to negotiations or in terms of final outcome (Enderlein, Trebesch, and von Daniels 2010; Cruces and Trebesch 2011). In particular, creditor losses were about the same, on average, in bond and bank restructurings: about 37 percent, albeit with large variations within both groups (for example, the bank-led debt rollovers of the early and mid-1980s involved much lower losses than the Brady deals of the 1989–97 period and most bond exchanges since then).[3]

What happened? One interpretation is that debtor countries, with a helping hand from a few creative lawyers, in effect created a new ad hoc institution that addressed the creditor coordination problem, namely, take-it-or-leave-it debt exchange offers, in which bondholders were asked to exchange their distressed bonds for new bonds with lower face value and/or longer maturity or lower coupon payments. A new paper (Bi, Chamon, and Zettelmeyer 2011) shows that in this setting, uncertain litigation and recovery prospects

---

2. For the policy proposals of the 1990s, see among others Sachs (1995), Eichengreen and Portes (1995), and Group of Ten, "The Resolution of Sovereign Liquidity Crises," May 1996, available at the Bank for International Settlements website, www.bis.org (accessed on December 16, 2011). For similar suggestions today, see, for example, Angela Merkel's May 19, 2010 speech to the German Parliament, www.bundeskanzlerin.de, or the November 28, 2010, statement by the Eurogroup arguing for collective action clauses.

3. See Cruces and Trebesch (2011). Argentina's default and debt restructuring were an exception on all of these fronts, with relatively low creditor participation (66 percent), protracted litigation, a long time to completion, and a high degree of coerciveness (a haircut of 75 percent). But even in the case of Argentina, the holdouts ultimately did not manage to derail the exchange offer, and Argentina regained market access through domestic issuance even before the exchange had been completed.

will limit the incentives to hold out—and that the more uncertain these are, the better the quality of the exchange offer. The latter may explain why most countries did not aim for high creditor losses: Everything else equal, imposing higher losses on creditors would have increased the probability of the exchange's failure. In some restructurings, the incentive to hold out was further limited through the use of "exit consents," in which bondholders accepting the offer voted to modify the nonpayment terms of the distressed bonds so as to remove typical legal protections (such as the prohibition of legal subordination). Finally, "minimum participation thresholds," in which countries announced that the offer would become effective only with sufficiently high participation, removed the possibility of pure coordination failures—that is, of creditors hesitating to accept the offer for fear that they would be the only ones to do so.

Not all of these legal tools (in particular, the use of exit consents, as explained below) would have general applicability in Europe today. However, the main lesson applies: Debt restructurings could be carried out relatively smoothly within the existing legal framework.

2. "Voluntary" Debt Exchanges Rarely Work

The European official sector has insisted that acceptance of any debt restructuring offer must be strictly voluntary for every creditor. The motivation for this appears to be twofold: allowing debtor countries to avoid the reputational and domestic costs of a coercive default (see below); and avoiding a "credit event" that would expose other sovereigns and financial institutions to contagion, including by triggering credit default swap (CDS) contracts, many of which are assumed to have been written by banks or other systemic financial players.

Unfortunately, voluntary exchange proposals do not have a very good track record. It is useful to distinguish two main types: "purely voluntary" operations, which are conducted at market interest rates and as such do not impose a haircut on creditors by construction; and "near-voluntary" operations, where the exchange is offered at preset terms but the haircut imposed is small.

Purely Voluntary Debt Exchanges. These are structured like normal debt management operations, in which a country retires old debt and issues new debt, typically at a longer residual maturity, or exchanges old debt against new debt. The interest rate on the new debt is determined through auction. Because in a distressed debt situation all but the shortest-term debt is typically considered very risky, purely voluntary exchanges tend to be very expensive in a debt crisis. For example, Argentina undertook its "mega swap" at a time when yields on its medium-term sovereign US debt were on the order of 16 percent.

Perhaps for this reason, such exchanges have also been rare. The three main cases in recent memory are these:

- Russia's GKO-to-eurobond exchange in July of 1998. In this exchange, about $4.4 billion worth of short-term local currency bonds were swapped into 7- and 20-year eurobonds.

- Argentina's mega swap of June 2001. This was a maturity-lengthening operation involving about $29 billion of mostly US dollar–denominated debt.

- Turkey's June 2001 debt exchange. This exchange swapped about US$7.7 billion in short-term local currency debt into $8.5 billion of mostly medium-term and dollar-linked new debt.[4]

All three exchanges were a success in the sense that creditor participation objectives were met or exceeded. However, only Turkey's exchange (in combination with fiscal adjustment, structural reform, and International Monetary Fund [IMF] financing) succeeded in averting an involuntary debt restructuring. In the other two cases, which also occurred in the context of IMF-supported programs, the debt swaps were followed by spectacular defaults (in the case of Russia, six weeks after the exchange; in the case of Argentina, after about six months). The economic costs that arose as a result of these defaults (and, in the case of Argentina, of last-ditch austerity efforts designed to prevent them) were arguably much worse than the costs that would have arisen if Russia or Argentina had attempted an earlier involuntary, but orderly, restructuring attempt instead of a voluntary debt swap.[5]

Near-Voluntary Exchanges. There are also a few cases of external debt exchanges, including Uruguay (in 2003) and the Dominican Republic (in 2005), that were conducted on predetermined (rather than market-determined) terms but were very investor friendly because the authorities avoided sending aggressive signals, the haircuts involved were typically small (13 and about 2 percent, respectively, on average), and all holdouts were eventually repaid (although the authorities did not commit to do so ex ante).[6] These near-voluntary exchanges were successes not only in that they achieved high creditor participation (93 and 94 percent, respectively) but in that a subsequent restructuring was avoided.

What explains why some voluntary or near-voluntary restructuring attempts have succeeded while Russia's and Argentina's attempts failed? It is not difficult to see why a voluntary exchange may *not* succeed. Almost by defi-

---

4. For details on the Russian GKO-to-eurobond exchange and Argentine mega swap, see Sturzenegger and Zettelmeyer (2007a). For details on the Turkey domestic debt swap, see IMF (2001, box 1).

5. For the case of Russia, see Kharas, Pinto, and Ulatov (2001); for Argentina, see Mussa (2002) and IMF Independent Evaluation Office (2004).

6. See Sturzenegger and Zettelmeyer (2007a). Belize's 2007 exchange arguably also belongs in this category, although it involved a higher haircut—about 24 percent, according to Cruces and Trebesch (2011).

nition, these are operations that help the debtor country deal with a liquidity shortage (typically in the form of a bunching of debt redemptions at a time when market access has disappeared or is becoming very expensive), but they do not have an impact on the country's solvency. Indeed, they typically *increase* the debt burden, as investors require compensation for taking on risk over a longer horizon.

However, in three of the five recent cases presented here, voluntary or near-voluntary exchanges did in fact work. What is different about cases such as Turkey or Uruguay compared to Argentina and Russia? Table 9.1 shows some basic fiscal indicators as well as some indicators of growth and competitiveness for the four countries during the year of their voluntary restructuring attempts (labeled year *t*), the two years after that, and the three preceding years. For comparison purposes, the same indicators are shown for Greece, taking 2011 as year *t*.

The main impression that emerges from the table is that based only on data up to year *t*, it would be very difficult to pick the two countries where voluntary restructurings worked. In particular, fiscal indicators for Uruguay and Turkey did not look any better than they did for Argentina and Russia. Debt and deficits were in fact higher in Uruguay than in Argentina, and while Turkey had the lowest public debt level of the group in the year before its voluntary restructuring, it also faced a seemingly impossibly high interest bill of over 12 percent of GDP. In the event, the combination of a restructuring that stretched out debt service, a large primary surplus, and high growth in the years after the restructuring brought the fiscal situation in Turkey back under control, but this would have been difficult to predict.

To the extent that *any* data in table 9.1 help distinguish the countries that avoided "hard" restructurings from those that did not, it is not the fiscal data but rather the behavior of exchange rates and exports. Among the five exchanges discussed above, the three that worked occurred after large devaluations that helped restore competitiveness, while the two that did not were part of a package of measures to defend a pegged exchange rate, and were eventually *followed* by large devaluations. Turkey's 2001 devaluation, in particular, led to an export boom that (combined with favorable external conditions) contributed to a fast recovery over the following years. This seems to have been a more important consequence of the devaluation than the fact that Turkey's public debt, which was partly denominated in foreign currency, almost doubled as a share of GDP (perhaps because even after this doubling, Turkey's debt, at 76 percent of GDP, was still lower than in most euro area countries today, and turned out to be sustainable).

3. "Haircuts" and Debt Relief Are Not the Same

The loss suffered by an investor as a result of a debt restructuring is often referred to as the "haircut." Market practitioners typically evaluate haircuts by comparing the *market* value of the new debt at the time of issuance to the

Table 9.1 Voluntary and near-voluntary debt restructuring attempts: Economic indicators

Country	Indicator	t–3	t–2	t–1	t	t+1	t+2
Argentina	Real GDP growth	3.9	−3.4	−0.8	−4.4	−10.9	8.8
	Inflation	0.9	−1.2	−0.9	−1.1	25.9	13.4
	Arg$ per US dollar (change)	0.0	0.0	0.0	0.0	206.5	−5.3
	Export volumes (change)	11.6	−0.7	2.7	4.3	0.7	5.0
	Primary balance	0.5	−0.8	0.4	−1.3	0.6	3.0
	Interest payments	2.6	3.4	4.1	4.6	2.4	1.9
	Overall balance	−2.1	−4.2	−3.6	−5.9	−1.8	1.1
	Government debt (federal)	37.6	43.0	45.0	53.7	134.6	138.0
Russia	Real GDP growth	−4.1	−3.6	1.4	−5.3	6.3	10.0
	Inflation	197.5	47.7	14.8	27.7	85.7	20.8
	Rubles per US dollar (change)	108.1	12.3	13.0	67.8	153.7	14.3
	Export volumes (change)	7.7	5.4	−1.3	4.7	−0.6	8.6
	Oil	16.4	7.7	−0.4	−3.1	−1.7	17.6
	Nonoil	3.7	4.1	−1.7	8.8	0.0	4.4
	Primary balance	−2.7	−3.2	−3.5	−3.6	2.9	7.5
	Interest payments	3.8	6.3	5.0	4.6	6.0	4.3
	Overall balance	−6.5	−9.5	−8.5	−8.2	−3.1	3.1
	Government debt (federal)	44.9	43.4	53.6	68.1	90.2	61.4
	Memorandum: Oil price (US$/barrel)	7.9	18.4	−5.4	−32.1	37.5	57.0
Turkey	Real GDP growth	3.1	−3.4	6.8	−5.7	6.2	5.3
	Inflation	84.7	64.9	55.0	54.2	45.1	25.3
	TrL per US dollar (change)	71.7	60.6	49.3	96.0	23.0	−0.4
	Export volumes (change)	0.8	−2.2	8.3	22.1	15.9	19.5
	Primary balance	3.4	1.5	4.3	5.0	3.4	4.0
	Interest payments	8.8	10.2	12.3	17.1	14.8	12.9
	Overall balance	−5.4	−8.7	−8.0	−12.1	−11.4	−8.8
	Government debt (federal)	31.0	39.8	38.2	75.7	70.5	63.2
Uruguay	Real GDP growth	−1.4	−3.4	−11.0	2.2	12.3	6.0
	Inflation	4.8	4.4	14.0	19.4	9.2	5.1
	Ur$ per US dollar (change)	6.7	10.1	62.1	30.4	−10.8	−13.3
	Export volumes (change)	6.5	−7.8	−9.1	6.9	22.1	12.4
	Primary balance	−1.5	−1.3	0.0	2.7	3.8	3.6
	Interest payments	2.6	2.9	4.6	6.0	6.0	4.9
	Overall balance	−4.1	−4.2	−4.6	−3.2	−2.2	−1.3
	Public sector debt	45.5	53.8	94.2	108.6	100.5	84.4
Memorandum:							
Greece	Real GDP growth	1.0	−2.3	−4.4	−5.0	...	...
	Inflation	4.2	1.4	4.7	2.9	...	...
	Euros per US dollar (change)	−6.9	5.7	5.0	−6.1	...	...
	Export volumes (change)	3.8	−18.0	4.8	8.7	...	...
	Primary balance	−4.8	−10.3	−4.9	−1.3	...	...
	Interest payments	5.0	5.2	5.5	6.7	...	...
	Overall balance	−9.8	−15.5	−10.4	−8.0	...	...
	Gross total government debt	110.7	127.1	142.8	165.6	...	...

Note: *t* denotes 1998 for Russia (July GKO-to-eurobond swap); 2001 for Argentina and Turkey (June "mega swap" and government debt swap, respectively); 2003 for Uruguay (May–June debt exchange); and 2011 for Greece. Fiscal variables are expressed in percent of GDP, all other variables are expressed in percent. Fiscal variables refer to general government except where otherwise noted.

Sources: Sturzenegger and Zettelmeyer (2007a) for Argentina, Russia, and Uruguay; IMF and Bloomberg for Turkey; IMF October 2011 *World Economic Outlook* for Greece. Column t numbers for Greece are projections.

face value of the old debt. For example, in market convention a haircut of 21 percent means that creditors receive new debt worth 79 cents for each euro of old face value.

Clearly, the market approach to calculating investor losses does not take the same approach to valuing old and new debt flows. One way of clarifying the difference between the two approaches is to interpret both as present values that are computed using different discount rates. The value of the new debt equals the present value of the promised cash flow discounted using the "exit yield" prevailing immediately after a debt exchange. In contrast, the face value of the old debt is equivalent to the present value of its cash flow discounted at the—typically lower—average precrisis coupon rate. The implication is that even when the new and old payment streams are identical, there could be a positive haircut (lower value of the new debt compared to the old debt) purely due to the difference in the discount rate. This does not seem reasonable.[7]

An alternative approach to measuring investor losses that avoids this problem is to discount *both* new and old payment streams using the exit yield, since this reflects the sovereign risk perceived by the market after a debt restructuring. This "net present value haircut" has an intuitive interpretation, namely, the loss suffered by an investor who accepts the exchange offer compared to a situation in which he or she had held on to the old debt and this old debt had been serviced with the same likelihood as the new debt.[8] This approach has by now become standard in the economic literature on sovereign debt crises (Sturzenegger and Zettelmeyer 2007a, 2008; Cruces and Trebesch 2011).

Now consider the perspective of the debtor country. Does, say, a 50 percent net present value haircut imply that the debt burden of the country has declined by 50 percent? Not necessarily, since—as just discussed—the magnitude of the haircut depends on the riskiness of the new debt after a debt restructuring. Consider two countries with identical pre- and postrestructuring debt profiles, and assume that in one country (say, country A, which has better structural policies) debt repayments after the restructuring are regarded as much less risky than in the other country. As a result, the value of the new debt will be higher in country A, and hence the haircut will be lower. Does this imply that the debt relief experienced by country A is lower than that experienced by country B? Clearly not: both countries received exactly the same amount of debt relief.

---

7. There is one situation in which the market is easier to justify, namely, in the event of a default in which the entire face value of the debt becomes contractually due and payable immediately. However, many debt restructurings are preemptive in the sense that they involve exchanging performing debt for new debt.

8. Hence, the net present value haircut in this definition measures the individual investor's temptation to seek a free ride, or equivalently—in the case of a successful exchange—the minimum threat (coercion) that the investor must have felt to join the exchange. See Sturzenegger and Zettelmeyer (2008) for details.

Table 9.2 Haircuts and debt relief in selected debt restructurings
(percent)

Exchange	Haircut	Debt relief estimate
Uruguay 2003, external	13.4	−5.3
Uruguay 2003, domestic	22.3	0
Argentina 2005, external	75.0	70.9
Pakistan 1999, eurobond	31.0	11.2
Ukraine 2000, external	28.9	10.2

Note: Haircut computed using exit yields prevailing after each debt restructuring. Debt relief is computed using expected borrowing yield in normal times. See Sturzenegger and Zettelmeyer (2007b) for details.

Source: Sturzenegger and Zettelmeyer (2007b).

Intuitively, it generally does not make sense to evaluate debt relief at the postrestructuring yield prevailing in the market, because this reflects a risky interest rate (which tends to remain elevated for some time after a debt exchange, as explained in the next section). In other words, it reflects the expectation, on the side of investors, that the country might quite possibly not repay. But the debtor country needs to evaluate its debt burden under the assumption that it *will* repay, that is, by discounting using a risk-free rate, or at most the borrowing rate in normal times. The definition of solvency requires that a country be able to transfer revenues across time, using normal capital market transactions—that is, saving at an international risk-free rate, or borrowing against future revenues at a normal borrowing rate—so as to match its promised debt service. Discounting future debt service at the abnormally high rate that tends to prevail immediately after a debt restructuring makes the future debt burden look smaller than it actually is. It amounts to saying that the country has access to a fantastic savings technology that would enable it to earn a high safe return on its current tax revenues, so as to match the future debt service. But the country does not have such access.

In practice, these different approaches to discounting can drive a big wedge between "haircuts" and "debt relief." They imply that debt relief from the country perspective is typically a lot lower than the haircut from the investor perspective. The reason for this is that debt restructurings usually involve a maturity extension. Hence, comparing the value of new debt with that of the old debt using a low discount rate will result in a smaller difference than if they are compared at a high discount rate, which shrinks particularly the distant future debt service on the new debt. Table 9.2, based on Sturzenegger and Zettelmeyer (2007b), shows the differences for some of the major exchanges of the 1998–2007 period. In most cases, the debt relief implied in these exchanges from the standpoint of the debtor was around 20 percentage points lower than the net present value haircut from an investor perspective. The outlier is Argentina's 2005 exchange, where both numbers are much closer together. The main reason for this is that the exchange happened so long after

Table 9.3 Haircuts implicit in the July 21, 2011 Greek debt exchange proposal (based on 30-year par bond option)

	Discount rate "new" bonds[a]		
Discount rate "old" bonds	3.50%	5.00%	9.00%
3.50%	−10.8	3.0	26.0
5.00%	−16.5	−2.0	22.2
9.00%	−31.9	−15.5	11.9

a. Refers to discount rate used for coupons. Collateralized principal was discounted at 3.787 percent, which was calibrated to achieve a net present value of the new par bond of exactly 79 percent assuming a 9 percent discount rate for the coupons.

Source: Author's calculations.

Argentina's 2001 default—and in the context of a booming economy—that its sovereign spread, as embodied in the secondary market yield prevailing after the January 2005 exchange, had almost reverted back to "normal" levels.[9] As a result, in this case there is hardly any difference between the haircut as computed by the exit yield and debt relief as computed using an estimated "normal" interest rate.

The difference between haircuts and debt relief can also be illustrated using the debt exchange proposal put forward by the Institute of International Finance (IIF) in the context of the July 21 EU heads of government declaration on the Greek crisis, which was later adopted by Greece (although it was superseded by a new plan announced on October 26). Table 9.3 shows the net present value haircuts, for alternative discount rates, that would have arisen in this proposal if the exchange had happened in late July 2011 with full participation (namely, all 81 eligible bonds) based on the terms outlined by Greece in a letter published on August 26, 2011. The haircuts are based on the assumption that all investors would have chosen a 30-year "par bond," which maintained and collateralized the principal using AAA-rated zero-coupon bonds, but extended its maturity far into the future, at a coupon that was about in line with the average coupon of the existing debt.[10] The present value of the principal is fixed at about 33 percent, which corresponds to a discount rate of about 3.8 percent (reflecting the almost risk-free nature of the collater-

9. In addition, when debt restructurings involve significant reductions in face value, their implied net present value debt reduction is less sensitive to the discount rate than in the case of maturity extensions. In the case of Argentina, the 2005 debt exchange reduced the face value of the debt that was tendered by about 43 percent (Sturzenegger and Zettelmeyer 2007a).

10. The bond also assumed a coupon payment of 4.0 percent for the first five years, 4.5 percent for years 6–10, and 5.0 percent for years 11–30. For details, see the letter to the minister of finance outlining the options for the Greek voluntary liability management operations, August 26, 2011, www.ase.gr (accessed on December 16, 2011).

alized principal). Together with a 9 percent discount rate on the coupons, this generates the present value of the new bond targeted by the exchange offer, namely, 79 cents on the euro.

Table 9.3 shows that if the exchange had gone through in late July, assuming an exit yield of 9 percent (not an unreasonable assumption given that medium to long-term Greek bonds were yielding 12 to 16 percent at around the time) the net present value haircut suffered by investors would have been about 12 percent—a bit lower than the haircut imposed by Uruguay in its very market-friendly 2003 external debt exchange. This is quite a bit less than the 21 percent haircut publicized by the IIF (100 minus the net present value of the new bonds assumed in the table), and it puts the plan in the "near-voluntary" category.[11] The table also shows that the 21 percent number could be rationalized by discounting the new bonds at 9 percent while discounting the old bonds at about 5 percent. This approach makes sense: Since the average coupon on the outstanding bonds was in the range of 4.5 to 5.0 percent, discounting at about that rate results in a market value of the old bonds that is approximately equal to their face value.

The discussion so far has focused on the investor losses implied by the IIF plan. But what about debt relief from the country perspective? As argued above, this needs to be computed by comparing the net present values of old and new debt using a discount rate that is no lower than the risk-free interest rate, and no higher than the expected country borrowing rate in normal times. On the assumption that the latter is not much higher than 5 percent (implying a spread of about 150 to 200 basis points over the German bunds), table 9.3 suggests that the debt relief implied by the July exchange proposal would have been somewhere between 0 and -10 percent. In other words, rather than reducing the debt burden by 21 percent, as the headline haircut figure that was widely publicized after the July 21 summit seemed to suggest, the exchange would have *increased* the debt burden by up to 10 percent in net present value terms.

Two factors would have changed the debt burden from the country perspective: the extension of coupon payments into the future, adding to the total nominal debt service; and the collaterization of the principal. The effect of the former on the net present value of the debt burden depends on whether the discount rate that is applied is higher or lower than the coupon rate on the new debt. A 5 percent discount rate would have been slightly higher than the average coupon on the proposed discount bond (which started at 4 percent and rose to 5 percent after 10 years); hence, based on this effect alone, the debt burden should have been slightly reduced (positive haircut). However, this is offset by the carry cost of collateralizing the principal: Since the country would have needed to borrow to purchase collateral, paying a lower interest rate than

11. The point that the net present value haircut implicit in the IIF proposal was much lower than the 21 percent headline figure was made almost immediately by a number of researchers and analysts, including Ghezzi, Aksu, and Garcia Pascual (2011). See also Kopf (2011) and Richard Cabral, "Greece's 2nd Bailout: Debt Restructuring with No Debt Reduction?" VoxEU, July 29, 2011, www. voxeu.org (accessed on December 16, 2011).

its borrowing rate, collateralization would have raised the debt burden compared to a situation where the principal would not have been collateralized. At a 5 percent discount rate, the net effect would have been a small increase in the debt burden. If the coupon payments are discounted using a 3.5 percent rate (approximately equal to the AAA long bond rate prevailing in July 2011), both effects go in the same direction, as the extension of coupon payments at a rate that exceeds the discount rate also increases the debt burden, resulting in a total increase of the net present value debt burden by 10.8 percent.

4. Default Can Be Costly and Contagious, but These Costs Are Generally Short-Lived

Empirical research on the costs of default for the debtor country suggests that these come mainly in two flavors: repercussions in international credit markets (in the form of loss of capital market access and higher borrowing costs, not only for the sovereign but also for the private sector), and the direct impact on the domestic financial sector, which is often heavily exposed to the government bonds that are being restructured (Panizza, Sturzenegger, and Zettelmeyer 2009; Borensztein and Panizza 2009; Cruces and Trebesch 2011; and Trebesch 2009). If the crisis is not well managed, it can lead to the collapse of the domestic financial system—creating bank insolvencies and a credit crunch, and also triggering bank runs and an impairment of the payments system. These occurred, for example, after the disorderly defaults of Russia (in 1998) and Argentina (in 2001), and they also accompanied the default of Ecuador (in 1999) and many other countries.

The existence of these effects is not in dispute, nor is the fact that other potential channels—trade sanctions and other direct sanctions, for example, which were debated at one point as a possible deterrent of default—have not mattered much in recent history. There is controversy, however, on two points.

First, it is not clear how large the output repercussions of these two channels are. Attempts to empirically relate defaults to declines in output suffer from the standard reverse causality problem: An economic downturn can be a cause as well as a consequence of a default, since it depresses a country's debt service capacity. Indeed, the raw data (see figure 9.1) suggest that most of the output decline around default episodes tends to *precede* the default. This said, some of this decline could be due to capital or deposit flight that anticipates the default, and in that sense is caused by it. Furthermore, the fact that a default can cause a banking crisis (as well as the other way around) is not controversial, and there is plenty of evidence in turn that banking crises cause and/or prolong recessions.[12] Hence, a general policy lesson is that debt restructurings should be undertaken in a way that protects the financial system and makes contingency plans for recapitalizing banks (for example, using new, performing bonds) and

---

12. See Dell'Ariccia, Detragiache, and Rajan (2008) and Jordà, Schularick, and Taylor (2011), among others.

Figure 9.1   Recent defaults and GDP growth

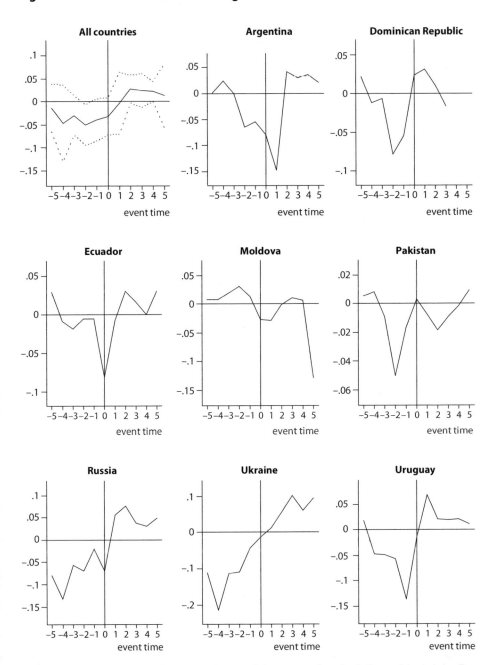

Note: The graphs plot the residuals of a regression that controls for country and year fixed effects and that includes all developing countries that had an income per capita greater than $500 in the year 2000.

Source: Panizza, Sturzenegger, and Zettelmeyer (2009).

dealing with bank runs. The defining feature of an "orderly" restructuring is that it does not drag the financial system into panic and insolvency.

A second area of disagreement, at least until very recently, was about the capital market repercussions of a default. There used to be a tension between academic economists and practitioners on this point: While practitioners (and particularly policymakers) seemed to take seriously the threat that defaulters would be "punished" by capital markets, economic researchers found at most small and passing effects of defaults on borrowing conditions. This controversy has to some extent been settled by a new paper, by Cruces and Trebesch (2011), who show that if the magnitude of defaults is measured more accurately—namely, using the net present value haircut as defined in the previous section—defaults have robust and fairly sizeable effects both on the costs of borrowing and on the length of the market exclusion period. An increase of one standard deviation in the haircut, which in their sample is an increase of 22 percentage points, implies an increase in borrowing cost by about 150 basis points in the first two years after a restructuring is complete, and of about 70 basis points in years 4 and 5. It also lowers the probability of reaccessing capital markets by about 50 percent in any given year.

However, even these stronger results do not seem to qualitatively challenge the finding of previous authors (e.g., Borensztein and Panizza 2009) that the costs of defaults are short-lived. Six years after a default, an impact of haircuts on borrowing costs can no longer be detected. And even though the average period of credit market exclusion in Cruces and Trebesch's sample is five years following a restructuring, the median is only three years, suggesting that there is a "tail" of a few countries with very long exclusion periods that distorts the average. Indeed, if one considers the seven main restructuring cases of the 1998–2005 period shown in figure 9.1, only one—Pakistan—suffered a market exclusion period of more than two years.[13] For the most part, countries that restructured their debts in the last 15 years were able to reaccess capital markets almost immediately after concluding a deal with creditors, albeit at temporarily higher borrowing costs.

Finally, the history of defaults teaches that the short-term pain of default can hit not just the debtor country but also other countries that are linked

---

13. Whether Argentina regained access to international borrowing after its 2005 debt exchange is hotly debated (see the chapter by Cline in this volume). Following its 2001 default, Argentina's central government did not issue any new bond in international markets. However, it borrowed from private nonresidents through other channels, particularly locally issued bonds. According to Cruces and Trebesch (2011), Argentina regained "partial" access to international capital market (meaning a return to positive net public borrowing from private external creditors) immediately following its 2005 restructuring, but not "full" access, defined as net transfers from private external creditors (new borrowing minus debt service) in excess of 1 percent of GDP. According to the World Bank's *Global Development Finance* database, net transfers from private external creditors to Argentina were about 0.8 percent of GDP during 2005–07, which is close to but below the usual threshold. Note that these data do not take into account local currency borrowing. See World Bank *Global Development Finance* database, 2011, http://data.worldbank.org/data-catalog/global-development-finance (accessed on December 16, 2011).

through trade and financial channels. The lesson of Russia's 1998 default is that these channels can sometimes operate between countries that have virtually no direct trade and financial relations, a result of common lenders who retreat from all financial markets that are viewed as sharing similar risk characteristics (Van Rijckeghem and Weder 2003). Hence, Russia's 1998 default did not just trigger balance of payments and debt crises in neighboring Ukraine and Moldova, but also precipitated a sudden stop of capital flows to countries such as Argentina, Chile, Brazil, Bolivia, Mexico, and Turkey, which suffered recessions or sharp slowdowns in growth, and in the case of Brazil a currency crisis that led to the floating of the real in February of 1999. In contrast, Argentina's 2001 default did not have sharp global repercussions (perhaps because it was largely anticipated), but it triggered a banking crisis, currency crisis, and eventually a debt restructuring in neighboring Uruguay.

The overall conclusion is that the costs of debt restructurings (1) can be severe, depending largely on whether they trigger a banking crisis; (2) can have severe costs for innocent bystanders that are hit by contagion; and (3) do not extend beyond the length of a typical cyclical downturn. Of course, all downturns—and particularly downturns triggered by banking crises—tend to have "permanent" effects on output levels in the sense that growth after the downturn does not typically make up for the lost output (Cerra and Saxena 2008). Other than in this very general sense, however, debt restructurings, as painful as they may be for a few years, do not seem to have permanent costs.

5. Precrisis Moral Hazard Is Much More Important than "Debtor Moral Hazard"

The economic literature on sovereign debt, particularly the theoretical literature, is obsessed with the possibility that a sovereign debtor might opportunistically decide not to repay. This phenomenon is variously referred to as "repudiation," "debtor moral hazard," or the "willingness-to-pay problem." The reason for this obsession is that the willingness-to-pay problem is the main distinguishing feature of sovereign debt compared to corporate debt. While there are standard domestic mechanisms that enforce corporate debt repayment, at least in countries with reasonable courts and legal frameworks, this is not generally true for sovereign debt. Hence, sovereign debt could not exist unless the willingness-to-pay problem were somehow overcome.

In practice, however, a lack of willingness to pay appears to play almost no role in explaining actual defaults. This does not necessarily contradict the theory: It could simply be that the costs of default for the debtor country (as surveyed in the previous section) are sufficiently large so as to more or less rule out repudiations; or it could be that the private costs of default for the policymakers in charge (who stand to lose power after a default, or perhaps merely find it embarrassing to meet their graduate school friends after defaulting) are likewise too large (Borensztein and Panizza 2009).

To be sure, there are occasional examples of such repudiations—that is, defaults at a time when the debt could have been serviced without unusually high domestic sacrifices. Typically, these happen after revolutions or other large political swings in which the new government refuses to take responsibility for the debts of the old government.[14] For the most part, however, defaults are preceded by exceptional economic distress, and often by adjustment efforts intended to avoid the default. To the extent that the behavior of policymakers in these episodes suggests a moral hazard problem, this does not appear to be that governments default too easily, but that they cling to adjustment and repayment in seemingly hopeless situations. In some cases, this behavior can be rationalized through the costs of default; in others, it looks like a "gamble for redemption" that is not in the best interests of the debtor country constituents.[15]

This is not to say, however, that moral hazard plays no role in causing debt crises. Indeed it does, but it is moral hazard of a different kind, which works through inadequate economic policies, rather than outright repudiation. *Conditional* on economic fundamentals, moral hazard plays very little role in causing default; however, it plays a big role in shaping the fundamentals that get countries into trouble in the first place. This brand of moral hazard includes a whole range of distortions to capture by special interests, including limited liability (policymakers who capture the upside of risky policies but not the full downside) and procrastination (policymakers who have short horizons because they may not expect to stay in power for very long). For every major default case in the 1998–2007 period, a story can be told that involves one or several of these factors (Sturzenegger and Zettelmeyer 2007a).

Importantly, these stories do not always involve profligate fiscal policies—often they are about allowing, and benefiting from, private sector debt accumulation. The recent European debt crisis represents a mix in this regard, ranging from a mainly fiscal story in Greece to a private debt story in Ireland. In both cases, however, the question of how to correct precrisis policy failures is a much bigger issue than the question of how to deter a country from defaulting.

Implications for Europe Today

The history of emerging-market debt crises has implications for Europe at two levels.

First, it teaches Europe lessons in financial architecture. The architecture of the European monetary Union was built on the premise that debt crises

---

14. The most recent example of such a repudiation was Ecuador's 2009 default. Earlier examples include Mexico in 1861, Russia in 1917, and Cuba in 1960. In addition, some governments display repudiation-like behavior *after* a default, by insisting on a debt restructuring offer that is widely viewed as understating the country's ability to pay. Argentina's 2005 default is the clearest recent example of such a case.

15. See Sturzenegger and Zettelmeyer (2007a, chapter 11) for a discussion.

could not happen, because countries would follow fiscal rules laid out in the Stability and Growth Pact. This turned out to be twice wrong: A large debt crisis did happen, in part because fiscal rules were ignored, but more importantly because of problems that could not have been prevented even if the Stability and Growth Pact rules had been followed to the letter—including large financial sector imbalances, in the form of a credit boom and a housing bubble, and a deterioration in competitiveness.

The history of emerging-market crises suggests that when Europe sets out to rebuild its architecture, it needs a financial safety net—because crises do happen, and debt restructurings are costly and should be avoided through a combination of financing and adjustment whenever possible. At the same time, it needs to pay more attention to incentives facing policymakers—because precrisis moral hazard at the expense of "innocent bystanders" that may include both national taxpayers and other countries is always an issue. A key question facing Europe today is how to reconcile the presence of implicit and future explicit safety nets with good incentives. This question goes beyond the scope of this article.[16]

Second, the history of emerging-market crises has some implications for how to handle a debt restructuring in Europe today if it must happen. Before developing these implications, it is important to recognize some differences between the current situation in Europe and typical emerging-market debt crises. These differences cut both ways. In some respects, they make the crisis more difficult to resolve; in others, they make if more manageable.

Three main facts complicate the European crisis compared with past emerging-market debt crises:

- Contagion is an even bigger problem, as painfully demonstrated by the behavior of financial markets in recent months. In part, this is because of direct financial links within Europe—for example, government bond holdings by European financial institutions, cross-border activities of European banking groups that may be threatened in a debt restructuring, and credit default swaps that may threaten the solvency of institutions that have written such protection. In addition, the fundamental problems underlying the debt crisis in one euro area country (high sovereign debt, lack of competitiveness, and hence poor medium-term growth prospects) are to some extent present in other European countries, particularly within southern Europe. If Greece, for example, cannot solve its problems without restructuring its debt, this might be viewed—rightly or wrongly—as a precedent that raises the chances of restructurings elsewhere. This is presumably one of the reasons why a Greek debt restructuring was (until recently) fiercely resisted by most European governments and by the European Central Bank.

---

16. For some answers, see Jeromin Zettelmeyer, "A Bridge to Somewhere: Building a Comprehensive Strategy for Resolving the Eurozone Debt Crisis, VoxEU," October 24, 2011, www.voxeu.org (accessed on December 16, 2011).

- Unlike their emerging-market counterparts, debt-ridden euro area countries do not have the option of currency devaluation (or only at enormous political and economic cost, via an exit from the euro area). While currency crises have sometimes triggered debt crises in countries with foreign currency debts, they have generally helped restore fiscal solvency *after* a debt restructuring, both by helping with fiscal adjustment (for example, by cutting the wage bill of the government in real terms) and by restoring competitiveness and growth. In the euro area, this instrument is not available.

- Finally, debt and deficits in some euro area countries are larger than they were in typical emerging-market debt crisis cases. This is true particularly for Greece, which has much higher debt-to-GDP levels than virtually any emerging-market country in recent history (with the exception of some small island economies[17]). In spite of large and for the most part successful fiscal efforts over the last two years, it also still has a primary deficit, implying that even a complete stop of debt service would not eliminate the need for further fiscal adjustment.

Against these complications, two main facts make a European debt restructuring easier to manage, in principle—that is, politics allowing—than in an emerging-market crisis case.

- In a technical and legal sense, the bonds of most euro area countries are very easy to restructure, because they are largely issued under domestic law and lack typical legal protections such as *pari passu* clauses (prohibiting legal subordination) or "negative pledge" clauses (prohibiting the issuance of new collateralized debt unless existing debt is enhanced in the same way) (Gulati and Smets 2011, Gulati and Zettelmeyer 2011). This means that collective action problems could be overcome even more easily in Europe than was the case in typical emerging-market crises. For example, once an agreement is negotiated with a majority of creditors, this agreement could be imposed on holdouts through an act of parliament that changes the payment terms of the bonds. Alternatively, the domestic legislature could "retrofit" collective action clauses to allow a majority of creditors to negotiate and agree to new payment terms on behalf of all creditors.[18] Yet alternatively, an exchange offer could be incentivized by legally subordinating the old debt to the new debt in the event of a new restructuring, or enhancing the new debt using collateral. Note that the first two options are not consistent with the notion of "voluntary" restructuring (since they coerce individual creditors who may disagree with the deal

---

17. The debt of Seychelles exceeded 140 percent prior to its 2009–10 debt restructuring (IMF 2011). Dominica and Grenada had public debt in the range of 120 to 130 percent of GDP before announcing debt restructurings in 2004 (IMF 2005).

18. See Buchheit and Gulati (2010) for the case of Greece.

agreed to by the majority), but the last one may well be (see Gulati and Zettelmeyer 2011 for details).

- From the perspective of managing a debt restructuring, membership in a currency union is a boon as well as a straitjacket. While it means that countries cannot devalue or inflate their way out of a crisis, it also implies that there is a supranational central bank that can both help safeguard the domestic financial system in the context of an orderly restructuring (by providing liquidity to banks and forestalling bank runs as banks are being recapitalized) and limit contagion (for example, through secondary market purchases of the public debt of "innocent bystanders" that are hit by the crisis and through funding to European banking groups).

The final step is to transpose the lessons from emerging-market debt restructurings into this European context. There are six main points that should be considered.

First, the restructuring offer should be comprehensive, covering all government bonds, and involuntary in the sense that holdouts should not be promised full repayment.[19] In the event that the exchange is successful and no payments are actually missed, an involuntary exchange offer will not in fact trigger CDS protection. Even if it does, the volume of this would be small in the case of Greece.[20]

Second, there are at least two straightforward and arguably fair ways of implementing a debt restructuring deal in Europe. One would be a standard debt exchange in which bondholders are offered an instrument with upgraded legal protections (see below). The other would be to use domestic law to "retrofit" a standard modification (collective action) clause on all domestic law bonds (for example, of the type that euro area heads of government have pledged to include in all new debt issuance beginning in June 2013; see Eurogroup 2010). After negotiating a restructuring agreement with banks and other large investors that hold a supermajority of bonds, this clause could be used to change the payment terms for all bondholders, hence eliminating the free rider problem. A hybrid between the two options is also feasible, in which a collective action clause is retrofitted but used only as a backup to incentivize a standard debt exchange offer.

Third, the *financial* terms of the new (or modified) debt instruments should be designed to do the following:

---

19. Even near-voluntary restructurings, such as in Uruguay (in 2003), did not promise holdouts full repayment. Although in most successful restructurings the volume of nonparticipating debt was so small that holdouts could be, and for the most part were, repaid in full, the related uncertainty was an important factor in the success of exchanges that did not benefit from collective action clauses. Restructurings that invoke collective action clauses are involuntary by definition.

20. According to market sources, there is approximately €4 billion in net CDS exposure, against approximately €200 billion in privately held Greek debt. See, for example, Felix Salmon, "Why the Greek CDS Market Is OK," Reuters, October 28, 2011, http://blogs.reuters.com.

- achieve sufficiently high debt relief to restore solvency, but no more (since unnecessarily high haircuts damage a country's reputation in credit markets),

- obviate a return to capital markets for at least six years (the window over which a restructuring typically triggers higher borrowing costs),

- avoid maturity extensions beyond 10–15 years, since a long maturity extension tends to drive a wedge between haircuts from an investor perspective and debt relief from a country perspective (except as one possibility in a menu of options, coupled with a par or quasi-par bond), and

- possibly include a GDP "kicker" to give investors some extra value without undermining the debt relief achieved in the restructuring.[21]

Fourth, the *nonfinancial* terms of the new or modified debt should include the standard creditor protections present in international bonds (but not currently present in typical euro area debt contracts), such as *pari passu*, negative pledge, cross-default, and acceleration clauses (Gulati and Zettelmeyer 2011). In addition, to the extent that the restructuring is implemented through a debt exchange offer, the new bonds offered to investors should be international bonds under foreign jurisdiction (e.g., that of England or Luxembourg) and with standard documentation. This "upgrade" with respect to legal protections implies a higher value of the new bonds from an investor perspective for any given payment terms (and hence for a given degree of debt relief). It is a way of minimizing the wedge between creditor losses and debt relief.

Fifth, restructurings should take place in the context of programs supported by the EU and IMF that both safeguard the banking system, by setting aside funds for recapitalization, and provide conditional financing of the remaining fiscal deficit. The latter is important both to allow time for gradual and orderly fiscal adjustment and to reassure the ECB that the domestic banking system, and with it ECB liquidity support, will not become a source of financing for the government in the absence of other sources.

Finally, European institutions, including the European Central Bank, should be used to prevent contagion—both by providing liquidity support to the European banking system and by intervening (or threatening to intervene) to cap sovereign risk premia of solvent countries.

To conclude: the experience of emerging-market debt crises shows that debt restructurings are costly and unpleasant, but manageable. Indeed, the costs of debt restructurings are to a large extent determined by how they are managed. There are vast differences in cost between a disorderly default that

---

21. Whether such a "kicker" is a good idea or not will depend in part on the credibility of growth-oriented reforms. If there is a gap between the commitment of the government to reform and the credibility of these reforms to the outside world, then GDP kickers that promise higher coupons if growth exceeds a certain level could turn very expensive, in the sense that the growth thresholds need to be set very low in order to generate some value to investors. In such circumstances the introduction of GDP kickers should be postponed until after the reforms begin to show fruit.

shuts down the financial system of a country and generates contagion, and a preemptive restructuring that does not. While Europe has every reason to avoid debt restructurings in fundamentally solvent countries, it also has the tools and institutions to manage debt restructurings and contain their costs if a restructuring should prove necessary.

References

Bi, Ran, Marcos Chamon, and Jeromin Zettelmeyer. 2011. *The Problem That Wasn't: Coordination Failures in Sovereign Debt Restructurings.* IMF Working Paper WP/11/265. Washington: International Monetary Fund.

Bini-Smaghi, Lorenzo. 2011. Private Sector Involvement: From (Good) Theory to (Bad) Practice. Speech at the Reinventing Bretton Woods Committee, Berlin, June 6. Available at www.ecb.int (accessed on December 15, 2011).

Borensztein, Eduardo, and Ugo Panizza. 2009. The Costs of Sovereign Default. *IMF Staff Papers* 56, no. 4: 683–741.

Buchheit, Lee C., and Mitu Gulati. 2010. *How to Restructure Greek Debt.* Duke Law Working Paper 47. Available at http://scholarship.law.duke.edu/working_papers/47.

Cerra, Valerie, and Sweta Chaman Saxena. 2008. Growth Dynamics: The Myth of Economic Recovery. *American Economic Review* 98, no. 1: 439–57.

Cline, William R. 1995. *International Debt Reexamined.* Washington: Institute for International Economics.

Cruces, Juan, and Christoph Trebesch. 2011. *Sovereign Defaults: The Price of Haircuts.* CESifo Working Paper No. 3604. Munich: Center for Economic Studies.

Dell'Ariccia, Giovanni, Enrica Detragiache, and Raghuram Rajan. 2008. The Real Effect of Banking Crises. *Journal of Financial Intermediation* 17, no. 1: 89–112.

Eichengreen, Barry, and Richard Portes. 1995. *Crisis? What Crisis? Orderly Workouts for Sovereign Debtors.* London: Centre for Economic Policy Research.

Enderlein, Henrik, Christoph Trebesch, and Laura von Daniels. 2010. *Sovereign Debt Disputes.* Berlin: Hertie School of Governance. Available at www.henrik-enderlein.de.

Eurogroup. 2010. Statement by the Eurogroup. Available at www.consilium.europa.eu. (accessed on December 16, 2011).

Ghezzi, Piero, Cagdas Aksu, and Antonio Garcia Pascual. 2011. *Greece: Assessing the New Debt Proposal.* Barclays Capital Economic Research, July 26, 2011.

Gulati, Mitu, and Frank Smets. 2011. The Evolution of Eurozone Government Debt Contracts. Duke University. Photocopy.

Gulati, Mitu, and Jeromin Zettelmeyer. 2011. Can a Debt Restructuring Be Both Voluntary and Deliver Real Debt Relief? The Case of Greece. Duke University. Photocopy.

IMF (International Monetary Fund). 2001. *Turkey: Eighth Review Under the Stand-By Arrangement.* IMF Country Report no. 01/137. Washington.

IMF (International Monetary Fund). 2005. *Eastern Caribbean Currency Union: 2005 Article IV Consultation—Staff Report and Public Information Notice on the Executive Board Discussion on the Eastern Caribbean Currency Union.* IMF Country Report no. 05/304. Washington. Available at www.imf.org.

IMF (International Monetary Fund). 2011. *Seychelles: 2010 Article IV Consultation and Second Review Under the Extended Arrangement, Request for Rephasing of Disbursements, and Financing Assurances Review—Staff Report; Staff Supplement; Public Information Notice and Press Release on the Executive*

Board Discussion; and Statement by the Executive Director for Seychelles. IMF Country Report no. 11/5. Washington. Available at www.imf.org.

IMF (International Monetary Fund) Independent Evaluation Office. 2004. *Report on the Evaluation of the Role of the IMF in Argentina, 1991–2001*. Washington.

Jordà, Òscar, Moritz Schularick, and Alan M. Taylor. 2011. *When Credit Bites Back: Leverage, Business Cycles, and Crises*. NBER Working Paper no. 17621. Cambridge, MA: National Bureau of Economic Research.

Kharas, Homi, Brian Pinto, and Sergei Ulatov. 2001. An Analysis of Russia's 1998 Meltdown. *Brookings Papers on Economic Activity* 1:1–50.

Kopf, Christian. 2011. *An Evaluation of the French Proposal for a Restructuring of Greek Debt*. CEPS Policy Brief No. 247. Brussels: Centre for European Policy Studies.

Mussa, Michael. 2002. *Argentina and the Fund: From Triumph to Tragedy*. Washington: Institute for International Economics.

Panizza, Ugo, Federico Sturzenegger, and Jeromin Zettelmeyer. 2009. The Economics and Law of Sovereign Debt and Default. *Journal of Economic Literature* 47, no. 3 (September): 651–98.

Reinhart, Carmen M., and Kenneth S. Rogoff. 2009. *This Time Is Different: Eight Centuries of Financial Folly*. Princeton: Princeton University Press.

Rogoff, Kenneth S., and Jeromin Zettelmeyer. 2002. Bankruptcy Procedures for Sovereigns: A History of Ideas, 1976–2001. *IMF Staff Papers* 49, no. 3: 470–507.

Sachs, Jeffrey D. 1995. Do We Need an International Lender of Last Resort? Frank D. Graham Lecture, Princeton University, April.

Sturzenegger, Federico, and Jeromin Zettelmeyer. 2007a. *Debt Defaults and Lessons from a Decade of Crises*. Cambridge, MA: MIT Press.

Sturzenegger, Federico, and Jeromin Zettelmeyer. 2007b. Creditors' Losses versus Debt Relief: Results from a Decade of Sovereign Debt Crisis. *Journal of the European Economic Association* 5, no. 2–3: 343–51.

Sturzenegger, Federico, and Jeromin Zettelmeyer. 2008. Haircuts: Estimating Investor Losses in Sovereign Debt Restructurings, 1998–2005. *Journal of International Money and Finance* 27, no. 5: 780–805.

Trebesch, Christoph. 2009. *The Cost of Aggressive Sovereign Debt Policies: How Much Is the Private Sector Affected?* IMF Working Paper WP/09/29. Washington: International Monetary Fund.

Trebesch, Christoph. 2010. *Delays in Sovereign Debt Restructurings: Should We Really Blame the Creditors?* Berlin: Hertie School of Governance.

Van Rijckeghem, Caroline, and Beatrice Weder. 2003. Spillovers Through Banking Centers: A Panel Data Analysis. *Journal of International Money and Finance* 22, no. 4: 483–509.

10

Sovereign Debt Restructuring: The Legal Context

LEE C. BUCHHEIT

Sovereign debtors are unique. Unlike corporate borrowers and individual debtors, overextended sovereign debtors have no institutional framework, such as a bankruptcy code, that will permit them to obtain debt relief without worrying about hostile creditor actions. Although proposals for such a transnational sovereign bankruptcy regime have been floating around for years, they are still floating.

How to Restructure Sovereign Debt

The legal context in which any sovereign debt restructuring must proceed assumes that individual creditors of all types (multilateral, bilateral, commercial) will be holding debt instruments that constitute legal, valid, binding, and enforceable obligations of the sovereign debtor. The challenge for the sovereign debt restructurer is to cajole or to bludgeon the holders of these instruments into giving debt relief; the creditors cannot be compelled to grant relief. Broadly speaking, there are two options for achieving this objective—carrots and sticks.

The Carrots

A variety of techniques can be used to entice a creditor into giving debt relief to a sovereign borrower. For example, in return for a stretch-out of maturities,

Lee C. Buchheit is a partner in the New York office of Cleary Gottlieb Steen & Hamilton LLP. He has been an advisor to the Greek government on its debt exchange efforts since late July 2011.

the interest rate on the debt can be raised. To balance the negative net present value effect of a principal haircut, the sovereign can offer credit enhancements, such as the posting of collateral security or guarantees from creditworthy entities to secure the residual amount of the restructured claim. Credit enhancements feature prominently in the July 21, 2011, restructuring package for Greek debt.

The financial problem with sweeteners of this kind is that they are (to use a pharmacological term) contraindicated for a sovereign in deep financial distress. In other words, they are expensive.

The legal problem with sweeteners is that they may run afoul of the sovereign's existing contractual covenants. The posting of collateral security to benefit a new creditor may violate a so-called negative pledge restriction (a promise not to create secured indebtedness in the future). An attempt to give legal seniority to new claims may violate the sovereign's *pari passu* clauses.

The Sticks

If a sovereign cannot, or does not wish to, pour honey over a debt restructuring proposal, it must find some other method of encouraging creditors to grant a measure of debt relief. There are, by the way, only three types of debt relief—an extension of maturities, a reduction of interest rates, and a haircut to principal. They can obviously be combined in limitless ways.

Over the last 30 years, a number of techniques have evolved to induce less-than-voluntary participation in a sovereign debt restructuring. Among these are the following:

- *Default, real or threatened.* In every sovereign debt restructuring of the last 30 years, except for the July 21, 2011, proposal for a Greek debt restructuring, the sovereign has either suspended payments on its existing debt before the restructuring was launched or threatened (explicitly or implicitly) a payment default on any debt instrument that did not join the restructuring. Sovereign debt restructurers have gotten quite expert in delivering this "abandon hope all ye who do *not* enter here" message.

- *Exit consents.* Staring with Ecuador in 2000, debt restructurings implemented through bond exchange offers have frequently used a technique known as exit consents. As participating bondholders tender their existing bonds into an exchange, they give the sovereign a proxy to vote at a bondholders' meeting to strip away features of the old bonds in a way that renders those instruments less attractive to prospective holdout creditors. For example, these voting proxies can permit the sovereign to strip out clauses in the old bonds such as the waiver of sovereign immunity, the choice of foreign governing law, the submission to foreign court jurisdiction, the acceleration provision, and the requirement to keep the bonds listed on an exchange. Because many bonds permit modifications of this kind to nonpayment terms with only a bare majority of the holders consenting, this approach can be an effective coercive technique. It does not make the new instruments being offered to creditors any prettier, but it makes the old instruments a whole lot uglier.

- *Collective action clauses.* Collective action clauses (CACs) are contractual provisions that permit a majority or supermajority of creditors to modify features of an instrument, including its payment terms (maturity, principal amount, or interest rate), with the consequence that the change is binding on any dissenting minority of the holders. CACs have been used in English law bonds since 1879. They were reintroduced into New York law–governed sovereign bonds (after an 80-year absence) in 2003 and now appear in most sovereign bonds governed by New York law. Three countries (Uruguay, the Dominican Republic, and Argentina) have "aggregated" CACs that permit a single vote of all bondholders across multiple series of bonds. CACs make a sovereign debt stock more malleable. In effect, the sovereign needs to win the hearts and minds of only 76 percent, not 100 percent, of its creditor group in order to implement the restructuring.

- *Local law.* If a sovereign's debt stock is governed by the sovereign's own law, it may be possible to change features of that law to facilitate a debt restructuring. Emerging-market sovereigns have generally not been able to issue bonds in international markets governed by their own law because investors feared some local legislative mischief down the road. The debt stocks of European peripheral sovereigns like Greece and Ireland, however, are predominantly local law governed. It remains to be seen whether one of these sovereigns will use this advantage to restructure those debts.

What Does History Teach?

What lessons can be gleaned from the past 30 years of sovereign debt restructurings, and how might those lessons be applied to the debt crisis in peripheral Europe? I offer six candidates, three involving measures designed to prevent a crisis or mitigate the severity of one that cannot be avoided, and three in the realm of how to handle a crisis once it erupts.

Lesson 1: Don't Let a Sovereign Debt Problem Become a Banking Sector Problem

Sovereign debt crises come in two forms: (1) those that are accompanied by a threat to the stability of the banking sector in the debtor country and/or important creditor countries, and (2) those that are not. Of these, the former are far more difficult and dangerous.

The debt crisis of the 1980s posed a clear and present danger to many of the world's international banks because of their precariously high exposures to emerging-market sovereigns, aggravated by the absence (or limited amount) of prudential reserves against that exposure. As a result, the debt restructuring technique adopted in 1982 (which lasted until the Brady Initiative in 1989) avoided any principal write-downs in order to preserve the accounting fiction that allowed the bank creditors to hold restructured sovereign credits on their books at par. This was an example, as the euro area peripheral sovereign debt crisis is today, of a situation in which the fragile balance sheets of creditor banks drove a debt restructuring technique that was in many respects artificial and visibly inadequate to deal with the problem. Nicholas Brady and his debt reduction plan came along only after seven years had passed, a period during which the creditor banks had built up their loan loss reserves.

When a sovereign debtor allows its own domestic banks to bulk up on government debt obligations, things can get even more complicated. Jamaica in the spring of 2010 was a good example. Well over half of the domestic law government bonds were in the hands of Jamaican financial institutions. Any restructuring of that debt stock involving a principal haircut would only have precipitated a domestic banking crisis, so no principal haircut was inflicted. Greece suffers a similar problem today.

Encouraging commercial banks to buy government bonds can be very tempting. This practice allows sovereigns to issue more debt, more cheaply, than they otherwise could. Encouragement can take the form of a zero risk weighting of such bonds for bank capital purposes, or easy access to a central bank discount window with little or no haircutting of any sovereign bonds offered as collateral. But the clear lesson of the last 30 years is this: when sovereign debt instruments are held predominantly by regulated financial institutions, it may prove impossible to address the sovereign's debt stock in a sensible way without triggering a banking crisis. The result? The sovereign's debt stock will probably be addressed, at least initially, in a less-than-sensible way.

Lesson 2: If It Can't Be Avoided, Don't Try

History tells us that sovereign debtors usually delay too long in facing up to an unsustainable debt stock. Mexico's international reserves in the summer of 1982 (the year Mexico declared its moratorium) "went negative"—whatever that means. The reasons are perfectly understandable. Politicians do not like to admit that they have ruined the economy (which is why most sovereign debt restructurings have begun only after a change in administration). Politicians hope that things can be held together until they leave office. Politicians routinely evince a profound belief in the efficacy of prayer.

Lesson 3: Keep Track

How often over the last 30 years have we seen a sovereign borrower lose the end of the string in terms of its debt stock? How much has been borrowed, by whom, on what terms, and pursuant to what documentation? For some countries, the answer has been—who knows?

Even an inept public debt management department is likely to know the extent of the central government's liabilities. The problem often resides in the unmonitored borrowings of ministries, parastatals, and subnational political units like provinces or municipalities. When these entities borrow, particularly from foreign lenders, the creditors are apt to see the loans as "quasi-sovereign" exposure. This perception usually means that a visit will be paid to the ministry of finance if the quasi-sovereign loan is not serviced. "The market will not distinguish between the liabilities of Petro Ruritania and the Republic of Ruritania," the Minister of Finance of Ruritania will be told by the aggrieved lender. I will let you fill in the remainder of this depressingly predictable speech.

An even more widespread problem relates to contingent obligations of sovereigns. Wrapping a government guarantee around a loan incurred by a state-owned enterprise, for example, allows that SOE to borrow on better terms. All will be well until the SOE can't pay the loan back and the once-contingent liability lands on the balance sheet of the sovereign guarantor.

Contingent liabilities may not be reported by the sovereign as forming part of its debt stock. Investors and analysts can thus be misled about the real state of the sovereign's financial picture, and this in turn leads to mispricing of credits.

Lesson 4: Ask for Enough Debt Relief

Once a sovereign debt restructuring becomes unavoidable, the worst possible outcome is for the country to endure all of the turmoil of a restructuring only to emerge from the process with a debt stock that prospective investors still view as unmanageable. The sovereign will not regain market access after a half-baked restructuring, thus ensuring that another debt restructuring must surely follow. The classic example is the three or four rounds of rescheduling that each of the Latin American countries limped through in the 1980s. It was not until those debt stocks were cut and the balance of the debt stretched out for 30 years under the Brady Initiative that new lending and investment began to flow back into the debtor countries.

The sovereign's existing lenders, of course, may sit on one shoulder and whisper advice such as, "Walk softly, you don't want to earn a reputation as an irresponsible debtor." Sitting on the sovereign's other shoulder, however, will be *future* creditors. They will whisper: "The more debt relief you extract from your current crop of lenders today, the more generous we will be in lending to you tomorrow." The sovereign must balance the need for debt relief today against the predictable consequences of a restructuring, in terms of higher interest rates and limited market access, in the future.

The trick, of course, is getting the balance right. How much debt relief is enough? And when does it begin to look as though the sovereign is just using a debt crisis as an excuse to force its creditors to underwrite a disproportionate share of the burden of adjustment?

Unfortunately, these are judgment calls, not matters of indisputable number crunching. For obvious reasons, neither the sovereign nor its creditors can be trusted to make this call unilaterally. There are two ways the matter has been handled. One approach locks the sovereign in a face-to-face negotiation with its lenders over the terms of the restructuring. If each side is doing its job in that negotiation, a balance will be struck.

For sovereigns whose debt stocks are too disparate to permit face-to-face negotiations with representative creditors, some neutral umpire must be found to pass upon the reasonableness and proportionality of the country's request for debt relief. By default, this job normally falls to the International Monetary Fund (IMF). An assessment of what a "sustainable" debt stock is for any country requires a balancing of economic, political, and social factors. To be blunt, how far can fiscal austerity be pushed before the social compact breaks down? The IMF has had to strike that balance many times in many places. It may not always get the balance right, but no other plausible candidate now exists to play this role.

Lesson 5: Be Ruthlessly Efficient

Sovereign debt crises never occur in isolation. They are usually accompanied by political, banking, economic, and sometimes social crises. Once they begin, however, it is in everyone's interest to conclude a debt restructuring as quickly as possible. This requires both political will and technical competence.

The Latin American debt crisis that began in 1982 languished for a full decade. The Latins still call it the "lost decade." Even the Brady bond exchange deals of the early 1990s sometimes took years to negotiate, document, launch, and close.

Fortunately, with bondholders replacing commercial banks as the dominant creditors, sovereign debt restructurings have been compressed into shorter timeframes. Mark to market institutional holders of sovereign bonds have an incentive to cooperate in a speedy resolution of the situation. For so long as their bonds are in default or near-default status, the market value of the instruments will be depressed. A successful debt restructuring, even one that calls for a principal haircut, can often restore market value to a portfolio. It is this alchemy that has allowed most sovereign bond restructurings to proceed more efficiently than the workouts of commercial bank loans in the 1980s.

Lesson 6: Be Evenhanded

Every creditor group caught up in a sovereign debt restructuring can make a plausible argument for why it should be treated more gently than all the others. Trade creditors, for example, will point to a history of preferential treatment in sovereign debt workouts. Commercial banks may argue that they will be the lenders of last resort when fickle bond markets have closed. Bilateral creditors may play the geopolitical card.

It is very dangerous for a sovereign debtor to begin discriminating among its creditor groups (that is, to hand out different treatment in a debt workout), absent a clear and convincing reason for doing so. In a corporate bankruptcy, once the senior and secured creditors are dealt with, everyone else gets lumped together as "general unsecured." A similar approach is wise in the sovereign context.

Differential treatment is sometimes appropriate—trade and supplier debt is a good example—and other creditors will normally accept the rationale for this. But when a sovereign appears to be picking favorites among its creditors without a compelling explanation, the result will be an aggravated sense of grievance on the part of the disfavored creditors.

PROS AND CONS OF ALTERNATIVE POLICY OPTIONS

11

Alternative Strategies for Resolving the European Debt Crisis

WILLIAM R. CLINE

The European debt crisis poses a severe challenge to the European and global economies. The crisis has spread from its original epicenter in Greece to Ireland and Portugal and, most recently, to Spain and Italy. This chapter examines two categories of policy options for dealing with the crisis. In the first, a menu of approaches is considered for dealing with liquidity and, potentially, solvency problems for these sovereign debtors. In the second, three major institutional changes are considered that could affect the outcome: expansion of the European Financial Stability Facility (EFSF); issuance of eurobonds jointly and severally guaranteed by euro area member states; and, as a more extreme possibility, exit from the euro by a country or number of countries.

The discussion first examines the severity of the debt problem in each of the five economies. The central framework is that of "debt sustainability." The main question is whether the country is on a fiscal path that will cause debt to spiral out of control or whether instead the debt burden relative to GDP can be held to, or brought down to, manageable proportions. A key diagnostic is a debt sustainability equation that calculates the size of the primary (noninterest) fiscal surplus that must be achieved to keep debt from rising relative to GDP. This equation states that this surplus, as a percent of GDP, must equal

William R. Cline has been a senior fellow at the Peterson Institute for International Economics since its inception in 1981. While on leave during 1996–2001, he was deputy managing director and chief economist of the Institute of International Finance. He thanks Yimei Zou for research assistance.

or exceed the excess of the interest rate over the nominal GDP growth rate, multiplied by the initial debt ratio (so the necessary surplus is higher if the initial debt ratio is higher). The discussion for four of the countries focuses in part on this required primary surplus. The analysis for Greece goes into greater detail, drawing on Cline (2011).

Beyond the solvency question addressed by this debt sustainability diagnosis, there is the question of liquidity. For this purpose the discussion considers magnitudes of amortization coming due. The existing support programs for Greece, Ireland, and Portugal are examined in light of these liquidity needs. For Italy and Spain, the broader question is raised regarding whether expansion of the EFSF, or other approaches, are necessary to ensure liquidity even if solvency seems plausible.

The analysis concludes with consideration of a matrix of impacts by policy approach and country, adding the implied effects for France and Germany as the main lender-of-last-resort economies. One such matrix is identified for country publics and governments of the seven euro area economies considered and also for the rest of G-7 (on a heuristic basis rather than estimated quantitatively). A second impacts matrix is identified for the banks of the corresponding countries. The patterns of suggested impacts may help diagnose how policy decisions would be likely to play out, and thus to provide a point of reference for the simulation exercise described in chapter 15 of this volume.

The overall thrust of the analysis here is that the European debt crisis is one of confidence and the maintenance of liquidity, rather than one of deep insolvency. Even for Greece the finding is that debt should be sustainable if the central expectations of the Greek adjustment package agreed to in July 2011 are attained, although an ambitious primary surplus will be required. For Ireland and Portugal the solvency condition should also be met, although liquidity strains might require going beyond the present arrangements toward one involving private sector involvement (PSI) more similar to that in the recent Greek package. Solvency is also the diagnosis for the sovereign debt of Spain and Italy, but if short-term loss of confidence were to dominate, meeting liquidity requirements could require mobilizing the broader measures of eurobonds and expansion of the EFSF. The most negative options are found to be deep debt forgiveness or even outright unilateral default. The option of exit from the euro is also viewed as potentially costly, including for a possible strong-country exit group that might seek to form a new currency—especially if public-good valuation of European monetary unity is taken into account.

Sustainability of Greek Public Debt

The first adjustment program to deal with the Greek debt crisis was launched in March 2010, with €80 billion in support from European governments and €30 billion from the International Monetary Fund (IMF), in comparison to total Greek government debt of €298 billion at the end of 2010.[1] The program assumed that Greece could reestablish access to private capital markets by 2012, starting at annual rates of about €30 billion and rising to about €70 billion annually in 2014–15. As it became clear in recent months that it would take considerably longer to restore market access, the need for a larger and longer-term support program became clear. German and Dutch authorities pushed for substantial PSI in any such additional effort, although the European Central Bank (ECB) opposed this approach out of concern about repercussions of rating agency classification as selective default. The new package agreed to in July 2011 did include major PSI, amounting to some €135 billion over 2011–20 in an initiative orchestrated by the Institute of International Finance. The new package pledged an additional €109 billion in euro area support. Crucially, the euro area support was to shift to more favorable lending terms (10-year grace, borrowing at EFSF funding rates, or about 3.5 percent) than in the original 2010 program (which involved interest rates of about 5.5 percent, rising to 8.0 percent by 2015–16).

The new package includes a large privatization effort, amounting to €50 billion. Skeptics have criticized the high debt ratio that the program involves, with the debt-to-GDP ratio peaking at 172 percent in 2012. However, gross debt exaggerates the burden. A considerable amount of the debt increase will correspond to funds set aside in zero coupon risk-free assets as collateral for the PSI. In addition, as much as 10 percent of GDP in the increase in gross debt was imputed in the IMF program to recapitalization of the banks, which should involve an increase in government claims.

Figure 11.1 shows the baseline trends for four key debt measures, before and after the July 2011 package. Even without the package, the IMF had projected the baseline gross debt-to-GDP ratio to fall to 130 percent of GDP by 2020, after peaking at 172 percent in 2012. With the package, there is an illusory greater buildup in the gross debt ratio (as just noted), but even the gross debt ratio is down to 113 percent of GDP by 2020. For the net debt ratio, which is more meaningful, the July package yields a central path falling from 120 percent of GDP in 2011 to 69 percent by 2020. The estimates here take account of an initial stock of government financial assets estimated by the Organization for Economic Cooperation and Development (OECD) at €76 billion (33 percent of GDP) at the end of 2010. For the third metric of debt burden, interest as a percent of GDP, figure 11.1 shows that in the prepackage baseline there would have been a considerable escalation, from 7.2 percent of GDP in 2011 to about 9 percent by 2016. The July 2011 package sharply reduced the central baseline, to 5.2 percent of GDP by 2020. These three metrics pertain to solvency. The fourth panel shown in figure 11.1 concerns liquidity.

---

1. This section draws on Cline (2011). For specific references, see that study. *Author's note*: By the time this volume went to press in early December, 2011, events had bypassed the July 21 package analyzed in this section. See the postscripts in chapter 1 and at the end of this chapter.

Figure 11.1 Alternative paths for Greek public debt, 2010–20

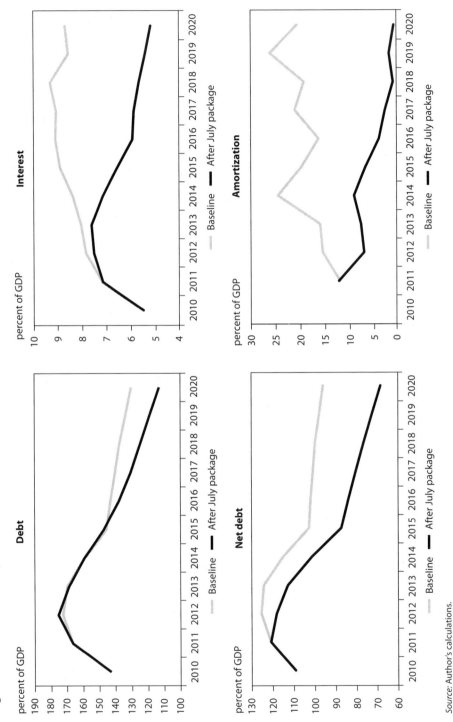

Source: Author's calculations.

It shows that prior to the package, amortization requirements would have escalated from 12 percent of GDP in 2011 to about 20 percent annually. With the package, in contrast, the amortization rate falls to 9.0 percent of GDP by 2014 and then steadily declines to 0.5 percent by 2020.

The central projections for the new package make the following assumptions for growth. After a decline in real GDP by 3.8 percent in 2011, real growth is 0.6 percent in 2012, then rises from 2.1 percent in 2013 to about 3 percent by 2016 and after. The primary surplus rises from –0.8 percent of GDP in 2011 to 1.5 percent in 2012 and 3.5 percent in 2013, then reaches a plateau of 6.4 percent by 2015 and after. This target is ambitious but feasible. Figure 11.2 shows alternative paths of the debt burden indicators if the growth path is 1 percentage point lower or higher, or if the primary surplus path is 1 percent of GDP lower or higher. Also shown is a variant in which the primary surplus does not reach higher than 3 percent of GDP (PS3). The central message of the figure is that there should be considerable progress even under alternative assumptions. Still, the variant with a ceiling of 3 percent of GDP for the primary surplus suggests that some alternative effort, such as greater privatization, might be needed if fiscal results did not exceed this outcome.

The PSI initiative involves 30-year par bonds with interest rates set at 4.0 percent for the first five years, 4.5 percent for the next five, and 5 percent thereafter; and 30-year discount bonds that cut face value 20 percent but boost the interest rates to 6.0, 6.5, and 6.8 percent for the respective periods. Both obtain collateralization of principal by zero coupon risk-free bonds, presumably German bunds. The exchange is calculated to involve a 21 percent haircut discounting at 9 percent, but arguably that is considerably too high a discount rate given the relatively secure postexchange conditions (even though only principal, not interest, is collateralized). From the standpoint of Greece there is little present value alleviation of the debt burden, as the original interest rates were on the order of 5 percent. The main contribution of the exchange is to remove the liquidity pressure by postponing amortization. The terms of the exchange are consistent with the intention of reaching high acceptance on a voluntary basis.

The Greek government plans to use €20 billion to repurchase debt from the secondary market. At an expected price of about 60 cents on the euro, repurchases are a relatively efficient way to reduce the debt burden. Any slippage in take-up of the exchange by bondholders can to some extent be offset by reallocating the funds that would otherwise have been earmarked for purchase of collateral for use in market buybacks.

Overall, the July package for Greece should provide a solid basis for management of Greek debt. The package helps ensure solvency and liquidity.[2] Its

2. Darvas, Pisani-Ferry, and Sapir (2011) reach the contrary conclusion and assert that 30 percent forgiveness of Greek public debt is necessary to restore solvency, which they judge as reducing the gross debt-to-GDP ratio to 60 percent by 2034. However, their projections, carried out in February 2011, do not take into account the more lenient official financing terms of the July 2011 package, or the impact of the PSI arrangement.

Figure 11.2 Impact of alternative growth and primary surplus assumptions for Greece, 2010–20

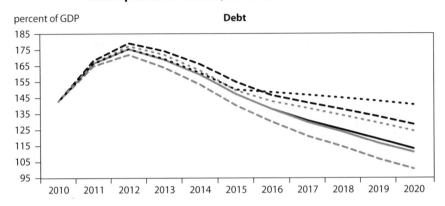

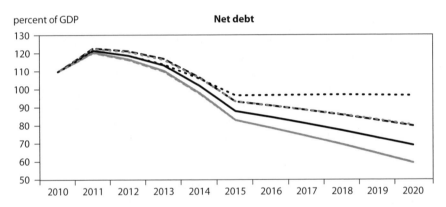

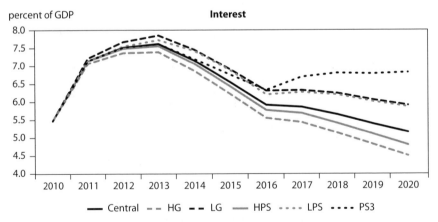

HG = high growth; LG = low growth; HPS = high primary surplus; LPS = low primary surplus
PS3 = primary surplus does not reach higher than 3 percent of GDP

Source: Author's calculations.

most challenging aspect will be achievement of the ambitious primary fiscal surplus and privatization targets.

Debt Sustainability in Ireland and Portugal

As shown in figure 11.3, spreads on 10-year sovereign bonds for Portugal and Ireland have shown the same pattern of climbing to crisis levels that has characterized spreads for Greece (albeit at somewhat lower levels). Like Greece, Ireland and Portugal have been forced to enter into adjustment programs supported by the International Monetary Fund and European Union. So far, however, neither Ireland nor Portugal has become a candidate for debt restructuring. Indeed, in announcing the July package for Greece, the official European statement explicitly stated that regarding PSI, "Greece requires an exceptional and unique solution.... All other euro countries solemnly reaffirm their inflexible determination to honour fully their own individual signature."[3]

Ireland

Public debt has increased rapidly in Ireland as a consequence of large fiscal deficits associated with the severe recession and the cost of supporting the banking system. In 2007, public debt was only 25 percent of GDP. The debt ratio then soared to 44 percent in 2008, 66 percent in 2009, 96 percent in 2010, and a projected 111 percent in 2011 (IMF 2011a, 39). From 2008 through 2011 the primary fiscal deficit excluding bank support averaged 8.4 percent of GDP, and interest payments averaged about 2.6 percent of GDP, placing the total fiscal deficit at an annual average of 11 percent of GDP (IMF 2011a, 27). Fiscal deficits not counting bank support thus cumulatively added about 44 percent of GDP to public debt over the four years.[4]

The banking system at its peak had assets five times the size of GDP (in comparison to 46 percent in the United States in late 2008 for banks and 170 percent for the financial sector broadly defined; see Cline 2010a, 305). With the bursting of the real estate bubble, the banks experienced major losses. In a context of international financial turmoil immediately after the collapse of Lehman Brothers, at the end of September 2008 the government of Ireland announced that it would guarantee the debt of banks. During 2009–10, public support to recapitalize the banks amounted to €46 billion, or 30 percent of GDP (IMF 2011a, 14). The government took full ownership of Anglo Irish Bank and provided major recapitalization support to the two other largest banks. It established the National Asset Management Agency (NAMA) as a "bad bank" to hold distressed real estate assets purchased from banks. By late

---

3. Council of the European Union, "Statement by the Heads of State or Government of the Euro Area and EU Institutions," July 21, 2011, www.consilium.europa.eu (accessed on October 28, 2011).

4. Simple addition is approximately valid considering that GDP was not rising (indeed, it fell from €189 billion in 2007 to about €160 billion in 2010–11).

**Figure 11.3   Greece, Ireland, and Portugal: 10-year sovereign bond
spreads over German bunds, January 2010–
September 2011**

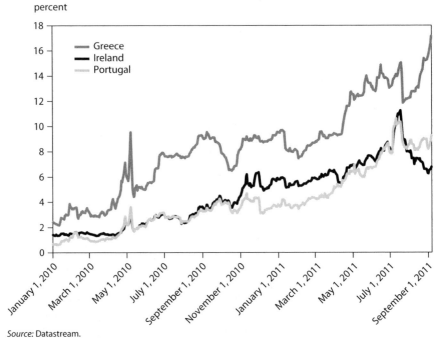

Source: Datastream.

2010, NAMA had acquired about €75 billion in such loans from banks at a
discount of about half of their value.[5]

The large public intervention to support the banks did imply partial
compensation in the form of increased public sector assets. The OECD (2011)
reports that general government financial assets rose from 29 percent of GDP
in 2007 to 50 percent by 2011. Net public debt rose from zero to 70 percent
of GDP over the same period, and is projected by the OECD to reach 76 percent in 2012. Considering the debt buildup contribution of about 40 percent
of GDP from fiscal deficits excluding bank support, the implication is that
capitalization and other bank support added about 30 percent of GDP to debt
even on a net basis. Although the cost of socializing bank losses is unusually
high in Ireland, it turns out that it was nonetheless overshadowed by the fiscal
losses associated with recession.[6]

---

5. Suzy Hansen, "The Reckoning," *Bloomberg Businessweek,* November 22, 2010.

6. This confirms even for Ireland the finding by Reinhart and Rogoff (2008, 45) that historically
it has been the recession-induced fiscal losses rather than direct banking costs that drive a large
increase in public debt in recessions associated with banking crises (typically by 86 percent in real
terms in the first three years after the crisis).

If net public debt is on the order of 75 percent of GDP, then at more normal sovereign borrowing rates on the order of 5 percent nominal interest (i.e., 300 basis points above German bunds), the interest burden would amount to about 3.5 percent of GDP. The equilibrium debt equation states that for the (net) debt ratio to remain constant rather than rise, the primary fiscal surplus as a percent of GDP needs to be at least equal to the product of the debt-to-GDP ratio and the difference between the nominal interest rate and the nominal growth rate of GDP (Cline 2010b).[7] The IMF (2011a) places average real growth for 2013–16 at 3.0 percent, and average (GDP deflator) inflation at 1.5 percent. With nominal growth at 4.5 percent and a nominal interest rate of 5.0 percent, the ratio of net debt to GDP could be held at 75 percent of GDP with a primary surplus of 0.37 percent of GDP. So at more normal medium-term conditions, Ireland should be solvent, since international experience suggests that such a small primary surplus should not be difficult to reach.

Excluding bank support costs, the primary balance was in deficit at an average of 9.2 percent in 2009–10, and 6.7 percent in 2011. The IMF program calls for the deficit to fall to 4.2 percent in 2012 and 1.4 percent in 2013, and then shift to a primary surplus averaging 1.8 percent of GDP in 2014–16. This surplus would be amply sufficient to avoid further escalation of the ratio of net debt to GDP and would provide modest scope for reducing it.

Nonetheless, Ireland is effectively cut off from markets, with the 10-year bond rate at about 8.5 percent at the end of August 2011 (figure 11.3). The decline from about 13 percent in early July reflected at least temporary success in ECB intervention in the bond market. The issue for Ireland would thus seem to be the need for classic (Bagehot) lender-of-last-resort temporary financing to a solvent entity during the time needed to restore more-normal market expectations after a panic. Ireland is in the fortunate position of having a large lender of last resort, the European Union.[8]

The official support should suffice to deal with the sovereign liquidity problem. Amortization of existing private medium and long-term debt amounts to €7 billion annually in 2012–13, €13 billion in 2014, and an average of €10 billion annually in 2015–20, though with spikes in 2016 and 2020 (European Commission 2011a, 38). Short-term debt was down to about €1 billion by end-June 2011, in contrast to €7 billion at end-2010 (NTMA 2011). Annual amortization is thus in the range of 5 to 9 percent of GDP, far lower than the prepackage Greek range of 20 to 25 percent for 2014–20. Ireland is thus under considerably less liquidity pressure than Greece was. Overall, for

---

7. That is: $\pi^* = \lambda(r - g)/(1 + g)$, where π^* is the primary surplus as a percent of GDP, λ is the sustained ratio of (net) debt to GDP, r is the interest rate, and g is the nominal growth rate. With low inflation and modest growth rates, the denominator approximates unity and the numerator is the focus of analysis.

8. Thus, in the current adjustment program, there is €45 billion in EU support, coming from the European Financial Stability Mechanism (€22.5 billion) and the EFSF (€17.7 billion) as well as from bilateral lending by the United Kingdom (€3.8 billion), Sweden (€0.6 billion), and Denmark (€0.4 billion). See European Commission (2011a, 40).

Ireland a diagnosis of fundamental solvency coupled with reasonably viable official liquidity support appears reasonable. Accordingly, the basic expectation should be that over the medium term, market interest rates on sovereign debt should return to more reasonable and sustainable levels, so long as Ireland makes progress as planned in fiscal adjustment.

Portugal

Contagion from Greece has hit Portugal with approximately the same severity and timing as it hit Ireland (figure 11.3). There were somewhat lesser effects for Portugal in the fourth quarter of 2010 and first quarter of 2011, but later there were somewhat more adverse effects, especially in the emerging trends in spreads following the July Greek package and subsequent ECB intervention in bond markets. Failure of a stabilization package to pass Parliament in March 2011 and the ensuing call for June elections prompted heightened market concerns and a ratings agency downgrade. In April the caretaker government sought support from the European Union and IMF. A statistical revision in April placed the 2010 fiscal deficit at 9.1 percent of GDP rather than the previously reported 7.3 percent. By May a proposed economic adjustment program received support from the main contending political parties. Support programs from the IMF and European Union were agreed upon by late May, providing up to €78 billion (46 percent of GDP) over 2011–14. Two-thirds is to come from the EU (divided evenly between the European Financial Stabilization Mechanism and EFSF) and one-third from the IMF (European Commission 2011b, 4, 15).

Portugal's debt problem is seen as one of both sovereign and external debt, with net external liabilities on track to reach about 120 percent of GDP in 2012 (European Commission 2011b, 7). The current account deficit stood at an average of 10.8 percent of GDP in 2006–10 and is projected at 8.7 percent of GDP for 2011.[9] Nonetheless, the internal rather than external debt problem is likely the more proximate, because as a member of the euro area Portugal does not face the typical external debt problem of severe exchange rate pressure and loss of external reserves. Even so, some form of internal devaluation and increased competitiveness is necessary for adjustment. More fundamentally, reforms are needed to overcome prolonged slow growth. Real GDP growth was an average of only 1.5 percent annually in 2000–07, well below the euro area average of 2.2 percent (although annual growth was approximately the same for Portugal and the euro area in 2008–10, at −0.4 and −0.6 percent annually).[10]

Excessive protection of employment in permanent contracts has created a two-tier labor market. The new adjustment program calls for liberalization of labor arrangements and a 5 percent cut in public sector wages, ingredients for

---

9. IMF, *World Economic Outlook* database, 2011, www.imf.org.

10. Ibid.

internal devaluation. The adjustment program seeks to reduce the fiscal deficit, which has already fallen from 9.1 percent of GDP in 2010 to a projected 5.9 percent in 2011, to a target of 3.0 percent by 2013 and 1.9 percent by 2015 (European Commission 2011b, 33). The primary deficit has fallen from 6.1 percent of GDP in 2010 to 1.7 percent in 2011, and is to reach a surplus of 2.1 percent of GDP by 2013.

Gross public debt has risen from 68 percent of GDP in 2007 to 93 percent in 2010, and is projected to peak at 115 percent in 2013–14 (IMF 2011b, 33). The OECD (2011) places net public debt at 68 percent of GDP for 2010, and projects it to rise to 80 percent of GDP by 2012. Net debt would thus remain almost as low as that in Ireland, and far below the 126 percent projected for prepackage Greece in 2012 (discussed above). With net debt at 80 percent of GDP, along with a postnormalization interest rate of 5 percent and nominal growth rate of 3.5 percent, the primary surplus required to achieve stabilization of the debt ratio would amount to 1.2 percent of GDP, lower than the target of 2.1 percent by 2013. Arguably Portugal is thus also solvent.

Liquidity pressure is relatively high, however. Short-term debt is high, at €20 billion in 2011 (IMF 2011b, 28), or 12 percent of GDP. Medium- and long-term debt amortization is moderate, at about €11 billion annually on average in 2011–13, or 6 percent of GDP. As in the case of Greece, however, there is a large one-time surge in financing requirements in 2011 for "other" uses (that is, other than fiscal deficit or amortization), primarily in bank support, amounting to €17 billion (10 percent of GDP).[11] The Portuguese adjustment program calls on substantial official support to cover the liquidity needs (€63 billion in EU and IMF disbursements in 2011–12, a rate of 18 percent of GDP annually) but transits relatively early to substantial renewed reliance on private market financing. Thus, "market access" disbursements, which will have fallen from about €40 billion annually in 2009–10 to €17 billion in 2011 and €9 billion in 2012, rebound to an average of €22 billion or 12 percent of GDP in 2013–14.

In the first review mission for the Portuguese adjustment program, the joint memorandum from the European Commission, ECB, and IMF emphasized that the decisions made at the July 21, 2011, European summit would substantially improve prospects for success. These decisions included lowering interest rates on EU support to near the EFSF's funding rate, extending maturities, and "most importantly . . . stand[ing] ready to provide financing until market access has normalized."[12] Nonetheless, Portugal, perhaps more than Ireland, may at some point need even broader reinforcement of liquidity support, conceivably along the lines of the Greek-style package that includes PSI. Although it is far too early to place much weight on recent trends, the

---

11. As in the Greek program, however, the IMF (2011b) country report does not analyze whether there is any corresponding increase in public sector assets associated.

12. International Monetary Fund, "Statement by the EC, ECB, and IMF on the First Review Mission to Portugal," Press Release no. 11/307, Washington, August 12, 1.

incipient divergence in spreads between Ireland and Portugal shown in figure 11.1 would tend to support this comparative ordering.

Confronting Market Pressures on Sovereign Debt in Spain and Italy

For most of the past 18 months, since the emergence of the European debt crisis in Greece, the working policy framework has been one of dealing with sovereign debt problems in three small, peripheral economies—Greece, Ireland, and Portugal—with the help of the far larger EU partner economies. Similarly, any Europe-wide or global threat to the financial system was limited so long as the vulnerable debt was just that of three smaller economies. Although some European banks outside these countries held substantial claims on the three sovereigns, these were nonetheless sufficiently limited to pose no major threat to neighboring banking systems, let alone those of the United States and elsewhere.

Thus, for the euro area as a whole, gross public debt stood at €7.88 trillion at the end of 2010; the combined gross public debt of the EP3 (Europe periphery 3) amounted to only €618.9 billion, or 7.9 percent of the total. Similarly, EP3 GDP at a combined €556.9 billion constituted only 6.0 percent of total euro area GDP (€9.27 trillion) in 2010.[13] Essentially, the euro area as a whole was patently capable of dealing with problems in the three peripheral members so long as the political will was present to do so. But if Italy and Spain were to enter seriously into the category of troubled sovereign debtors, the leverage for financial backstopping would change sharply. Adding these two countries would boost the periphery debtor totals to €3.10 trillion for gross public debt, and €3.17 trillion for GDP. Based on euro area GDP shares, the leverage for nontroubled to troubled debtor countries—a sort of financial backstopping-capacity metric—would then shift from 16.7 to 1 with only the EP3 in the troubled category, to only 1.5 to 1 after adding Italy and Spain to the troubled group. The potential scope of the European debt crisis thus threatened to escalate sharply in July 2011 when market spreads began to surge for sovereign debt of Italy and Spain.

The replacement of national currencies with the euro in 1999 had in effect converted currency risk for debt of member countries such as Italy and Spain into sovereign credit risk. However, in the context of modern industrial country experience and especially that of high-income European economies, sovereign risk was widely regarded to be minimal. As a result, the spread above German bund rates for 10-year treasury obligations went from being high for some countries, especially Greece, to virtually zero for most of the posteuro period (figure 11.4).[14] Only beginning in 2010 did the myth of zero intra-euro

---

13. IMF, *World Economic Outlook* database, 2011, www.imf.org.

14. Most of the pre-euro difference in interest rates reflected differential inflation expectations, however, rather than perceived differential sovereign credit risk.

Figure 11.4   Government bond yields in seven euro area economies, 1990–2011Q1

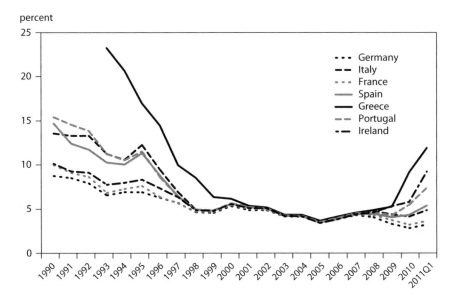

percent

Source: International Monetary Fund, *International Financial Statistics,* Washington (CD-ROM, monthly), 2011.

area sovereign risk explode. As shown in the figure, the postmyth hierarchy of bond rates is largely similar to the pre-euro profile (albeit this time for credit rather than inflation reasons), with German and French rates low, Italian and Spanish rates intermediate, and Greek rates high. The two exceptions are Ireland and Portugal, which were in the low and intermediate group, respectively, before the euro but have jumped to the high group (lower only than Greece) since 2010.

As recently as 2007, government bond rates in Italy were only about 30 basis points above those in Germany; for Spain the spread was only about 10 basis points. In 2008, 2009, and 2010, the spread for Italy rose to 70, 110, and 130 basis points; and for Spain, to 40, 75, and 150 basis points. By the first quarter of 2010, however, the spread had risen to 165 basis points for Italy and 215 basis points for Spain.

Still, sovereign spreads on the order of 200 basis points were essentially still modest for Italy and Spain. The implications for fiscal costs were attenuated by the fact that the German base rate had eased substantially, from 4.2 percent in 2007 to 2.7 percent in 2010 and 3.1 percent in the first quarter of 2011. However, as shown in figure 11.5, in July 2011 contagion to Spain and Italy from the European debt crisis entered a more forceful phase. Spreads above the German bund rose from about 200 basis points for the two countries at the beginning of July to a peak of 380 basis points in the first week of August 2011. Instead of providing a quarantine to halt contagion, the Greek

Figure 11.5   Italy and Spain: 10-year spread above German bund rate

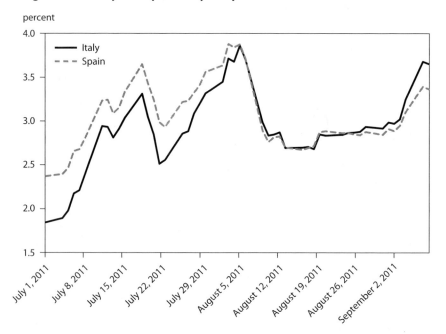

Source: Datastream.

package appears to have exacerbated it, probably because of the perception of increased risks to investors associated with the move toward PSI.

Soon after the Greek package was agreed to, bond market intervention by the ECB in its Securities Markets Program (SMP) helped cut back the spreads, which dropped by about 100 basis points by the end of August. The ECB boosted the outstanding stock of its holdings in the SMP from €74 billion on August 5 to €116 billion on August 26.[15] Even if all of these purchases were of Italian and Spanish bonds, however (and they were presumably not, because of likely purchases for Irish and Portuguese obligations), the amounts were small relative to total debt: about €40 billion compared to €2.48 trillion (of which about two-thirds was owed by Italy and one-third by Spain). A sustained reduction of one-fourth in the risk spread (from about 380 to 280 basis points) for purchases of only 1.6 percent of the stock of debt was perhaps too much to expect, and within a few days the spread was back up to about 360 basis points for Italy and 340 basis points for Spain (figure 11.5).

It is useful to examine the debt sustainability metrics for Italy and Spain at spreads of 300 basis points instead of 200. At the end of 2010, net general government debt stood at 99.1 percent of GDP for Italy and 40.2 percent for

---

15. European Central Bank, Weekly Financial Statements, August 9 and 30, 2011, www.ecb.int (accessed on December 8, 2011.)

Spain; the ratios are projected at 100.6 percent and 45.7 percent, respectively, at the end of 2011 (OECD 2011). (For reference, gross public debt stood at 119 percent in Italy and 60 percent in Spain, Maastricht criterion.) Even allowing a 300 basis point base for the German bund (versus 200 basis points in August 2011), spreads of an additional 300 basis points and hence borrowing costs of 6 percent could imply relatively manageable debt burdens. For Italy the IMF projects nominal GDP growth for 2012–16 at 3.4 percent annually (1.4 percent real).[16] The 100 percent ratio of net debt to GDP could be kept stable by achieving a primary surplus of 2.6 percent of GDP.[17]

In April 2011 the IMF projected the average primary surplus for Italy in 2012–16 at 1.8 percent of GDP. It would thus have required only 0.8 percent of GDP in additional fiscal tightening to reach the debt-stabilizing target primary surplus. The August 2011 fiscal package is much more ambitious: It plans to cut the total fiscal deficit (including interest) from 3.8 percent of GDP in 2011 to 1.4 percent in 2012 and zero in 2013, an improvement by 3.5 percentage points of GDP from the baseline deficit prior to the package.[18] By implication, the primary surplus would stand about 3 percent of GDP higher than in the previous baseline, reaching 4.8 percent of GDP—well above the 2.6 percent required for debt ratio stability and hence sufficient to provide scope for gradual reduction in the debt ratio.

For Spain, a low initial debt ratio in principle means that achieving debt stability should be even easier. There are two important caveats: Spain begins from a position of primary deficit rather than surplus; and contingent liabilities from the banking system could arguably impose a debt problem. Spain's low initial net debt ratio of 40 percent of GDP, combined with projected nominal GDP growth at 3.5 percent annually in 2012–16 (half real, half GDP deflator increase) means that the debt ratio would remain constant if the primary surplus were 1 percent of GDP.[19] The IMF projected the average annual primary balance at –2.3 percent of GDP for 2012–16, however. One way to interpret this baseline is that the result would be an increase in net debt from 40 percent of GDP to about 50 percent over a five-year period, still a moderate level (the same as in Germany in 2010 [OECD 2011]).

With respect to contingent liabilities from bank problems, Eurostat has compiled data on contingent government liabilities associated with guarantees extended in the financial crisis.[20] For Spain, these stand at €60 billion, or 5.6 percent of GDP. The comparable figure for France is 4.7 percent of GDP,

---

16. IMF, *World Economic Outlook* database, 2011, www.imf.org.

17. That is, 2.6 percent = 1.0 × (6 percent – 3.4 percent).

18. James Mackenzie and Gavin Jones, "Italy delivers tough austerity measures," Reuters, August 12, 2011.

19. That is, 1 percent = 0.4 × (6 percent – 3.5 percent). Moreover, it could be argued that Spain could safely allow the net public debt ratio to rise somewhat above its relatively low 40 percent level.

20. Eurostat, Supplementary Tables on Financial Turmoil, 2011, http://epp.eurostat.ec.europa.eu.

and for the United Kingdom 24.7 percent of GDP. By at least this indicator, then, Spain does not seem to be disproportionately vulnerable to a surge in public debt from socialization of banking losses.

Overall, both Italy and Spain would seem to warrant the diagnosis that sovereign debt is solvent. Moreover, even at recent high spreads, the incremental burden of borrowing at the higher rates as long-term debt comes due would appear to be limited. The amortization of medium- and long-term debt coming due in 2012 amounts to €195 billion in Italy (Ministero dell'Economia e delle Finanze 2011) and €47 billion in Spain (Dirección General del Tesoro y Política Financiera 2011). Suppose that both countries needed to pay even 7 percent interest instead of 4 percent (an exorbitant 500 basis point spread rather than 200 basis points above bunds) on these tranches of debt coming due. The annual extra fiscal cost would amount to 3 percent of the amounts involved, or about €6 billion annually on the 2012 vintage for Italy and about €1.5 billion on that for Spain. These numbers translate to about 0.40 percent of GDP for Italy and 0.15 percent of GDP for Spain. Although not inconsequential, especially for Italy, so long as the high borrowing cost were only temporary and spreads returned to more normal levels by 2013 and after, the impact on longer-term solvency would be de minimis.

The spread levels for Italy and Spain shown in figure 11.5 are a far cry from those that would typify the classic problem of credit rationing (Stiglitz and Weiss 1981; Cline 1984, 210). Credit rationing occurs when the credit supply curve turns vertical and additional lending is not forthcoming even at extremely high interest rates. Such a cutoff from market access is indeed what is represented by the spreads shown for Greece and, to a lesser extent, those for Ireland and Portugal (figure 11.3).

Another way to differentiate the market gauge of creditworthiness across these economies is to use the concept of loss equivalent probability (LEP) (Cline and Barnes 1997). This measure tells the probability of complete loss versus complete payment that is implied by the spread, given the risk-free interest rate.[21] With the 10-year bund at 2 percent, the Greek spread at 15 percent in late August implied an LEP of 0.54. The Irish spread at 6.5 percent translated to an LEP of 0.29; the Portuguese spread of 9.0 percent, an LEP of 0.39. In other words, purchasing the Greek obligation at late-August prices was a bit worse than flipping a coin to determine whether the paper paid completely or paid nothing. The LEPs for Italy and Spain remain much lower. With their spreads at 2.8 percent, their LEP now stands at 0.067. There is ap-

---

21. Discounting at the risk-free interest rate, the loss equivalent probability is the ratio of the present value of the spread to the present value of the bond if fully paid. Thus,

$$LEP = \frac{s\Gamma}{1/(1+i)^T + (s+i)\Gamma}$$, where s is the spread, i is the risk-free interest rate, T is the term of

the bond (10 years, in this case), and Γ is a discounted present value term: $\Gamma = \sum_{t=1}^{T} \frac{1}{(1+i)^t}$ (Cline and Barnes 1997, 36).

proximately a 93 percent chance that they will pay fully, but a 7 percent chance they will pay nothing, according to recent market valuations.

The LEP calculations underscore the diagnosis that markets seem to have been exaggerating expected losses for the three crisis economies, at least in contrast to the analysis presented here. Even the LEPs for Italy and Spain seem considerably overstated. Especially for Italy and Spain, however, if market concerns were to intensify and these two economies were to enter into the territory of credit rationing, the implied magnitudes of emergency lending could be very large indeed. In Italy, short-term debt is €195 billion; medium- and long-term amortization over 2012–15 is €574 billion. In Spain, short-term debt is €64 billion; amortization over 2012–15 is €191 billion. An official financing program to take both countries fully out of the markets through 2015 would require a total of €1.0 trillion. That amount would far exceed the €440 billion envisioned for the EFSF (even without considering the amounts already earmarked for the "program" economies).

For its part, the ECB has a balance sheet of €2.1 trillion.[22] Providing €1 trillion in emergency financing to Italy and Spain through the ECB could thus imply a 50 percent increase of its balance sheet. That is not inconceivable, considering that in response to the financial crisis the ECB increased its balance sheet from €1.15 trillion at end-2006 to €1.85 trillion at end-2009. However, such a large additional expansion could prompt concerns among those worried about inflation risk, even though such lending would replace private financing rather than increase total financing to the two governments.

It is crucial, then, that contagion to Italy and Spain be stanched. If these two economies were to enter into acute debt crisis, the financial support needs could swamp EU capabilities—as suggested by the earlier calculation of an ad hoc "financial backstop leverage capacity" of only 1.5 to 1 (instead of about 17 to 1) if Germany, France, and other noncrisis countries are compared in economic size to a group of five crisis countries that would include Italy and Spain (rather than just the three economies now in crisis, Greece, Ireland, and Portugal).

Policy Options for Debt Crisis Resolution

Traditionally, debt crisis resolution involves an initial determination of whether the problem is one of liquidity or solvency. The sovereign is judged to be solvent if, with realistic adjustment measures (including privatizations), it is plausible that in the medium term the debt can be fully honored at pre-crisis interest rates. In this case, the (Bagehot) central-banking principle of lender-of-last-resort lending to banks to stem a panic applies to the sovereign. This approach was adopted in the first phase of the Latin American debt

---

22. European Central Bank, Weekly Financial Statements, September 6, 2011, www.ecb.int (accessed on December 8, 2011.)

crisis in the 1980s, and during more recent crises including that of Korea in 1998. In the opposite case, where it is patently obvious that debt has reached levels impossible to manage, the initial determination is that the sovereign is insolvent, and that some form and extent of debt forgiveness by creditors is unavoidable. Instead of new lending, the solution involves debt restructuring. For the 1980s debt crises that involved primarily bank debt, this restructuring began in a mild form with concerted lending by large banks, and took a much more concrete form in the Brady Plan conversions into long-term obligations collateralized by zero coupon US Treasury bonds, typically with forgiveness of about 30 percent of the debt obligation.

Inevitably the illiquidity-insolvency dichotomy is a policy metaphor or framework rather than an unambiguous distinction. Political will has classically been a critical ingredient in determining whether the country sought to fully honor the debt or instead asked for debt forgiveness. Thus, whereas Chile had much higher debt ratios than Venezuela at the beginning of the Latin American debt crisis, Chile eventually avoided even Brady debt reduction, whereas Venezuela insisted upon it. The "debt overhang" literature seeks to instill a more purely economic basis for the distinction, based on the notion that new investment and growth will suffer if potential investors fear that excessive debt will cause the government to tax future profits from real sector investment projects rather than allow reasonable returns.

Official Refinancing Only

The continuum of debt policy options thus begins with the mildest form of liquidity problem, in which an official sector lender of last resort provides financing to tide over the sovereign until panic subsides and there is a return to market access. This "official refinancing only" (ORO) option characterizes the adjustment programs presently in place for Ireland and Portugal.

Refinancing with Voluntary PSI

The next basic debt policy option involves more extensive refinancing coupled with private sector involvement of a form that in some sense does not involve forgiveness. The early stage of the Latin American debt crisis was precisely of this form, because banks rescheduled debt. Later, by 1985–87, the banks entered into more substantial PSI through commitments to provide additional new lending rather than merely roll over principal (Baker Plan). This option can be described as "refinancing with voluntary full-value PSI," or RVPSI. This category describes the July package for Greece, with its increase in EU financing coupled with the private holder exchange offer led by the Institute of International Finance. That initiative is voluntary; some holders will not exchange, and the debt held by those that do not will not become superseded in any formal way, such as by a statement that the Greek government will no longer honor debt not exchanged. Private creditor participation despite the lack of compulsion reflects the internalization of "free rider" externalities, or collective action, by a finite number of relatively large private holders of the debt that benefits them as a group if most participate.

The terms of the Greek PSI package maintained precrisis interest rates but extended maturities sharply to 30 years, while providing zero coupon risk-free collateral of the principal. As noted above, the widely publicized haircut of 21 percent for the initiative is based solely on the use of a 9 percent "exit" discount rate. Arguably that rate is too high to reflect the much-improved security of the obligations; at a discount rate of 5 percent there would be no haircut at all. This is one reason to be optimistic that the 90 percent participation sought by Greece may well be achieved.

Market Buybacks

Market buybacks (MBs)—sovereign repurchases of debt at a discount in the secondary market—are an important market-oriented form of debt relief. The ECB has already conducted substantial purchases of bonds of Greece, Ireland, Portugal, Italy, and Spain in its Securities Markets Program. However, so far there is no mechanism for the conveyance to Greece of savings from the difference between the ECB's purchase price and the face value of these bonds. In contrast, the July 2011 Greek package specifically provided for the use of some of the official support funds for the repurchase of some €20 billion in Greek public debt.

Critics of buybacks have argued that by repurchasing debt at a higher price than it otherwise might be extinguished in a debt reduction deal, buybacks are not helpful (the classic statement is Bulow and Rogoff 1988). The problem with this critique is that it ignores that the ideal anti-monde is not still deeper forgiveness and greater damage to credit reputation, but full honoring of the debt on its original terms and thereby maintenance of a long-term reputation for creditworthiness. For Greece in particular, with recent market prices on the order of 50 cents on the euro, the use of official support from the European Union for the purpose of market repurchases offers an important opportunity for improving debt sustainability without jeopardizing credit reputation. Market buybacks are strictly voluntary on the part of the sellers, so long as the country is not engaging in strategic positioning by stating that it cannot meet debt repayments but does have funds to repurchase at a discount.

In the context of the present crisis, the most relevant formulation of the buyback option would seem to be in two alternative forms. For the cases of Italy and Spain, the relevant form would be bond market intervention through ECB purchases in its SMP. The benefit would be indirect in terms of reducing market borrowing rates, rather than direct in the form of reduction of debt at a repurchase discount. In contrast, for Greece, Ireland, and Portugal, there would seem to be considerably more scope for direct debt reduction through repurchases, presumably financed by EU funding from the EFSF.

So the MB options become MB-SMP and MB-Ctr, for SMP intervention and country-government repurchases, respectively.

Exchange Offer with Maintenance of Value

Still toward the mild end of the debt restructuring spectrum is an exchange offer with maintenance of value (EOMV). In effect, this instrument for bonds is the analog of a comprehensive debt rescheduling for bank loans with no reduction in value. The Uruguay restructuring in 2003 is the most widely cited prototype for this approach. After extensive cooperative consultation with creditors, the exchange converted existing market debt into longer maturities at interest rates unchanged from the prior obligations, usually adding five years to the maturity (but also including options with longer maturities [Sturzenegger and Zettelmeyer 2006, 216–17]). Discounting at the yield curve of new US bonds, the bulk of claims exchanged involved present value haircuts on the order of 8–12 percent (Sturtzenegger and Zettelmeyer 2006, 220), relatively low for international restructuring experience. The outcome reflected the authorities' goal of preserving credit reputation and enlisting high participation, which reached 89–99 percent depending on the category of debt.

Restructuring with Moderate Debt Reduction

Next in order of severity is a formal, comprehensive debt restructuring with moderate debt reduction (RMDR). The Brady Plan deals for Mexico, Argentina, and Brazil in 1989–92 are in this category. They involved conversion of claims to 30-year bonds with a 35 percent reduction in value (Cline 1995, 234). These were either "discount bonds" that formally reduced the principal but continued to pay interest rates at originally contracted levels, or "par bonds" that kept 100 cents on the dollar in face value but reduced interest rates to well below their original levels. The Brady bonds were backed by zero coupon US Treasury bonds, which were cheap at the time because of high interest rates. In the precedent-setting Mexican deal, funding for these "enhancements" came from the IMF, the World Bank, and the Export-Import Bank of Japan (Cline 1995, 221).

Restructuring with Deep Debt Reduction

The sixth and most extreme form of restructuring is restructuring with deep debt reduction (RDDR), similar to RMDR but with much deeper debt forgiveness. The prototype is the Argentine debt restructuring of 2005, which imposed a haircut of approximately 70–75 cents on the dollar (Sturzenegger and Zettelmeyer 2006, 193). Excluding official aid initiatives for highly indebted poor countries (HIPCs), such deep debt reduction is rare and reflects aggressive unilateralism by the debtor. Thus, prior to the Argentine exchange,

I (Cline 2003, 5) estimated that with a target primary fiscal surplus of 4.5 percent of GDP, Argentina could achieve debt sustainability with a haircut of 47 percent. The Argentine negotiating tactics were unilateral and did not involve negotiations with bondholders' committees (Porzecanski 2005). Among foreign holders of Argentine debt, the acceptance ratio of the exchange offer was only 60 percent (Mussa 2006, 438).

This option inevitably involves lasting damage to the sovereign's credit reputation. Of the modest amount of external debt Argentina was subsequently able to issue, the bulk was in politically motivated purchases by Venezuela.[23] As of mid-2006, Argentina's B3 credit rating by Moody's stood only slightly above those of Cuba and Nicaragua. The contemporary higher ratings of Brazil (Ba3) and investment-grade Mexico (Baa1), combined with international relationships between ratings and spreads, meant that whereas Argentina could be expected to pay risk spreads of 600 basis points, Brazil could expect 350 basis points and Mexico 100 basis points. By implication, the present value of future excess interest costs as a legacy of the unilateral default was on the order of 20 percent of one year's GDP (Cline 2007, 79–80).[24]

Unilateral Default

Finally, at the severe extreme of the continuum is unilateral default (UD) *sine die*, the indefinite suspension of payment with at most a vague expression of intent to convene with creditors at some future date to work out a debt reduction agreement. UD could transit to RDDR (or conceivably RMDR) but with great uncertainty. Usually it is a domestic political upheaval that precipitates UD (such as that by Argentina at the end of 2001).

Three Additional Policy Options for Restructuring

Three overarching policy options are crucial to add to what essentially amounts to a restructuring options menu, just discussed. These are substantial expansion of the EFSF, fiscal integration and euro area bonds, and exit from the euro. These may be labeled EFSFX, EB, and EXIT.

EFSF Expansion

The existing support programs for the three troubled debtor countries amount to EU and euro area commitments of €189 billion for Greece (including both

---

23. From 2005 through 2007, Venezuela purchased $5 billion in Argentine bonds. "Slush and garbage: The imbroglio over a cash-stuffed suitcase," *Economist,* January 3, 2008.

24. The view that Argentina enjoyed rapid growth despite its default ignores the fact that much of the growth was from a deeply depressed level of GDP in 2002, a level that was far lower than would have been expected in the absence of the unilateral default, as well as from the good luck of high international commodity prices later in the decade.

the March 2010 program and the July 2011 expansion), €40.2 billion for Ireland, and €51.4 billion for Portugal. Of the total of €281 billion, €48.2 billion is to come from the EU-wide European Financial Stability Mechanism—€22.5 billion for Ireland and €25.7 billion for Portugal. The €80 billion support for Greece in the March 2010 program predated the EFSF and came from euro area member states, but this would ideally be transferred to the EFSF and enjoy its now more favorable lending terms. The programs already in place thus imply EFSF commitments on the order of €230 billion. In comparison the amount currently authorized for the EFSF is a total of €440 billion.

As discussed above, the lender-of-last-resort capacity needed to deal with potential liquidity problems in Italy and Spain could be on the order of €1 trillion. Adding the amount already set aside for the three acute-problem countries, the total of €1.23 trillion is approximately three times the current size of the EFSF. Economist and former Greek labor minister Louka Katseli has called for a tripling of the size of the EFSF.[25] Application of the EFSFX policy option might thus be conceptualized as expanding the current authorization threefold.

An important limitation of the EFSF is that in practice its borrowing capacity seems likely to be limited to the guarantee portions provided by the stronger (AAA) countries. Together, Greece, Ireland, Portugal, Italy, and Spain account for 36.7 percent of the guarantee commitments of the EFSF.[26] None has a rating of AAA.[27] In order to attain lending capacity of €1.2 trillion, with only two-thirds of potential member guarantees available, the EFSF total would need to reach €1.8 trillion, a quadrupling of the present authorized amount. With a share of 27.1 percent, Germany would then have exposure of €490 billion, or 19 percent of GDP. At a share of 20.4 percent, France would have exposure of €367 billion, also 19 percent of GDP. The increased exposure could weaken prospects for at least France's country rating (currently AAA).

Fiscal Integration and Euro Area Bonds

An important potential alternative to debt restructuring, in the European cases, is the development of institutional arrangements to permit country issuance of public debt jointly and severally guaranteed by euro area (or EU) members, so-called eurobonds (the EB option). Access to such guarantees would sharply reduce borrowing costs, especially for Greece, Ireland, and Portugal, though also for Italy and Spain; but it might marginally raise borrowing costs for France, Germany, the Netherlands, and other euro area members.

25. Dow Jones, August 8, 2011.

26. European Financial Stability Facility, "EFSF Framework Agreement," Paris, 2010, www.efsf.europa.eu (accessed on December 8, 2011.)

27. Standard and Poor's currently rates the five countries as follows: Spain, AA; Italy, A+; Ireland, BBB+; Portugal, BBB–; Greece, CCC. Standard and Poor's, "Sovereigns Ratings List," 2011, www.standardandpoors.com (accessed on December 8, 2011.)

Delpla and von Weizsäcker (2010) have proposed a variant of this approach in which EU countries would pool their debt up to a limit of 60 percent of GDP for each member for joint liability, in "blue bonds." For a member with total debt exceeding this level, the excess amount would be ineligible for the joint guarantee, thereby having the status of "red bonds." Although this arrangement might have appeal for the longer term, under current circumstances the borrowing at the margin for all of the countries under stress—with the sole exception of Spain—would have to be in red bonds. Gross public debt stands far above 60 percent for Greece, Ireland, Portugal, and Italy, as noted above. Nor would the refinancing of the stock of existing debt, up to a 60 percent of GDP limit, have much near-term benefit. As shown in figure 11.4, until very recently there have been virtually no sovereign spreads, so the bulk of the debt outstanding will have been contracted at relatively low interest rates, and the service on that earlier debt is not the principal problem.

Eurobonds would transform the monetary (euro area) and economic (EU) union into a transfer union. One study estimates that the eurobond approach would boost German interest rates by enough to raise annual borrowing costs by 1.9 percent of GDP.[28] Some counter that the much wider market for consolidated EU debt would increase liquidity and provide some offsetting interest rate reduction. In Germany especially, however, the notion of a transfer union (through eurobonds or otherwise) has been anathema, and seems to linger as an option only because an alternative—the breakup of the euro—is even more unattractive.

It is useful to consider what might be the redistributive effects of sovereign debt pooling in the euro area. Figure 11.6 shows what might be called stylized-fact spreads by (Standard and Poor's-type) ratings categories. For single A to CCC, the data are median spreads above US Treasuries for 35 emerging-market economies from December 1997 to February 2010 (Jaramillo and Tejada 2011, 9). There were no AA or AAA countries in the data set, and for these categories the figure sets a spread of zero for AAA and an interpolated value of 55 basis points for AA.

Appendix table 11A.1 reports current S&P ratings for each of the euro area member countries, along with 2011 GDP and end-2010 gross public debt as reported by the IMF. Using the spreads of figure 11.6, for the euro area, weighted average spreads can be imputed at about 43 basis points (average of GDP weights and gross debt weights). The zero spread (in principle) AAA debt of Germany, France, Austria, the Netherlands, and Finland, together with the 55 basis point (imputed) AA debt of Spain, Slovenia, and Belgium (AA+) dominates the overall group. The table shows that if debt pooling shifted the pricing for all members to the weighted average, the consequence would be modest increases in debt costs by about 0.35 percent of GDP for Germany and

---

28. The study is by Kai Carstensen of Ifo Institute for Economic Research, as reported in "An Unpalatable Solution," *Economist,* August 20, 2011.

Figure 11.6 Stylized-fact spreads by sovereign ratings

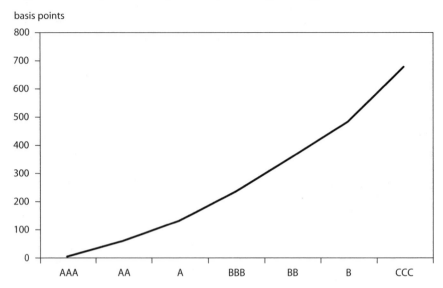

basis points

Source: Jaramillo and Tejada (2011); Standard and Poor's, "Sovereigns Ratings List," 2011, www.standardandpoors.com. See text.

France, but large interest savings for Portugal (1.9 percent of GDP annually), Ireland (1.3 percent), and Greece (albeit at a too-large-to-be-plausible 9.0 percent of GDP). The averaging of creditworthiness would produce modest net interest cost savings for the group as a whole, at 0.19 percent of annual GDP. Intuitively, the net gain from pooling reflects the nonlinearity of the spread with respect to the successively lower credit rating categories.

Although extremely heuristic, this exercise suggests that some of the recent estimates of fiscal costs of fiscal integration may be overstated. If the estimate here is anywhere near correct, then another way of looking at the cost of fiscal integration is to ask whether it would be worth about one-third of one percent of GDP annually to the strong, larger economies to ensure that the euro area avoids breakup caused by the debt problems of the weaker economies. At the same time, the more fundamental consideration is that the right to borrow in eurobonds would be equivalent to the right to tax euro area members, and arguably that right should not be granted without a fiscal union that imposes much more effective control over member states' fiscal performance than has been possible so far under the Maastricht obligations.

Euro Exit

Finally, an even more fundamental policy option is exit from the euro (the EXIT option), either by the weakest member(s), or by a core of strong economies that would create its own new single currency, leaving the euro free to devalue.[29] Some economists argue that a debt-growth trap cannot be escaped by Greece and other weak peripheral economies because they are in the straitjacket of the single currency and do not have the option of spurring growth through devaluation and stimulus to the export sector. That argument ignores both the possibility for "internal devaluation" through such reforms as labor market liberalization and the fact that devaluation would impose a windfall loss through effective increase in euro-denominated debt relative to GDP.

There would also be the loss of welfare associated with the single currency.[30] There are few measurements of welfare gains from the single currency. A 2007 study by the OECD focusing on structural reform found that euro area countries had "undertaken more comprehensive and far-reaching reforms than other OECD countries over the past decade," but that reform intensity had "fallen since the advent of EMU in 1999."[31]

In principle the welfare gains from the single currency could be large, because of optimal currency considerations; if so, exit could impose large welfare costs on the economy leaving if the country is small, and on all members if the breakup involved a large group of countries. Alternatively, the euro could be viewed as a political good, worth a considerable amount in terms of "contingent valuation" welfare but with little economic benefit or even net economic costs.[32] If so, the fracturing of the euro would sacrifice the welfare value of the political goal otherwise achieved. There could also be large market disruption costs from breakup of the euro, although these might be modest if the change involved only the temporary exit of a small member. There would be institutional barriers to overcome; one ECB study concluded that "a Member State's exit from EMU, without a parallel withdrawal from the EU, would be legally inconceivable" (ECB 2009, 4). Such a withdrawal would sacrifice the gains from participation in free trade and factor movement provided by the European Union, suggesting that the existing legal arrangements might need to change if some form of exit were to be pursued.

---

29. The latter is proposed by Hans-Olaf Henkel, former head of the Federation of German Industries. "A Sceptic's Solution—A Breakaway Currency," *Financial Times*, August 30, 2011.

30. The European Commission in 2008 issued a report on the Economic and Monetary Union at the 10-year mark that found the euro a "resounding success" that had "secured macroeconomic stability and boosted cross-border trade, financial integration, and investment" (European Commission 2008, 3). However, the report did not attempt to quantify welfare gains, and also noted that slow productivity growth and growing concerns about income distribution have qualified the success.

31. OECD, "Euro Riddle," *OECD Observer* no. 260, March 2007, www.oecdobserver.org (accessed on October 29, 2011).

32. In the environmental economics literature, contingent valuation is the economic value attached to a particular environmental good based on sample surveys.

Table 11.1   Relevance of policy options for seven European economies

Policy	Greece	Ireland	Portugal	Italy	Spain	France	Germany
ORO		x	x				
RVPSI	x	x	x				
MB-SMP	x	x	x	x	x		
MB-Ctr	x	x	x				
EOMV		x	x	x	x		
RMDR	x	x	x				
RDDR	x						
UD	x						
EFSFX				x	x		
EB		x	x	x	x		
EXIT	x	x	x			x	x

ORO = official refinancing only; RVPSI = refinancing with voluntary full-value private sector involvement; MB-SMP = market buyback through Securities Markets Program intervention; MB-Ctr = market buyback directly by countries; EOMV = exchange offer with maintenance of value; RMDR = restructuring with moderate debt reduction; RDDR = restructuring with deep debt reduction; UD = unilateral default; EFSFX = expansion of European Financial Stability Facility; EB = euro area bonds; EXIT = exit from the euro

Source: Author's calculations.

Benefits and Costs of Alternative Options for Stakeholders

Suppose there are m policy options and n stakeholders. Then for each of the stakeholders, the welfare effects of the policy decisions taken can be conceptualized as $\underset{n\times1}{W} = \underset{n\times m}{\beta'}\ \underset{m\times1}{X}$, where β is a matrix of impact coefficients by policy and party, and X is a vector of policy activities. Arriving at a policy solution can then be viewed from the standpoint of a global planner, who would maximize some (weighted) sum of the elements of W, or from the standpoint of a strategic uncooperative game, in which there may or may not be a stable Nash equilibrium.

Table 11.1 sets forth a mapping of the policy options available to countries, indicating which options are relevant for which countries. For Greece, events have already bypassed ORO; the July 21 program was RVPSI along with MB-ctr; the October 26 program, closer to RMDR. More drastic restructuring options (forced RMDR, RDDR, or, in the case of political breakdown, unilateral default) remain open, however, in case the current approach does not suffice. Ironically, the most market friendly of the nonvoluntary restructurings, exchange offer with maintenance of value, has already been superseded by the voluntary restructuring as a consequence of its escalation to a 50 percent haircut in the October 26 agreement.[33] If EOMV were offered there would presumably be no takers for the voluntary 50 percent haircut.

---

33. The main text of this chapter was completed in mid-September. The October 26 agreement is described in the postscript.

For Ireland and Portugal, the relevant spectrum essentially moves up one row in the table and begins with ORO, running down through RMDR but not plausibly extending to RDDR or UD. The option of EOMV might become relevant by 2014 when there are substantial increases in private new borrowing required. The option of EFSF expansion seems of little relevance to Greece, Ireland, and Portugal, because the currently agreed-upon size should suffice to provide the lender-of-last-resort function for the three. The EB seems relevant for Ireland and Portugal but not Greece, simply because Greece is sufficiently further along in debt difficulty that its eligibility for a plausible eurobond scheme would seem doubtful. The question of exit from the euro is ultimately relevant for all three economies, and has received the most discussion for Greece.

Italy and Spain are in the position of prospectively needing support but being too large for support to take place in the existing framework, except in the form of market intervention by the ECB. For these two economies, the most relevant policy options are expansion of the EFSF so that it becomes large enough to provide financing to them and issuance of eurobonds if some regime becomes available for that purpose. Neither economy seems anywhere near conditions that might induce them to exit from the euro in a desperate effort to increase competiveness through devaluation. However, if the options of eurobonds and major borrowing from the EFSF remain unavailable, and if the ECB refuses to engage in the potentially large SMP purchases that might be needed for a lender-of-last-resort operation, it is conceivable that Italy and possibly Spain might need to adopt an exchange offer with maintenance of value. The reason is that there are large maturities coming due in 2012, and if market conditions were such that private refinancing were essentially frozen, there might be little alternative to a temporary suspension followed by the most market-friendly involuntary restructuring, the EOMV. However, even the EOMV could be extremely disruptive. It would likely trigger a flight of bank deposits, possibly requiring capital controls.

Finally, as the lenders of last resort rather than the crisis-enveloped recipients, France and Germany are not likely candidates for receiving assistance from any of the crisis resolution options (although they would be crucially involved in decisions about the use of these options to help their partners). For them, the most relevant policy option is that of exit from the euro toward a strong-subgroup initiative (call it the New Franc).

Of the 77 combinations of policies (11) and countries (7), there are thus 33 that are relevant. Table 11.2 presents a heuristic evaluation of the impact of each of these 33 policies on the publics (and by extension the governments) of each of the seven euro area economies considered, as well as on the rest of the G-7 major industrial countries (RG-7). The entries are on a scale of –5 for extremely adverse to +5 for extremely favorable. To facilitate reading of the table, all zero (neutral impact) entries are omitted. France and Germany are considered jointly for the option of euro exit, as it would make little sense for one to leave without the other, so 32 options remain.

Table 11.2   Illustrative impact of policy option on publics/governments

			GR	IR	PT	IT	SP	FR	DE	RG-7
1	ORO	IR		4						
2	ORO	PT			4					
3	RVPSI	GR	5							
4	RVPSI	IR		2						
5	RVPSI	PT			2					
6	MB-SMP	GR	3							
7	MB-SMP	IR		3						
8	MB-SMP	PT			3					
9	MB-SMP	IT				3				
10	MB-SMP	SP					3			
11	MB-Ctr	GR	3							
12	MB-Ctr	IR		3						
13	MB-Ctr	PT			3					
14	EOMV	IR		1						
15	EOMV	PT			1					
16	EOMV	IT				−1	−1	−1	−1	−1
17	EOMV	SP				−1	−1	−1	−1	−1
18	RMDR	GR	3							
19	RMDR	IR		1						
20	RMDR	PT			1					
21	RDDR	GR	−2	−1	−1	−1	−1			
22	UD	GR	−5	−2	−2	−2	−2	−1	−1	−1
23	EFSFX	IT				4			−1	1
24	EFSFX	SP					4		−1	1
25	EB	IR		4					−1	
26	EB	PT			4				−1	
27	EB	IT				4		−1	−2	1
28	EB	SP					4	−1	−2	1
29	EXIT	GR	−2					−1	1	
30	EXIT	IR		−2				−1	1	
31	EXIT	PT			−2			−1	1	
32	EXIT	FR,DE	−2	−2	−2	−2	−2	−3	±2	−2

GR = Greece; IR = Ireland; PT = Portugal; IT = Italy; SP = Spain; FR = France; DE = Germany; RG-7 = remaining G-7 countries; ORO = official refinancing only; RVPSI = refinancing with voluntary full-value private sector involvement; MB-SMP = market buyback through Securities Markets Program intervention; MB-Ctr = market buyback directly by countries; EOMV = exchange offer with maintenance of value; RMDR = restructuring with moderate debt reduction; RDDR = restructuring with deep debt reduction; UD = unilateral default; EFSFX = expansion of European Financial Stability Facility; EB = euro area bonds; EXIT = exit from the euro

Note: Impacts are ranked from −5, extremely adverse, to +5, extremely favorable. No ranking (blank cell) means there is a neutral (zero) impact.

Source: Author's calculations.

For Greece, the table indicates that achieving success with the July 21 program (including PSI) would have been an extremely favorable outcome. As Greece has been forced to shift toward moderate debt reduction (Brady-style), the effect should likely remain positive, but less so because of reputational damage.[34] If Greece sought HIPC or Argentina-style deep debt reduction, the effect is imputed at negative, because of the severe reputational effect. Market buybacks are favorable whether by the ECB (SMP) or the country (not only in Greece but also in Ireland and Portugal, as well as Italy and Spain, though in these last two countries it is assumed that only the ECB is making market purchases). Ireland and Portugal obtain favorable results (score of 4) from success of the current official-refinancing-only packages; their results are less favorable but still positive if they find it necessary to resort to a Greek-style package (RVPSI), and barely favorable if they must enter into moderate debt reduction. If Greece enters deep debt reduction, there are adverse spillover effects for Ireland, Portugal, Italy, and Spain (–1 in each case). If Greece goes into unilateral default, these adverse effects are larger, and some adverse effect occurs even for France, Germany, and RG-7 because of the shock to general financial market confidence.

Recourse to formal restructuring through EOMV is shown has having a moderate positive effect for Ireland and Portugal, although lower than that of refinancing with voluntary PSI (because of reputational cost). Because both countries already have official support programs that largely take care of financing needs through 2013, there would not need to be market panic associated with development of such offers. In contrast, in the far larger cases of Italy and Spain, neither one of which currently enjoys prospective official financing capable of meeting rollover needs, EOMV would likely unleash such market havoc that the impact would seem likely to be negative not only for the countries themselves but also for other euro area partners and for the international economy (G-7). This option would probably require an announcement of a temporary moratorium, triggering bank runs as depositors sought to transfer assets outside of the country in question. Capital controls could become necessary to stem the bank runs. Hence table 11.2 shows negative rather than positive entries for the EOMV for Italy and Spain, and also shows negative spillover to Germany and France and to the rest of the G-7.

Access to eurobonds is placed at a quite favorable impact (4) for Ireland, Portugal, Italy, and Spain. (Again, Greece is considered not eligible.) However, if Italy and Spain access the eurobond market, there is a negative effect for France (–1) from potential liability (or simply the modest increase in interest rates discussed above), and an even larger negative impact for Germany (–2) because of the "political bad" of exposure as the ultimate European lender of last resort, combined with the large potential volumes of Italian and Spanish borrowing. There is a similar but smaller negative effect for Germany even if the measure is just expansion of the EFSF. In contrast, the RG-7 has a mildly positive effect from expansion of the EFSF as well as eurobond access, because of the perceived market-stabilizing effects.

---

34. As discussed below, the voluntary 50 percent haircut agreed to on October 26 is difficult to interpret as anything but at least a moderate debt reduction, despite the voluntary characterization.

Finally, the last five rows of the table posit that euro exit would be negative for all parties except, possibly, Germany. Exit by Greece, Ireland, or Portugal would on balance be negative for each of them because long-run integration losses would exceed short-term gains in competitiveness. France would perceive mild negative effects because of the loss of the political good of the historic monetary integration initiative, whereas the corresponding effect in Germany might be a perception of improvement. If France and Germany were both to leave the euro and enter a strong New Franc union, all partners would suffer; France would pay an even larger "political bad" cost. In contrast, Germany could perceive even greater "political good" gains, but in long-term economic effects Germany could experience loss as New Franc appreciation brought an end to its ready export market; hence the sign for Germany is ambiguous. There would be a sizable loss perceived by the rest of the G-7 because of an essentially backward step in global financial integration, although a likely currency appreciation of the New Franc could benefit RG-7 current accounts in the medium term.

A similar exercise can be conducted with respect to effects of alternative policies on banking systems. European banks have sizeable holdings of claims on the five economies in question, and an important risk in the European debt crisis is that it returns Europe, and to a lesser extent the international economy, toward the financial crisis environment of 2008–09 as a consequence of undermining European banks. Hence separate consideration of the banks is warranted.

Table 11.3 shows the qualitative results for the banks. The first policy option, ORO in Ireland and Portugal, is positive for the French and German banks because it provides official support to shore up the sovereigns and hence the bank holdings of the sovereign debt. The impact is especially favorable for Irish banks, from ORO for Ireland, and for Portuguese banks, from ORO support for Portugal, because typically the holdings of home country sovereign debt are particularly high for the banking system in question.

The July 21 Greek package was highly favorable for Greek banks for this same reason, but mildly negative for German and French banks, which perceived the PSI as equivalent to a 21 percent haircut (as discussed above). A shift to this mode to shore up Irish and Portuguese public debt would on balance remain positive for Irish and Portuguese banks but less so than simple ORO; the effects would again be mildly negative for French and German banks, this time only about half the size (in each case) as for the impact of Greece because of the relative sizes of the debt and economies in question.

Market purchases of bonds by either the ECB (SMP) or the countries would have favorable effects for the banks of the country in question by strengthening sovereign bond prices. The magnitudes in the cases of Italy and Spain would be sufficient to have a noticeable impact for French and German banks and, mainly because of lesser financial market turmoil, US and other G-7 banks.

Exchange offers with maintenance of value would cause moderate losses to banks in Ireland and Portugal. If applied in Italy or Spain, the impact would

Table 11.3   Illustrative impact of policy option on banks

			GR	IR	PT	IT	SP	FR	DE	RG-7
1	ORO	IR		4				1	1	
2	ORO	PT			4			1	1	
3	RVPSI	GR	4					−1	−1	
4	RVPSI	IR		2				−0.5	−0.5	
5	RVPSI	PT			2			−0.5	−0.5	
6	MB-SMP	GR	3							
7	MB-SMP	IR		3						
8	MB-SMP	PT			3					
9	MB-SMP	IT				3		2	2	1
10	MB-SMP	SP					3	2	2	1
11	MB-Ctr	GR	3							
12	MB-Ctr	IR		3						
13	MB-Ctr	PT			3					
14	EOMV	IR		−1						
15	EOMV	PT			−1					
16	EOMV	IT				−2	−1	−1	−1	−1
17	EOMV	SP				−1	−2	−1	−1	−1
18	RMDR	GR	−3					−1.5	−1.5	
19	RMDR	IR		−3				−0.75	−0.75	
20	RMDR	PT			−3			−0.75	−0.75	
21	RDDR	GR	−4					−2	−2	
22	UD	GR	−5	−1	−1	−1	−1	−3	−3	−1
23	EFSFX	IT				3		1.5	1.5	1
24	EFSFX	SP					3	1.5	1.5	1
25	EB	IR		4				2	2	
26	EB	PT			4			2	2	
27	EB	IT				3		3	3	1
28	EB	SP					3	3	3	1
29	EXIT	GR	−2							
30	EXIT	IR		−2						
31	EXIT	PT			−2					
32	EXIT	FR,DE						−1	−1	

GR = Greece; IR = Ireland; PT = Portugal; IT = Italy; SP = Spain; FR = France; DE = Germany; RG-7 = remaining G-7 countries; ORO = official refinancing only; RVPSI = refinancing with voluntary full-value private sector involvement; MB-SMP = market buyback through Securities Markets Program intervention; MB-Ctr = market buyback directly by countries; EOMV = exchange offer with maintenance of value; RMDR = restructuring with moderate debt reduction; RDDR = restructuring with deep debt reduction; UD = unilateral default; EFSFX = expansion of European Financial Stability Facility; EB = euro area bonds; EXIT = exit from the euro

Notes: Impacts are ranked from −5, extremely adverse, to +5, extremely favorable. No ranking (blank cell) means there is a neutral (zero) impact.

Source: Author's calculations.

be relatively larger for the own-country banks considering the point of departure (large magnitudes, no official financing), and there would be adverse spillover effects on banks in partner and other G-7 banks, again because of the much larger magnitudes involved for these two sovereigns than for Greece, Ireland, and Portugal.

Restructuring with moderate debt reduction would adversely affect banks of the country in question, as well as French and German banks because of their holdings. Restructuring with deep debt reduction would impose larger losses, and unilateral default even larger losses.

Expansion of the EFSF with corresponding increased official support to Italy and Spain would benefit the banks in those countries and to a lesser extent in France, Germany, and RG-7. There would be corresponding and potentially larger gains from access to eurobond borrowing.

Finally, exit from the euro would likely impose losses on Greek, Irish, or Portuguese banks, as they would be exposed to euro debt but now their domestic currency basis would be devalued. If France and Germany were to exit and form a new currency that appreciated, banks could also face some losses because of reduced competitiveness of their economies.

Conclusion

The European sovereign debt crisis is a crisis of confidence. With the possible exception of Greece, the levels of public debt, especially net debt, are manageable at reasonable interest rates. Even in Greece, the July 2011 package provided sufficient interest rate relief on EU support, and sufficient liquidity relief through conversion to 30-year maturities in the PSI, that under central projections the net debt, interest burden, and amortization rates were all consistent with debt sustainability. Ambitious primary surplus and privatization targets would, however, need to have been largely achieved to ensure sustainability.

Contagion from Greece has driven market interest rates to levels that, for Ireland and Portugal, could make insolvency a self-fulfilling prophecy. Thus the key policy challenge is to ensure official liquidity support and, if needed, PSI such that, together with fiscal adjustment, confidence can be restored and interest rates reduced back to levels consistent with sustainable market access. The euro area has gone a long way toward mounting efforts capable of carrying out this task, especially in the creation of the EFSF but also in the market intervention by the ECB. Contagion to Italy and Spain after the July Greek package has substantially increased the stakes and scope of the crisis, and if the recent market pressures persist, it might be necessary for a much enlarged EFSF to offer support, or for borrowing to begin in jointly and severally guaranteed eurobonds, or both. An examination of fiscal plans and debt dynamics reinforces the conclusion, however, that for these much larger economies the debt problem is one of liquidity from temporary loss of confidence rather than insolvency that would necessitate large haircuts and debt reductions.

An attempt to illustrate the pros and cons of alternative policy options, from the vantage points of the main countries involved as well as their banking systems, highlights the challenges in cooperative decision making that may lie ahead. However, the broad implication is that even for the stronger economies (and Germany in particular), the indirect benefits of sustaining the euro seem likely to warrant the escalation of support efforts that may become necessary. At the same time, such approaches as the eurobond would imply a move toward much greater fiscal integration and more centralized control of fiscal performance than has proven feasible under the current Maastricht arrangements.

Postscript[35]

Subsequent to the September 13–14, 2011 conference at which this paper was presented, several major developments occurred by the time this volume went to press in early December. First, on October 27, 2011, EU leaders announced that representatives of private banks and insurers had agreed to reduce the face value of their holdings of Greek public debt by 50 percent. At the same time, they announced their intention to use leverage to increase the lending capacity of the EFSF. Second, in early November, in the face of domestic political impasse on adjustment measures governments fell in both Greece and Italy, with technocratic interim prime ministers taking power (Lucas Papademos in Greece and Mario Monti in Italy). Third, on December 9, 2011 the European Council of EU heads of state tentatively agreed (except for the United Kingdom) on legislative strengthening of fiscal balance commitments (and new mechanisms for EU—or euro area—enforcement and penalties for countries violating these commitments); on moving forward the start of the €500 billion ESM to July 2012; and on providing €200 billion in lending to the IMF, together with supplementary funds to be sought from other countries, in support of an increased capacity for IMF crisis lending to European countries.

The move toward a large haircut on Greek debt represented a shift downward in the menu of policy options (table 11.1), from refinancing with voluntary PSI (RVPSI) to restructuring with somewhere between moderate and deep debt reduction (RMDR and RDDR, respectively). Ironically, the prominent Greek economist who would soon become the new prime minister, Lucas Papademos, wrote in the *Financial Times*[36] that forcing deep debt reduction would be counterproductive, because the July 21 arrangement yielded a sustainable debt burden and there would be serious contagion effects from a forced deeper reduction—the same diagnosis arrived at in this chapter and in Cline (2011).[37] By December, however, the epicenter of the European debt crisis had moved to the much larger venue of Italy (and by association Spain). The initial market quotes soon after the December 9 Council of Europe meeting were less than

---

35. December 14, 2011.

36. Lucas Papademos, "Forcing Greek Restructuring Is Not the Answer," *Financial Times,* October 21, 2011.

37. As noted in the postscript to Chapter 1, the president of the European Council stated in December 2011 that the earlier attempts to force PSI "had a very negative effect on the debt markets" (European Council 2011).

reassuring.[38] The euro area had still not made good on its October 27 pledge to leverage the EFSF to create a strong firewall, and increasingly the signals from the ECB were that its SMP interventions would be temporary and modest.

Increasingly it was becoming clear that the euro had created a collection of economies with no capacity to print their own money as the ultimate backstop to ensure payment of their sovereign debt.[39] When coupled with the conspicuous absence of a credible lender of last resort because of constraints on the ECB and German-led opposition to major leveraging of the EFSF and issuance of euro bonds, the result was to create a financial minefield for sovereign debt. It will require skill and some luck for the European and international financial systems to pass safely through this dangerous terrain.

---

38. By December 13, yields on 10-year Italian public bonds were 6.69 percent (Datastream).

39. For a discussion of the transformation of currency risk to sovereign risk under the euro, see Cline and Williamson (2011).

Appendix

Table 11A.1   Euro area member GDP, gross general government debt, and S&P ratings

Country	GDP (billions of euros)	Debt (billions of euros)	Rating	Index	Spread (basis points)	Impact[a]	Percent of GDP
Austria	284.0	198.4	AAA	1	0	0.8	0.30
Belgium	351.0	340.9	AA+	1.5	25	0.6	0.17
Cyprus	17.5	10.8	BBB+	3.5	179	−0.1	−0.84
Finland	180.3	87.2	AAA	1	0	0.4	0.21
France	1,946.3	1,639.7	AAA	1	0	7.0	0.36
Germany	2,498.8	1,998.9	AAA	1	0	8.5	0.34
Greece	230.2	326.9	CC	8	677	−20.7	−9.01
Ireland	153.9	148.0	BBB+	3.5	179	−2.0	−1.31
Italy	1,548.8	1,843.2	A+	2.5	91	−8.9	−0.58
Luxembourg	41.4	6.8	AAA	1	0	0	0.07
Malta	6.2	4.2	A	3	127	0	−0.57
Netherlands	590.3	375.9	AAA	1	0	1.6	0.27
Portugal	172.8	144.0	BBB−	4.3	272	−3.3	−1.91
Slovakia	65.9	27.7	A+	2.5	91	−0.1	−0.20
Slovenia	36.1	13.4	AA	2	55	0	−0.05
Spain	1,062.6	638.8	AA	2	55	−0.8	−0.07
Total	9,186.1	7,804.8				−17.1	−0.19
GDP-weighted:				1.69	37.5		
Debt-weighted:				1.87	47.8		

a. Change in annual interest costs, billions of euros.

Note: See discussion of table in text.

Sources: IMF, *World Economic Outlook* database, 2011, www.imf.org; Standard and Poor's, Sovereigns Ratings List, 2011, www.standardandpoors.com.

References

Bulow, Jeremy, and Kenneth Rogoff. 1988. The Buyback Boondoggle. *Brookings Papers on Economic Activity* 2: 675–704. Washington: Brookings Institution.

Cline, William R. 1984. *International Debt: Systemic Risk and Policy Response*. Washington: Institute for International Economics.

Cline, William R. 1995. *International Debt Reexamined*. Washington: Institute for International Economics.

Cline, William R. 2003. *Restoring Economic Growth in Argentina*. World Bank Policy Research Working Paper 3158. Washington: World Bank.

Cline, William R. 2007. Global Financial Architecture and Emerging Capital Markets. In *Monetary Policy and Financial Stability: From Theory to Practice*. Proceedings of the 2006 Monetary and Banking Seminar, Central Bank of Argentina. Buenos Aires: Central Bank of Argentina.

Cline, William R. 2010a. *Financial Globalization, Economic Growth, and the Crisis of 2007–09*. Washington: Peterson Institute for International Economics.

Cline, William R. 2010b. A Note on Debt Dynamics. Peterson Institute for International Economics, Washington, May. Processed.

Cline, William R. 2011. *Sustainability of Greek Public Debt*. Policy Brief 11-15. Washington: Peterson Institute for International Economics.

Cline, William R., and Kevin J. Barnes. 1997. *Spreads and Risk in Emerging Markets Lending*. IIF Research Papers No. 97-1. Washington: Institute of International Finance.

Cline, William R., and John Williamson. 2011. *The Current Currency Situation*. Policy Briefs in International Economics 11-18 Washington: Peterson Institute for International Economics, (November).

Darvas, Zsolt, Jean Pisani-Ferry, and André Sapir. 2011. *A Comprehensive Approach to the Euro-Area Debt Crisis*. Bruegel Policy Brief 2011/02. Brussels: Bruegel.

Delpla, Jacques, and Jakob von Weizsäcker. 2010. *The Blue Bond Proposal*. Bruegel Policy Brief 2010/03. Brussels: Bruegel.

Dirección General del Tesoro y Política Financiera. 2011. *Government Debt: Maturity Profile of Outstanding Debt as of 06/30/11*. Madrid. Available at www.tesoro.es (accessed on December 8, 2011).

ECB (European Central Bank). 2009. *Withdrawal and Expulsion from the EMU: Some Reflections*. Legal Working Paper Series 10. Frankfurt: European Central Bank.

European Commission. 2008. EMU@10: Successes and Challenges after Ten Years of Economic and Monetary Union. *European Economy* no. 2. Brussels: European Commission.

European Commission. 2011a. *The Economic Adjustment Program for Ireland*. Occasional Papers 76, Directorate-General for Economic and Financial Affairs. Brussels: European Commission.

European Commission. 2011b. *The Economic Adjustment Program for Portugal*. Occasional Papers 79, Directorate-General for Economic and Financial Affairs. Brussels: European Commission.

European Council. 2011. Remarks by Herman Van Rompuy, President of the European Council following the first session of the European Council. EUCO 155/11, December 9. Brussels.

IMF (International Monetary Fund). 2011a. *Ireland: First and Second Reviews under the Extended Arrangement and Request for Rephasing of the Arrangement*. IMF Country Report No. 11/109 (May). Washington.

IMF (International Monetary Fund). 2011b. *Portugal: Request for a Three-Year Arrangement under the Extended Fund Facility*. IMF Country Report No. 11/127. Washington.

Jaramillo, Laura, and Catalina Michelle Tejada. 2011. *Sovereign Credit Ratings and Spreads in Emerging Markets: Does Investment Grade Matter?* IMF Working Paper WP/11/44. Washington: International Monetary Fund.

Ministerio dell'Economia e delle Finanze. 2011. *Outstanding Public Securities (Breakdown by Maturity)*, July 31. Rome.

Mussa, Michael. 2006. Reflections on the Function and Facilities for IMF Lending. In *Reforming the IMF for the 21st Century*, ed. Edwin M. Truman. Washington: Institute for International Economics.

NTMA (National Treasury Management Agency). 2011. *Maturity Profile of Debt* (August). Dublin. Available at www.ntma.ie.

OECD (Organization for Economic Cooperation and Development). 2011. *Economic Outlook* no. 89. Paris.

Porzecanski, Arturo C. 2005. From Rogue Creditors to Rogue Debtors: Implications of Argentina's Default. *Chicago Journal of International Law* 6, no. 1: 311–26.

Reinhart, Carmen M., and Kenneth S. Rogoff. 2008. *Banking Crises: An Equal Opportunity Menace.* NBER Working Paper 14587. Cambridge, MA: National Bureau of Economic Research.

Stiglitz, Joseph, and Andrew Weiss. 1981. Credit Rationing in Markets with Imperfect Information. *American Economic Review* 71, no. 3: 393–410.

Sturzenegger, Federico, and Jeromin Zettelmeyer. 2006. *Debt Defaults and Lessons from a Decade of Crises.* Cambridge, MA: MIT Press.

12

The Euro Area Crisis:
Policy Options Ahead

GUNTRAM B. WOLFF

The global financial crisis quickly affected the euro area economies. The initial response of significant fiscal expansion to address shortfalls in domestic demand due to corrections in housing and asset markets was followed by a phase of gradual fiscal retrenchment. What started as a Greek fiscal crisis with significant market risk premia on the Greek sovereign quickly transformed itself into a crisis affecting five euro area economies. Greece, Ireland, and Portugal are under financial assistance programs. Spain and Italy face heavy market pressure from elevated yields on their sovereign debt.

This is not the place to describe the developments of the last two years and the fundamental policy mistakes that have been made. Clearly, the handling of Greece and the responses of the Eurogroup and the European Council have not been enough to stop the fire from spreading. In short, the euro area is in a precarious situation.

Against this background, this chapter discusses a number of the policy proposals that are on the table. In particular, it examines the conceptual and legal limits and opportunities of the approaches, setting them in the general economic context. The chapter is structured as follows. The first section sets out the issue in broad macroeconomic terms. A discussion of debt restructuring follows in the second section. The third section discusses the eurobond, paying special attention to the concept of a "joint and several" guarantee and its implications for the euro area governance setup. The next section discusses the solution involving the European Financial Stability Facility (EFSF) and

Guntram B. Wolff is deputy director of Bruegel.

the European Stability Mechanism (ESM), pointing to its limits, as well as the solution proposed by Daniel Gros. The last section discusses the possibility of euro area breakup, which would be a disaster. The chapter concludes with four major recommendations.

The Issue

The current euro area crisis is characterized by a combination of an overhang in public and/or private debt and significant adjustment needs in terms of price competitiveness. The combination of these two factors renders this crisis especially dangerous, resulting in a very fragile banking sector and weak economic growth.

Figure 12.1 illustrates the ratio of net external financial assets to GDP in Greece, Portugal, Ireland, Spain, and Italy. Net external liabilities currently exceed 100 percent of GDP in Greece and Portugal and are close to that in Ireland. Spain is at around 90 percent. Only in Italy are the net external liabilities more limited, not exceeding 20 percent of GDP. Large external liabilities reflect the past increases in domestic net liabilities, which have increased differently in the different sectors of the economies. Figure 12.2 shows the net financial assets of the different sectors of the economy. As would be expected, households are typically holders of net assets, while corporations and governments have a net debt position. The figure also reveals clearly that in Greece the main driver of large liability positions is the government sector, while in Spain, Portugal, and Ireland, the large accumulation of liabilities results from the corporate sector. In Italy, large government debt is offset by large asset holdings of the household sector so that the net position of the economy is more balanced.

These net positions conceal very large gross financial asset and liability positions (figure 12.3). Ireland certainly stands out with financial assets and financial liabilities of around 18 times GDP. But the numbers for the other countries are also nonnegligible, easily constituting stocks of assets and liabilities exceeding several years' worth of income.

Such large stocks can render economies susceptible to changes in the prices of assets and liabilities. Suppose that assets react differently to changes in economic circumstances than do liabilities. Any economic event then has the potential to dramatically change the net asset position of an economy. Take again the extreme case of Ireland, where assets are mostly in the form of debt and liabilities mostly in the form of shares (figure 12.4). In 2007, Ireland was only in slight net external liability (less than 20 percent), while by 2009 this number had climbed to almost 100 percent. An important part of this increase is related to valuation effects.[1]

A large part of the increase in net liabilities is in the form of debt, i.e., securities other than shares (bonds) and loans (figure 12.4). This comes as a heavy

---

1. An extensive discussion of valuation effects can be found in European Commission (2010).

Figure 12.1 Net external financial liabilities, 2009

percent of GDP

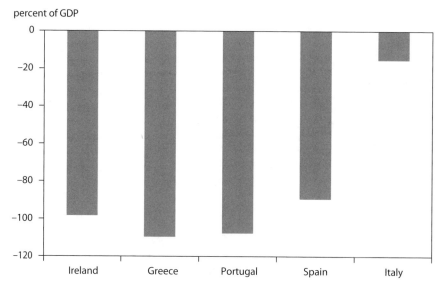

Source: Eurostat database, http://epp.eurostat.ec.europa.eu.

Figure 12.2 Net financial assets in domestic sectors, 2009

percent of GDP

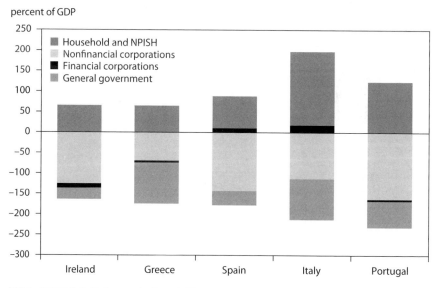

NPISH = Nonprofit institutions serving households

Source: Eurostat database, http://epp.eurostat.ec.europa.eu.

Figure 12.3   Gross assets and liabilities, 2009

percent of GDP

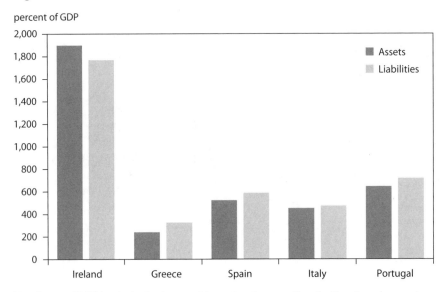

Note: Assets and liabilities obtained as the sum of three categories—securities other than shares, loans, and shares and other equity.

Source: Eurostat database, http://epp.eurostat.ec.europa.eu.

Figure 12.4   Net assets and liabilities across categories, 2009

percent of GDP

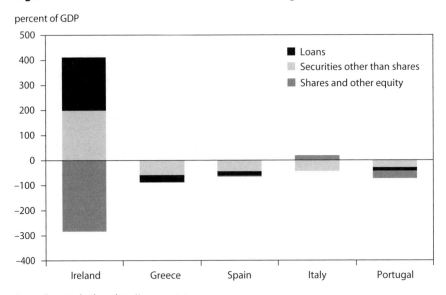

Source: Eurostat database, http://epp.eurostat.ec.europa.eu.

Figure 12.5 Divergence in competitiveness, 1994–2010
(unit labor cost-adjusted real effective exchange rate)

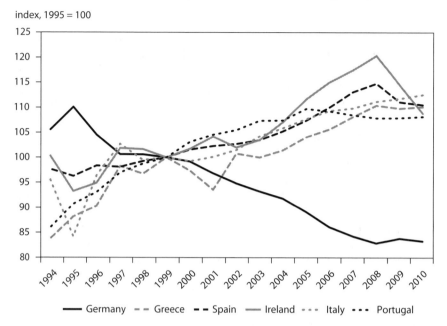

index, 1995 = 100

Germany ▬▬ Greece – – Spain ▬ ▬ Ireland ▬ Italy ··· Portugal ···

Source: European Union, Directorate General for Economic and Financial Affairs, Price/Competitiveness Database.

burden to the economies concerned, since in a recessionary environment the value of the debt remains unchanged while income and nonfinancial assets go down massively.

This high external and internal debt burden combines with significant competitiveness adjustment needs. Figure 12.5 summarizes the divergence in competitiveness based on unit labor costs for the economies concerned. As can be seen, there has been a continuous divergence in relative unit labor costs since 1999. The crisis has not massively corrected this divergence in competitiveness except in the case of Ireland and to some extent Spain.

The five economies discussed in this chapter therefore face a double challenge. On the one hand, they have to deal with a large debt burden. This debt burden is too high in a situation where interest rates on public debt increase and credit availability to firms and households is restricted. The situation is all the more difficult when income is falling due to the recession, which in part is aggravated by the public budget consolidation needs. On the other hand, the economies in question need to increase their competitiveness in order to be able to service their foreign debt. This is particularly relevant for those economies that hold large external debt positions. Repaying external debt requires running current account surpluses, which can currently be achieved only with a strong increase in exports. (While the Italian export performance is not good and price competitiveness indicators are not looking good either, this is somehow less of an issue in Italy, where the external debt problem is more limited.) The combination of the two factors—i.e., the need for a competitiveness adjustment and the debt overhang—renders the current situation toxic. While downward wage adjustments may help on the competitiveness and export side, they may also reduce the overall income (depending on the time profile of job creation), rendering debt repayment more difficult.

Below I discuss the different policy options for addressing this situation.

Debt Restructuring

One obvious option to get rid of a debt overhang is to default on this debt. This will imply a transfer of resources from the creditor to the debtor, thereby alleviating the situation of the debtor. But a debt restructuring certainly comes at a price. In this section I discuss only sovereign debt restructuring and leave aside the important issue of household and corporate debt overhang and restructuring. Restructuring in these two sectors is governed by clearer rules, though these vary greatly from country to country. Conceptually, I think of a debt restructuring as a significant decrease in the face value of sovereign debt.[2]

A significant debt restructuring may limit future borrowing capacity. Empirical evidence on this is, however, limited. In fact, if the debt reduction is sufficient to bring down the primary deficit to zero, there is no borrowing requirement. The discipline imposed by markets may even be the kind of limit needed to prevent future debt increases. Of course there is also the option to use limited fiscal transfers from the creditor countries to smooth the impact on expenditure and revenues of a tax cut. The decision when to do the debt cut therefore does not depend on the level of the primary deficit if foreign lenders are willing to accept temporary budget help to more gradually decrease the primary deficits.

A more serious issue to explore is the impact of a debt restructuring on the banking sector and financial industry at large. I have argued elsewhere that this should be systematically explored by the euro area institution in charge of it, the European Systemic Risk Board.[3] It is not straightforward to make such an assessment, as it depends on numerous different channels.

A necessarily preliminary assessment by Darvas (2011) comes to the conclusion that a restructuring of Greek debt may not be a significant problem for financial stability. I do not want to replicate all the arguments here, but exposure in terms of debt, credit default swaps (CDS), and financial functions

---

2. There exists a large and sometimes imprecise body of terminology for describing different forms of debt restructuring. Basically, the forms can all be thought of in terms of the different sizes of the reduction of the debt's face value.

3. Guntram B. Wolff, "ESRB Should Act on Sovereign Risk," May 5, 2011, www.bruegel.org (accessed on November 15, 2011).

Table 12.1 Exposure of banks to sovereigns as tested in stress test (billions of euros)

Country	Greece	Ireland	Portugal	Spain	Italy
France	10.1	2.1	4.8	14.6	53.0
Germany	7.9	1.0	3.6	18.6	36.8
Greece	54.4	0.0	0.0	0.0	0.1
Ireland	0.0	12.5	0.2	0.3	0.8
Portugal	1.4	0.5	19.6	0.3	1.0
Spain	0.4	0.1	5.5	231.7	7.4
Italy	1.4	0.2	0.4	3.2	164.0

Source: European Banking Authority, July 2011.

of the rest of the euro area is limited. The major fallout would come for the Greek banking system itself. The financial assistance program for Greece, however, already foresees some means to address such a problem, and further capital for bank recapitalization could be provided.

Instead, I want to focus on banking sector exposure to sovereign debt of the five euro area countries discussed, using some recent data from the European Banking Authority's (EBA's) stress test. Table 12.1 provides data on how much of the debt of a given country is held in the banking systems of seven different countries that are part of the current exercise. EBA and the national authorities designed the stress tests such that in every country at least 75 percent of the total assets of the banking system would be covered.

A number of interesting observations can be made. First, sovereign bonds of a country are typically held by the banks located in the same country. Second, a debt restructuring in Greece or Ireland would have very limited direct effects on the banking sectors of the other countries having difficulties. Spain has significant exposure to Portugal and Italy. The banking systems of Greece, Ireland, and Portugal have no exposure to Italy. Italy in turn has no significant exposure to the other four countries. A debt restructuring in any of the five countries would therefore have a limited impact on any of the other peripheral economies.

Turning to the exposure of France and Germany to the five countries discussed, France is much more exposed than Germany, with overall French exposure at €85 billion and overall German exposure at €68 billion. Relative to GDP, France would thus incur much greater losses. However, the largest part of the difference comes from exposure to the Italian sovereign. In the cases of Greece, Ireland, and Portugal, the differences are of small macroeconomic relevance.

Addressing the insolvency of Greece,[4] but potentially also of Ireland and Portugal, by a significant haircut on the existing debt would lead to relatively limited direct losses for the banking systems in France and Germany as well

---

4. The insolvency of Greece is discussed in length in Darvas, Pisani-Ferry, and Sapir (2011).

as the banking systems of the other four countries. Only the banking system of Greece itself is heavily exposed to its own sovereign.

In the case of Greece, a 50 percent haircut—which is considered necessary by many economists—would basically wipe out the entire equity of the Greek banking sector. Large-scale financial instability in Greece would need to be avoided in order to prevent Greek problems from spreading in the region.[5] One would have to agree to a nationalization and recapitalization of the Greek banking system, potentially involving foreign banks. The financial means needed for this are quite limited. A recapitalization fund of around €25 billion would be sufficient. Greece's first financial program already foresees €10 billion for the banking system, so another €15 billion would have to be found.

If a country has such a credit event and restructures debt, what happens to its relations with the ECB? The ECB has repeatedly claimed that it would not be able to accept collateral of a government that had recently defaulted. However, there is no clear rule that would force the ECB to do so, and the decision would be at the discretion of the governing council. Obviously the rating of a defaulted country would be very low. Economically, however, the quality of restructured debt would be much higher, as a much lower debt burden would stand against the same revenue stream. It therefore sounds plausible that the ECB would continue accepting defaulted bonds as collateral. And the ECB would certainly provide unlimited liquidity to the financial system if needed, as it has an obligation to contribute to the financial stability of the system.

Major restructuring of Greek debt would, however, lead to a reassessment of the appropriate price of the other sovereigns concerned. Clearly, prices include the implicit assumption that other euro area sovereigns would partly pay up for the current exposure of the financial sector. A restructuring would thus be a credible signal that banks can actually lose money on sovereign debt. Note that this contagion does not come from the direct exposure of the financial system, which implicitly enjoys the national sovereign backstop.[6] The contagion comes from a reassessment of the size of the haircut.

The difficulty of the situation comes from the fact that this reassessment of the potential losses can, by itself, render a default more likely. For Italy, most economists would probably agree that there is no solvency issue unless the market is driving up the interest rate, thereby triggering a self-fulfilling liquidity-solvency crisis.[7] The doubt about Italy started because major structural difficulties surfaced when the finance minister started to have political difficulties. The resulting spreads render the political as well as economic situation in Italy more difficult. On the other hand, the resulting spreads have also

---

5. Greek banks are important players in Bulgaria, Romania, and some of the republics of the former Yugoslavia.

6. For a discussion of the feedback loop between exposure of the banking system to its own national sovereign and responses to this situation, see Marzinotto, Pisani-Ferry, and Wolff (2011).

7. Paul de Grauwe, "The European Central Bank as a Lender of Last Resort," VoxEU, August 18, 2011, www.voxeu.org (accessed October 16, 2011).

helped to increase the pressure for much-needed reform. At current interest rates, Italy could survive for quite a long time without major economic implications in terms of debt sustainability. However, doubts about fiscal sustainability could certainly have become self-fulfilling very quickly if the banking system had experienced a bank run.[8]

In the following section, I therefore want to discuss ways to address self-fulfilling crises or true insolvency.

Eurobond: Possibilities and Difficulties

The most widely discussed eurobond concept is certainly the Blue Bond/Red Bond concept proposed by Jacques Delpla and Jakob von Weizsäcker (2010). They suggest that sovereign debt in euro area countries be split into two parts. The first part, the senior "blue" tranche of up to 60 percent of GDP, would be pooled among participating countries and jointly and severally guaranteed. The second part, the junior "red" tranche, would keep debt in excess of 60 percent of GDP as a purely national responsibility.

One of the advantages of this proposal is that it maintains a large incentive for market discipline and prudent lending behavior by the financial industry. The red debt would certainly be a very expensive way of borrowing from the market, and parliaments would have a strong incentive to reduce the red part of the debt.

A central concept that needs to be understood when discussing a common eurobond (in this case the Blue Bond) is the concept of joint and several guarantees. *In extremis*, this implies that every country can be held fully liable for all the debt issued under the scheme. At a pinch, if all countries but one (say all countries except Luxembourg) decided not to service their obligations, the remaining country would need to service the total stock of debt. This example shows that a true joint-and-several guarantee has vast implications for national fiscal policy:

1. A clear mechanism needs to be developed that ensures that every country is obliged to service its blue debt under all circumstances. In other words, the seniority of blue debt needs to be established. This needs to be done not only at the country level but also at the European level so that the group of euro area countries participating can control the payment obligation of every other country.

2. In the case of a bond issued by a bank, seniority can be easily established by a simple contract. This contract is enforceable in law, and the bank can be taken to court. For a sovereign, this becomes much more difficult as the sovereign needs to commit itself to respect its own contract. This is not a trivial thing to do. De facto, it can be credibly done only if the coun-

---

8. I therefore see in principle no alternative to the ECB's Securities Markets Program at this stage. See Wolff (2011).

try ceases to be the sovereign and gives up sovereignty to a supranational institution.

3. The introduction of a eurobond would thus have to involve a change in the EU treaty. This change in the treaty would have to specify what areas of sovereignty would be given to the European Union. EU competence would certainly have to extend to setting the level of the budget deficit. It may even include a veto on the composition of revenues and expenditure so as to force the national finance ministry and parliament to first pay the interest on the eurobond. Such a huge transfer of sovereignty from national parliaments to the European level should then go hand in hand with a massive stepping up of democratic accountability at the European level. In other words, the European Parliament would be given some form of EU budget authority.

4. Giving up such a degree of sovereignty at the national level and passing it to the European level would have to involve changes in constitutions of several euro area member states.

Overall, the introduction of a common euro area bond involving joint and several liability will have to involve massive changes in the legal and institutional setup of the European Union and its member states. It does not appear likely that these could take place in a short period of time. On the contrary, even if a decision to go ahead with a eurobond was taken today, it would probably take two years to implement it.

The assessment that massive legal and institutional changes are needed to introduce eurobonds is also confirmed in the recent German Constitutional Court ruling. Karlsruhe makes it clear that all major decisions with a major budgetary impact can be taken only by a democratically elected parliament.[9] While the ruling allows the setup of an EFSF, the size thereof may not be extended beyond a value that would de facto severely inhibit budgetary autonomy.[10] It is also clear that the German court again stresses the intergovern-

---

9. "In this context, the Bundestag, as the legislature, is also prohibited from establishing permanent mechanisms under the law of international agreements which result in an assumption of liability for other states' voluntary decisions, especially if they have consequences whose impact is difficult to calculate." Federal Constitutional Court, Press Office, press release no. 55/2011, September 7, 2011, www.bundesverfassungsgericht.de (accessed on November 15, 2011).

10. "Article 38 of the German constitution [www.artikel5.de/gesetze/gg.html#art38] requires, in connection with the tenets of the principle of democracy (Article 20.1 and 20.2, Article 79.3), that the decision on revenue and expenditure of the public sector remain in the hand of the German Bundestag as a fundamental part of the ability of a constitutional state to democratically shape itself. As elected representatives of the people, the members of parliament must remain in control of fundamental budget policy decisions in a system of intergovernmental governance as well. When establishing mechanisms of considerable financial importance which can lead to incalculable burdens on the budget, the German Bundestag must therefore ensure that later on, mandatory approval by the Bundestag is always obtained again." Federal Constitutional Court, Press Office, press release no. 55/2011, September 7, 2011, www.bundesverfassungsgericht.de (accessed on November 15, 2011).

mental nature of the European Union, in which democratic legitimacy comes exclusively from the nation state. Already in the ruling of 2009 on the Lisbon Treaty, the court demanded a strengthening of the national legislature. Ultimately, the court denied that the European Parliament could be the source of democratic legitimacy.[11] In this sense, the latest court decision does not come as a surprise. It stands in a long tradition of, on the one hand, not stopping the European integration process while, on the other hand, setting clear limits. A further integration step introducing eurobonds with joint and several liability is thus conceivable from the Constitutional Court's point of view only under a new treaty setting up a democratically legitimate EU structure. In parallel, the German constitution would need to be changed (certainly Article 23 but others as well).

In the area of economics, an important critique that has recently been voiced on the Blue Bond and Red Bond proposal is that the split of the debt into a senior and junior tranche would increase the overall interest burden. This would make it very difficult to introduce it for high-debt countries such as Italy. According to the Modigliani-Miller theorem, however, the overall interest burden should remain unchanged. Even if not all of the assumptions of Modigliani-Miller are fulfilled, and the overall interest burden does increase, the increase could still be offset by the greater liquidity of the Blue Bond. Overall, then, the validity of this criticism is not established.

The criticism shows, however, that a simple introduction of Blue and Red Bonds would not immediately solve the crisis and could not prevent self-fulfilling liquidity crises from becoming solvency crises. It has therefore been proposed that the Blue/Red Bond concept be introduced gradually. Under this approach, all newly issued debt, including the debt that is rolled over, would be issued in blue debt up to a predefined threshold. In contrast to a "big bang" introduction, where every bond would be split into a junior and senior tranche, the gradual introduction of Blue Bonds has a number of important advantages and disadvantages.

---

11. "At its current position of integration and despite entry into force of the Treaty of Lisbon, the European Union still has not achieved a configuration which corresponds to the level of legitimacy required for constitutionally defined democracy. Not only from the perspective of the [German] Constitution, however, is the issue of the participation of Germany in the European Union not about the transference of a federal state model to the European level. It also concerns the extension of the current [German] federal constitutional model to the dimension of supra-national cooperation. The Treaty of Lisbon has decided against the idea of a European federal constitution in which a European Parliament acts as a constitutionally representative body with a newly constituted people at the center. It is not possible to detect [in the Lisbon Treaty] an intention of founding a state as the end-goal. When measured against the principles of free and equal choice and the requirements of strong majority rule, the European Union does not correspond to the federal level in the [German] federal state. The Treaty of Lisbon therefore does not alter the fact that the Bundestag is the representative body of the German people in the center of an interwoven democratic system" (Editors' translation of German text in Bundesverfassungsgericht [Federal Constitutional Court], 2 BvE 2/08 of 30/06/2009, paragraphs No. (1-21), www.bundesverfassungsgericht.de [accessed on November 15, 2011]).

It would enable a country like Italy, with a relatively long debt maturity, to issue only blue debt for several years. This would help the country for several years to avoid refinancing difficulties. However, eventually, there would come a day when the Blue Bond capacity was exhausted and the refinancing of maturing debt would have to be done with red debt. It is possible that, at this stage, the interest rate would become prohibitive, leading to a default.

One disadvantage of the gradual approach has to do with its political economy. Up front, there are no incentives to address structural weaknesses of the economy, in particular the day when Red Bonds become the only way of financing in the next election cycle. Once only Red Bonds are available for financing, there will be enormous pressure from all sides to increase the ceiling of Blue Bonds. If such a scenario is to be avoided, all countries would need to commit to carry out very strong structural reforms up front, while at the same time forcing the banking sector to get rid of all bonds maturing after the deadline when only Red Bonds were available for refinancing. Only if the banking sector is freed of such bonds could a restructuring be possible. But how can the banking system sell these bonds if all market participants know that there will eventually be a large haircut? Banks would incur massive losses from the beginning.

Legally, moreover, it is doubtful whether a gradual introduction of Blue Bonds would be acceptable. In fact, by introducing senior bonds, all remaining bonds would be put at a disadvantage. This would certainly be challenged in court.

Given these difficulties, a gradual introduction of Blue Bonds does not appear to be feasible. Instead, it appears more sensible to split all debt in two parts up front. This solution would not, however, solve urgent funding pressures now. The most feasible eurobond concept, therefore, appears to be the transformation of all national debt into common eurobond debt with joint and several liability in exchange for a massive transfer of sovereignty to the European level.

The EFSF/ESM Solution

Given the difficulties associated with a massive transfer of sovereignty and a country's political unwillingness to effect such a transfer, other solutions have so far been sought. The EFSF/ESM solution that is currently being pursued explicitly avoids joint and several guarantees. Instead, the EFSF is an international financial institution that can borrow on the market with guarantees of the national member states. The mechanism by which borrowing is done is quite complicated and is currently being redrafted following the agreement of July 21, 2011.[12]

---

12. A summary is given in a recent note by Credit Suisse. See Michelle Bradley, Helen Haworth, Thushka Maharaj, and William Porter, "EFSF (R)evolution," Credit Suisse, August 16, 2011, https://research-and-analytics.csfb.com (accessed on November 15, 2011). Political and legislative discussions are still not settled.

The basic feature of the mechanism is that every state gives a certain guarantee (in the new amendments, there is no cash deposit anymore). But the debt issued by the EFSF is guaranteed only to a certain percentage by the member state (it is therefore similar to a jumbo bond in the German subnational bond market[13]). This means that large overguarantees have to be given by the AAA countries to secure an AAA rating of the debt issued by the EFSF.

If any of the large risks were to materialize, especially if Italy came to the brink, one possibility alluded to in a recent letter by President José Manuel Barroso to the European Council would be to increase further the size of the EFSF, possibly to €1 trillion or €1.5 trillion. This is a very mechanical approach, which ignores the fact that the EFSF relies on a sufficiently large number of strong core euro area issuers to support peripheral countries in crisis. In fact, the possibility of contagion beyond the periphery severely challenges the very logic on which the EFSF rests. The very structure of the EFSF/ESM makes it possible to envisage a scenario whereby recourse to it after the crisis starts would sequentially weaken one country after another until the crisis hit core countries. Should Italy need to be rescued using the EFSF, for instance, France would inevitably be hit. The EFSF architecture, instead of being a vector of stability, would become a vector of instability—an incubating vehicle for financial distress. The endgame would be Germany providing support to all the rest of the euro area, which would exceed its fiscal capacity.

In brief, contagion, which spreads with centripetal force to the core, challenges the logic of the EFSF and the mutual limited guarantee mechanism through which it operates to provide durable and credible assistance to affected countries. Thus, a mechanism excluding joint and several guarantees could easily fail when the crisis spreads to Italy.

Given these shortcomings, Daniel Gros has proposed registering the EFSF/ESM as a bank.[14] He argues that given the cascading effects described above, the size of the EFSF cannot simply be increased. Instead, the EFSF could get unlimited access to refinancing at the ECB. The ECB obviously can provide unlimited liquidity. This solution would keep the management of debt problems in the hands of finance ministers, but at the same time provide a liquidity backstop that is needed in case of generalized breakdown of liquidity and confidence, as in the case of self-fulfilling liquidity crises. To date, I have not seen a convincing counterargument. Indeed, this solution appears feasible and would ensure ECB independence from individual countries.

Euro Breakup

Any fiscal solution is incomplete, as fiscal transfers or a common assumption of debt does not address the wage and cost divergence of the last 10 years. A

---

13. See Schulz and Wolff (2009).

14. Daniel Gros, "August 2011: The Euro Crisis Reaches the Core," VoxEU, August 11, 2011, www.voxeu.org (accessed on November 15, 2011).

Figure 12.6 Manufacturing share of value added, 1995–2007

index, 1995 = 100

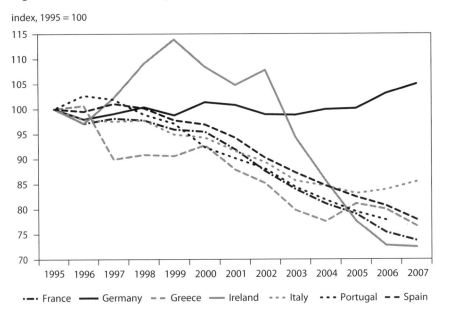

Source: Organization for Economic Cooperation and Development.

fiscal solution is thus a necessary but possibly not a sufficient solution. Even with large fiscal transfers, entire countries of the euro area will remain highly uncompetitive, and value added in manufacturing and industry will remain low. Figure 12.6 shows the massive decline in manufacturing as a share of value added experienced by the five countries at issue since the beginning of the euro. Value added and employment have dramatically decreased. With the collapse in construction, service sector activity, and all activity related to imports, a significant redeployment of resources from this nontradable sector to the tradable sector is needed.

Economically, this shift of resources is achieved by changing the price of tradables relative to nontradables. In economies with a flexible exchange rate, this is achieved by a depreciation of the currency, but this option does not exist in the euro area. In the euro area, wages have to fall significantly (or productivity has to increase without a concurrent wage increase) in order to regain competitiveness. Certainly wage increases in the core euro area countries would help somewhat, but the gains would be of second order, as the export structure of most of the southern countries includes only moderate exports to the core area countries, whereas reductions in the unit labor cost in the country itself will directly impact on all exports.

In the absence of major price adjustments, unemployment is likely to rise even further. This, in turn, will increase political instability. At some stage, there may be a populist call for dropping out of the euro area. There are also other reasons why a euro exit could be contemplated. The large increase in the cost of debt would certainly give rise to a call for more monetary policy flexibility. If this is not met by the ECB via the Securities Markets Program, populist calls to regain monetary independence may arise. It is also possible that a member state might not accept the conditionality and therefore decide to leave the euro.

I will start by discussing the hypothetical exit of one country, followed by a discussion of a split of the euro area into two.

Suppose one country decides that it wants to leave the euro. The first question is how this can be done in practice. Once a rumor of the exit reached the market, there would immediately be a bank run and all capital would flee the country. Practically, the decision would have to be announced on a Friday evening. One would then probably have to introduce a couple of days of bank holidays to avoid a bank run. A law would have to be passed to transform all domestic contracts from euros to the new currency. What would need to be done with all the contracts signed under the law of a country other than the one concerned? The baseline assumption would be that these contracts remain in euros. For all circulating cash, one could offer a period of one month to exchange at a fixed exchange rate. Most of the larger amounts of cash would leave the country anyway, but quantitatively this is of less importance. Before the final new cash would be introduced, some form of interim cash would need to be quickly printed.

Does the EU treaty provide for an exit from the Economic and Monetary Union (EMU)? Athanassiou (2009) of the ECB has provided a comprehensive study on the question. In the pre-Lisbon treaty, there was no legal provision for EMU/EU exit. The Vienna Convention on the Law of Treaties recognizes limited rights of withdrawal (from treaties), but the relevance of this provision was disputed (The European Court of Justice's argument: because the European Union is a legal system sui generis, the transfers of sovereignty are permanent). However, Greenland's withdrawal from the European Communities was allowed in 1982, so apparently a withdrawal was conceivable as a last resort, though there was no possibility of expelling a country. In the Lisbon Treaty, the EU negotiated an exit clause (Article 50), but no specific EMU provision. In other words, it is legally impossible to withdraw from the EMU only. An EMU exit would therefore have to involve a simultaneous European Union exit.

More important than these practical and legal/constitutional issues, however, are the economic challenges to a euro area breakup. The euro area is a highly integrated financial system with very large cross-border asset and liability positions. Even a small country like Greece holds more than €200 billion of assets in the form of debt (bonds and loans) abroad. It owes nearly €450 billion abroad (see table 12.2). A redenomination could lead to large mismatches in assets and liabilities. What matters for such mismatches is, of course, the law of the contract. Government bonds issued in the country are usually issued under domestic law. But foreign law would apply, for example, to corporate bonds issued on international markets.

Table 12.2　Assets and liabilities, end-2007
(billions of euros)

Country	Debt assets	Debt liabilities
Germany	5,000	4,578
France	4,100	4,425
Italy	1,602	2,412
Spain	1,114	2,086
Ireland	2,506	2,000
Portugal	310	464
Greece	223	448

Source: Lane and Milesi-Ferretti (2007).

It appears likely that these differences in the place of contract of the different debt obligations, together with the large ensuing devaluation, would lead to massive asset and liability mismatches. The gains and losses for each economic agent are difficult to predict, as little is known about the place of contract of the different economic relations. It appears almost certain that as a result we would observe massive chains of bankruptcies. It is difficult to come up with precise economic estimates of this. Some analysts have tried to do so. UBS claims that the cost for a southern seceding country would amount to between €9,500 and €11,500 per person.[15] But frankly, such numbers are at best a good guess. Certainly a breakup would exact a massive cost in terms of civil unrest, banking sector collapse, capital controls, loss of trust, etc.

An even more serious issue is the chain reaction that a decision by one country to leave would trigger. Basically, once the market knows how a euro area exit would work, it would have a blueprint for the future. The market would then start to immediately bet against all the other countries that are at risk of leaving. This would not only concern the financial sector; all other businesses as well as households would stop entering into contractual relations with the countries in question (resulting in, e.g., no delivery of goods against trade credit). From this moment onward, the euro would stop being the euro, as a euro in Lisbon would not be the same as a euro in Frankfurt or Paris. In sum, one country leaving would trigger a domino effect of further countries leaving, and the euro area would eventually break up.

As a gradual and successive unraveling of the euro would come with very high economic—to say nothing of political—costs, some commentators have recently advanced the idea of splitting the euro in two.[16] A "neuro" would be used by the countries of the former Deutsche mark zone. A "seuro" would be used essentially by the Mediterranean countries and Ireland. The big question

---

15. See Deo, Donovan, and Hatheway (2011).

16. See, for example, the piece by Hans-Olaf Henkel, former head of the Federation of German Industries: "A Sceptic's Solution—A Breakaway Currency," *Financial Times*, August 30, 2011.

is whether France belongs to the neuro or seuro area. Certainly France is torn between the two groups in terms of geography, history, politics, and economics, and either choice would be a disaster for Europe as well as for France.

A breakup of the euro would thus be a huge economic, political, and historical mistake.

Conclusion

Europe is at a crossroads. In this chapter I have sketched a number of possible avenues that are currently being debated. Politically and economically, four major steps need to be taken:

1. The Greek problem needs to be solved.

2. The ECB, potentially in combination with the EFSF, needs to document its full resolve to act. The EFSF or another institution needs to exercise tough conditionality.

3. Credible structural reforms to address weak economic performance need to be enacted.

4. Further integration steps calling for a common EU treasury need to be started.

References

Athanassiou, Phoebus. 2009. *Withdrawal and Expulsion from the EU and EMU: Some Reflections.* ECB Legal Working Paper Series No. 10. Frankfurt: European Central Bank. Available at www.ecb.int (accessed on November 15, 2011).

Darvas, Zsolt. 2011. Debt Restructuring in the Euro Area: A Necessary but Manageable Evil? Bruegel Policy Contribution 2011/07. Brussels: Bruegel. Available at www.bruegel.org (accessed on November 15, 2011).

Darvas, Zsolt, Jean Pisani-Ferry, and André Sapir. 2011. *A Comprehensive Approach to the Euro-Area Debt Crisis.* Bruegel Policy Brief 2011/2. Brussels: Bruegel. Available at www.bruegel.org (accessed on November 15, 2011).

Delpla, Jacques, and Jakob von Weizsäcker. 2010. *The Blue Bond Proposal.* Bruegel Policy Brief 2010/03. Brussels: Bruegel. Available at www.bruegel.org (accessed on November 15, 2011).

Deo, Stephane, Paul Donovan, and Larry Hatheway. 2011. *Euro Break-up—The Consequences.* UBS Investment Research Global Economic Perspectives. September 6.

European Commission. 2010. Competitiveness and Current Account Divergences in the Euro Area. In *Quarterly Report on the Euro Area* 9, no. 1. Brussels: European Commission, Directorate General for Economic and Financial Affairs. Available at http://ec.europa.eu (accessed on November 15, 2011).

Lane, Philip R., and Gian Maria Milesi-Ferretti. 2007. The External Wealth of Nations Mark II: Revised and Extended Estimates of Foreign Assets and Liabilities, 1970–2004. *Journal of International Economics* 73 (November): 223–50.

Marzinotto, Benedicta, Jean Pisani-Ferry, and Guntram Wolff. 2011. *An Action Plan for the European Leaders.* Bruegel Policy Contribution Issue 2011/09. Brussels: Bruegel. Available at www.bruegel.org (accessed on November 15, 2011).

Schulz, Alexander, and Guntram B. Wolff. 2009. The German Sub-national Government Bond Market: Structure, Determinants of Yield Spreads and Berlin's Foregone Bail-out. *Journal of Economics and Statistics* 229, no. 1: 61–83.

Wolff, Guntram. 2011. *Changing of the Guard—Huge Challenges Ahead for the New ECB President*. Bruegel Policy Contribution 2011/10. Brussels: Bruegel.

13

Comments on Policy Strategies

Sustainability, Financial Backstopping, and the Restructuring of Greek Debt

GERTRUDE TUMPEL-GUGERELL

William R. Cline has prepared a very comprehensive description of the European debt crisis that puts the focus on debt sustainability (chapter 11). Debt sustainability was the aim of the tough consolidation program in Greece. I remember that this program was heavily criticized by market participants and rating agencies when it was designed last spring. Would it have been better to continue with a 15 percent deficit? Bill describes very well the potentially detrimental effects of worsening confidence. He is convinced that in principle solvency and liquidity risks can be contained and explains why even Greece could remain solvent. This was always the working assumption of many actors in Europe, including the authorities.

In my view there are three risks: the political process in Greece, the political process in Europe, and the macroeconomic scenario. In chapter 11, Cline describes the considerable benefits for program countries as a consequence of the European Council decisions taken on July 21. It seems that Ireland and Portugal are now more on track to address their problems despite the large costs of stabilizing the financial sector (approximately 30 percent of GDP).

Gertrude Tumpel-Gugerell was a member of the Executive Board of the European Central Bank from 2003 to 2011, responsible for market operations (from 2003 to 2006), for human resources, budget, and organization (2006–11), and for payment systems (2003–11). Rodrigo de Rato has been chairman of Bankia and of Caja Madrid since 2010. He was the managing director of the International Monetary Fund from 2004 to 2007.

The author concludes that markets seem to exaggerate in their assessment of country conditions. We have to keep in mind the powerful combination of negative news and self-fulfilling prophecies via rating assessments and changes in investor behavior.

The concept of financial backstopping capacity that is used in chapter 11 is rather mechanistic. The stability of the euro area is a technical as well as a confidence issue. Of the three options mentioned in chapter 11, the expansion of the European Financial Stability Facility (EFSF) has the highest likelihood of being implemented. Fiscal integration refers to the medium term and only in this context does the debate about eurobonds make sense. EFSF bonds are a sort of eurobonds, as are bonds issued by the European Investment Bank. Eurobonds have a zero percent chance of being approved for the time being. There is no alternative to internal devaluation, consolidation, and structural reform.

Turning to chapter 12, by Guntram Wolff, I fundamentally disagree that we can be sure that a restructuring of Greek debt would have no impact on financial stability. Greece and Argentina are not comparable. The European Central Bank (ECB) has taken a number of unconventional measures, like lifting the rating threshold for collateral or buying government bonds to keep monetary policy effective. The discretionary powers of the ECB are considerable. This could be seen during the crisis when no single change in the legal framework was necessary. There is a rule in the EU treaty that allows the ECB to lend to sound banks, and therefore lending to insolvent banks is forbidden. Let me conclude by saying that a lot depends on the political process—in Greece and in Europe as a whole.

Strategies to Resolve the Sovereign Crisis in the EMU

RODRIGO DE RATO

The current sovereign debt crisis on the periphery of the Economic and Monetary Union (EMU) has shown that monetary union is not feasible any more without economic and fiscal union. The crisis has brought Europe face to face with one of the most difficult choices in its history: either move toward complete integration or else disintegrate. Strategies to resolve the crisis may pursue one or the other of these two goals, with major risks in either direction: A strategy of continuity implies a firm commitment to the euro and to economic and political integration, while any "clean break" strategies involve either abandoning the monetary union project (with a return to national currencies) or else redefining it (by creating a multispeed Europe).

For the time being, the EMU member states remain committed to monetary union and have focused all their efforts on the strategy of continuity, which on the face of it seems the least costly and, potentially, the most beneficial in the mid- to long term. In fact, it is the only option that would allow

Europe to consolidate its position as a third pole of global influence, counterbalancing the United States and China.

What has been done so far? The sovereign crisis has acted as a catalyst of European integration. Measures taken since May 2010 entail a notable—though insufficient—advance over the previous situation. They include

- establishment of mechanisms to assist countries in financial difficulty;
- coordination of economic policy, through the European semester review budgetary policy of member states, the Euro-Plus Pact, the "Six-Pack" legislative improvements in the Stability and Growth Pact, and the creation of pan-European financial supervisors;
- strengthening of disciplinary mechanisms; and
- intervention of the ECB in government debt markets.

These measures should not be seen as all that can be done, but as the first steps toward a true economic and fiscal union that will guarantee the future of the monetary union. Achieving that goal will require brave decisions that may not be readily accepted by public opinion in all countries. The measures to be taken can be categorized according to whether they are orthodox or heterodox, though these categories are not exclusive.

The following are some of the *orthodox* measures that should be adopted in Europe: The first and most important measure is to rebuild confidence in sovereign issuers and in European financial institutions by ensuring that sovereign debt regains its risk-free status in the euro area. This is fundamental in the short term and will call for action in various areas. Measures to expand the EFSF and make it more flexible must be swiftly implemented. Ideally, the EFSF should be given greater independence vis-à-vis member states and ought to be significantly enlarged, as it is no longer big enough to perform its new duties effectively. But if additional commitments by member states are completely ruled out, due to political constraints and the risk of some countries losing their AAA rating, proposals should focus on how to make EFSF money go further. For example, the EFSF could offer guarantees against a portion of losses on sovereign bonds instead of buying them. Thus offering a guarantee of 20 percent would increase the facility's firepower by five times. Alternatively, the EFSF could be turned into a bank and allowed to borrow money from the ECB—a virtually unlimited source of funding—using sovereign bonds as collateral, although this alternative would eventually affect triple-A countries. But debtor countries must make a firmer commitment to fiscal consolidation.

A second set of measures would involve reforms to stimulate growth, which is crucial to ensuring debt sustainability. According to International Monetary Fund (IMF) studies, successful reforms could boost the potential growth of euro area countries by 0.50 to 1.25 percentage points, depending on each country's particular situation. Growth could be stimulated by closer integration: Growth is higher in the countries whose markets are most integrated, as they benefit from the impact of greater competitiveness on investment and innovation. In many areas, there is also a need for harmonization. The euro area financial sector, for example, should be subject to uniform regulation and be supervised by pan-European agencies (that is, national supervisors should be removed). There should also be specific reforms to deregulate and give greater flexibility to the labor market and the markets for goods and services.

A third set of measures should seek closer political and economic integration. This is a medium- to long-term goal, which will most likely require amending the EU treaties and will have to be ratified by all member states. The goal can be met in the following ways:

- improved economic governance, through establishment of an economic policy coordinating body, or "economic government," led by a European finance minister, to which countries would surrender part of their sovereignty in fiscal matters;

- a more stabilizing role for the EU budget, through a more flexible budgeting process (at present, a budget is drawn up every seven years, without the possibility of incurring a deficit), a higher budget (it is currently 1.1 percent of EU GDP), and the decoupling of the budget from national contributions (that is, the transfer of taxes to the EU level); and

- joint guarantee of government debt, which might evolve to a two-speed fiscal union inside the euro area, with the trading of a convergence process.

At the global level, multilateral institutions could launch initiatives that might be described as orthodox. For example, the IMF could create a "debt facility." In 1973 the IMF created an "oil facility," so that countries with a current account surplus could lend to countries with a deficit that were unable to raise funds at "reasonable" interest rates in the markets.

14

Does the Euro Have a Future?

GEORGE SOROS

The euro crisis is a direct consequence of the crash of 2008. When Lehman Brothers failed, the entire global financial system started to collapse and had to be put on artificial life support. This took the form of substituting the sovereign credit of governments for the bank and other credit that had collapsed. At a memorable meeting of European finance ministers in November 2008, they guaranteed that no other financial institutions that are important to the workings of the financial system would be allowed to fail, and their example was followed by the United States.

Angela Merkel then declared that the guarantee should be exercised by each European state individually, not by the European Union or the euro area acting as a whole. This sowed the seeds of the euro crisis because it revealed and activated a hidden weakness in the construction of the euro: the lack of a common treasury. The crisis itself erupted more than a year later, in 2010.

There is some similarity between the euro crisis and the subprime crisis that caused the crash of 2008. In each case a supposedly riskless asset—collateralized debt obligations (CDOs), based largely on mortgages, in 2008, and European government bonds now—lost some or all of their value.

Unfortunately the euro crisis is more intractable. In 2008 the US financial authorities that were needed to respond to the crisis were in place; at present in the euro area one of these authorities, the common treasury, has yet to be brought into existence. This requires a political process involving a number of sovereign states. That is what has made the problem so severe. The political will to create a common European treasury was absent in the first place;

George Soros is chairman of Soros Fund Management, LLC.

and since the time when the euro was created the political cohesion of the European Union has greatly deteriorated. As a result there is no clearly visible solution to the euro crisis. In its absence the authorities have been trying to buy time.

In an ordinary financial crisis this tactic works: With the passage of time the panic subsides and confidence returns. But in this case time has been working against the authorities. Since the political will is missing, the problems continue to grow larger while the politics are also becoming more poisonous.

It takes a crisis to make the politically impossible possible. Under the pressure of a financial crisis the authorities take whatever steps are necessary to hold the system together, but they only do the minimum and that is soon perceived by the financial markets as inadequate. That is how one crisis leads to another. So Europe is condemned to a seemingly unending series of crises. Measures that would have worked if they had been adopted earlier turn out to be inadequate by the time they become politically possible. This is the key to understanding the euro crisis.

Where are we now in this process? The outlines of the missing ingredient, namely a common treasury, are beginning to emerge. They are to be found in the European Financial Stability Facility (EFSF)—agreed on by 27 member states of the European Union in May 2010—and its successor, after 2013, the European Stability Mechanism (ESM). But the EFSF is not adequately capitalized and its functions are not adequately defined. It is supposed to provide a safety net for the euro area as a whole, but in practice it has been tailored to finance the rescue packages for three small countries: Greece, Portugal, and Ireland; it is not large enough to support bigger countries like Spain or Italy. Nor was it originally meant to deal with the problems of the banking system, although its scope has subsequently been extended to include banks as well as sovereign states. Its biggest shortcoming is that it is purely a fund-raising mechanism; the authority to spend the money is left with the governments of the member countries. This renders the EFSF useless in responding to a crisis; it has to await instructions from the member countries.

The situation has been further aggravated by the recent decision of the German Constitutional Court. While the court found that the EFSF is constitutional, it prohibited any future guarantees benefiting additional states without the prior approval of the budget committee of the Bundestag. This will greatly constrain the discretionary powers of the German government in confronting future crises.

The seeds of the next crisis have already been sown by the way the authorities responded to the last crisis. They accepted the principle that countries receiving assistance should not have to pay punitive interest rates and they set up the EFSF as a fund-raising mechanism for this purpose. Had this principle been accepted in the first place, the Greek crisis would not have grown so severe. As it is, the contagion—in the form of increasing inability to pay sovereign and other debt—has spread to Spain and Italy, but those countries are not allowed to borrow at the lower, concessional rates extended to Greece.

This has set them on a course that will eventually land them in the same predicament as Greece. In the case of Greece, the debt burden has clearly become unsustainable. Bondholders have been offered a "voluntary" restructuring by which they would accept lower interest rates and delayed or decreased repayments; but no other arrangements have been made for a possible default or for defection from the euro area.

These two deficiencies—no concessional rates for Italy or Spain and no preparation for a possible default and defection from the euro area by Greece—have cast a heavy shadow of doubt both on the government bonds of other deficit countries and on the banking system of the euro area, which is loaded with those bonds. As a stopgap measure the European Central Bank (ECB) stepped into the breach by buying Spanish and Italian bonds in the market. But that is not a viable solution. The ECB had done the same thing for Greece, but that did not stop the Greek debt from becoming unsustainable. If Italy, with its debt at 108 percent of GDP and growth of less than 1 percent, had to pay risk premiums of 3 percent or more to borrow money, its debt would also become unsustainable.

The ECB's earlier decision to buy Greek bonds had been highly controversial; Axel Weber, the ECB's German board member, resigned from the board in protest. The intervention did blur the line between monetary and fiscal policy, but a central bank is supposed to do whatever is necessary to preserve the financial system. That is particularly true in the absence of a fiscal authority. Subsequently, the controversy led the ECB to adamantly oppose a restructuring of Greek debt—by which, among other measures, the time for repayment would be extended—turning the ECB from a savior of the system into an obstructionist force. The ECB has prevailed: the EFSF took over the risk of possible insolvency of the Greek bonds from the ECB.

The resolution of this dispute has in turn made it easier for the ECB to embark on its current program to purchase Italian and Spanish bonds, which, unlike those of Greece, are not about to default. Still, the decision has encountered the same internal opposition from Germany as the earlier intervention in Greek bonds. Jürgen Stark, the chief economist of the ECB, resigned on September 9. In any case the current intervention has to be limited in scope because the capacity of the EFSF to extend help is virtually exhausted by the rescue operations already in progress in Greece, Portugal, and Ireland.

In the meantime the Greek government is having increasing difficulties in meeting the conditions imposed by the assistance program. The troika supervising the program—the EU, the IMF, and the ECB—is not satisfied; Greek banks did not fully subscribe to the latest treasury bill auction; and the Greek government is running out of funds.

In these circumstances an orderly default and temporary withdrawal from the euro area may be preferable to a drawn-out agony. But no preparations have been made. A disorderly default could precipitate a meltdown similar to the one that followed the bankruptcy of Lehman Brothers, but this time one of the authorities that would be needed to contain it is missing.

No wonder that the financial markets have taken fright. Risk premiums that must be paid to buy government bonds have increased, stocks have plummeted, led by bank stocks, and recently even the euro has broken out of its trading range on the downside. The volatility of markets is reminiscent of the crash of 2008.

The authorities are doing what they can to forestall an immediate breakdown. The Greeks are meeting the troika's demands so as to receive the next installment of the rescue package. The ECB is allowing banks to borrow dollars for up to three months instead of just one week, as has been the case. The Bundestag is expected to pass legislation establishing the EFSF. These steps will delay the climax from September to December.

Unfortunately, the capacity of the financial authorities to take additional measures has been severely restricted by the recent ruling of the German Constitutional Court. It appears that the authorities have reached the end of the road with their policy of "kicking the can down the road." Even if a catastrophe can be avoided, one thing is certain: the pressure to reduce deficits will push the euro area into prolonged recession. This will have incalculable political consequences. The euro crisis could endanger the political cohesion of the European Union.

There is no escape from this gloomy scenario as long as the authorities persist in their current course. They could, however, change course. They could recognize that they have reached the end of the road and take a radically different approach. Instead of acquiescing in the absence of a solution and trying to buy time, they could look for a solution first and then find a path leading to it. The path that leads to a solution has to be found in Germany, which, as the EU's largest and highest-rated creditor country, has been thrust into the position of deciding the future of Europe. That is the approach I propose to explore.

To resolve a crisis in which the impossible becomes possible it is necessary to think about the unthinkable. To start with, it is imperative to prepare for the possibility of default and defection from the euro area in the case of Greece, Portugal, and perhaps Ireland. To prevent a financial meltdown, four sets of measures have to be taken. First, bank deposits have to be protected. If a euro deposited in a Greek bank were lost to the depositor, a euro deposited in an Italian bank would then be worth less than one in a German or Dutch bank and there would be a run on the banks of other deficit countries. Second, some banks in the defaulting countries have to be kept functioning in order to keep the economy from breaking down. Third, the European banking system has to be recapitalized and put under European, as distinct from national, supervision. Fourth, the government bonds of the other deficit countries have to be protected from contagion. The last two requirements would apply even if no country defaulted.

All this would cost money. Under existing arrangements no more money is to be found and no new arrangements are allowed by the German Constitutional Court decision without the authorization of the Bundestag. There is no alternative but to give birth to the missing ingredient: a European treasury with the power to tax and therefore to borrow. This would require a new treaty, transforming the EFSF into a full-fledged treasury.

That would presuppose a radical change of heart, particularly in Germany. The German public still thinks that it has a choice about whether to support the euro or to abandon it. That is a mistake. The euro exists and the assets and liabilities of the financial system are so intermingled on the basis of a common currency that a breakdown of the euro would cause a meltdown beyond the capacity of the authorities to contain. The longer it takes for the German public to realize this, the heavier the price they and the rest of the world will have to pay.

The question is whether the German public can be convinced of this argument. Angela Merkel may not be able to persuade her own coalition, but she could rely on the opposition. Having resolved the euro crisis, she would have less to fear from the next elections.

The fact that arrangements are made for the possible default or defection of three small countries does not mean that those countries would be abandoned. On the contrary, the possibility of an orderly default—paid for by the other euro area countries and the IMF—would offer Greece and Portugal policy choices. Moreover, it would end the vicious cycle now threatening all of the euro area's deficit countries whereby austerity weakens their growth prospects, leading investors to demand prohibitively high interest rates and thus forcing their governments to cut spending further.

Leaving the euro would make it easier for them to regain competitiveness; but if they are willing to make the necessary sacrifices they could also stay in. In both cases, the EFSF would protect bank deposits and the IMF would help to recapitalize the banking system. That would help these countries to escape from the trap in which they currently find themselves. It would be against the best interests of the European Union to allow these countries to collapse and drag down the global banking system with them.

It is not for me to spell out the details of the new treaty; that has to be decided by the member countries. But the discussions ought to start right away because even under extreme pressure they will take a long time to conclude. Once the principle of setting up a European treasury is agreed upon, the European Council could authorize the ECB to step into the breach, indemnifying the ECB in advance against risks to its solvency. That is the only way to forestall a possible financial meltdown and another Great Depression.

IV

POLICY SIMULATION GAME

15

The Simulation Exercise: A Real-Time Economic and Political Stress Test

STEVEN R. WEISMAN with SILVIA B. MERLER

On its second day, the Peterson Institute for International Economics conference "Resolving the European Debt Crisis" moved from assessment to action, or at least simulated action. The result was a highly unusual, provocative, and productive stress test of the political and economic system, illuminating the opportunities and difficulties that face Europe.

About 50 participants—most of whom had been present on day 1 and absorbed the lessons of the papers, panels, and discussions—met on day 2 in a large room at the conference center to square off in a mock crisis "war game." The game was designed to reflect the actual deteriorating situation caused by market pressure on several troubled economies in the euro area. Tables were arrayed around the periphery of the room. A large screen in front showed market movements and developments.

One set of participants played roles representing the European Central Bank (ECB), the International Monetary Fund (IMF), commercial banks, political analysts, and the governments of Greece, Ireland, Italy, Portugal, Spain, France, and Germany as well as the United States. (No sitting officials from any of these governments or institutions participated in the exercise.) At one

Steven R. Weisman is editorial director and public policy fellow of the Peterson Institute for International Economics. He was the chief international economics correspondent of the New York Times and served as a member of the editorial board of the Times, specializing in politics and economics. Silvia B. Merler is a research assistant at Bruegel.

end of the room were more than 15 "market participants" drawn from actual market players from specialized financial firms who traded in real time and thus rendered periodic judgments on debt and equity prices and spreads. Also participating were players in the role of the rating agencies. Others in the game provided expertise on legal and accounting issues.

The goal of the players was to grapple with immediate—sometimes minute-by-minute—responses to events in a condensed time frame of several hours meant to represent the period starting in September 2011 and ending in mid-2012. Participants representing policymakers voted their preferences on major policy choices. These choices were in turn informed and influenced by the periodic infusion of new data from the market participants as well as from growth forecasts supplied by the game organizer.

As might have been expected, the exercise reflected and also presaged events in the real world. Greece remained at the center of the action amid the delays and debates over crisis resolution, and soon after the game started, contagion began moving from the periphery to the core, with spreads on Italian, Spanish, and also French bonds widening in each round of trading. In the end, the players were able to devise collaborative mechanisms to provide additional assistance to ailing countries of the euro area, much as political figures in Europe have struggled to do. The market reaction in the game suggested that the approach of applying massive lending "firepower" could help quell the serious risk of contagion spreading from the periphery to the core of Europe, while still leaving doubts about the long-term economic prospects in the region.

The main feature of the mechanism produced by the game was a dramatic expansion in the lending and borrowing capacity of the European Financial Stability Facility (EFSF) with collateralized financing from the ECB. The scheme would make available substantial additional resources—depending on haircuts applied in repurchase agreements—of between €3 trillion and €5 trillion through the new leveraged EFSF mechanism. (See details below.) The ECB played a pivotal role in the game in assisting the euro area leaders to set up this arrangement. The EFSF also lent to Greece, enabling it to undertake market buybacks of debt. The market participants responded positively, reducing Greece's rates somewhat. Confidence was expressed that the new leveraged facility could effectively address the liquidity crises of the ailing countries, while guarding against the spread of contagion from the periphery to the core of Europe.

But for all these positive developments, many players articulated lingering concerns about the euro area's long-term growth and financial prospects. They also expressed unease over the possibility of a massive rescue mechanism reducing the incentive for countries facing sovereign debt problems—particularly Spain and Italy—to continue steps toward fiscal consolidation and reform. Moreover, many players saw the likelihood of fiscally and financially troubled countries being tested yet again by the markets.

The game also illustrated many familiar shortcomings in policymaking in Europe, especially the difficulty of making decisions rapidly among a multitude of players. Players representing Germany, in particular, were uneasy over the potential for a political backlash and possible legal or constitutional challenges to the expanded lending and borrowing powers of the EFSF, and by extension the ECB. They were concerned as well about open-ended new lending unaccompanied by additional conditions imposed on the recipient countries. Previous expansions of the role of both the ECB and the EFSF these entities have already raised similar concerns in the real world, they noted. Supporters of this program argued, however, that it was needed to help countries that were on track in implementing their fiscal and structural reforms but still plagued by skeptical markets and the effects of a slowing national, regional, and world economy.

The exercise also dramatically illustrated the difficulties involved in explaining the complexities of the EFSF initiative to other players, to the public, and especially to the markets. Players from the ECB, the IMF, and the United States—which supported the expansion of the EFSF based on what the US players said was a model that had worked in Washington and New York in 2008–09—had to explain how the program would work to skeptical players in other parts of the room. (The United States team also stepped in several times to lend a hand to Europe, by announcing new dollar swaps with the ECB and a third round of bond purchases known as "quantitative easing.") On top of this problem, participants from the euro area countries, often convening separately to discuss their possible decisions, encountered difficulties in arriving at a consensus on how to proceed. On the other hand, it was notable that, contrasting with some of the discussions of the first day of the conference, no support surfaced among the players for the option of breaking up the euro area, which many said would be the worst of all possible "solutions" to the sovereign debt crisis in Europe.

Players and Objectives

The simulation game was directed by Andrew Gracie of Crisis Management Analytics (www.crisismanagementanalytics.com). Gracie, a former member of the Bank of England's Financial Stability Group, has had experience running simulated games for central banks globally. The game was also played under the Chatham House Rule, which meant that the information from it could be disseminated to the public as long as there was no identification of, or attribution to, any of the individuals involved.

Before the start of the game, Gracie's team presented a series of descriptions of the players and their objectives.

- *The euro area governments* (Germany, France, Italy, Spain, Ireland, Portugal, and Greece) were to achieve the best economic outcome subject to political limitations. Each country was represented by one person playing the role of the government. Another player representing the banking sector was to try to maximize shareholder value in light of the sinking value of sovereign bonds, demands to recapitalize, and difficulties in interbank lending. The third team member played the role of "political analyst" and provided periodic updates on the constraints facing elected governments. Team members were to undertake decisions on fiscal adjustments and bank recapitalizations while negotiating multilateral solutions with their counterparts.

- *The ECB* had a primary objective of maintaining monetary and financial stability subject to balance sheet risk and other constraints on its role as a player in seeking reform in ailing European countries. The bank was expected to play a decision-making role in the sovereign debt crises, bank solvency, policy rates, and liquidity provision.

- *The IMF* aimed to support global financial stability, constrained by the need to protect its resources and credibility, and to cooperate with the ECB and other players on sovereign debt crisis resolution, bank recapitalization, and fiscal and economic reform in ailing countries.

- *The G-7 countries and the United States* had the objective of pushing for a solution to the EU debt crisis, stabilizing the global economy, and preserving the integrity of the international financial institutions. The United States team represented both the Treasury and Federal Reserve Board.

- *Credit rating agencies* were to render ratings on sovereign and bank debt and also preserve their own credibility.

- *Market participants,* arrayed at one end of the room, were to observe the interconnected decisions and make investment decisions about bonds, spreads, and values of currencies, gold, and equities. Their decisions, transmitted to a screen in front of the game players, would in turn affect choices by policymakers.

The Game: First Phase (September to December 2011)

The exercise began with market participants driving sovereign debt spreads up for euro area peripheral countries, particularly Greece and Italy. In response, the French and the German governments opened consultations with the IMF and the ECB about the possible use of the EFSF, in coordination with the IMF, for the recapitalization of Greek banks, which were heavily exposed to Greek debt that was now plummeting in value. The ECB gave qualified support for such a proposal but cautioned that the public needed to understand the rationale for using public funds in this way. The Portuguese government supported the use of the EFSF to help Greece but said such a step was so far unnecessary for other countries.

The ECB noted that it had addressed the sovereign debt crisis with its initiative to purchase bonds under the Securities Markets Program (SMP), but that it wanted to bring this program to an end and turn some of that responsibility over to the EFSF. The French government, meanwhile, called on the IMF to assess the recapitalization needs of Greek banks in light of their exposure to Greek government debt. But there were indications of concerns about the exposure of French banks as well, and French banks opened private discussions with some of the non-euro area private market players (not disclosed to other players in the game) to see if they might participate in a recapitalization plan. The French political analyst said the public would support bank recapitalization but that involvement by foreigners might be a sensitive issue.

In a signal of fears about possible contagion from Greece, the Portuguese and Spanish governments met and committed themselves to far-reaching structural reforms. Italy, seeing widening spreads on its 10-year bonds as telegraphed by the market players, turned to the ECB for help through the SMP. But the ECB demurred, expressing reservations about the adequacy of Italy's fiscal consolidation steps. Italy responded with promises of further steps, including a wealth tax, labor reforms, and other steps to liberalize the economy.

The disclosure of the first round of decisions by various players brought the game to a new phase. The German government took a tough stance in relation to Greece and called for further Greek debt restructuring, stirring fears of an adverse market reaction among other euro area governments. At another gathering of Eurogroup leaders France reiterated the proposal for Greek bank recapitalization with EFSF funds. The German government supported this proposal. Greek banks took a different view, saying that any such step should await a resolution of how much in enforced losses would be demanded of holders of Greek bonds as part of the so-called private sector involvement (PSI) by creditors. The issue of such enforced haircuts came in the form of euro area banks voting to support the PSI framework of July 2011. That accord had called for a stretch-out of the maturities of Greek sovereign debt and a moderate debt buyback. Euro area leaders agreed to strengthen the capitalization of Greek banks with €10 billion, though the IMF raised doubts about this commitment made without a further assessment of the adequacy of the proposed PSI. The ECB, meanwhile, decided against making any changes in its policy interest rates but emphasized its readiness to supply liquidity and keep open the SMP.

Market participants continued to put pressure on French banks, giving rise to new concerns at the ECB about the spread of contagion to the French financial system. Accordingly the ECB joined with the Federal Reserve Board of the United States to set up a new three-month facility offering dollar swaps for European banks under pressure to supply dollars. Seeing a rise in the Euribor/OIS spread, which measures the difference between the rate at which banks lend to each other in euros and the overnight index swap rate based on the expected federal funds rate—an important index of banks' lack of mutual confidence—the ECB decided to cut interest rates by .25 percent and introduce a new 12-month liquidity facility. To further bolster the European financial system, the Federal Reserve announced a $400 billion long-term bond purchasing program, a third round of its so-called quantitative easing program.

But a further blow was delivered to the French banking system when Spanish banks reduced credit lines to French counterparties.

Much of the action of the game continued to focus on Italy as its government bonds came under increasing market pressure. Again, Eurogroup leaders called on the government in Rome to act and report more frequently on its progress in implementing structural reforms. Italy objected to being seen as a distressed country, but nonetheless agreed to deliver quarterly reports to the Eurogroup. To placate Italian sensibilities, euro area participants let the Italian government announce its additional austerity package first and disclose the quarterly reporting commitment afterward. In response, the Eurogroup said the EFSF would be ready to support Italy with bond purchases if necessary, and it expressed a further wish for a transition to a new government in Rome.

It was at this point that the discussions between players representing the ECB and the Eurogroup led to the major innovation of the simulation exercise: a dramatic expansion of the lending capacity of the EFSF with collateralized financing from the central bank itself, a mechanism designed to expand the EFSF's "firepower" to deal with the danger of contagion in Europe.[1] The concept was outlined in the game to a group of European leaders meeting in a session of the European Council. It was apparent that the ECB had been in discussions about such a plan with the US delegation, because American officials in the game supported this step, saying that it followed similar actions by the US Treasury and the Fed in 2008-09, at the start of the global financial crisis.

The new leveraged EFSF mechanism was designed to supply between €3 trillion and €5 trillion in funding, depending on the size of haircuts applied in repurchase agreements between the ECB and the EFSF. Of particular interest was the ECB's suggestion that it wanted to shed its burden as a conditional lender and turn that function over to the EFSF. The EFSF, as a creation of the euro area states in 2010, would have more legitimacy in making politically sensitive judgments about the extent to which debtor country actions were addressing their financial crises, according to this view. As one observer at the game put it, this solution would free the ECB from interventions in various European economies so that it could protect its balance sheet and concentrate on monetary policy. The problem, however, was that the EFSF capacity to lend was still seen as too small in the face of growing liquidity crises in Europe. It was explained that the new leveraged EFSF mechanism could generate between €3 trillion and €5 trillion, but there was some confusion among some players over exactly how this financing was to be generated. ("What did the ECB do?" one market participant asked.)

Expanding the capacity of the EFSF was seen by the Eurogroup players as necessary for protecting Italy, Spain, and other countries endangered by

---

1. In reality, subsequent to the simulation game, the actual ECB in Frankfurt opposed a similar proposal.

potential contagion from Greece. But the exact role of the facility was ambiguous in the view of other players, who saw it as an instrument that could also be used to help Greece and support banks. The mechanics of the proposed instrument were complex. As explained by various players, the EFSF would use €100 billion of its own funds (derived from European governments) to buy Italian debt, for example. The facility would then take this debt to the ECB as collateral for a loan. The ECB would accept this debt as collateral but only after applying a haircut or discount to the amount that could be counted. If the haircut were 15 percent, the ECB would lend €85 billion to the EFSF. The EFSF would then take that €85 billion, buy an additional equivalent amount of Italian debt, and take that Italian debt back to the ECB, which would turn around and lend €72 billion to the EFSF against this additional collateral (again applying a haircut of 15 percent). Repeating this process numerous times would multiply the total lending capacity of the EFSF severalfold beyond the initial €100 billion—6.67 times in this example.

With the haircut of 15 percent, the leverage would be about 6.67 to 1. But if the haircut were 10 percent, the leverage would be about 10 to 1. On this basis, the instrument was described in the game as giving the EFSF—which has been authorized €440 billion in resources—a lending capacity or "firepower" of €2 trillion to €3 trillion, after allowing for some direct lending to Greece, Ireland, and Portugal.

It was noted in the game that this mechanism—called a "repo" operation, in which the borrower of the money against collateral promises to repurchase the underlying asset—was modeled on one used by the Federal Reserve and the US Treasury when they set up the Term Asset-Backed Securities Loan Facility (TALF) to revive consumer and business credit at a time in 2008–09 when the asset-based securities market had shut down. (The Treasury tapped funds from the Troubled Asset Relief Program [TARP] to buy subordinated debt in the TALF structure in order to insulate the Federal Reserve from losses up to the point of its subscription of debt.)[2]

Along with the repo mechanism, the players began outlining a separate operation for Greece, involving direct EFSF lending to Athens so that it could undertake debt buyback. Once the market participants understood what these two measures would entail, they reacted positively, reducing rates on Greek bonds slightly. But market participants also wanted to know exactly how "unlimited" the ECB funding of the EFSF would be, and they wanted to know more about its power to enforce reforms and fiscal consolidation in recipient countries. The ECB, the IMF, and the Treasury and Federal Reserve stepped in to explain the mechanics, the risks, and the rationale, citing the experience of the TALF. They also said that the operations would be sterilized by the ECB, with either term deposits or sales of other assets.

---

2. The same repurchase mechanism discussed during the simulation game was reportedly raised as a possibility by the US Treasury Department in actual discussions with Europeans in September and October, though it reportedly met with considerable skepticism and resistance.

Aside from the markets, Germany expressed the greatest skepticism and concern about the new mechanism. It viewed the scheme as a setup to issue eurobonds by another name. Germany was also concerned over whether such an expansive role for the EFSF would comply with the German constitutional ban on extending German credit without the approval of voters. If the EFSF suddenly came to be seen as a bank, German representatives in the game said, the voters would object. Credit rating agencies in the game were also skeptical, though they assigned an AAA rating to the EFSF.

The developments did not entirely quell the turmoil in the markets. Stocks tumbled 10 percent and the euro-dollar exchange rates and interbank lending showed signs of stress. To protect themselves, German banks cut their exposure to lending to all countries except for France and Germany itself. Irish banks engaged in generalized deleveraging. Portuguese banks discussed the possibility of reducing credit to Italian counterparties, and Italian banks started curbing lending to all foreign banks apart from German ones. Reflecting the uneasiness in the markets, the French political analyst said the government in Paris was losing support ahead of elections in 2012.

The Game: Second Phase (January 2012 to mid-2012)

As the second phase began there was a general weakening of the global and regional economic outlook. The focus shifted increasingly to France, whose bond spreads with Germany had earlier begun to rise in the face of market skepticism over French banks and the country's general fiscal outlook. Indeed, as this phase progressed, French bond yields gradually decoupled from Germany and instead began to trade in a range between the euro area core, on the one hand, and Italy and Spain, on the other. A meeting of the Eurogroup discussed whether the EFSF proposal needed a change in the EU treaty. All participants looked to Germany for clarification. The IMF and the ECB joined in expressing concerns about Greece's investment and growth prospects. The IMF stressed that although the Greek program was on track, the market was evidently not convinced. There would have to be a delay in the IMF's review of Greece, and also a postponement of the next tranche of funding needed by Athens. The ECB agreed that Greece had not fallen down on its austerity commitments but rather faced a deteriorating macroeconomic outlook.

The IMF accordingly outlined in more detail how Greece would use its EFSF funding, focusing on a proposal for it to buy back its debt at a premium slightly above current market prices. This action would reduce Greece's existing stock of debt and thereby enhance its fiscal sustainability and allow it to use any savings to help recapitalize its banking system. By employing the leveraging mechanism with the ECB, discussed in the first phase of the game, the EFSF was moreover able to conserve its own resources.

But the buyback proposal raised fresh doubts among some players, including Germany, which expressed concern that a buyback would squander the new fund's limited resources and ease pressure on Greece to reform. Greece countered by asserting that its problems were caused by market behavior, not Athens's failings. The buyback proposal raised qualms among the rating agencies, however. The credit rating team acknowledged that the Greek operation would help avert a more serious default, but the agencies nevertheless decided to downgrade Greek debt. They argued that, in the context in which Greek debt was distressed and the scale of the buybacks was massive, the discounted buyback would constitute grounds for a selective default, which by definition is a temporary status. This decision drew protests and objections from the architects of the EFSF lending and buyback schemes. They pointed out that Greece had already negotiated a PSI program of voluntary stretch-outs and buybacks of debt with its creditors. The new buybacks, they said, amounted to a kind of second round of efforts to ease Greece's debt burden—but did not by themselves constitute a default. The rating agencies said that after one month, they would raise the rating on Greek debt assuming Greek debt levels had been reduced.

As the game drew to a close, the markets seemed impressed that the short-term liquidity problems of Greece and other countries were being addressed by the EFSF scheme. Spreads on bonds of peripheral countries declined and liquidity constraints eased as equities rallied somewhat. "It solves all the market problems for Greece," said one market player. But he added that "what is needed is a path for sovereigns to run budget surpluses," and that the solution devised in the game was short term and posed new risks in the future. Some commented that open-ended assistance could weaken incentives for peripheral countries to reform and end up encouraging them to monetize their debts rather than undertake structural improvements. The fear of the markets was that this solution, while impressive as a stopgap, could become—in the cliché of the moment—a case of "kicking the can down the road" without solving underlying problems.

To reinforce the point, market players urged Greece to sell off (i.e., privatize) its government-owned enterprises, as another way of reducing indebtedness. As always, there remained skepticism in Germany, where the political analyst reported that as a consequence of the decisions taken in the game, Germans' support of their government was bound to decline. The analyst further asserted that the German Constitutional Court would not have agreed to the creation of the EFSF had it known that the facility would be undertaking such a sweeping program.

Postgame Discussion

Following the game, a general discussion among participants led to the conclusion that it sometimes takes crises to produce solutions, and that the process of arriving at solutions is usually messy. There was widespread agreement that the failure to communicate the complexity of the solutions slowed the players' ability to act. The feeling among many was that even though the "solution" devised in the game settled the market turmoil over Greece, lingering concerns continued to surround Italy, Spain, and even France. The general view was that in spite of all the actions of the game, the overall economic outlook for Europe remained weak.

Reviewing the two days of meetings, C. Fred Bergsten, director of the Peterson Institute for International Economics, said that one lesson to emerge was the need for government entities "to put more money on the table" to impress the markets. Another, he said, was that Europeans working together can make progress as long as they communicate effectively among themselves and with the markets. In the absence of a European fiscal union, Bergsten said, the game underscored the ECB's crucial role as the one institution with the resources and stature to broker a solution. He said that although concerns about large amounts of funding without conditionality were perhaps justified, the counterargument was that European authorities had already made demands on Greece to get its house in order, and that countries (like Spain) already doing the right thing were being unfairly battered by market skepticism.

Jean Pisani-Ferry, director of Bruegel, said the game players stemmed the spread of contagion from the periphery to the core of Europe. But he cautioned that the session produced only medium-term solutions. It was also notable, he said, that in spite of some discussion of it on day 1 of the conference, no one had called for dismantling the euro area.

In the game at least, the ECB emerged as a single strong voice focused on finding solutions, said Pisani-Ferry. In the real world, however, the ECB along with others in Europe have been more opposed to using the EFSF as a lending vehicle. A feature of the game was that the French and German governments took the lead, whereas in reality other members of the euro area would demand to have a say in approving such a step. Pisani-Ferry said that the difficulty Europeans had in communicating—among themselves and to the markets—was striking. "This was perhaps due in part to failings of those in charge of the communication," he said. "But the deeper issue arose from the fact that meetings took place in a rush, with the need to compromise and negotiate under pressure. We didn't know how deep and how broad the agreement was, so there was a difficulty in communicating it to the markets and in answering questions without jeopardizing the consensus. You had policymakers obsessed with agreeing among themselves, not concentrating on a focused message for the market." Pisani-Ferry said further that the game did not address the painful difficulties of achieving fiscal consolidation and reform in the peripheral European countries or the bleak long-term economic outlook casting a shadow over Europe. "It was about putting money on the table," he said. He concluded that a game like this one could not replicate in full the myriad political pressures in the real world that impede quick actions like those discussed among the players.

But the consensus among the players was that the game succeeded in clarifying the issues and options facing Europe and in outlining a possible path toward resolution of its sovereign debt crisis.

About the Contributors

Alan Ahearne lectures in economics at the National University of Ireland in Galway. He is also a nonresident research fellow at Bruegel and a member of the Board of the Central Bank of Ireland. Ahearne was recruited as a special advisor to Irish Minister for Finance Brian Lenihan in March 2009. Previously, he worked as a senior economist at the Federal Reserve Board's Division of International Finance. He holds a master's degree from University College Dublin and a PhD from Carnegie Mellon University.

Lee C. Buchheit is a partner at Cleary Gottlieb Steen & Hamilton LLP, New York, where his practice focuses on international and corporate transactions, including euro currency financial transactions, sovereign debt management, privatization, and project finance. He heads a Cleary Gottlieb team providing legal advice to the Greek government. In 2010, he received *International Financial Law Review*'s inaugural Lifetime Achievement Award for his contributions to international finance. He has taught at the School for International and Public Affairs, Columbia University; Harvard Law School; and Yale Law School and is a visiting professorial fellow at the Centre for Commercial Law Studies, University of London. Buchheit holds a BA degree from Middlebury College, a JD from the University of Pennsylvania Law School, and a Diploma in International Law from Cambridge University.

William R. Cline has been a senior fellow at the Peterson Institute for International Economics since its inception in 1981. While on leave during 1996–2001, he was deputy managing director and chief economist of the Institute of International Finance. Since 2002 he has held a joint appointment with the Center for Global Development. He has been a senior fellow at the Brookings Institution (1973–81); deputy director for development and trade research, US

Treasury Department (1971–73); Ford Foundation visiting professor in Brazil (1970–71); and lecturer and assistant professor of economics at Princeton University (1967–70). He graduated summa cum laude from Princeton University in 1963 and received his PhD in economics from Yale University in 1969. He is the author of 23 books, including *Financial Globalization, Economic Growth, and the Crisis of 2007–09* (2010), *Global Warming and Agriculture* (2007), and *The United States as a Debtor Nation* (2005).

Guillermo de la Dehesa is chairman of Centre for Economic Policy Research (CEPR), a member of the Group of Thirty, and chairman of the IE Business School. He has been an international advisor to Goldman Sachs Europe since 1988. He is also an independent director of Banco Santander. He was deputy governor of the International Monetary Fund and the World Bank and deputy general manager of the Bank of Spain. He has also served in the government of Spain as secretary of state for economy and secretary general of commerce. He has published extensively on economic issues and is the author of *Europe at the Crossroads* (McGraw Hill, 2005), *Winners and Losers in Globalization* (Blackwell, 2005) *Saving Globalization from Itself* (Blackwell, 2007), and *Globalization of Labour and Migration* (forthcoming).

Rodrigo de Rato has been chairman of Bankia and of Caja Madrid since 2010. He was managing director of the International Monetary Fund from 2004 to 2007. Prior to leading the IMF, de Rato was vice president for economic affairs and minister of economy for the government of Spain. He regularly attended the European Union's economic and finance ministers' meetings and represented the European Union at the G-7 Finance Ministers' meeting in Ottawa, Canada, in 2002, when Spain held the EU presidency. He was also in charge of foreign trade relations for the government of Spain and represented Spain at the World Trade Organization's ministerial meetings in Seattle in 1999, in Doha, Qatar in 2001, and Cancún, Mexico, in 2003. He was a member of Spain's parliament from 1982 to 2004. de Rato holds a degree in law and PhD in economics from the Complutense University of Madrid, as well as an MBA from the University of California, Berkeley.

Zaki Laïdi is professor at Sciences Po Paris and founder of the French think tank Telos. He was member of the French Commission on the White Paper on Foreign Policy and European Affairs. From 2000 to 2004, hewas special advisor to Pascal Lamy, who was then serving as the European commissioner for trade. Laïdi has written extensively on globalization and European affairs. His recent publications include *The Great Disruption* (Polity, 2007), *Norms over Force: The Enigma of European Power* (Palgrave, 2008) and *EU Foreign Policy in a Globalized World* (Routledge, 2008).

Pedro Lourtie is the former secretary of state for European affairs of Portugal (2009–2011). Prior to this position, he was chief of staff to the Portuguese prime minister from 2006 to 2009 and diplomatic adviser in the prime minister's office from 2005 to 2006. He also served as political counselor at the European Commission's delegation in Washington from 2004 to 2005 and in the permanent representation of Portugal to the European Union in Brussels from 1999 to 2004. Lourtie holds a degree in economics from the Instituto Superior de Economia e Gestão (ISEG/UTL) and an MA in European economic studies from the College of Europe in Bruges, Belgium.

Silvia B. Merler has been a research assistant at Bruegel since May 2011. Her research focuses on the macroeconomics of the euro area. She joined the Fondazione ENI Enrico Mattei (FEEM) as a junior researcher in October 2010, where she worked on the MYCRODIN project (on the competitiveness of firms, regions and industries in Europe) and the POLINARES–Policy for Natural Resources project. She holds a master of science and bachelor's degrees in economics from Bocconi University, Italy.

Riccardo Perissich is executive vice president of the Council for the United States and Italy at the Italian branch. He was senior counselor in APCO Worldwide's Rome office, as well as director of public and economic affairs at Telecom Italia Group and Pirelli. Perissich worked for more than two decades at the European Commission, where he coordinated the Single Market Program and served as director general for industry from 1990 to 1994. He is the author of *The European Union, An Unofficial History*.

Daniela Schwarzer is head of the research division of European integration at the German Institute for International and Security Affairs, Stiftung Wissenschaft und Politik (SWP), in Berlin. In 2010, she became a member of the team of academic advisors to the Polish secretary of state for European affairs in preparation of Poland's EU Council presidency in 2011. In 2007-08 she was a member of the working group "Europe" of the Whitebook Commission on Foreign and European Policy in the French foreign ministry and a visiting researcher at the French Institute for International Relations in Paris. She previously worked with the *Financial Times Deutschland* as editorialist and France correspondent. Schwarzer studied in Tübingen, Reading (UK) and at Sciences Po Paris. She holds a PhD in political economy from the Freie Universität Berlin, cosupervised by the London School of Economics.

George Soros is chairman of Soros Fund Management, LLC. As one of history's most successful financiers, his views on investing and economic issues are widely followed. His philanthropic organization, the Open Society Foundations, supports democracy and human rights in over 70 countries. Soros is the author of *The Soros Lectures: At the Central European University* (2010), *The Crash of 2008 and What it Means: The New Paradigm for Finance Markets* (2009), *The Age of Fallibility: Consequences of The War on Terror* (2006), *The Bubble of American Supremacy* (2005), *George Soros on Globalization* (2002), *Open Society: Reforming*

Global Capitalism (2000), *The Crisis of Global Capitalism: Open Society Endangered* (1998), *Soros on Soros: Staying Ahead of the Curve* (1995), *Underwriting Democracy* (1991), *Opening the Soviet System* (1990), and *The Alchemy of Finance* (1987). His essays on politics, society, and economics appear frequently in major periodicals around the world.

Loukas Tsoukalis is professor of European integration at the University of Athens, president of the Hellenic Foundation for European and Foreign Policy (ELIAMEP), and visiting professor at the College of Europe in Bruges. Previously, he was special advisor to the president of the European Commission. He has taught at many universities, including Oxford, London School of Economics and Political Science, European University Institute in Florence, and Sciences Po Paris. He holds a BA degree in economics from the University of Manchester, an MA degree and a PhD from University of Oxford.

Gertrude Tumpel-Gugerell was a member of the Executive Board of the European Central Bank from 2003 to 2011, responsible for market operations (2003–06), for human resources, budget, and organization (2006–11), and for payment systems (2003–11). She worked for more than 20 years at Oesterreichische Nationalbank, serving as vice governor from 1998 to 2003. She was also chair of the Banking Advisory Committee of the European Union from 2002 to 2003 and alternate governor of Austria to the International Monetary Fund from 1997 to 2003. Tumpel-Gugerell holds a Master of Science degree and a PhD in economics and social sciences, both from the University of Vienna.

Steven R. Weisman is editorial director and public policy fellow of the Peterson Institute for International Economics. He was the chief international economics correspondent of the New York Times and served as a member of the editorial board of the Times, specializing in politics and economics. Before serving as chief international economics correspondent, he was chief diplomatic correspondent and won the Edward Weintal Prize in 2004 for his reporting on diplomacy and international affairs, awarded by the Walsh School of Foreign Service at Georgetown University. He is the author of *The Great Tax Wars: Lincoln to Wilson—The Fierce Battles over Money and Power That Transformed the Nation* (Simon and Schuster, 2002), which received the Sidney Hillman Award in 2003 for the book that most advances the cause of social justice.

Guntram B. Wolff is deputy director of Bruegel. He worked for the European Commission's Directorate General for Economic and Financial Affairs, where he researched on the macroeconomics of the euro area and the reform of euro area governance. Prior to joining the Commission, Wolff was an economist in the economics and research departments of the Deutsche Bundesbank, where he coordinated the research group on fiscal policy. He holds a PhD from the University of Bonn, where he was a research fellow at the Center for European

Integration Studies (ZEI). He has taught economics at the University of Pittsburgh and is currently an adviser to the International Monetary Fund.

Jeromin Zettelmeyer is director for policy studies at the European Bank for Reconstruction and Development, responsible for research and country economic analysis. From 1994 to 2008, he worked at the International Monetary Fund, including as an economist in the European II Department, as deputy head of regional studies in the Western Hemisphere Department, where he led research on Latin America, and, for over 10 years, in the Research Department, where his research interests included financial crises, sovereign debt, international financial architecture, and economic growth. He is the coauthor of *Debt Default and Lessons from a Decade of Crises* (MIT Press, 2007). Zettelmeyer is a graduate of the University of Bonn and holds a PhD from MIT.

Index

Pact for the Euro, 86
Pakistan
  haircut versus debt relief, 173*t*
  impact of default, 177*f*, 178
Papademos, Lucas, 229
Papandreou, George, 13, 20, 32
par bonds, 216
pari passu clauses, 182, 184, 188
PASOK party (Greece), 20, 25, 28–32, 34
pension reforms
  Italy, 100, 106
  Portugal, 65–66, 66*t*, 67*f*
  Spain, 118–19
peripheral countries. *See also specific country*
  defined, 54*n*
PIGS [acronym], 95
policy options. *See* alternative policy options
political situation. *See also specific country*
  alternative policy choices and, 214
  delay in crisis response and, 190
  disagreements within euro area, 79
  euro area breakup, 250–51, 261
  eurobonds, 246
  European integration, 257–58
  repudiation, 180
  as risk factor, 253–54
populism
  crisis management and, 117
  within euro area, 79
  Greece, 32–33
  Italy, 102–103
Portugal, 51–94
  overview, 4
  alternative policy options, 214–15
    banking sector impact, 226–28,
      227*t*
    comments on, 253–56
    public/government impact, 223–26,
      224*t*
    by relevance, 222*t*, 223
  asset holdings, 236, 237*f*–238*f*, 250*t*
  austerity measures, 77, 79–80, 83, 85
  banking sector, 87
    alternative policy impacts, 226–28,
      227*t*
    stress test, 240–43, 241*t*
  bond interest rates, 75–81, 203, 204*f*
  budget deficits
    bond yields and, 74
    in euro area context, 56
    projections, 69, 69*t*
    solvency and, 207
    vulnerability and, 65–68

competitiveness deficit
  correction of, 88
  debt sustainability and, 206
  euro area comparison, 239, 239*f*
  precrisis, 56–58, 71–72
construction sector, 57, 57*f*
contagion, 75–77, 81, 206
credibility deficit, 81
currency devaluation, 58, 68
current account deficit, 56, 70–74, 71*f*, 72*f*,
  206
debt crisis, 74–87
  contagion, 75–77, 81, 206
  in context of euro area crisis, 52–55
  EFSF flexibility and, 82–83, 86
  European hesitation about, 80–82,
    90–93
  market sentiment about, 78–82
  request for financial assistance, 86–87
  timeline, 91*t*–93*t*
debt levels, 206–207, 236, 237*f*
debt restructuring, 84–87, 89, 206–207
debt sustainability, 203, 206–208
default by, 260–61
economic performance, 55, 56–74, 87–88
euro exit, 261
export growth, 69–72, 70*f*, 71*f*, 88–90
fiscal policy, 68, 73–74, 85, 88
interest rate spreads, 75
international investment position, 73, 73*f*
labor costs/productivity, 56, 58, 59*f*, 68, 70,
  206–207
liquidity needs, 198, 207
political situation, 74, 86–87, 89–90, 206
recession, 56, 73, 83–84, 88
ring-fencing strategy toward, 55, 81
in simulation game, 267–68
social situation, 90
sovereign rating, 86, 218*n*, 231*t*
Stability and Growth Program (PEC IV),
  86–87
structural reforms, 60–64, 79, 85, 88
  education, 60, 61*f*, 70
  energy dependency, 62, 62*f*
  labor legislation, 63*f*, 63–64, 64*f*
  public sector and business, 62–63, 66,
    68*f*
  research and development investment,
    60–62, 61*f*
  social security, 65–66, 66*t*, 67*f*
tax rates, 72, 88
unemployment, 56
wages, 56, 58, 206

Other Publications from the Peterson Institute for International Economics

WORKING PAPERS

94-1 APEC and Regional Trading Arrangements in the Pacific
Jeffrey A. Frankel with Shang-Jin Wei and Ernesto Stein

94-2 Towards an Asia Pacific Investment Code Edward M. Graham

94-3 Merchandise Trade in the APEC Region: Is There Scope for Liberalization on an MFN Basis?
Paul Wonnacott

94-4 The Automotive Industry in Southeast Asia: Can Protection Be Made Less Costly? Paul Wonnacott

94-5 Implications of Asian Economic Growth Marcus Noland

95-1 APEC: The Bogor Declaration and the Path Ahead C. Fred Bergsten

95-2 From Bogor to Miami...and Beyond: Regionalism in the Asia Pacific and the Western Hemisphere
Jeffrey J. Schott

95-3 Has Asian Export Performance Been Unique? Marcus Noland

95-4 Association of Southeast Asian Nations and ASEAN Free Trade Area: Chronology and Statistics Gautam Jaggi

95-5 The North Korean Economy
Marcus Noland

95-6 China and the International Economic System Marcus Noland

96-1 APEC after Osaka: Toward Free Trade by 2010/2020 C. Fred Bergsten

96-2 Public Policy, Private Preferences, and the Japanese Trade Pattern
Marcus Noland

96-3 German Lessons for Korea: The Economics of Unification
Marcus Noland

96-4 Research and Development Activities and Trade Specialization in Japan
Marcus Noland

96-5 China's Economic Reforms: Chronology and Statistics
Gautam Jaggi, Mary Rundle, Daniel H. Rosen, and Yuichi Takahashi

96-6 US-China Economic Relations
Marcus Noland

96-7 The Market Structure Benefits of Trade and Investment Liberalization
Raymond Atje and Gary Clyde Hufbauer

96-8 The Future of US-Korea Economic Relations Marcus Noland

96-9 Competition Policies in the Dynamic Industrializing Economies: The Case of China, Korea, and Chinese Taipei
Edward M. Graham

96-10 Modeling Economic Reform in North Korea Marcus Noland, Sherman Robinson, and Monica Scatasta

96-11 Trade, Investment, and Economic Conflict Between the United States and Asia Marcus Noland

96-12 APEC in 1996 and Beyond: The Subic Summit C. Fred Bergsten

96-13 Some Unpleasant Arithmetic Concerning Unification
Marcus Noland

96-14 Restructuring Korea's Financial Sector for Greater Competitiveness
Marcus Noland

96-15 Competitive Liberalization and Global Free Trade: A Vision for the 21st Century C. Fred Bergsten

97-1 Chasing Phantoms: The Political Economy of USTR Marcus Noland

97-2 US-Japan Civil Aviation: Prospects for Progress Jacqueline McFadyen

97-3 Open Regionalism C. Fred Bergsten

97-4 Lessons from the Bundesbank on the Occasion of Its 40th (and Second to Last?) Birthday Adam S. Posen

97-5 The Economics of Korean Unification
Marcus Noland, Sherman Robinson, and Li-Gang Liu

98-1 The Costs and Benefits of Korean Unification Marcus Noland, Sherman Robinson, and Li-Gang Liu

98-2 Asian Competitive Devaluations
Li-Gang Liu, Marcus Noland, Sherman Robinson, and Zhi Wang

98-3 Fifty Years of the GATT/WTO: Lessons from the Past for Strategies or the Future C. Fred Bergsten

98-4 NAFTA Supplemental Agreements: Four Year Review
Jacqueline McFadyen

98-5 Local Government Spending: Solving the Mystery of Japanese Fiscal Packages Hiroko Ishii and Erika Wada

98-6 The Global Economic Effects of the Japanese Crisis Marcus Noland, Sherman Robinson, and Zhi Wang

98-7 The Relationship Between Trade and Foreign Investment: Empirical Results for Taiwan and South Korea
Li-Gang Liu, The World Bank, and Edward M. Graham

99-1 Rigorous Speculation: The Collapse and Revival of the North Korean Economy Marcus Noland, Sherman Robinson, and Tao Wang

Trade Protection in the United States: 31 Case Studies* Gary Clyde Hufbauer, Diane E. Berliner, and Kimberly Ann Elliott
1986 ISBN 0-88132-040-4
Toward Renewed Economic Growth in Latin America* Bela Balassa, Gerardo M. Bueno, Pedro Pablo Kuczynski, and Mario Henrique Simonsen
1986 ISBN 0-88132-045-5
Capital Flight and Third World Debt* Donald R. Lessard and John Williamson, eds.
1987 ISBN 0-88132-053-6
The Canada-United States Free Trade Agreement: The Global Impact* Jeffrey J. Schott and Murray G. Smith, eds.
1988 ISBN 0-88132-073-0
World Agricultural Trade: Building a Consensus* William M. Miner and Dale E. Hathaway, eds.
1988 ISBN 0-88132-071-3
Japan in the World Economy* Bela Balassa and Marcus Noland
1988 ISBN 0-88132-041-2
America in the World Economy: A Strategy for the 1990s* C. Fred Bergsten
1988 ISBN 0-88132-089-7
Managing the Dollar: From the Plaza to the Louvre* Yoichi Funabashi
1988, 2d ed. 1989 ISBN 0-88132-097-8
United States External Adjustment and the World Economy* William R. Cline
May 1989 ISBN 0-88132-048-X
Free Trade Areas and U.S. Trade Policy* Jeffrey J. Schott, ed.
May 1989 ISBN 0-88132-094-3
Dollar Politics: Exchange Rate Policymaking in the United States* I. M. Destler and C. Randall Henning
September 1989 ISBN 0-88132-079-X
Latin American Adjustment: How Much Has Happened?* John Williamson, ed.
April 1990 ISBN 0-88132-125-7
The Future of World Trade in Textiles and Apparel* William R. Cline
1987, 2d ed. June 1999 ISBN 0-88132-110-9
Completing the Uruguay Round: A Results-Oriented Approach to the GATT Trade Negotiations* Jeffrey J. Schott, ed.
September 1990 ISBN 0-88132-130-3
Economic Sanctions Reconsidered (2 volumes) Economic Sanctions Reconsidered: Supplemental Case Histories Gary Clyde Hufbauer, Jeffrey J. Schott, and Kimberly Ann Elliott
1985, 2d ed. Dec. 1990 ISBN cloth 0-88132-115-X
ISBN paper 0-88132-105-2
Economic Sanctions Reconsidered: History and Current Policy Gary Clyde Hufbauer, Jeffrey J. Schott, and Kimberly Ann Elliott
December 1990 ISBN cloth 0-88132-140-0
ISBN paper 0-88132-136-2

Pacific Basin Developing Countries: Prospects for the Future* Marcus Noland
January 1991 ISBN cloth 0-88132-141-9
ISBN paper 0-88132-081-1
Currency Convertibility in Eastern Europe* John Williamson, ed.
October 1991 ISBN 0-88132-128-1
International Adjustment and Financing: The Lessons of 1985-1991* C. Fred Bergsten, ed.
January 1992 ISBN 0-88132-112-5
North American Free Trade: Issues and Recommendations* Gary Clyde Hufbauer and Jeffrey J. Schott
April 1992 ISBN 0-88132-120-6
Narrowing the U.S. Current Account Deficit* Alan J. Lenz
June 1992 ISBN 0-88132-103-6
The Economics of Global Warming William R. Cline
June 1992 ISBN 0-88132-132-X
US Taxation of International Income: Blueprint for Reform Gary Clyde Hufbauer, assisted by Joanna M. van Rooij
October 1992 ISBN 0-88132-134-6
Who's Bashing Whom? Trade Conflict in High-Technology Industries Laura D'Andrea Tyson
November 1992 ISBN 0-88132-106-0
Korea in the World Economy* Il SaKong
January 1993 ISBN 0-88132-183-4
Pacific Dynamism and the International Economic System* C. Fred Bergsten and Marcus Noland, eds.
May 1993 ISBN 0-88132-196-6
Economic Consequences of Soviet Disintegration* John Williamson, ed.
May 1993 ISBN 0-88132-190-7
Reconcilable Differences? United States-Japan Economic Conflict* C. Fred Bergsten and Marcus Noland
June 1993 ISBN 0-88132-129-X
Does Foreign Exchange Intervention Work? Kathryn M. Dominguez and Jeffrey A. Frankel
September 1993 ISBN 0-88132-104-4
Sizing Up U.S. Export Disincentives* J. David Richardson
September 1993 ISBN 0-88132-107-9
NAFTA: An Assessment Gary Clyde Hufbauer and Jeffrey J. Schott, rev. ed.
October 1993 ISBN 0-88132-199-0
Adjusting to Volatile Energy Prices Philip K. Verleger, Jr.
November 1993 ISBN 0-88132-069-2
The Political Economy of Policy Reform John Williamson, ed.
January 1994 ISBN 0-88132-195-8
Measuring the Costs of Protection in the United States Gary Clyde Hufbauer and Kimberly Ann Elliott
January 1994 ISBN 0-88132-108-7
The Dynamics of Korean Economic Development* Cho Soon
March 1994 ISBN 0-88132-162-1

Food Regulation and Trade: Toward a Safe and
Open Global System   Tim Josling,
Donna Roberts, and David Orden
March 2004   ISBN 0-88132-346-2
Controlling Currency Mismatches in Emerging
Markets   Morris Goldstein and Philip Turner
April 2004   ISBN 0-88132-360-8
Free Trade Agreements: US Strategies and
Priorities   Jeffrey J. Schott, ed.
April 2004   ISBN 0-88132-361-6
Trade Policy and Global Poverty
William R. Cline
June 2004   ISBN 0-88132-365-9
Bailouts or Bail-ins? Responding to Financial
Crises in Emerging Economies
Nouriel Roubini and Brad Setser
August 2004   ISBN 0-88132-371-3
Transforming the European Economy
Martin Neil Baily and Jacob Funk Kirkegaard
September 2004   ISBN 0-88132-343-8
Chasing Dirty Money: The Fight Against
Money Laundering   Peter Reuter and
Edwin M. Truman
November 2004   ISBN 0-88132-370-5
The United States and the World Economy:
Foreign Economic Policy for the Next Decade
C. Fred Bergsten
January 2005   ISBN 0-88132-380-2
Does Foreign Direct Investment Promote
Development?   Theodore H. Moran,
Edward M. Graham, and Magnus Blomström,
eds.
April 2005   ISBN 0-88132-381-0
American Trade Politics, 4th ed.   I. M. Destler
June 2005   ISBN 0-88132-382-9
Why Does Immigration Divide America?
Public Finance and Political Opposition to
Open Borders   Gordon H. Hanson
August 2005   ISBN 0-88132-400-0
Reforming the US Corporate Tax
Gary Clyde Hufbauer and Paul L. E. Grieco
September 2005   ISBN 0-88132-384-5
The United States as a Debtor Nation
William R. Cline
September 2005   ISBN 0-88132-399-3
NAFTA Revisited: Achievements and
Challenges   Gary Clyde Hufbauer and
Jeffrey J. Schott, assisted by Paul L. E. Grieco and
Yee Wong
October 2005   ISBN 0-88132-334-9
US National Security and Foreign Direct
Investment   Edward M. Graham and
David M. Marchick
May 2006   ISBN 978-0-88132-391-7
Accelerating the Globalization of America: The
Role for Information Technology
Catherine L. Mann, assisted by Jacob Funk
Kirkegaard
June 2006   ISBN 978-0-88132-390-0
Delivering on Doha: Farm Trade and the Poor
Kimberly Ann Elliott
July 2006   ISBN 978-0-88132-392-4

Case Studies in US Trade Negotiation, Vol. 1:
Making the Rules   Charan Devereaux,
Robert Z. Lawrence, and Michael Watkins
September 2006   ISBN 978-0-88132-362-7
Case Studies in US Trade Negotiation, Vol. 2:
Resolving Disputes   Charan Devereaux,
Robert Z. Lawrence, and Michael Watkins
September 2006   ISBN 978-0-88132-363-2
C. Fred Bergsten and the World Economy
Michael Mussa, ed.
December 2006   ISBN 978-0-88132-397-9
Working Papers, Volume I   Peterson Institute
December 2006   ISBN 978-0-88132-388-7
The Arab Economies in a Changing World
Marcus Noland and Howard Pack
April 2007   ISBN 978-0-88132-393-1
Working Papers, Volume II   Peterson Institute
April 2007   ISBN 978-0-88132-404-4
Global Warming and Agriculture: Impact
Estimates by Country   William R. Cline
July 2007   ISBN 978-0-88132-403-7
US Taxation of Foreign Income
Gary Clyde Hufbauer and Ariel Assa
October 2007   ISBN 978-0-88132-405-1
Russia's Capitalist Revolution: Why Market
Reform Succeeded and Democracy Failed
Anders Åslund
October 2007   ISBN 978-0-88132-409-9
Economic Sanctions Reconsidered, 3d ed.
Gary Clyde Hufbauer, Jeffrey J. Schott, Kimberly
Ann Elliott, and Barbara Oegg
November 2007
              ISBN hardcover 978-0-88132-407-5
     ISBN hardcover/CD-ROM 978-0-88132-408-2
Debating China's Exchange Rate Policy
Morris Goldstein and Nicholas R. Lardy, eds.
April 2008   ISBN 978-0-88132-415-0
Leveling the Carbon Playing Field:
International Competition and US Climate
Policy Design   Trevor Houser, Rob Bradley, Britt
Childs, Jacob Werksman, and Robert Heilmayr
May 2008   ISBN 978-0-88132-420-4
Accountability and Oversight of US Exchange
Rate Policy   C. Randall Henning
June 2008   ISBN 978-0-88132-419-8
Challenges of Globalization: Imbalances and
Growth   Anders Åslund and
Marek Dabrowski, eds.
July 2008   ISBN 978-0-88132-418-1
China's Rise: Challenges and Opportunities
C. Fred Bergsten, Charles Freeman, Nicholas R.
Lardy, and Derek J. Mitchell
September 2008   ISBN 978-0-88132-417-4
Banking on Basel: The Future of International
Financial Regulation   Daniel K. Tarullo
September 2008   ISBN 978-0-88132-423-5
US Pension Reform: Lessons from Other
Countries   Martin Neil Baily and
Jacob Funk Kirkegaard
February 2009   ISBN 978-0-88132-425-9
How Ukraine Became a Market Economy and
Democracy   Anders Åslund
March 2009   ISBN 978-0-88132-427-3

**Australia, New Zealand,
and Papua New Guinea**
D. A. Information Services
648 Whitehorse Road
Mitcham, Victoria 3132, Australia
Tel: 61-3-9210-7777
Fax: 61-3-9210-7788
Email: service@dadirect.com.au
www.dadirect.com.au

India, Bangladesh, Nepal, and Sri Lanka
Viva Books Private Limited
Mr. Vinod Vasishtha
4737/23 Ansari Road
Daryaganj, New Delhi 110002
India
Tel: 91-11-4224-2200
Fax: 91-11-4224-2240
Email: viva@vivagroupindia.net
www.vivagroupindia.com

**Mexico, Central America, South America,
and Puerto Rico**
US PubRep, Inc.
311 Dean Drive
Rockville, MD 20851
Tel: 301-838-9276
Fax: 301-838-9278
Email: c.falk@ieee.org

Asia (*Brunei, Burma, Cambodia, China,
Hong Kong, Indonesia, Korea, Laos, Malaysia,
Philippines, Singapore, Taiwan, Thailand,
and Vietnam*)
East-West Export Books (EWEB)
University of Hawaii Press
2840 Kolowalu Street
Honolulu, Hawaii 96822-1888
Tel: 808-956-8830
Fax: 808-988-6052
Email: eweb@hawaii.edu

Canada
Renouf Bookstore
5369 Canotek Road, Unit 1
Ottawa, Ontario KlJ 9J3, Canada
Tel: 613-745-2665
Fax: 613-745-7660
www.renoufbooks.com

Japan
United Publishers Services Ltd.
1-32-5, Higashi-shinagawa
Shinagawa-ku, Tokyo 140-0002
Japan
Tel: 81-3-5479-7251
Fax: 81-3-5479-7307
Email: purchasing@ups.co.jp
*For trade accounts only. Individuals will find
Institute books in leading Tokyo bookstores.*

Middle East
MERIC
2 Bahgat Ali Street, El Masry Towers
Tower D, Apt. 24
Zamalek, Cairo
Egypt
Tel. 20-2-7633824
Fax: 20-2-7369355
Email: mahmoud_fouda@mericonline.com
www.mericonline.com

United Kingdom, Europe
(*including Russia and Turkey*)**, Africa,
and Israel**
The Eurospan Group
c/o Turpin Distribution
Pegasus Drive
Stratton Business Park
Biggleswade, Bedfordshire
SG18 8TQ
United Kingdom
Tel: 44 (0) 1767-604972
Fax: 44 (0) 1767-601640
Email: eurospan@turpin-distribution.com
www.eurospangroup.com/bookstore

**Visit our website at:
www.piie.com
E-mail orders to:
petersonmail@presswarehouse.com**